Global
POP,
Local
LANGUAGE

Global

POP

LANG

Edited by

Harris M. Berger and
Michael Thomas Carroll

University Press of Mississippi / *Jackson*

'Local
UAGE

www.upress.state.ms.us

The University Press of Mississippi is a member of the
Association of American University Presses.

The editors would like to extend their thanks to Pat
Browne, director of Bowling Green State University Press,
and to Gary Burns, editor of *Popular Music and Society*, for
allowing us to reprint the essays from the special issue of
Popular Music and Society (Vol. 24.3, fall 2000), which
carried the subtitle, "Global Popular Music: The Politics
and Aesthetics of Language Choice."

The essays by Tony Mitchell, Paul D. Greene and David
R. Henderson, María Elena Cepeda, and Edward Larkey
all are reprinted in this volume as they appeared in the
original publication. The essays by Alex Perullo and John
Fenn, Morgan Gerard and Jack Sidnell, and Cece Cutler
are revised versions of the original publication.

Library of Congress Cataloging-in-Publication Data

Global pop, local language / edited by Harris M. Berger and
Michael Thomas Carroll.
    p. cm.
In part, originally published in Global popular music: the
politics and aesthetics of language choice, a special issue of
Popular music and society (v. 24.3, fall 2000).

ISBN 1-57806-535-6 (alk. paper) — ISBN 1-57806-536-4
(pbk.: alk. paper)

1. Popular music—History and criticism. 2. Music and
language. 3. Sociolinguistics. I. Berger, Harris M., 1966–
II. Carroll, Michael Thomas, 1954–
ML3470 .G54 2003
781.63′01′4—dc21   2002152727

British Library Cataloging-in-Publication Data available

Contents

**Part Three. Music and Words: Language Choice
and Dialect in Song and Performance**

Acknowledgments

The editors of this volume would like to thank Pat Browne of Bowling Green State University Popular Press and Gary Burns of the journal *Popular Music and Society* for permission to reprint some of the chapters included here. We would also like to thank the Department of Performance Studies at Texas A&M University for support of this project in its various stages.

Introduction

The Politics and Aesthetics of Language Choice
and Dialect in Popular Music

—*Harris M. Berger*

In the 1999 film *The Talented Mr. Ripley*, a wealthy industrialist asks an earnest young man named Tom Ripley to travel to Italy in order to lure home to New York his ne'er-do-well son, Dickie.[1] It is an unlikely misunderstanding that draws Tom, a restroom attendant who works on the side as a classical pianist, into the world of the powerful and privileged. But seizing unforeseen opportunities is Tom's defining character trait, and he happily agrees to the industrialist's proposal. Before leaving, Tom learns that Dickie is a jazz aficionado, and to prepare for his task he quickly educates himself about that music. Arriving in Italy, Tom arranges a "chance meeting" with Dickie, fabricates for himself a new identity as a forgotten college friend, and, playing on his feigned love for jazz, slowly insinuates himself into Dickie's life. At first cool and haughty, Dickie soon warms to Tom, and their relationship is suffused with homoerotic overtones.

In a pivotal scene, the two attend a performance at Dickie's favorite jazz club, a raucous basement hotspot in Naples. Early in the evening, Dickie sits in with the house band on saxophone while Tom and assorted friends watch from the audience. At the climax of the performance the group breaks into a rendition of the song "Tu vou' fa l'Americano" (You want to be American). Another audience member, played by the well-known Italian vocalist Fiorello, sings the lead in Italian, while Dickie, well familiar with the tune, sings along fluently at the mike in the same language. Halfway through the song, Fiorello drags a reluctant Tom up to the stage to join in. In many scenes, the dramatic tension in the film centers on the constant threat that Tom's deception will collapse. At this juncture it is clear to the film audience—if not to Dickie—that Tom doesn't know the song and fears that if he can't sing along, he will lose his credibility as a jazz buff. But Tom is a quick study. Though the tempo shifts into high gear, the Anglophone Tom soon masters the Italian lyrics, and together the three belt out the final chorus to the delighted applause of the nightclub crowd.[2]

For most viewers, it is the machinations of Tom's deception that are the focus of attention in this complex performance. I have chosen to begin this introduction with a description of this scene, though, because it evocatively illustrates some of the key dynamics of the topic of this edited volume—the politics and aesthetics of language choice and dialect in popular music. To monolingual Anglophone Americans living outside major urban areas, this issue may seem exotic. For all the growth of Latin music in the United States, English still dominates the American mass media and many realms of social life. But for many throughout the world (including non-English speakers in the United States), questions of language choice are a crucial part of musical experience. Musicians, listeners, and culture workers must constantly ask themselves such questions as: Which languages or dialects will best express my ideas? Which will get me a record contract or a bigger audience? What does it mean to sing or listen to music in a colonial language? A foreign language? A "native" language? And even within societies where a single language dominates the cultural landscape, subtler questions of dialect inform many aspects of song, including the syntax or word choices of the lyrics, the diction of the singers, and the politics and aesthetics of the interpretations made by critics, music industry gatekeepers, and listeners. We can get a glimpse into the complex dynamics of language choice in popular music by exploring the *Ripley* example in more detail.

Two elements of context are important for understanding this scene—the significance of jazz in U.S. cultural history and the representation of Italy in the American popular imagination. From its emergence around the turn of the twentieth century as a working-class African American music to its complex entanglements with Tin Pan Alley pop to its eventual acceptance by the academy as an "art music," jazz is a musical style freighted with a complex and often contradictory set of meanings. The *Ripley* narrative draws on this history to develop its two major characters. Dickie is an alienated young bourgeois who builds his personal identity by performing a music marked in American culture for both "high art" formal sophistication and a deeply racialized version of emotional authenticity. Tom, on the other hand, is a genuinely working-class young man who must affect a knowledge

of jazz to make the same *déclassé* moves that come so naturally to his privileged "friend"; he thus serves as an ironic counterpart to Dickie. Like jazz,
Italy, too, has a range of contradictory meanings in the American imagination. It has been variously envisioned as the homeland of Western high culture,
as a place of convivial peasants, or as a site of chronic underdevelopment,
crime, clannishness, and poverty. Interestingly, the upward mobility that
many Italian Americans experienced in the decades after World War II parallels the canonical status that jazz achieved in the American academy during that period.

Both this larger cultural context and the lives of the characters play out
richly in the musical and linguistic performances of "Tu vou' fa l'Americano."
Though high-status forms of jazz such as bop and postbop can be heard in
much of the *Ripley* soundtrack, the style of "l'Americano" is markedly different. With attention-grabbing tempo changes and splashy brass and reed hits
accompanying Fiorello's dramatic singing, this song is closer in style to commercial jazz, or even jazz-tinged Las Vegas show music, than to postbop. More
easily overlooked but perhaps most important for the scene is the question of
language choice. Let us assume for the sake of argument that the presumptive
audience for this American-produced film is non-Italian speakers. For such an
audience, the lyrics of the song are only grasped in fragments. Clearly the song
involves an *"Americano,"* and a range of English phrases and loan words—
"whiskey and soda," "baseball," and *"rock e roll"*—can be heard as well. The
rest of the lyrics, however, are a blur. Here, the choice of language and dialect
combines with the musical style, the other elements of the performance, and
the larger social context to give the scene its rich meanings.

On a basic level, the choice of presenting a song in Italian draws the
viewer's attention away from the referential content of the lyrics and toward
the other features of the performance—the melody, the arrangement, the
actor's stage behavior, and so forth. Interestingly, this choice also places the
movie audience in a position similar to that of Tom, an outsider who must
scramble to make sense of the social and linguistic world around him. But
even though the words convey almost no referential content to its presumptive viewers, the sound of the Italian language still serves a semiotic
function. To my reading, the referentially incomprehensible Italian words
are not devoid of meaning. Taking an approach similar to that found in
C. K. Szego's essay in this volume, I suggest that the words of "l'Americano"

operate collectively as a highly sensual sign, an aural evocation of the diverse images of Italy described earlier—high-culture sophistication, romantic conviviality, and, perhaps, clannishness, crime, and poverty. The musical performances of the individual actors reference these meanings to develop their characters. Placed in Dickie's mouth, the Italian lyrics index his privileged upbringing of European vacations and private schools while highlighting his insider knowledge of European jazz. Stumblingly performed by Tom in his first chorus and more smoothly performed in the out-chorus, the same lyrics raise the specter of his unmasking and attest to his unique "talent," his ability to adapt to new situations and perpetuate his deception.

Additional levels of meaning come into play for those who speak Italian or are aware of the history of "Tu vou' fa l'Americano." Best known through Sophia Loren's performance in the 1960 film *It Started in Naples*, the song is a rambling litany of criticism in which the singer castigates his or her interlocutor for affecting an American style of conduct.[3] The song's use of English loan words and images from the American mass media highlights Italy's fascination with the United States, even as it critiques the latter country's postwar cultural imperialism. In the context of *Ripley*, such lyrics add an additional layer of irony to the performance. Those particularly well familiar with the Italian language will also recognize that the song is not set in standard Italian but in the Neapolitan dialect, thus positioning the singer within Italy's complex regional politics. But even for non-Italophones, the combination of Italian-language lyrics and English-language loan words makes it clear that this song is sung from the perspective of an Italian and has something to do with the United States. If Italian-language jazz is read as a sign of sophistication, then Italian-language jazz larded with a tantalizingly obscure cultural reflexivity would be doubly sophisticated.

In sum, I suggest that this scene depicts a working-class European American man struggling to display competence in an African American musical genre with Italian-language lyrics and English-language loan words in order to feign a typically leisure-class performance of racially and ethnically marked emotional authenticity. This formulation is certainly awkward. I have, however, chosen to express my interpretation in this manner in order to highlight the complex ways in which language choice and dialect combine with other elements of the musical performance to produce rich meanings and link the situated event with large social contexts.

The issue of language choice in popular music involves a wide range of phenomena. First, consider just the acts of music making and music listening. In its most narrow sense, the expression "language choice in music" will be used here to refer to the selection of one language rather than another in a musical context. This includes, for example, the lyricist's decision to compose in one language rather than another, the performer's consideration of language when selecting songs for his or her repertoire, and the interpretive processes that listeners employ with respect to the languages of the songs around them. In a broader sense, however, language choice in music also includes codeswitching (the shifting from one language, dialect, or register to another within a single piece or performance) and a range of even more fine-grained devices by which composers or performers combine individual elements of one language, dialect, or register (syntax, lexicon, morphology, phonetics, or even language-distinctive literary themes) with those of another.

As several of the contributors to this volume show (Alex Perullo and John Fenn; Paul D. Greene and David R. Henderson; Morgan Gerard and Jack Sidnell), language choice in music is not sharply demarcated from language choice in other expressive forms or in aesthetically unmarked situations. In a 1994 article, Steven Feld and Aaron A. Fox point out that music and language can be combined in an extraordinarily wide variety of ways—from the setting of words to melody in song to the use of "musical speech surrogates" (such as talking drums) to the musical elements of verbal art to an array of hybrid forms that includes "chant, recitative, *sprechgesang* (sung speech), *sprechstimme* (dynamically, rhythmically, and intonationally heightened speech), preaching, and lamentation" (30–31). Considering, for example, the contributions to this volume on hip hop in Italy (Tony Mitchell) or the talk of West Indian drum & bass MCs in Toronto (Gerard and Sidnell), we see that language choice and dialect are issues that can play out anywhere that music and language are combined. Additionally, considerations of language may also be important to those forms of social interaction that spring up around musical performance. Feld and Fox emphasize that verbal discourses about music are another way in which music and language may come together (32–33). Clearly, issues of language choice may be important in these contexts. Further, several of the essays in this volume draw special attention to those forms of talk that occur in situations defined by music making and music listening but which do not explicitly discuss music. For example, Perullo and Fenn show how Chichewa- and Swahili-speaking hip hop fans in East Africa incorporate English-language expressions from American rap into their everyday interactions, and the authors illustrate the importance of such language choices for the fan's social experiences.

The issue of language choice in music is not limited to situated interaction, and the essays in this volume explore the wide range of ways in which this topic is informed by large-scale social contexts. On a basic level, institutions such as the culture industry or the state may censure, regulate, or shape the use of language in music. This issue deserves careful attention, and María Elena Cepeda, Sue Tuohy, Maria Paula Survilla, and others address this important concern. The explicit institutional management of language choice is one manifestation of the broader phenomena of "language ideology." In a review of the topic, Kathryn A. Woolard and Bambi B. Schieffelin explain that the term is often used to refer to groups of ideas within a given society about the meanings associated with particular languages, dialects, registers of speech, or ways of talking (57–58). This subject is not an obscure one. From the mass media to educational institutions to everyday spheres of social interaction, we are surrounded by discourses that depict particular languages as sophisticated or crude, native or foreign, appropriate or inappropriate for business, literature, science, or religion. Language ideologies such as these tie language choice in popular music to larger social contexts. In many parts of the world, for example, native languages or regional dialects may be iconic of the colonized peoples or marginalized groups that speak them; songs set in such languages may function as a powerful affirmation of identity for their singers or listeners. This dynamic represents the most straightforward expression of language ideology in music.

While examples of this dynamic can certainly be found, real world situations often contradict what Woolard and Schieffelin refer to as the simplistic "equation of one language/one people" (61), and the politics of language choice in music can be made far more complex as a result. Phenomena such as bilingualism, linguistic appropriation, and hybridity are as common as the affirmation of group identity through language and are central for many of the studies in this volume. It is also worth emphasizing that while language choice in music may reflect prevailing language ideologies, that influence is

often a two-way street; that is, rather than merely reproducing existing ideologies, singers, culture workers, and listeners may use music to actively
think about, debate, or resist the ideologies at play in the social world
around them.

Whether exploring the aesthetics of the performance event or the politics of the culture industry, the essays in this volume illustrate the relevance
that language choice in popular music has for a wide range of concerns. But
before discussing the individual contributions, I want to describe two sets
of social dynamics distinctive to this topic that make it a particularly powerful focus of inquiry for anyone interested in expressive culture. The first set
of dynamics stems from the unique status that language has in society. In
the last fifty years, scholars from a wide range of disciplines have emphasized that linguistic behavior does not merely describe but actually constitutes many spheres of social life. For instance, depending on the speaker and
the context, performative utterances such as "I sentence you to five years in
prison" do not just depict a social situation, they establish and constitute it.
While judicial performatives like this one do not have the force of law when
uttered in music events, legal discourse is not the only sphere in which language constitutes social reality. Much of our identity in everyday life is
achieved through linguistic behavior, and, capitalizing on this fact, singers
and songwriters use forms of talk from the social world around them to
publicly think about, enact, or perform their identities. Construed broadly
to include the use of multiple dialects and registers, the issue of language
choice in music is central to these processes. This idea is richly expressed in
Perullo and Fenn's discussion of the mimetic functions of musical and linguistic performance. Describing how Malawian youth incorporate expressions from American hip hop into their conversations, they explain that the
participants are more concerned with "the 'doing' of speech acts" than they
are with the referential accuracy with which these expressions are used. It is
"through this 'doing,'" Perullo and Fenn explain, that the participants
"enacted membership in localized rap scenes. The meaning of language in
these cases lies not in the semantic realm [that is, the referential content that
the words have in their original speech community], but in a participation-
through-doing that is socially meaningful" and is at least partially constitutive of identity for the youth. Such a "participation-through-doing" is
important in many kinds of popular music. When a singer uses, for example,

a high-status foreign language, a despised local dialect, or a formal linguistic register in song, he or she may be exploring, performing, or enacting a social identity rather than merely describing it.[4]

Perhaps the earliest awareness of these phenomena in popular music can be found in Peter Trudgill's important study "Acts of Conflicting Identity: The Sociolinguistics of British Pop-song Pronunciation." Building on the earlier theoretical work of Le Page, Trudgill presents a detailed phonetic analysis to show how the vocalists of British Invasion bands like the Beatles and the Rolling Stones partially incorporated elements of American dialects—often specifically African American dialects—into their singing. Trudgill argues that the hybrid dialect of these songs resulted from a combination of the high regard that these British singers had for American rock and their incomplete understanding of American English. The use of American features diminished across the span of the 1960s, presumably as British rockers became comfortable in having made the music their own, and Trudgill shows how British punk singers from the mid-1970s created a different image for themselves by combining the American-English hybrid dialect of late-1960s rock with phonetic features associated with the urban working class of southern England. Trudgill points out that the Le Page—inspired approach used in his article attends to the "the phatic and self-expressive more than the communicative function of language" (Le Page qtd. in Trudgill 159). By treating linguistic behavior in music as the titular "acts of conflicting identity," Trudgill is a key precursor to the scholars in this volume who focus on the achievement of performance events through linguistic practice (Gerard and Sidnell) or who take concepts or theoretical orientations like mimesis (Perullo and Fenn), social interactionism (Anthony McCann and Lillis Ó Laoire), or phenomenology (Szego) as intellectual touchstones. In all of this, language's ability to at least partially constitute some forms of social reality makes the issue of language choice in music a uniquely important one.

A second set of dynamics specific to language choice in music emerges from the issue of comprehensibility. While musical styles from unfamiliar cultures may be more or less accessible or legible to outsider audiences, the presence of a referential function in language makes songs in unfamiliar tongues inaccessible in a distinctive way. It is obvious, of course, that a listener cannot comprehend the meaning of lyrics that are set in a language that he or she doesn't understand. But as the essays in the volume show, the question of comprehensibility plays out in complex and culturally specific ways in popular musics around the world. In some contexts, such as the Hawaiian one examined by Szego, music listeners may be attracted to the romance of songs with incomprehensible (or only partially comprehensible) words and may invest the sounds of those words with powerful meanings. Alternatively, listeners may place considerable value upon the comprehensibility of lyrics and avoid songs set in languages that they do not understand. Singers from marginalized speech communities may learn to sing in dominant languages in order to gain access to wider markets, even if they do not speak or understand those dominant languages; alternatively, such singers may stick with their native tongue to resist "selling out" or to capitalize on the attraction that their "exotic" language may have for others. And these are only the most obvious dynamics. As Cece Cutler shows, songwriters in a number of countries compose melodies set to texts of foreign-sounding gibberish, intending that a foreign-speaking lyricist will later replace the gibberish with meaningful foreign-language words. On the institutional level, such issues are mediated by music industry gatekeepers and their ideas about how comprehensibility informs a song's potential for sales—whether or not such ideas accurately describe listener tastes.

While these two sets of concerns thread themselves through many of the contributions to this volume, the issues that the studies explore are quite diverse, and I and my co-editor have grouped the essays into three sections based on the questions they address. The essays in the first section use language choice in popular music to shed light on the topic of globalization and culture; closely related, those in part two center on issues of national, regional, or ethnic identity. Finally, the essays in the third section provide detailed explorations of the situated performance event itself and the music and words found there. If the studies in the first two sections largely focus on the selection of one language over another in a particular musical style or physical locale, those in the last section use analytic tools from linguistics, literary studies, and music to reveal how performers manipulate the formal features of the musics and languages around them to achieve their expressive ends. Of course, these two levels of focus—the macrosocial and the microsocial—are deeply intertwined. As social theorists such as Anthony Giddens have argued (see, for example, *Constitution* and *Central Problems*), macrosocial patterns are constituted by the actions of agents, and all situated conduct is informed by larger social contexts. Thus, while the more macro-oriented studies seek to uncover large-scale patterns, they recognize that those patterns are patterns of situated action. Likewise, even the most fine-grained analyses locate the performances and social processes that they explore within larger political and economic contexts and make them speak to broader social issues. A number of authors in this volume—for example, Greene and Henderson, Szego, and Dave Laing—attend equally to both of these levels.

The problem of globalization and culture is of central importance for many of the studies in the volume. In contemporary parlance, the social processes that are referred to as "globalized" are ones that spread over large geographical areas without regard for national governments or their borders and institutions. For example, phenomena such as multinational corporations, guest workers, mass migrations, global satellite media, and the Internet all involve social or economic processes that are constituted across national boundaries as much as they are constrained by them. Older theories about the relationship between expressive culture and its social base become highly problematic in such contexts. Updating an earlier generation's fears about the homogenizing effects of the mass media, some critics of globalization have warned that the transnational proliferation of (often Western) popular music will lead to a "graying out" of local musical styles. More recent work, however, emphasizes that globalization may also produce new musical styles, and such research seeks to understand the distinctive social and cultural formations (such as hybridized ethnic musics or continent-spanning music subcultures) that emerge from the shifting demographics, mobile populations, and proliferating media technologies of globalization. The role of language choice in music here requires careful consideration. What do "native," regional, national, and colonial languages mean to the diverse youth of the postcolonial world, and how do these meanings play out in globalized practices of music consumption and production? How does the comprehensibility of music lyrics inform the marketing and promotion of popular styles by the global culture industry? How does language choice in music link globalization to issues of gender, class, and social change?

Mitchell, Perullo and Fenn, Wallach, and Greene and Henderson use the issue of language choice in popular music to examine what happens to expressive culture when such global processes are at work. Spread around

the planet by the transnational music industry, hip hop is clearly a globalized phenomena. Building on the ideas of Russell A. Potter, Tony Mitchell
compares rap music from five different countries to reveal common patterns
of indigenization and reappropriation. In each country, rappers creatively
combine the English of African American hip hop with a range of regional
and subordinated languages to articulate local identity and resist the hegemony of dominant languages and groups. A different set of themes emerges
in Perullo and Fenn's comparison of hip hop in Tanzania and Malawi. Here,
an ethnography of musical and linguistic practices in the countries' respective scenes is contextualized with regards to the larger frames of political
change, linguistic history, and the development of local music industries.
Perullo and Fenn show that although both countries experienced European
colonization, political, economic, and musical conditions unique to each
nation have resulted in differing patterns of language choice. Where
Mitchell's work highlights the commonalties that can be found across different locales in rappers' responses to globalization, Perullo and Fenn underscore the importance of unique local histories and the issue of agency in
producing distinctively local reactions to globally circulating styles. It is
worth noting that while Mitchell emphasizes the similarities between the
hip hop scenes of varied geographical locations, the similarities he finds are
abstract ones; that is, Mitchell finds related cultural dynamics, not identical
music styles. In all five scenes, African American hip hop is indigenized
(combined with local musics and languages to create a unique local style),
and neither Mitchell nor any other author in the collection subscribes to the
view that the global media are producing a planetary musical homogeneity.

The disappearance of local languages represents a different facet of the
problem of culture and globalization. In recent years, linguists have noted
that the number of languages spoken in the world is shrinking and that the
economic and political hegemony of the United States may be leading to
the emergence of English as a worldwide lingua franca. Wallach's analysis of
punk and metal in Indonesia speaks richly to the so-called Global (or
World) English phenomenon. After placing the emergence of Indonesia's
underground rock scenes within the context of the country's political and
linguistic history, Wallach uses ethnographic data to reveal the musicians'
and listeners' perspectives on the question of language choice in their music.
In the past, Indonesian punk and metal bands sang almost exclusively in

English. Countering the predictions of linguistic gray-out theorists, Wallach shows that in recent years, a number of factors—including the diminished fears of censorship and political reprisals after the demise of the repressive Soeharto regime—have led these singers to introduce native languages into their music. While the musical style of Indonesian underground music is (with some recent exceptions) largely indistinguishable from that of its Western counterparts, the style of the lyrics is a different story, and Wallach's analysis shows how the lyrics of the new native-language songs speak in an emergent, English-influenced register.

The blending of features from two different languages and the indigenization of Western music styles are central to the final essay in this section, Greene and Henderson's study of popular music in Nepal. In the last twenty years, discourses of modernization and Westernization have been crucial in all spheres of Nepali life, and the emergence of Nepali-language rock music has accompanied these changes. In the sphere of interpersonal relationships, for example, traditional arranged marriages are giving way to Western-style dating and "love marriages," and Greene and Henderson illustrate how musicians and listeners use the new Nepali pop to think about these issues. In a particularly powerful section of the analysis, Greene and Henderson show how Nepali grammatical constructions depict emotions as active and persons as passive; for example, sentiments like love or sadness are expressed in Nepali as literally "adhering" to their human subjects. Borrowing structures from English grammar, recent pop musicians in Nepal have created new linguistic constructions in a modified Nepali in which the person is the agent of the affect. Throughout their detailed discussion, Greene and Henderson shed light on the wealth of musical and linguistic devices through which musicians forge new discourses about development, affect, and interpersonal relationships.

Szego's study of Hawaiian chant, discussed in more detail later, provides a different perspective on cross-cultural interaction and social change. Using analytic tools from linguistics to examine the reception of song, she explore the interpretive processes by which native youth possessing only a fragmentary knowledge of Hawaiian make sense of traditional music set in that language. The essay speaks to issues of globalization by offering new ways to study those situations in which broad cultural or historical gaps separate a song's initial site of composition and its reception.

If the essays in the first section focus on globalization, those in the second examine nationalism, regionalism, and ethnicity. Exploring individual songs or larger institutions, the politics of identity is the primary concern here, and the issues are as complex as they are important. In a rich analysis, Cepeda's essay reveals how entrenched power relations within the American music industry (and beyond) have shaped the recent upsurge of Latin(o) music sales in the United States and how that growth has in turn been interpreted by journalists and others in the print and broadcast media. Drawing on the work of Reebee Garofalo, Cepeda shows that marketing categories like "rhythm and blues," "country," "pop," and "Latin music" operate as code words within the industry, compartmentalizing listening audiences via race and ethnicity, obscuring the hybridity of U.S. Latino/as, and marginalizing musicians of color. Language is crucial to these processes in several ways. First, a performer's choice of language is often dictated by his or her record company, and to a large extent such choices determine how a song will be marketed. But language in popular music can also be politicized in more subtle ways, and Cepeda illustrates how a range of techniques (such as the pairing of Spanish-language lyrics with stereotypical themes or the use of mock Spanish by journalists and media figures) can be used to trivialize Latino/a artists or reinforce derogatory images.

The politics of ethnic or regional identity is critical in popular musics outside the United States as well. Surveying the broad sweep of languages and musical styles in postwar Germany, Edward Larkey finds different dynamics at work. Here, the complex interplay between regional dialects and the national standard language is enriched by the presence of a Turkish-speaking guest-worker population and the prominence of English-language rock and rap from the United States and the United Kingdom. Larkey shows how the state cultural bureaucracy in the former East Germany limited the use of English in popular music and shaped the content of German-language songs. Musical expression in the regional dialects and the language of guest workers is used to affirm marginalized identities, and Larkey illustrates how the treatment of sexuality in English-language rock has been selectively incorporated into the styles of German-language music.

Maria Paula Survilla's essay on rock music in the Republic of Belarus resonates strongly with Larkey's work, although clearly the Belarus case is more extreme: the Belarusans not only struggled with the cultural restrictions imposed by the Soviet Union but also with more than a century of the earlier Russian imperial hegemony that attempted to suppress all forms of indigenous culture, including language. As Survilla reveals, Belarusan musicians and lyricists in the early 1990s used Western-style rock music as a vehicle for expression in the Belarusan language, which, owing to the longstanding Russian domination, was rapidly being forgotten by the urban population. The Belarusan rock bands successfully linked themselves with a long tradition of national literary movements in the country, and their use of the Belarusan language in song, Survilla argues, presents a complex "package" of meanings that resonates with the local cultural identity and history.

The issue of musical production under conditions of state cultural management is tied to questions of ethnicity, region, and nation in Sue Tuohy's essay on *hua'er*, a folk-song genre of Northwest China. A meeting place for Turkic-speaking central Asians, Han Chinese from various regions, Tibetan Buddhists, and a variety of other groups, Northwest China is a highly multicultural and multilinguistic place. *Hua'er* is a key form of expression for many of these peoples, and the songs have traditionally employed a stylized version of local dialects and a richly metaphoric and allusive use of language. Disparaged by both local religious authorities and Chinese scholars of the past, the genre has been celebrated by the Communist government as a music of the people and an icon of regional culture. Tuohy's analysis shows how the cultural bureaucracy's national promotion of *hua'er* has attempted to broaden the music's listenership by removing many of its distinctively local features, including the Northwestern dialects that are at its core. These changes are much debated by local scholars and musicians, and Tuohy explains how the national standard language (Mandarin) *hua'er* of the Cultural Ministry's music festivals coexists with the traditional dialect *hua'er* of informal local performances and the music of professional *hua'er* singers from the Northwest who seek to carve out for themselves regional and national careers in the wake of China's market reforms.

If the essays by Cepeda, Larkey, Survilla, and Tuohy demonstrate how singing in a subordinated native language may serve as a resistant affirmation of identity for marginalized peoples, then those by Laing and by McCann and Ó Laoire illustrate something quite different: that in some situations, no clear-cut one-to-one correspondence between a language and a social group can be found. Drawing on the work of Gareth Stedman-Jones, Laing traces out the history of images of "the cockney" in English popular culture from the eighteenth century to the present. He argues that such images do not describe an extant social group so much as they construct one. London has been a multicultural city since at least the mid-eighteenth century, and, Laing argues, Cockney figures—from those in *Pickwick Papers* to *My Fair Lady*—have operated historically as a nativist fantasy of the authentically "English" Londoner. Even though "cockney English" and cockney characters are media constructs, they have been richly imagined in music, theater, and film. Laing shows how the phonetic norms, stereotypical poetic devices (like backslang and rhyming slang), and character traits of "cockney culture" have been employed in rock music to express reactionary or xenophobic attitudes. The essay ends with a close reading of the music of the late rock singer Ian Dury, a performer who employed and cleverly subverted the traditional cockney images to construct a scathing vision of English culture.

As interested in highlighting the complexities of identity politics as Laing, McCann and Ó Laoire critique what they call the "two-traditions hypothesis" of Irish folk music. According to this perspective, Ireland possesses two distinct song traditions—one expressed in the Irish (or Gaelic) language and the other expressed in English.[5] In every way (literary style, musical technique, cultural sensibility), the hypothesis asserts, the two traditions are completely distinct, and the Gaelic language is more authentically "Irish." Contesting this widely held position, McCann and Ó Laoire trace out the history of the two-traditions hypothesis from its roots in nineteenth-century romantic nationalism through its incarnation in the adjudication of present-day music festivals. A discussion of contemporary singing practices in the country is used to show how the same musical style is expressed in songs of both English-speaking and Gaelic-speaking regions and how singers move fluidly between songs in the two languages. In the two-traditions hypothesis, McCann and Ó Laoire find an arbitrary and divisive identity politics that elevates some styles and regions at the expense of others, and the authors urge scholars to attend to the concrete reality of musical practices in social interaction. If the early essays in this section show that language choice and dialect are the symbolic battleground upon which struggles for identity are played out, the cockney and Irish examples show that such a terrain may be filled with mirages and that the lines of allegiance and opposition in these conflicts are not always clear-cut.

Focused on the level of individual songs and performances, the volume's last three essays explore the techniques and devices that musicians use to manipulate language in popular music and the interpretive practices that listeners employ to make sense of them. No less sensitive to politics than the earlier essays, the authors of these studies place their analyses of songs and performances within broader contexts and show how situated acts of music making and listening respond to larger social forces. In so doing, these close readings uncover the subtlety with which musicians employ musical and linguistic codes, provide nuanced interpretations of individual musical styles, and offer new tools for the analysis of music and language. Perhaps most important, these studies reveal on-the-ground performers and listeners to be agents creatively responding to the social world around them.

Gerard and Sidnell's study of drum & bass MCs in Toronto examines a facet of language choice unexplored by the previous authors—the interactive techniques that bind together musicians and audience members in the performance event. Though drum & bass has its musical roots in Jamaican popular styles and though many of its MCs are of West Indian origin, only a few of the syntactic and phonetic elements of Jamaican Creole can be found in their verbal displays. The authors show that, while these features are missing, the MCs use interactive techniques associated with Jamaican pop traditions to engage the audience and manage the event. Pronouns and other naming words, directives, questions, and descriptions of the performance itself are among the wide range of devices that the MCs use to make the performance happen. Unlike many of the other authors in this volume, Gerard and Sidnell analyze specific instances of musical and verbal performance (rather than generalized practices, songs, or discourses), thus placing the reader close to the site of musical production and reception.

A fitting conclusion to the volume, the last two essays address the issue of comprehensibility and illustrate how musicians and listeners deal with songs whose lyrics are set in languages they do not understand. Focused on the processes of reception and examining the shaping influence of educational institutions (rather than government cultural bureaucracies or the music industry), Szego's study of music making in a private school for native Hawaiians brings a unique array of issues to light. Until the Hawaiian cultural revival movement of the 1970s, the use of the Hawaiian language had been discouraged by educators at Honolulu's Kamehameha Schools, and the vast majority of students there had little or no proficiency in the language. Though the addition of Hawaiian classes in the early 1990s resulted, at that time, in only a limited increase in the students' comprehension, the language's status as an icon of native identity has been enhanced by the strong emphasis placed on the study and performance of *mele* (intoned Hawaiian poetry).[6] Exploring both the official classroom pedagogy and the students' perspectives, Szego's compelling and detailed analysis reveals the wealth of interpretive devices through which students make sense of Hawaiian-language lyrics whose referential content they only partially grasp. Turning from the Hawaiian case study to broader theoretical issues, Szego suggests how reception-oriented research can yield new perspectives on the problem of cross-cultural interaction and the dynamics of cultural revival.

While Szego examines how listeners interpret lyrics in languages that they do not understand, Cutler turns our attention toward an equally surprising situation: one in which musicians compose lyrics in languages they cannot speak. In many parts of the world, musicians whose languages are marginal to the popular music mainstream will compose lyrics in a foreign-sounding gibberish when writing their songs, intending such gibberish to be replaced by meaningful lyrics in a dominant language at some future point. (Larkey notes this practice in his essay on German-language pop as well.) The practice is called *chanter en yaourt* (literally, singing in yogurt) by musicians in France, and Cutler's study of the "yogurt lyrics" of the French rock group Montecarl offers what is, to my knowledge, the first detailed linguistic analysis of this complex phenomenon. Sophisticated yet accessible, Cutler's discussion shows that non-Anglophone rockers in France possess a surprisingly deep understanding of the sound structures of English, even when intentionally producing utterances with no lexical meaning. Cutler suggests that, for the French rockers, certain language sounds and constructions from English are given special emphasis in the music and serve to index the language as a whole. The overall analysis is used to shed new light on the issue of English-language dominance in global popular musics.

Viewed together, the essays in this volume discuss a range of unexplored phenomena and shed new light on old problems. The issue of language choice is a meeting place not only for different expressive modalities but also for scholars from a varieties of disciplines including, but not limited to, ethnomusicology, folklore, literature, cultural studies, linguistics, and anthropology. By taking language choice in global popular music as our focus, my co-editor and I hope this volume contributes to an interdisciplinary dialog about performance, popular culture, and the social life of music.

Notes

1. The film is based on a 1976 novel by Patricia Highsmith. This scene does not appear in the novel.

2. In everyday parlance, the term "lyrics" is used informally to refer to the words to which the melody of a song is set. In academic music studies, the more formal expression "text" is often used for this purpose. Because this volume seeks an interdisciplinary audience and because the word "text" has a complex range of meanings in contemporary intellectual life, I have chosen to use the informal terminology in this introduction.

3. The song is performed twice in the film. The first time, it is sung largely in English with a short section in Italian. The second time, it is sung in Italian with the English loan words noted earlier.

4. In a related connection, see Feld and Fox's discussion of the pragmatic, agentive, and indexical dimensions of musical and linguistic practices and their rich cross-cultural analysis of lament genres.

5. See note 2 in McCann and Ó Laoire's essay for a discussion of the varying usages of the terms "Irish language" and "Gaelic language."

6. In more recent years, Hawaiian schools have introduced language emersion programs, and some students today have substantial proficiency in Hawaiian.

Works Cited

Feld, Steven, and Aaron A. Fox. "Music and Language." *Annual Review of Anthropology* 23 (1994): 25–53.

Garofalo, Reebee. *Rockin' Out: Popular Music in the USA*. Boston: Allyn and Bacon, 1997.

Giddens, Anthony. *Central Problems in Social Theory: Action, Structure, and Contradiction in Social Analysis*. Berkeley: U of California P, 1990.

———. *The Constitution of Society: Outline of a Theory of Structuration*. Berkeley: U of California P, 1984.

Highsmith, Patricia. *The Talented Mr. Ripley*. Harmondsworth: Penguin, 1976.

Potter, Russell A. *Spectacular Vernaculars*. New York: SUNY P, 1995.

Stedman-Jones, Gareth. "The 'Cockney' and the Nation, 1780–1988." *Metropolis: London Histories and Representations since 1800*. Ed. D. Feldman and G. Stedman-Jones. London: Routledge, 1989. 272–324.

Trudgill, Peter. "Acts of Conflicting Identity: The Sociolinguistics of British Pop-song Pronunciation." *On Dialect: Social and Geographical Perspectives*. Ed. Peter Trudgill. Oxford: Basil Blackwell, 1984. 141–60.

Woolard, Kathryn A. and Bambi B. Schieffelin. "Language Ideology." *Annual Review of Anthropology* 23 (1994): 55–82.

Language

CHOIC

and

GLOBAL

Popular MUSIC

Part One

Doin' Damage in My Native Language

The Use of "Resistance Vernaculars" in Hip Hop in France, Italy, and Aotearoa/New Zealand

—*Tony Mitchell*

In *Spectacular Vernaculars*, Russell A. Potter applies Deleuze and Guattari's comparison of Kafka's use of Prague German as a "minor language" with the use of English by African-Americans to what he regards as the heteroglossaic, marginal vernacular forms of African-American rap, which he sees as a de-territorialization of "standard" forms of English (66–68; cf. Deleuze and Guattari 16–17). Potter sees African-American rap as a form of "resistance vernacular" which takes the minor language's variation and re-definition of the major language a step further and "deform[s] and reposition[s] the rules of 'intelligibility' set up by the dominant language." He concludes that African-American rappers "have looked more towards the language and consciousness of the ghetto in search of a more authentically black identity" (69). But it is arguable that the ghetto vernacular practiced by many African-American rappers has become so atrophied and ossified in its relentless repetition of a severely limited range of expletives that any claims for "resistance" have long passed their use-by date. As Paul Gilroy noted in 1994: "Hip hop's marginality is as official, as routinized, as its overblown defiance; yet it is still represented as an outlaw form." He goes on to identify a need to interrogate "the revolutionary conservatism that constitutes [rap's] routine political focus but which is over-simplified or more usually ignored by its academic celebrants" (51). In this essay I examine the use of indigenous languages other than English in rap music in Zimbabwe, Switzerland, France, Italy, and Aotearoa/New Zealand as more appropriate examples of "resistance vernaculars" which re-territorialize not only major Anglophone rules of intelligibility

3

but also those of other "standard" languages such as French and Italian. In the process, I also argue that rhizomic, diasporic flows of rap music outside the United States correspond to the formation of syncretic "glocal" subcultures, in Roland Robertson's sense of the term, involving local indigenizations of the global musical idiom of rap. The assertion of the local in hip hop cultures outside the United States also represents a form of contestation of the importance of the local and regional dialect as a "resistance vernacular" in opposition to a perceived U.S. cultural imperialism in rap and hip hop, and often corresponds to what Lily Kong has described, in reference to popular music in Singapore, as an expression of "inscribed moral geographies."

I start with an example from Zimbabwe that challenges the standard rhetoric about the Afrodiasporic and Afrocentric aspects of African-American rap and hip hop (e.g., Rose). In the title track of *Doin' Damage in My Native Language*, an EP produced in the United States in 1992, Zimbabwe Legit (brothers Dumisani and Akim Ndlouvu) provide English translations of key expressions employed in their Zimbabwe regional tribal dialect, Ndbele (Jones III). These English expressions ("Power to the people"; "The ghettos of Soweto"; "You know where to find me—in Zimbabwe") serve for the Anglophone listener both to locate Zimbabwe Legit firmly in its county of origin, Zimbabwe, and to indicate the proximity of that country to South Africa. In addition, the brothers Ndlouvu prioritize their native dialect as the main source of their art of rhyming, which finds local equivalents for certain rhetorical attributes of African-American "nation conscious" rap. The back sleeve cover and the CD itself highlight and celebrate words in Ndbele as a form of "concrete poetry," but Zimbabwe Legit's raps also incorporate Shona, the more "standard" language of Zimbabwe. So the linguistic "damage" done by Zimbabwe Legit is directed not only against the English language of their colonizers—which Zimbabwe Legit needs to use in order to be accessible in the United States—but also against standard linguistic practices in Zimbabwe. This concern for linguistic authenticity is furthermore linked to broader notions of authenticity and Afrocentricity. In a track entitled "To Bead or Not to Bead," the brothers Ndlouvu criticize African-American rappers who assimilate African fashions such as hair beading. This track is entirely in English, and includes an apparent reference to the rhetorical embrace of the Italian-American Mafia by African-American gangsta rappers:

Some MCs would rather be Italian / Now sportin' beads and a black medallion / Medallion on your chest, but do you feel it in your heart? / Jump off the bandwagon and pull the cart. (Qtd. in Jones 106)

Despite its inventiveness and its "authentic" African origins, Zimbabwe Legit was a distinctly minor voice in the chorus of African-American hip hop in 1992, and the group subsequently disappeared without a trace from the United States music industry. An entry about Zimbabwe Legit on the Rumba-kali African hip hop website describes it as the first African hip hop crew to break into the United States and European markets. When Zimbabwe Legit's Ndlouvu brothers were college students in the United States, they secured a record deal and an unreleased album produced by African-American hip hop producer, Mr. Lawng (for the Black Sheep label). Dumi Ndlouvu later went on to become part of the rap group called the Last 8th, and he now goes by the name Doom E. Right.

Another marginalized African rap group which shares Zimbabwe Legit's multilingual dexterity is Positive Black Soul, a duo from Senegal who rap in a combination of English, French, and their native Senegalese language, Wolof, thus managing to address two major global linguistic groups in the African diaspora as well as those in their own locality. In the track "Respect the Nubians," Positive Black Soul identifies itself in English in relation to African-American rap as "a brother man from another land known as the motherland." In "Djoko" (Unity), rapped in a mixture of Wolof and French, they address more local concerns, describing themselves as "a brand new (political) party . . . we are underprivileged, but we want the good life." Their multi-lingual rhymes enable them to address their immediate constituency as well as audiences in the United States and the world at large (the album sleeve contains the lyrics to all their tracks in English translation). Unfortunately the United States and the world at large didn't seem to be listening, and the first album by this innovative group did very poor business in the English-speaking world.

Deleuze's notion of the "rhizome" is aptly applicable to hip hop culture and rap music, which has rapidly become globalized and transplanted into different cultures throughout the world. This rhizomic process is expressed directly in the work of another rap group, Silent Majority, which is based in Switzerland and raps in a mixture of English, Jamaican patois, French, Spanish, and Swahili. Referring to themselves as "funky multilinguals," Silent Majority's members foreground their collective linguistic dexterity in a track entitled "Dans une autre langue" (In another language). In it, guest Spanish rapper MC Carlos from the bilingual Lausanne-based group Sens Unik states:

Ok! ok! el rap es americano / Pero, si el americano fuero amarillo / Mi musica saria una musica de chino / . . . . / La musica es contagiosa y al ritmo es una planta / Que cresce de Nueva York a Martignan

[Ok! ok! rap is American / But if American was yellow my music would be Chinese music / . . . . / Music is contagious and rhythm is a plant / That grows from New York to Martignan]

This use of the trope of rap music as a "plant" neatly corresponds to Deleuze's "rhizome" and serves to emphasize the "glocalization" of rap, which, although a worldwide phenomenon, is, like African-American rap, still very much concerned with roots, family, locality and neighborhood. As Sens Unik's MC Rade puts it in the same track, in a mixture of French and English: "Our music is not a pale copy of the United States, Lausanne on the map, rhymin' is the art, part of a global thing." Perhaps one of the most peripheral examples of the global linguistic indigenisation of rap as a "resistance vernacular" is the Nuuk Posse from Greenland, which uses its distinctly minority language (Inuit) to rap about the domination of their country by the Danish language (Barnes 1997).

The variety of ethnic origins among French rappers, from the French Caribbean to the Arab populations of North Africa to other parts of Europe, is notable. The origins of French hip hop in the immigrant and working class housing projects of the *banlieues* (outer suburbs) of French cities, as displayed in Matthieu Kassovitz' 1995 film *La Haine* (Hate), are also notable. A broad variety of musical inflections ranging from hard-core rap to reggae and raggamuffin distinguish French rap from U.S. rap and give it features more in common with British and Italian hip hop. The "adaptation" period of French hip hop in the 1990s involved the growth of hard-core rap and Zuluism (based on Afrika Bambaataa's Zulu Nation), where African-American models were adapted directly to French realities, but other concepts, such as Afro-centrism, could not be translated wholesale into the French context. André Prévos shows how French rap crews like IAM attempted to circumvent the "return to Africa" ideology prevalent among some U.S. rappers in order to avoid playing into the hands of French right-wing anti-Arab movements like Le Pen's National Front ("Post-Colonial"). Consequently IAM constructed an elaborate "Pharaonic" ideology and mythology which boasts about Africa, but not black or Arabic Africa, rather adapting the Africa of Ancient Egypt into a religious symbology. They also mythologize their native Marseilles, a marginalized city with a high non-European immigrant population, as "*le côté oscur*" (the obscure side) of France, and rap in Marseilles dialect. As Steve Cannon has noted, there is in Afro-French rap "a closer physical and therefore less mythical relationship of (black) rappers in France to the '*pays d'origine*' [African homeland] than in the USA" (164). Cannon also notes that, despite the fact that only six percent of the population of France consists of non-European immigrants, rap and hip hop have become a vital form of anti-racist expression for ethnic minorities:

studies of hip hop in France in the 1980s and 1990s suggest that not only is the most numerical participation in both production and consumption of hip hop "products" among people of minority ethnic origin, but also that hip hop in France is characterized to a great extent by its role as a cultural expression of resistance by young people of minority ethnic origin to the racism, oppression, and social marginalization they experience within France's *banlieues* and in its major towns and cities. (155)

Rap's rich impact on the French language was also illustrated by the publication in 1998 of a controversial dictionary of French urban slang partly derived from French rap, *Comment tu tchatches?* (How do you talk?) by a Sorbonne professor, Jean-Pierre Goudaillier. This charts the language of the French *banlieues*, known as *Cefron*, "a melting pot of expressions that reflect the ethnic make-up of the communities where it is used, borrowing words from regional dialects as well as Arab, Creole, Gipsy and Berber languages" (Bell). It also reveals that French rappers and North African immigrant youth are not, as the French mass media sometimes portrays them, an illiterate and uneducated subclass; rather, they are often talented linguists who speak French and *Cefron* as well as thier native "home" language. In "The Rapper's Tongue," Prévos suggests that the French rappers' use of the "reverse" slang languages "*verlan*" and "*veul*," in which words are syllabically reversed, represents a hip hop vernacular which contests the rules of standard French. Combined with the use of borrowings from English, Arabic, Gypsy expressions, and words from African dialects, the vernacular of some North African immigrant French rappers displays a rich linguistic dexterity which constitutes another form of "resistance vernacular."

Like a number of other non-Anglophonic countries, the first compilation of rap music in Italy was almost entirely in English. Called *Italian Rap Attack* and released in 1992 by the Bologna-based dance label Irma, it included a brief sleeve note by radio DJ Luca De Gennaro declaring that "rap is a universal language, in whatever language and whatever part of the world it is performed." But in fact the only Italian-language track on the compilation was Frankie Hi NRG's "Fight da faida," with its half-English, half-Italian refrain urging resistance against Mafia blood feuds. This track deservedly became the most re-released and most famous Italian rap track of the 1990s. It was a courageous declaration of resistance against the Mafia, and, in marked contrast to the celebration of Martin Scorsese's Italian-American mafioso stereotypes in American gangsta rap, it became one of the dominant polemics of "nation conscious" Italian rap. Frankie Hi NRG's barrage of internal rhymes also illustrated the greater facility for rhyming that the Italian language had over English, while his use of a brief burst of a woman rapping in Sicilian dialect was also a first:

Padre contro figlio, fratello su fratello / Partoriti in un avello come carne da macello; / Uomini con anime / Sottili come lamine, / taglienti come il crimine / Rabbiosi oltre ogni limite, / Eroi senza terra / Che combattono una guerra / Tra la mafia e la comorra, Sodoma e Gomorra, / Napoli e Palermo, / Succursali dell'Inferno.

[Father against son, brother against brother, / Born in a grave like butcher's meat; / Men with minds / As sharp as blades, / Cutting like crime / Angry beyond limits, / Heroes without land / Fighting a war / Between the mafia and the camorra, Sodom and Gomorrah / Naples and Palermo / Regions of hell.]

Although there are Italian posses based in the major cities like Rome and Milan, a notable feature of Italian rap is a tendency to manifest itself in smaller and more marginal regional centers. If Turin and Naples became major localities for rap music, Sicily, Sardinia, Calabria, and Puglia were just as important. A nationwide network of *centri sociali* (social centers), which were often set up in occupied disused buildings, became the focal point for Italian hip hop culture. As Italian rappers began experimenting in their native language, they also Italianized U.S. hip hop expressions like "*rappare,*" "*scratchare,*" and "*slenghare*" (to use slang) and began to rap in their regional dialects. Some rappers also revived the oppositional political rhetoric of the militant student groups of the 1970s, and in some cases began to excavate Mediterranean regional folk music roots which had been neglected since the Italian folk music revival of the late 1960s. A distinctive musical syncretism also emerged among the Italian rap groups that pushed out the parameters of hip hop and more often than not became fused with raggamuffin reggae ("ragga"), dance hall, and ska influences. This led to the coinage of the term "rappamuffin" in a 1992 Flying Records compilation of Italian rap and ragga entitled *Italian Posse: Rappamuffin d'Azione.* The Sud Sound System, based in Salento on the Southern Adriatic Coast, took this even further, referring to their hybridized music as "tarantamuffin," referring back to the dance tradition known as tarantella. The hybridizations of both Sud Sound System and the Marseilles-based Marsilia Sound System were studied by the French ethnomusicologist George Lapassade and his Italian collaborator Piero Fumarola, and as Felice Liperi has indicated, the use of dialect in Italian rap was partly a consequence of both technical considerations and the choice of polemical subject matter:

Clearly the motivation was not only cultural, it was also technical. Italian DJs and musicians who chose the musical idiom of rap, which is based on the relation between words and rhymes, found dialect a more malleable language in which to combine rhythm and rhyme. But it is also true that once they found themselves talking about the domination of the mafia in the south and urban disintegration, a more coherent use of the language of these localities came spontaneously. Dialect is also the language of oral tradition, and this brings it closer to the oral culture of rap. (201)

This is particularly evident in the work of the Bari-based group Suoni Mudu, which superimposes a street map of Bari on its name and enacts a mock Mafia murder on the cover of its polemical 1996 mini-album, *Mica casuale sara* (Hardly by chance). The CD cover includes the lyrics to their track "Citt e camina (L'ambiente)" (City and hearth [where I live]) in both Barese dialect and "standard" Italian. This begins with an address to local Christian Democrat and neo-fascist politicians and then proceeds to mark out a criminal cartography of Bari:

[Ind'a Libbertà acchemmà] [nne l'omertà / Ind'a Sambasquàle acchemmà]
[nne u criminale] / A Japigiè stene na Coop addò vennèvene la robba / A Carrassi uno
scippo] [ogni due passi.

[A conspiracy of silence rules in Libertà / Organized crime rules in San Pasquale /
There was a co-op in Japigia which sold drugs / In Carrassi a bag gets snatched every
two meters.]

The track exposes a conspiracy between the government, the police, the Mafia and their Calabrian and Neapolitan equivalents (the *'Ndrangheta* and the *Camorra*), and expresses similar sentiments to those of "Fight da faida," but they are articulated very differently. The loping ragga beat gives the track a sense of grim resignation as well as denunciation, and the sung refrains— "*Poverannù*" (poor us) and "*Ste fatt'u sccèhe*" (the die is cast), which use a female voice—draw on local musical idioms to express a sense of grief. Barese dialect is also used for its musical attributes, as in the line "Ask me for two hits (of heroin), there, give him two hits," which in Barese is sing-song: "*Dì dù, da dà, de dù.*" As Goffredo Plastino has noted, "dialect is also used for its different musicality with regard to Italian, for the greater possibilities of rhythmic and musical organisation of phrases which it allows" (100). The use of local expressions, the perorations through the main precincts of Bari, and the roll call of politicians also give the track a specificity and sense of locality which "Fight da faida" lacks. Suoni Mudu provides a detailed and intimate cartography of the Bari criminal underworld which is fleshed out by its idiomatic use of the "minor language" of Barese dialect. "Fight da faida," on the other hand, like the Rome-based rappers Menti Criminali (Criminal Minds), addresses the whole of Italy by using standard Italian. As a member of Menti Criminali put it, "my rhymes are written in [Standard] Italian so that what I experience and feel is clear from Sicily to Milan." But this kind of clarity often involves sacrificing a sense of local identity which is vital to the regional diversity of Italian rap. In the case of the Sardinian group Sa Razza, rapping in Sardinian dialect serves as a means of defending local (and national) pride. As the group puts it in its track entitled "The Road": "We prefer Sardinian slang rap. You have to defend your pride in being Sardinian, brother.

That's why we're rapping, here the only hope is for my people to survive. Survive on the road" (Qtd. in Pacoda 42). For the Sicilian group Nuovi Briganti, rapping in the dialect of Messina is a way of maintaining contact with the poor and dispossessed people of its locality, who have difficulty expressing themselves in "standard" Italian:

We are based in one of the most devastated areas of the city, and the people in the neighbourhood have difficulty expressing themselves in [Standard] Italian. They've been used to speaking dialect since they were children. And they were our first reference point, the people who have followed us since we began. And rap is about communication. (Qtd. in Pacoda 42)

A more paradoxically polemical use of Italian dialect as "resistance vernacular" occurs in a track by the Calabrian group South Posse, which was based in Cosenza until it disbanded in 1995. In "Semplicemente immigrato" (Simply immigrated), Luigi Pecora, an Italian of Ethiopian origin, also known as Louis, uses the dialect of Cosenza as a way of expressing his adopted Calabrian "roots." As Plastino has stated, here "dialect serves the function of identifying the privileged interlocutors of a discussion, the people of Cosenza, and challenging them to a dialogue. At the same time . . . it is a way of elaborating a personal style" (98). Influenced by the dialect ragga-rap of Sud Sound System, Pecora wrote "Simply Immigrated" in dialect as a way of expressing his ability to belong to Cosenza, and to get closer to the inhabitants, who he addresses as "brothers":

Eppure molti dicono tutto il mondo è paese / Eppure troppi dicono vattene al tuo paese / Ma dicu ma moni tu chi cazzu vu I mia / Ca signu vinutu druacu a lavurà pe fatti mia . . .

[Many people say all the world's your home town / Too many people say go back to where you came from / I'm telling you what the fuck do you want me to do / I came here to work and mind my own business.]

The simplicity of the language used here is abetted by musical repetitions of particular words, and there is a shift in the track from the direct address of "I" and "you" to "he" and then "we," indicating that the narrator identifies with both the immigrant and the native Italian. The use of dialect here is strategic, an act of defiance, and to emphasize this Pecora raps the first two lines in standard Italian before shifting into dialect in the second two.

As Plastino notes, this mixture of dialect and Italian corresponds to

the way a young person from Cozsenza talks today, which is what Luigi Pecora wanted to identify himself with to communicate more clearly. . . . The reference to "roots" is made to indicate the need to establish an exclusively linguistic relationship to one's region. (100)

But South Posse also uses dialect to rap about racism, in the context of both the discrimination against southern Italians by northern Italians and the exclusion of immigrants from Africa, who are often refered to as "extra-comunitario," a euphemism used to describe non-Europeans.

In spite of the fact that Aotearoa/New Zealand is on the opposite side of the globe in relation to Italy, we find that there too indigenous language is used in rap as a form of "resistance vernacular." The native inhabitants of Aotearoa, the Maori, constitute about thirteen percent of the 3.36 million population of Aotearoa, but forty percent of Maori are in the lowest income group, and twenty-one percent are unemployed, compared with 5.4 percent for *pakeha* (persons of European origin). Seventy-five percent of the Maori population is under thirty years of age, but forty percent of Maori youth are out of work and four out of ten leave school without having graduated. Since the 1980s, steps have been taken by Maori towards a renewal of their cultural and social traditions, and to regenerate *te reo Maori* (the Maori language), which is only spoken by about eight percent of the inhabitants of Aotearoa. This establishes it as a "minor language," although it is the language of the indigenous inhabitants of Aotearoa, the *tangata whenua* (people of the land). The syncretization of aspects of traditional Maori *waiata* (song) and imported African-American musical forms is one which many Maori popular groups and performers have pursued in different ways and to varying degrees throughout the history of Maori popular music. Given the implausibility of entertaining strict notions of authenticity and purity in relation to Maori cultural traditions (or to any contemporary indigenous musical forms), the combination of traditional *waiata* (song) and popular musical forms from the United States is part of a cultural project of self-assertion and self-preservation which is linked with a global diaspora of musical expressions of indigenous ethnic minorities' social struggles.

Maori rappers were quick to adopt the trappings of hip hop culture and to explore its affinities with indigenous Maori musical and rhetorical forms.

This is illustrated by the way concepts such as *patere* (rap), *whakarongo mai* (listen up) and *wainua* (attitude) are easily assimilated into hip hop discourse. The first Maori rapper to release a recording was Dean Hapeta (D Word), with his group Upper Hutt Posse. Hapeta was part of a "lost generation" of Maori youth who didn't have the benefits of learning the Maori language at school, as is now customary, and thus had to learn it himself. This informed the militancy with which he uses the Maori language in his raps. As Hapeta says, "Although I love and respect Hip-Hop, being Maori I only take from it what doesn't compromise my own culture. But in spite of this I have found them both very compatible" (Qtd. in Frizzell 48; cf. 50).

Hapeta and other Maori and Pacific Islander rappers and musicians have substituted Maori and Polynesian cultural expressions for the African-American rhetoric of hip hop, while borrowing freely from the musical styles of the genre (and it is an indication of the strong position traditionally held by women in Maori and Pacific Islander societies that the misogynist aspects of U.S. hardcore rap are totally absent from its Maori and Pacific Islander appropriations). The result is a further syncretization of an already syncretic form, but one which is capable of having strong musical, political, and cultural resonances in Aotearoa. In their 1996 album *Movement in Demand* (a title derived from Louis Farrakhan), Upper Hutt Posse combine the use of traditional Maori traditional instruments, militant *patere* and *karanga* (raps and calls to ancestors) and invocations of the spirits of the forest (*Tane Mohuta*) and the guardian of the sea (*Tangaroa*), and rhetoric borrowed from the Nation of Islam. The album also draws on the group's reggae and ragga inclinations, funk bass rhythms, blues guitar riffs, and hardcore gangsta-style rapping which switches from English to *te reo Maori*. One of the album's tracks, "Tangata Whenua" (The people of the land) is entirely in Maori, a choice which runs the risk of receiving virtually no radio or TV airplay, as the national media in New Zealand still regard the Maori language as a threat to its Anglophone hegemony. Nonetheless, Hapeta completed a powerful video for "Tangata Whenua," which was previewed on a Maori language television program. It tells the story of a polluted river, a consultation with a *kaumatua* (elder), traditional Maori gods destroying a factory, and an expression of Maori sovereignty:

Ko Papatuanuku toku Whaea, ko te whenua ia / Ko Ranginui toku Matua, kei runga ake ia / Whakarongo mai ki te mea nui rawa / He take o te Ao / He kaupapa o toku whakapapa /

*Ko IO MATUA KORE, te matua tuatahi / E ora! koutou! toku Iwi, / Whaia te wairua o te
ahi / Whakatikangia te kupu, te mahi, / Whakatahea nga hee o Tauiwi, / Kia rere ai nga
hiahia, nga moemoeaa, / O te hinengaro / Kia toko ai hoki te whakaaro moohio / Taangata
Whenua—Ko Te Pake—Whakapapa / Taangata Whenua—Ko Te Take Me Te Mana /
Taangata Whenua—Ko Te Hana O Te Haa / Taangata Whenua—Te Ahi Kaa*

[Papatuanuku is my mother, the earth / Ranginui is my father, he is above / Listen
to the thing it's very important / A root of the world / A foundation level of my
genealogy / It is Io-matua-kore, the first parent Live! you all! my people, / Pursue the
spirit of the fire / Make correct the words, the work / Cause the wrongs of Tauiwi
(the foreigner) to pass away / So the desires, dreams, can flow / Of the conscience / So
wise thoughts can rise up also / People of the land—The durable lineage / People of
the land—The root and the authority / People of the land—The glow of the breath /
People of the land—The ever burning fire]

The track starts with a woman chanting a *karanga* (call to ancestors), and
includes the sound of the *purerhua* (bull roarer), a traditional Maori instrument consisting of a piece of greenstone or wood rotated on a piece of string
which makes a whirring noise associated with sounding the alarm. The track
draws on key concepts in Maori philosophy, which are familiar to some
pakeha, such as *whakapapa* (lineage), *mana* (authority), *tangata* (man), and
kaupapa (strategy or theme of a speech). It also draws extensively on Maori
oral traditions and rhetorical figures. The track is not translated into English
on the lyric sheet of the album, which suggests that it is addressed to Maori
only, although most New Zealanders know the meaning of the term "*tangata
whenua.*" To adapt Zimbabwe Legit's phrase, in "doin' damage in [*his*] native
language," Dean Hapeta and the Upper Hutt Posse use the rhetoric, idioms,
and declamatory styles of hip hop to express Maori resistance and sovereignty, and in so doing, they indigenize it. Rap becomes subservient to an
expression of Maori philosophy and militant dreams, and is thus absorbed
into the wider project of Maori sovereignty. On 1 January 2000, Hapeta
released *Ko Te Matakahi Kupu* (The word that penetrates), a twenty track rap
album entirely in Maori, under his Maori sobriquet, Te Kupu (D Word).

From our consideration of hip hop scenes in places like Zimbabwe, Italy,
Greenland, and Aotearoa/New Zealand, we see that the the rhizomic globalization of rap is not a simple instance of the appropriation of a U.S./
African-American cultural form; rather; it is a lingustically, socially, and politically dynamic process which results in complex modes of indigenization and

syncretisim. The global indigenization of rap and hip hop has involved appropriations of a musical idiom which has become a highly adaptable vehicle for the expression of indigenous resistance vernaculars, their local politics, and what Kong calls the "moral geographies" of different parts of the world. The "minor languages" of Maori and Italian dialects, together with the use of *verlan* and *veul* in French and the languages of other ethnic minorities within dominant languages such as French and English, however, pay a price for their status as "resistance vernaculars." While the use of these vernaculars can be regarded as constituitive of deliberate strategies to combat the hegemony of the English language in both the global popular music industry in general and in hip hop in particular (which, its African-American linguistic variants notwithstanding, still represents a dominant language), their limited accessibility in both linguistic and marketing terms largely condemns them to a heavily circumscribed local context of reception. In contrast, a hip hop group such as the Swedish crew Looptroop reflect the continuing dominance of the English language and American culture in the formation of global pop:

We've all had English in school since we were 10 years old and there's a lot of sitcoms and films on TV that are English/American. The whole of Europe is becoming more and more like America basically. I guess we're fascinated with the language. But the way rap in Swedish sounds is a little bit corny and I think it's great that people as far away as Australia can understand us. I think that's the main reason why we rhyme in English. (Qtd in McDuie 31)

What Looptroop risks in their embrace of the Anglophonic and American homogenization of Europe, of course, is the erasure of any distinctively local or even national features in their rapping and breakbeats. In contrast, Maori rapper Danny Haimona of Dam Native sees the popularity of U.S. gangsta rap and R&B among young Maori and Pacific Islanders as the biggest threat to their appreciation of their own culture expressed in local indigenous hip hop:

There's such an influx of American stuff, and we need to quell it, and we need to give these kids some knowledge on what's really up. . . . Kids don't want to be preached to, so what I'm trying to do is put it on their level, and take all the good influences from hip hop, and bring it close to home. There is a good vibe out there for New Zealand hip hop, but it's being poisoned by the Americanisms—the Tupacs and the Snoop Doggy

Doggs. You have to have a balance, and Dam Native are trying to help kids work out that they have their own culture, they don't have to adopt Americanisms. (Qtd. in Russell 18)

In this context, the choice of local indigenous "resistance vernaculars" is an act of cultural resistance and preservation of ethnic autonomy, and as such, it is a choice that overrides any global or commercial concerns.

Note

Throughout this essay, translations from French, Italian, and Spanish are by Tony Mitchell; translations from Maori are by Dean Hapeta and Tony Mitchell.

Works Cited

Barnes, Jake. Review *Kaataq* (CD), by Nuuk Posse. *The Wire* 158 (April 1997): 65.

Bell, Susan. "Talk of Town Irks Academie." *The Australian* 20 Jan. 1999. (Rpt. from the London *Times*.)

Cannon, Steve. "Paname City Rapping: B-boys in the Banlieues and Beyond." *Post-Colonial Cultures in France*. Ed. Alec Hargreaves and Mark McKinney. London: Routledge, 1997. 150–66.

Deleuze, Gilles, and Félix Guattari. *Kafka: Toward a Minor Literature*. Tr. Dana Polan. Minneapolis: U of Minnesota P, 1986.

Frizzell, Otis. "Hip Hop Hype." *Pavement* (NZ) 8 (Dec. 1994): 44–50.

Gilroy, Paul. "'After the Love Has Gone': Bio-Politics and Etho-Poetics in the Black Public Sphere." *Public Culture* 7.1 (1994): 49–76.

Goudailler, Jean-Pierre. *Comment tu tchatches: dictionaire du français contemporain des cités*. Paris: Maisonnuveau et Larose, 1997.

Jones, K. Maurice. *The Story of Rap Music*. Brookfield: Millbrook P, 1994.

Kong, Lily. "The Politics of Music: From Moral Panics to Moral Guardians." International Association of Geographers' Conference, U of Sydney, 1999.

La Haine. Dir. Matthieu Kassovitz. Egg Pictures, 1995.

Liperi, Felice. "L'Italia s'è desta. Tecno-splatter e posse in rivolta." *Ragazzi senza tempo: immagini, musica, conflitti delle culture giovanili*. Ed. Massimo Canevacci et al. Genoa: Costa & Nolan, 1993. 163–208.

McDuie, Duncan. "A Looped Nordic Sample." *Revolver* (Sydney) 1 Nov. 1999: 31.

Pacoda, Pierfrancesco, ed. *Potere alla parola: Antologia del rap italiano*. Milan: Feltrinelli, 1996.

Plastino, Goffredo. *Mappa delle voci: rap, raggamuffin e tradizione in Italia*. Rome: Meltemi, 1996.

Potter, Russell A. *Spectacular Vernaculars*. New York: SUNY P, 1995.

Prévos, André. "Post-colonial Popular Music in France: Rap Music and hip hop culture in the 1980s and 1990s." *Global Noise: Rap and Hip Hop Outside the USA*. Ed.Tony Mitchell. Middletown, CT: Wesleyan UP, 2001 (forthcoming).

———. "The Rapper's Tongue: Linguistic Inventions and Innovations in French Rap Lyrics." American Anthropological Association Meeting, Philadelphia, 1998.

Robertson, Roland. "Glocalization: Time-Space and Homogeneity-Heterogeneity." *Global Modernities*. Ed. Mike Featherstone, Scott Lash, and Roland Robertson. London: Sage, 1995. 25–44.

Rose, Tricia. *Black Noise: Rap Music and Black Culture in Contemporary America*. Hanover, NH: Wesleyan UP, 1994.

Russell, John. 1997. "Rhymes and Real Grooves: Dam Native." *Rip It Up* (NZ) 240 (Aug. 1997): 18.

"Zimbabwe Legit." Rumba-kali African Hip Hop Website. rumba-kali.www. cistron.nl/zimbabwe.ht. 1999.

Discography

Dam Native. *Kaupapa Driven Rhymes Uplifted*. BMG/Tangata Records, 1997.

Menti Criminali. *Provincia di piombo*. X Records, n.d.

Positive Black Soul. *Salaam*. Island Records, 1996.

Silent Majority. *La majorité silencieuse*. Unik Records, 1994.

South Posse. *1990–1994*. CSOA Forte Prenestino, n.d.

Suoni Mudu. *Mica casuale sarà*. Drum & Bass, 1996.

Te Kupu. *Ko Te Matakahi Kupu*. Universal/Kia Kaha, 2000.

Upper Hutt Posse. *Movement in Demand*. Tangata Records, 1996.

Various. *Italian Rap Attack*. Irma Records, 1992.

Zimbabwe Legit. *Zimbabwe Legit*. Hollywood Basic, 1992.

Language Ideologies, Choices, and Practices in Eastern African Hip Hop

—Alex Perullo and John Fenn

Hip hop emerged as a musical and cultural force during the late 1970s in the United States and has followed a global trajectory ever since. Artists and fans around the world filter North American hip hop styles through their own local musical, social, and linguistic environments, making hip hop a highly visible (and audible) example of the intersection of global and local youth cultures. Young people in Tanzania and Malawi, neighboring African countries in the eastern region of the continent, are no exception to this creative process. Both countries have vibrant hip hop communities that draw on youth knowledge of international, as well as local and national, hip hop music and culture. Youth in the two countries listen to the same popular American stars and hold similar ideas about and interpretations of their lives and music. Yet Tanzanian and Malawian hip hop scenes diverge in the social and cultural significance of local musical practices, which include performing as well as dancing, dressing, and talking about rap music. This tension between the similar and the different serves as an analytic backdrop for what follows.

In this essay, we examine the language choices made by Tanzanian and Malawian hip hop fans and performers to compare rap musical practices in the two nation-states. Patterns of language use in the two countries share a dualistic structure: Tanzanian youth draw on English or Swahili, and Malawian youth rely mainly on English or Chichewa. The English language is a common component, representing elements of a shared colonial history. However, language-use patterns diverge with respect to local responses to broader historical forces within the region, preventing a sweeping analysis based on a presumed shared history or experience within East Africa. It is necessary to examine the local social and economic dimensions of rap musical practice in relation to both a (potentially) shared regional history as well as country-specific social, economic, political, and cultural systems, especially as reflected in language use and choice. Such analysis provides a broader understanding of hip hop's development in eastern Africa and its social and cultural importance in both Tanzania and Malawi. What are the similarities and differences, and how do they play out in musical practice? What is distinctive about general language use in each country, and how do these factors affect local hip hop musics? What are the tensions between "regionwide" and "country-specific" historical factors?

Following ideas outlined in Paul Kroskrity's *Regimes of Language*, we treat the processes of language choice in Tanzanian and Malawian rap practices as functions of explicit and implicit language ideologies that underlie social life. Language ideologies are people's beliefs and interests concerning the structure and use of language within social life. These ideologies motivate the ways individuals use languages in both music-specific and more general social situations. In the first section of this essay, Alex Perullo analyzes the relationship between language choice and meaning in rap lyrics, the development of vernacular words and rap aliases, and the influence of commercialization on the burgeoning hip hop scene to comprehend the use of English and Swahili in Tanzania. In the second section, John Fenn examines Malawian hip hop scenes, exploring the ways youth strive to express themselves in both English and Chichewa as they generate and interpret the "messages" and meanings of rap music. Each author draws on ethnographic fieldwork conducted separately over the past several years, and their respective analyses reflect current trends and situations in the two countries. As these are constantly changing, this essay also serves as an indicator of future avenues for research into language choices and popular musics.

Swahili and English in Tanzanian Hip Hop

The choices of language in Tanzanian rap music, whether English, Swahili, or a combination of the two, reflect particular ideologies held by hip hop musicians. English-language rap tends to borrow from popular American hip hop that emphasizes life's pleasures and the prowess of individual rappers. Songs are often about parties, friends, or praise for the group and the individual rappers in the group. Though also influenced by American hip hop discourses, rap in Swahili moves away from the more celebratory rap and focuses on social problems pertinent to Tanzanians, such as government corruption, lack of jobs and opportunities for youth, police violence, and health concerns such as HIV/AIDS. These issues confront the youth of the country everyday, and, by addressing them in a language that is understood throughout the country, artists believe that they are educating their fans and listeners. While artists who use English also rap about important social issues and those who use Swahili discuss life's pleasures, generally the two languages offer different avenues for rapping and reach different audiences within the Tanzanian hip hop scene.

The separate uses of English and Swahili are a result of a number of factors, including language history in Tanzania, language valuation and evaluation, and commercialism. The history of language in Tanzania is perhaps the most important of these factors. As in most other African countries, colonialism dramatically affected local language choices among indigenous populations. German colonialism, which lasted roughly from 1884 until 1919, was unique in that the colonial government did not force people to learn German. Instead, administrators encouraged the use of Swahili, as they considered local people's mastery of German a threat. Saida Yahya-Othman, a professor of linguistics at the University of Dar es Salaam, explains:

Sous les Allemands, le Swahili était utilis non seulement dans la vie courante, mais aussi dans l'administration et le commerce. L'apprentissage de l'Allemand n'était pas encourage, en grande partie de peur que les "indigènes" n'aient ainsi accès aux informations officielles. De ce fait, le Swahili prospéra considérablement durant cette administration Allemande.

[Under the Germans, Swahili was not only used in daily life, but also in administration and commerce. The learning of German was not encouraged, mainly for fear that the "indigenous" people would have access to official information. For this reason, Swahili prospered considerably during the German administration.] (79)

Though the Germans' approach to language may have kept specific information out of the hands of local peoples, it also encouraged the prosperity of Swahili, making it possible for large portions of the population to learn the language.

After World War I, the British took control of Tanganyika, the former name of Tanzania, and pushed the use of English in certain school and administration situations, in particular the education of teachers, clerks, and chiefs. Yet the British also insisted that Swahili be the sole language of primary education throughout the country. By the 1950s, the British support of Swahili made it the universal language of communication between the country's cultural groups (Iliffe 529) and allowed the country's liberation party, the Tanganyika African National Union (TANU), to gain support throughout the territory to oppose British rule. Unlike Kenya and other neighboring East African countries, where no one local language dominated, Tanganyikans were able to establish a national independence movement mainly because of Swahili's widespread use (Temu 212).

Though several communities continue to use local languages such as Sambaa, Haya, and Sukuma, in most parts of the country Swahili has become the primary language. Dialects of Swahili have developed as people have integrated it into their own systems of pronunciation, syntax, and vocabulary, but native Swahili speakers understand these dialects, even though they vary at all levels of language structure.[1] While indigenous languages are rapidly disappearing throughout the country, a few rap groups have employed non-Swahili and non-English languages in their music. The X-Plastaz from Arusha, Tanzania, for instance, occasionally use the language of the Maasai people in their raps, though they primarily rely on Swahili. In other areas of the country, particularly Dar es Salaam, rappers tend to include only a few words from local languages and rarely rap entire songs in a language other than Swahili or English.

English is still taught in secondary and college education but is spoken by less than 5 percent of the Tanzanian population (Yahya-Othman 82). Though a small minority, English speakers have a great deal of power and resources, though not necessarily wealth, in Tanzania. Many are professors, politicians, or business owners and are in control of newspaper, radio, and television companies. For these reasons, English is considered the language of political and economic power, especially in international commerce and politics. Most other Tanzanians who have access to radio and television or who have gone through secondary education comprehend basic elements of the language and can appreciate some English rap lyrics sung by Tanzanians and, to a lesser extent, those sung by foreign rap groups.

The historical processes that allowed Swahili to be the most widely spoken language in Tanzania and English to be the dominant political and economic language created a unique environment for hip hop culture to develop. As youth aspired to rap, the choice between English and Swahili came from the musicians' backgrounds, their association with each language, and their particular language abilities. Many of the more affluent youth, largely those who had access to learning English, rapped in that language, mixing American vernacular and phrasing into their music. Other youth, even those who could speak English, relied on Swahili, as it gave them a voice to speak to broader audiences about issues relevant to Tanzanians. As rap became more a part of both rural and urban life, Swahili dominated the country's hip hop scenes, though English continued to play a significant role within several rap groups.

To better comprehend how English and Swahili developed in hip hop culture, we must look at the early history of rap music in Tanzania. As the Tanzanian government liberalized the country's economy in the mid-1980s, both audio and video cassettes of American hip hop artists were imported by companies or brought into the country by individual travelers.[2] The introduction of cassettes caused an immediate interest in rap music, partially because foreign music was forbidden under the former government's strict socialist policies. Cassettes of rap music were also important for Tanzanian youth, since hip hop music reflected their sense of identity as poor, black, and outcast youth. Yet American hip hop artists were also successful, eloquent, and popular— powerful images for youth with little confidence in their own place in society. Even if Tanzanians could not understand the lyrics, the commanding visual images of artists such as Tupac Shakur, L.L. Cool J, and Ice T, accompanied by their strong, often angry, voices was taken by many Tanzanian youth as iconic of the autonomy and success they hoped to obtain themselves. Nigga J from the group the Hard Blasters remarked, "In that time [1989] I liked to listen to rap like Public Enemy. They really attracted me to rapping because I saw the way black men liked the music and the way they searched for their own voice." For artists such as J, trying to rap or imitate American rappers was a means to overcoming their social and political situation and attaining the success that they envisioned American rappers had achieved.

Perhaps most importantly for Tanzania, hip hop was a means for the country's youth to bond together and collectively speak out against their problems. Initially, youth participated in hip hop as an enjoyable way to distinguish themselves from other members of society, such as their parents and elders. However, as the first generation of rappers and rap groups, particularly Kwanza

Unit, the Deplomatz, G.W.M. (Gangsters with Matatizo), and the Hard Blasters, arose in the early 1990s, hip hop became both a marker of group identity and a vehicle for social commentary. It gave artists a voice to speak about their opinions and concerns in a way that they could not do elsewhere. As Nigga J stated, "We have to speak about the problems that are nearest to us. I speak about the hard life here because it is something that I experience and I live in this environment. You can strengthen or destroy society by the words you use." J's comment on the power of words is apropos to the philosophy many rappers have toward their art. Jobless after they finish school and influenced by drugs and alcohol, many Tanzanian youth spend their time loitering on the streets and working at informal jobs to make money. In this context, rappers' words can, as J makes clear, positively and dramatically influence youth culture. This style of educational lyrics ties into the country's socialist past, where aiding others was encouraged as a way to promote equality among the country's people.

Many Tanzanians taught themselves to rap by imitating the lyrics, mannerisms, and gestures of American hip hop artists. Mr. II, who also uses the name II Proud and is currently one of the most popular rappers from Tanzania, explained that he would listen to rap cassettes repeatedly until he could mimic the English lyrics. Though he did not speak English at the time, he would sound out the words until he had a sense of the rhyming and "flow" of the song. After establishing the song's feel, Mr. II would create his own lyrics and rap over the music from an American rap tape. While learning to rap, Mr. II often studied the music of the American artist Tupac Shakur, a ubiquitous rap icon in Tanzania and other parts of Africa. In explaining his relationship with Tupac Shakur, Mr. II stated, "I use Tupac like a role model, except that the things that we speak about are different. He discusses his environment in the States, while I discuss my environment here." Though Mr. II assimilated Tupac Shakur's delivery and rhyming into his own music, he never lost sight of his own identity as a performer and artist in Tanzania. Other Tanzanians follow a similar course in acquiring rap skills and use American hip hop as a springboard to develop their own identity as rap artists.

Despite the growth of hip hop music during the late 1980s, it was not until the early 1990s that the first album of Tanzanian rap appeared. Saleh J (otherwise known as Saleh Aljabry) released the first Tanzanian rap album, *Swahili Rap*, with lyrics mostly in Swahili but with sections, particularly choruses, in English.[3] The album became an immediate sensation all over the country and, in many ways, set a high standard for future Tanzanian rappers. Most of the songs were based on the music and rhythms of American songs, such as Vanilla Ice's "Ice Ice Baby" and Naughty by Nature's "O.P.P." Instead of translating the song from English to Swahili, however, Saleh J used the American rap as a framework to develop his own ideas—ideas pertinent to Tanzanian lifestyles. For instance, on his version of "Ice Ice Baby," Saleh J turned a song about a drive-by shooting and self-praise into a warning about AIDS and multiple sexual partners (Remes, "Global," 6). Throughout the song, Saleh J also uses English words and phrases from Vanilla Ice's original version to identify the song to listeners.

Saleh J's album marked a significant transition in Tanzanian rap. Until that point, most youth who recorded music and many who performed used English as their primary language. A trend, however, was growing in live performances to use Swahili, particularly at the "Yo! Rap Bonanza" competitions organized by Kim and the Boyz in the early 1990s (see Haas and Gesthuizen 284). Still, artists were unsure about using Swahili since it was not the language used in "original" American rap music. The album *Swahili Rap*, however, legitimized rapping in Swahili and inspired others to drop English from their lyrics. Inspecta Harun, leader of the rap group Magangwe Mob, commented, "So, then came a period when this fierce musician rapped in Swahili named Saleh Aljabry. He really moved me because he rapped in Swahili. This was at a time when Tanzanian [artists] had not proved ourselves." Encouraged by Saleh J's album, local rappers were given confidence to pursue rap music in the more dominant local language, though English remained a popular choice for youth who wanted their raps to remain "true" to the American music they heard.

The trend of rapping in Swahili about important issues that Saleh J began in the early 1990s continues today. Swahili lyrics often speak directly to social and cultural issues pertinent to the country's youth. Mr. II is the most prominent rap artist using this style. He has released five albums to date, each critiquing different aspects of life in Tanzania. The song "Hali Halisi" is one such example.

Washikaji zangu kibao wako jela, eti wazuruaji / Dada zangu wengine hawapendi kuwa malaya . . . / Mi nasema sawa, vijana kupagawa sawa / Hii ni hali halisi

[Many of my friends are in jail for they don't have work / Others of my sisters don't like to be prostitutes . . . / I'm saying it's alright for youths to go crazy / This is the real situation]

Throughout the song, Mr. II explains what he sees as the real situation: his friends are in jail; there are no jobs; and his female friends earn their living as prostitutes. In other parts of the song, he criticizes the government for not assisting local youth and for destroying education by not supporting teachers. Similar to the way that Julius Nyerere—leader of the country's independence movement and the nation's first president—sparked a nationalistic fervor by using Swahili during Tanganyika's independence, Mr. II uses Swahili to connect to the country's youth, hoping they will take action to address their problems.[4]

English-language lyrics often support ideological interests different from those upheld by Swahili lyrics. One group that uses English is Kwanza Unit (the First Unit, also known as the K.U. Crew). Kwanza Unit formed in 1992 and became one of the top rap groups in Tanzania. In their lyrics, the group borrows heavily from American rap discourses in their English language songs. Take, for example, the song "Inahouse," which describes a party with women, cigars, and other "pleasures":

Ladies in lingerie, passion, ménage à trois . . . / I'm sipping older sex Mafioso . . . / I'm in my silk robe, puffing a cigar, laying on my waterbed / I'm about to be fed by this Puerto Rican love child

Kwanza Unit's lyrics use themes—such as women, wealth, and ability to do whatever one wants—that are common to many popular American rap songs heard in Tanzania. More telling, however, is the choice of words used by the group; "ménage à trois," "Puerto Rican love child," "Mafioso," and even "waterbed" indicate the group's in-depth knowledge of American and European culture. Kwanza Unit's talent lies in their ability to draw from their vast knowledge of these cultures and present their own unique sound to Tanzanian audiences. Even though many Tanzanians might not understand the meaning of words such as "Mafioso," they can relate to the song because certain aspects of it—such as the smooth, upfront delivery of the lyrics and the use of common rap words "sex," "love," and "ladies"—resemble the American rap songs with which they are so familiar.

What is important for Tanzanian hip hop, however, is that Kwanza Unit develops their music without stories of violence or vulgar language, even though these themes are prominent in the rap music they hear from the United States.[5] When I asked rappers about their selectivity in copying certain elements of American music and not others, they stated that the expression of themes such as violence and vulgar language was frowned upon by Tanzanians and considered disrespectful, while the topic of male/female relations was more appropriate and found in most Tanzanian music. Though Kwanza Unit moves beyond typical discussions of love and sex employed in Tanzanian music, the themes in their lyrics still fall under the rubric of "male-female relations." Part of the reason for the disinterest in some American themes is that older hip hop artists and people in charge of performance, radio, and other events continually monitor the content of rap lyrics. Taji Liundi, a radio DJ who assisted in bringing hip hop to a broader audience through his radio shows in the mid-1990s, stated that he discouraged artists from incorporating vulgar language into their music: "So I started telling people that you must have music that is entertaining, but it must also have a social message. And that is what they started doing. If they brought music in that had cursing, I wouldn't play it." While the restrictions placed on artists are not censorship, since artists are never forced to alter their songs, older hip hop artists are central to maintaining a common vision for local hip hop music and emphasizing its social importance. Those youth who want their music aired on the radio or who want to perform at major rap events need to be cognizant and respectful of the social, political, and linguistic ideologies of the older rappers.

By rapping in English but limiting themselves to themes that are appropriate in Tanzania, Kwanza Unit reaches their niche audience—affluent East African youth familiar with American and European cultures. Additionally, their use of English is a strategy to communicate with people outside Tanzania, employing American rap discourses as cues to signal outside listeners to the group's understanding of hip hop music and their legitimacy as rappers. Unfortunately for groups such as Kwanza Unit, their music is lost on a majority of the Tanzanian population who either do not understand or have no interest in English lyrics. The audience referred to as "affluent youth" are a minority of the urban population. Many do not remain in Tanzania, as they travel outside the country to attend college or find work. Since Kwanza

Unit's music, even some of their Swahili rap, does not engage the larger population, the group has only had a steady fan base of diehard rap fans and has recently been moved to the periphery of the larger hip hop scene.[6]

The choice between English and Swahili becomes more complicated when considering the use of vernacular words and phrases—such as the American words "gangster" and "fresh" or the Swahili words "*bongo*" (wisdom) and "*msela*" (urban "sailor")—in hip hop lyrics and conversations. The creation and incorporation of new words and the altering of the meaning of old words are central to Tanzanian hip hop culture. Pieter Remes points out in his study of urban youth and language in Mwanza, Tanzania, that, in using vernacular words, "Tanzanian youth are pursuing distinction, as they mediate societal and parental expectations as well as their own desires and perspectives" ("Karibu" 270). Borrowing from Pierre Bourdieu, Remes uses the notion of distinction to highlight how youth employ vernacular words to set themselves apart from others in Tanzanian society. Such usage creates a sense of identity and a common culture, one with which many youth all over the country relate and identify. By creating words that are only understood by other youth, they are separating themselves from their parents, elders, and even other youth who do not participate in hip hop culture. They are also creating a vast network of rap fans who can interact with one another through their own use of language.

Depending on the language used, rappers incorporate vernacular words into their music and conversations in different ways. English words often develop from American, European, and, more recently, South African rap lyrics and from the rappers' in-depth knowledge of foreign cultures. This is a common aspect of Swahili in general, as many words, such as "*pasipoti*" (passport), "*polisi*" (police), and "*kompyuta*" (computer), have developed from American, European, and Arabic linguistic influences. Tanzanian rappers, however, incorporate other words such as "ghetto" (*geto*), "fresh," "microphone" (mic), "nigga," "flava," and "mission" into their music. These words, borrowed from American rap artists, demonstrate a person's in-depth knowledge of rap music and his or her desire to identify with an international hip hop culture.

One area in which American vernacular words feature prominently is in the use of rap aliases. Rap groups such as Underground Souls, Rough Niggas, G.W.M., Dogg Posse, Dream Team, East Side Killers, East Side Group, Hard Blasters, and Mob 'n' Genius (FBI) use names of American rap groups or words found in American rap songs to identify themselves with American culture. Almost all Tanzanian rappers use pseudonyms as a way to self-identify with a particular American group. In a 1999 interview, one of the members of Kibo Flava, a rap group from the Kibo section of Dar es Salaam, explained the origins of his rap name and its importance to him: "My rap name is Ice II. I chose this name because of the musician there [in America], Ice T. I am fascinated by his raps and the way he started [rapping]. People said I resembled his rapping style." Through hearing and reading about the music of Ice T, Ice II perceived himself, and was perceived by his peers, to be much like his American counterpart. By using the name Ice II, he hoped to show his fans with whom he wanted to be associated and whom he most resembled in terms of the flow and delivery of his lyrics. Further, Ice II believed that a particular English word from an American rap artist would help promote his career as a rapper. Many rap fans in Tanzanian knew the name Ice T and understood that Ice II was emulating his style and identity by using that name. Other rappers use the same approach as Ice II, searching for American names that most resemble their music or their approach to music and thereby acknowledging their heritage as followers in an American musical tradition. Still, while rappers can be complemented on their resemblance—in name and music—to other artists, they would be insulted if someone said that they sounded exactly like another rapper. Even if rappers borrow from American rap icons, they must still show that they are creative and have a unique style of rapping.

Rap artists and aficionados also use *maneno ya mtaani* (Swahili vernacular words) in their music and conversations. New words develop so quickly that even fluent speakers of Swahili have to interact continually with hip hop fans and artists in order to follow conversations, jokes, and rap lyrics. Working with one group in Arusha, for example, Perullo spent a significant portion of daily conversations discussing vernacular words. Each day, several new words appeared, including terms for "police" (*momwela, makuda, njagu,* and *ndata*), "English" (*ung'eng'e* and *umombo*), and "woman" (*sambra, nyusti,* and *dem*). These words develop from numerous sources, such as other local languages, the transformation of Swahili words, or the Swahilization of English words. Though some words never leave a particular community, others become widespread through rap songs and concert performances.[7] For instance, Magangwe Mob, a local hip hop group, popularized the word "*ngangari*" with their song of the same name. "*Ngangari*," which loosely translates as a tough-minded, resilient person, was used in the Temeke district of Dar es Salaam to describe members of the government opposition party, Civic United Front (CUF).[8] Because of the song, however, "*ngangari*" became a term that was used nationwide.

Though the use of vernacular is not solely a hip hop phenomenon, the creation of new words has become a central part of Tanzanian hip hop culture. Youth create their own identities in part through language, thereby separating themselves from other Tanzanian social groups. Of course, this is a common phenomenon all over the world, as language is a powerful means to assert group identity and separateness from the dominant culture. For example, in his study of African American communities in the United States, "Black Talking on the Streets," Roger Abrahams examines how the invention of new words and the innovative use of old ones are an important part of the community members' relationships with one another. Similarly, by creating their own words, the youth of Tanzania identify with one another and create group solidarity. American hip hop musicians and fans experience the same processes of language creation but tend to rely almost exclusively on one language, such as English or Spanish. Tanzanian youth develop a unique music through the junction of two languages, English and Swahili.

Most rap musicians consider hip hop to be a voice for youth culture in Tanzania and a way to speak about the "reality" of living in a "Third World" society. The choice between English and Swahili lies in the musicians' conception of and association with each language and the processes by which they attach meaning and value to each language, a concept Debra Spitulnik terms "language valuation and evaluation" (164), a phrase that depicts language as value laden, always undergoing social evaluations and judgments that are embedded in constructions of power. In Tanzania, for instance, members of the media, such as radio owners, DJs, and station managers, often regard Swahili as a weak language since it is used by poor, rural people. English, on the other hand, is an international and therefore powerful language. The apparent language valuation and evaluation is that English offers more opportunities within European and American societies and is therefore more valued than Swahili.

Many Tanzanian rap musicians, however, do not value and evaluate English in the same way. Dolasoul, also called Balozi, is fluent in both English and Swahili. For him, each language has a distinct importance based on the audience that his music reaches. In a letter to Perullo, he wrote:

Wherever I go on the face of this planet, I will always represent the thoughts of my people, ideas and views and speak on their behalf. I stand for the Truth and the Vision of a better tomorrow. Using my language "Swahili" and English as a second option if the need be. . . . I also try to provide solutions and give a wake up call to my people.

Most of the tracks [on my album] will be in Swahili—I just want to make my Language more acceptable internationally and at the same time I wouldn't like to leave too many people in the Dark so there will be about 3 Tracks in English.

For Dolasoul, rap music provides him with the means to represent his people and speak about changes that can be made for "a better tomorrow." The choice of language, whether English or Swahili, is based on his valuation and evaluation of that language within a particular context. In other words, language ideology, or Dolasoul's interest in using language to reach a certain group of people, affects his choice of language, whether English or Swahili.

Artists who are unable to rap in both English and Swahili cannot switch languages like Dolasoul. Yet in the early years of hip hop, when English was more valued for rapping, many youth learned to compose and use English in their music. Songs in this style were often simple and repetitive, but they maintained the status quo by rapping in the dominant language of that genre. As Swahili became the more accepted language, a flood of new artists appeared who were better able to compose and rap in their own language. The change of language choice by the hip hop community was due to an acceptance and legitimization of Swahili over English, which had previously been thought to be the most appropriate language for hip hop.

One other area that needs to be addressed is the influence of commercialism on language choice in hip hop, an issue that is intertwined with the question of language valuation and evaluation. Making records and finding ways to sell those records are constant challenges for Tanzanian musicians. Though Tanzania exceeds other African countries, such as Malawi, in recorded rap, the majority of rappers are never able to record an album since they have no way of paying recording studio fees.[9] Only through continual performance, sponsorship from local businesses, or employment at other jobs can rappers afford to record a single or an album in a local studio. Yet members of the hip hop community also consider language choice to be intrinsically tied to their ability to make and sell records.

Many Tanzanian rap artists stated that between 1994 and 1999—a period when independent radio stations played far more foreign than local music— English, rather than Swahili, was more beneficial for attaining airtime on local radio stations. These artists commented that Tanzanian radio stations, such as Radio One, often featured a great deal of hip hop music but almost none in Swahili. To these artists, radio personnel valued English over Swahili and therefore made an effort to play English hip hop. In an interview, how- ever, one of the hip hop DJs from Radio One stated that his station had no access to local Swahili music for their shows since so few recordings existed. Though at that time a great deal of Swahili rap was available, especially rap singles, most of it was poorly recorded. In another interview, Ruge Mutahaba, the program director at Clouds FM (a popular, youth-oriented station that began in 1998) said that in order for stations to remain professional, the music they played needed to be of a quality comparable to that of American, European, and other African countries. The English rap, he continued, tended to be of better quality, while the Swahili rap was usually recorded on cheap, multitrack cassette recorders. For this reason, stations initially focused their efforts on promoting English-language rap music.

Though radio station employees dismissed the notion of favoring one lan- guage over another, many hip hop performers believed that English was the stronger language for gaining airplay, sponsorship, and recording opportu- nities. By mid-1999, however, well-recorded Swahili rap swelled the local market and forced many stations to search for high-quality copies of local material. Stations that initially ignored local Swahili hip hop began to work with local musicians to gather as much of this material as possible. English rap continued to exert its influence, with several groups releasing singles in English or even albums (such as Dolasoul's *Balozi Wenu*) that combined English and Swahili. Where many groups had initially rapped in English, believing this would give them more radio play, by the end of the decade local attitudes had changed, and fans and artists pushed Swahili rap onto the airwaves. The shift in language choice within the local music industry was largely due to the success of several artists who used Swahili and the push by a few radio DJs to promote a local hip hop scene that focused more on social and political issues relevant to Tanzania.

Swahili became the more powerful language choice within the hip hop scene because of a desire among youth to build a national hip hop culture that promoted local rather than foreign values, ideas, and language. But the shift only occurred because of the interest in Swahili during live performances and the release of several high-profile albums, particularly Mr. II's (well-received) 1998 album *Niite Mr. II*, which was the first highly successful album of Swahili rap since Saleh J's album appeared in 1992.[10] These albums proved that Swahili rap could be commercially successful, despite beliefs by those in the local music industry that English-language rap would become more popular.[11]

Since Tanzania's music economy is still developing and changing, it will continue to influence language choice in Tanzanian hip hop. Artists pay attention to the demands of record companies, radio stations, sponsors, and promoters in the hope of finding support for their music.[12] Although commercialism is not the sole contributor to language choice—as this section has shown—it has a powerful presence in Tanzanian hip hop culture. Many artists desire financial success and fame, such as is portrayed in American hip hop videos, and will bend some of their creative style to accommodate commercial interest. Further, as artists find success in other countries, the international community may desire more music in English, depending on their interest in Tanzanian rap. Tanzanian artists may therefore monitor national and international music industries to inform their language choices.

Tanzanian hip hop artists choose between English and Swahili, relying on both languages to construct a unique soundscape for their music. They rely on their knowledge of the historical, commercial, and political dimensions of their social identities, using language to position themselves within the national and international hip hop culture. As hip hop "develops" in Tanzania, the performers' choice of languages and their visions of those languages will change as hip hop music and culture themselves continue to change. Clearly, however, neither language will dominate the local rap scene, as each plays a significant role in Tanzanian society and will continue to do so for the near future.

The Message Inside: Rap and Language Choices in Malawi

The English language pervades rap musical culture in Malawi, but it occurs alongside and is often interspersed with Chichewa. This dual presence reflects the general daily linguistic environment of Malawi, where English and Chichewa interweave as the two dominant elements of the social and linguistic environments. Much of the discourse about rap music, including newspaper articles, discussions with and among youth, and radio broadcasts, takes place in English, but young people acknowledge that at times Chichewa is more appropriate, especially with regard to conveying "messages" in certain situations. The general concept of "messages" in music comes up often when discussing rap with Malawian youth, and exploring this topic can illuminate their ideas about the social functions of this music and the importance of language as a vehicle for transmitting meaning effectively. Being able to transmit messages to peers often means knowing or guessing which language(s) audience members understand, just as being able to comprehend and interpret messages in rap music from the United States means having a strong grasp of English and some sort of understanding of its cultural context.

Language choices in Malawi take place when both consuming and producing rap musical culture—receiving and transmitting messages—and youth hold varying notions about "appropriate" and "effective" language use. The diversity of perspectives on this topic arises from the complex weave of social, economic, political, and cultural forces that young people experience. Language ideologies underpinning popular musical practices in general and those of Malawian rap in particular reside in these differing perspectives. A brief description of the general linguistic topography of Malawi and the recent development of the country's rap scenes, followed by several specific cases illustrating language use in musical practice, will provide material for considering the nexus of popular music, language, and the social construction of identity for Malawian youth.

The legacy of Hastings Kamuzu Banda forms a backdrop for contemporary linguistic practice in Malawi. Throughout his three-decade rule of the country, Banda maintained strict national policies on all aspects of life in Malawi, including language. He championed Chichewa, a dialect of Chinyanja, as the national language of Malawi, despite the fact that it was only spoken in the central region (Banda's home district). His policies affected language use in education, the print media, and the national radio. Other regional languages, such as Chitumbuka, were barred from media and educational institutions, effectively providing Chichewa with a linguistic monopoly. The situation changed in 1994, however, when a referendum brought about multiparty democracy, the end of Banda's reign, and concomitant alterations in policy. Due to Banda's institutionalization of Chichewa, it continues to have a strong presence in Malawi as both a lingua franca and an official language, but its status as the "national language" has come into question as of late (see Kishindo).

The English language has a social and political history in Malawi due to British colonial rule as well as because of Banda's language policies. Throughout Banda's presidency, English served as the language of governmental proceedings, business, education, and elite society (Kishindo 275), and alongside Chichewa, it continues to be an official language in Malawi. The situation here is parallel to that of English and Swahili in Tanzania. Today, primary school students throughout Malawi begin learning English in Standard 1 and continue to learn it throughout primary and secondary school; in secondary levels and in university, English is the language of instruction as well as a topic of study.[13] While English appears daily in markets, on the radio, and in newspapers, it has not completely supplanted local or regional languages as a means of communication, mainly due to widespread differential access to education between genders and economic classes. Code switching is a common phenomenon in Malawi among people who can speak and understand both languages (Kayambazinthu), and English words can easily appear in Chichewa speech when there is no Chichewa equivalent, for example, "democracy" or "hip hop." In some cases, English words are transformed into Chichewa, such that "computer" becomes *"computala."* Again, the situation is similar to that of Tanzania.

Language choice potentially carries political overtones in Malawi, especially given the strong regional divisions between national political party affiliations. Chichewa—originally spoken only in the central region of the country—has come to symbolize the historical (pre-1994) dominance of that region in Malawian politics and economics. Negative feelings surrounding this perception clash with the current rhetoric of national unity, especially in certain intellectual and political circles based in other regions and languages. Regional and ethnic identities are important in Malawian society and often are carried on the back of language choice. Choosing or refusing to speak a certain language in particular situations can communicate one's stance on issues of politics and identity in contemporary Malawi.[14] While such politicized discourse currently does not enter into Malawian rap, it does form part of the general linguistic backdrop against which Malawian rap musical culture continues to emerge.

Banda's strict national policies extended to cultural phenomena as well, and he celebrated "traditional" Malawian expressive forms over "foreign" influences in expressive practices such as dress and music (Phiri 159–61). Censorship was rampant in Banda's Malawi, and all arts suffered as means of expression for anything other than approved messages or themes (see Chimombo chap. 1). In the 1994 general elections, the political opposition to Banda won the presidential office as well as a majority in parliament, and a general liberalization of national policies followed. There was a subsequent profusion of expressive practices that, up until that point, had been suppressed and seemingly nonexistent in the public sphere. For example, several individuals told Fenn that after the election, males were able to wear earrings, grow their hair long or into dreadlocks, and, perhaps most important, express themselves freely in song lyrics. Under Banda, these phenomena were not permissible and would likely have led to harassment or prosecution by governmental or quasi-governmental forces.

In conjunction with expressive freedom in cultural practices, the economic sector opened as the market became deregulated. Banda-era economic policies favored politicians and pro-Banda businesspeople; a chameleon-like confederation of private and government interests controlled the economy, relying on a model that is best described as capitalism without the free markets.[15] The rich (politicians and businesspeople) prospered, while widespread poverty dominated most of the population (see Lwanda, 16–33). Of particular relevance to musical culture in Malawi, during Banda's rule only a handful of licensed merchants could sell cassettes, with street vendors being regulated and relatively rare. Selection and availability of cassettes were low, and rap music was almost always dubbed from cassettes purchased abroad. After 1994, however, the informal economic sector of street vending was deregulated, and stalls flooded the streets and markets. Highly prized items such as (pirated) cassettes became more widely available, leading to spikes in popularity for many types of music. Rap was one of these, and several Malawian youth stated that it was around this time that they first started listening to this music extensively.

Since 1994, youth involvement with rap has surged around the country. From the large urban centers of Blantyre and Lilongwe to the more rural areas of Nkhata Bay or Chitipa, rap music and its associated paraphernalia (such as T-shirts and posters) blanket the cultural landscape. Vibrant rap scenes have emerged in urban and rural areas. While in some ways discrete from one another, the local scenes are also connected through a nationwide institutional network of radio and newspapers. Such connections extend to the global level, as Malawian youth partake of the latest trends in hip hop culture from the United States, South Africa, the United Kingdom, and the Caribbean via such media as satellite television and video cassettes. Following Sara Cohen's work on scenes in popular music, we suggest that these Malawian hip hop scenes should be viewed as dynamic instances of both local and global culture. That is, they serve as social and physical sites for musical practices that are an emergent mixture of local and global streams of influence. Such streams of influence involve more than just the sounds of imported rap music; they include styles of behavior and dress from around the world as well as elements of the local economy, society, and culture. One significant component of rap musical practice in Malawi that illustrates the confluence of multiple influences and forces is language choice.

Language choice is fueled by language ideology, but language ideology is not necessarily a unilinear force that binds together speakers of a language. As Kroskrity points out, in any context there are often multiple language ideologies that interact and inform language use (12). These multiple ideologies may be held by one individual and called upon in different situations, or they may spread across individuals, providing apparently conflicting explanations even when describing the same phenomenon. Multiple language ideologies do not necessarily compete to describe some absolute truth but rather reflect the differing interpretive and experiential positions held by individuals with regard to their own and others' language choice or use.

Several examples gathered during fieldwork in Malawi will illustrate the enactment of language ideologies underlying rap musical practice there. As mentioned previously, English and Chichewa stand as the two main languages of rap music in Malawi; they are also the two main and "official" languages for general communication. Other languages are widely spoken, primarily within specific geopolitical regions. For example, Chitumbuka and Chitonga are found in the north and Chiyao and Chilomwe in the south. Singing rap music in languages other than English or Chichewa, however, is not at the core of rap musical practice in Malawi. Recalling that language choice in Malawi can mark ethnic, political, and social identity in general, rap music performance practices rarely stray from the English/Chichewa paradigm that characterizes the national or "official" level of Malawian language practice. The following examples, then, deal only with the choice between Chichewa and English and the ideologies that contribute to such choices.

Language choice related to rap music in Malawi cuts across processes of both production and consumption. In terms of the production of rap music, the choice involves the languages used in composing and performing rap songs. Malawi is unlike Tanzania in that there is not as strong an infrastructure for the manufacture and sale of rap music recordings. In Blantyre, home to most of Malawi's recording studios, only two are accessible to youth interested in recording their songs: MC Studios and GME Studios. There, performers usually cut a "single," meaning not only one song but also only one copy of that song. For economic reasons, most youth are not able to reproduce their music for distribution, and the common practice is to get the song to a sympathetic DJ in the hopes that he or she will play it on the air at least once. The political economy of making rap music in Malawi reflects the general situation of popular music there—a lack of economic and material resources for producing music coupled with widespread poverty and subsequent lack of a lucrative music market.

The situation for rap, however, is even more desperate. Many youth interested in recording their songs told Fenn that they have even less access to jobs or other income-generating activity than adults do and as a result have very little money to put toward their music careers. Furthermore, while many youth involved with rap music expressed hope for rap's future in the Malawian music market, there was strong agreement that right now, people (mainly adult consumers) are not interested in hearing Malawian rap, preferring instead to listen to reggae or "traditional sounds," usually performed in Chichewa. Consequently, locally produced rap is not widely heard, and English-language rap music from North America or the United Kingdom dominates the airwaves and cassette stalls.

There is, however, another option for performance and presentation of local rap music. "Rap and ragga" competitions are dynamic spaces in which young performers can make their music heard. Competitions may be sponsored by profit-oriented private organizations or individuals, but more often they are held by nongovernmental organizations (NGOs) dedicated to youth issues. Such groups may be local or attached to international donor aid programs and will offer cash prizes in addition to T-shirts, hats, and posters promoting their cause. Participating in competitions forms an important portion of rap musical practice and discourse in Malawi.

During competitions, participants perform original lyrics over prerecorded instrumental backing tracks. Performers might find these instrumental tracks on cassettes purchased from street vendors, record them from the radio, or create original instrumentals at places such as MC Studios. The first option is the most common, and due to financial constraints, contestants will often share instrumentals within a single competition. Also, groups or individual performers may have only one instrumental in their possession and will sing numerous original compositions to this lone track over the course of several competitions. In general, "copyright" or cover songs are not permitted in competitions, and thematic lyrics are sometimes a requirement for participation. This is especially so if the event is sponsored by an NGO dedicated to particular interests, such as HIV/AIDS awareness and education.

In competitions observed in the town of Mzuzu (northern Malawi), English was the predominant language for rapping, but performers also used Chichewa. When members of Mzuzu Crew, a group that sang in Chichewa about AIDS, discussed their choice of language with Fenn, they all agreed that Chichewa allowed more people to understand their message.[16] They anchored this explanation in their belief that more people understand Chichewa than English, and thus the importance of their message warranted communication in Chichewa. Many performers (and competition veterans) in Blantyre echoed the explanation that a song's message was more likely to be understood in Chichewa. The belief that there is a prevalence of Chichewa speakers over English speakers draws on the positioning of Chichewa as the "national" language of Malawi. Youth often referenced this notion by referring to Chichewa as "our language" and glossing over current debates in the political sphere about Malawi's multiple languages. Young rappers, then, replicated broader language ideologies concerning widespread use of Chichewa by positing—for the most part, correctly—that audience members would easily understand rap in that language.

Mzuzu Crew also performed a song in English at the same competition, but this song had a very different theme. Drawing on young Malawians' interpretations of rap music from the United States, the lyrics focused on celebrating the rappers' skills and invoked a "party and good times" atmosphere. The performers held no strong opinion about why they used English in this second song. Their lack of an ideological stance attached to the use of English in combination with the "lighter" themes in these lyrics recalls the distinction made by Tanzanian rappers presented in the previous section. Such a distinction was also echoed by some performers in Blantyre, who stated that rapping in English often involves talking about oneself or "boosting." In these cases, the implied criticism was that using English in a rap song might preclude meaningful content or messages, the underlying belief about language being that many youth who sang in English did not know the language well enough to create meaningful lyrics in it and were instead rehashing themes found in imported rap music.

However, several other performers in Mzuzu stated that they specifically employed English in their songs when they wanted a majority of people to comprehend their messages. This reflects another commonly held belief—that more people in towns regularly use English over Chichewa.[17] Conflicting interpretations of the effectiveness of English over Chichewa were also held by performers in Blantyre and serve to highlight the intersection of processes of differential identity construction with processes of language valuation and evaluation.[18] Such conflicting interpretations also underscore the multiplicity of language ideologies, especially as refracted through individuals' language experiences. Choosing a language to rap in at a competition often means choosing the "right" language to reach the audience, as language is a means to pass along particular messages to particular audiences. But depending on an individual youth's background and situation in life, the choice will be based in a variety of considerations: What language might the majority of the audience understand (or might the performer believe them to understand)? In what language is the performer particularly proficient (and how does this proficiency influence the performer's vision of the audience's language skills)? What kind of image does he or she want to project via language (or what language carries importance among peers)?

Urban dwellers often see themselves as living in a more sophisticated environment than their rural counterparts, with command of English serving as a status marker connecting youth to a more cosmopolitan sphere.[19] Such a perception extends to the regional level as well, with individuals living in Blantyre or Lilongwe—Malawi's two large urban centers, located in the south and central regions, respectively—often viewing other areas of Malawi as devoid of material, cultural, or intellectual sophistication. Such biases or prejudices (simplified here for the sake of brevity) are not necessarily politically motivated, even though regionalism is rampant in Malawi and language choice can carry political overtones and generate political debate. Rather, motivations behind valuation and evaluation of English in rap music arise from a widely held belief that youth gravitate toward English as more fashionable or international than Chichewa—a notion expressed in interviews Fenn conducted as well as in nonrap-related conversations.

No matter which languages are statistically more prevalent or actually used and understood more, contrasting language ideologies are important because they illustrate the diversity of perspectives that inform individual choices in language use. Such choices arise in shared social contexts and reflect the array of concerns held by youth in Malawi as well as the myriad influences on language practice, such as implicit notions of sophistication or cosmopolitanism. The idea that one language or another more effectively carries a song's message within a polyglot society implicates language ideology as a factor in popular music practice. Choice of language in rap performance practices is a key element in analyzing both semantic and socially symbolic meanings of words and linguistic practices; in the case of Malawi, such choices are influenced by a combination of the broader social, political, and historical forces that act upon language use in general.

In addition to serving as conduits for messages, language choices also enter into the ways that youth conceptualize and articulate their places within Malawi's rap scenes. Language choices and underlying ideologies can serve either to differentiate or unify individuals, drawing and redrawing lines of social interaction. Several discussions with young people in Nkhata Bay about their self-descriptions as "O.G.s," "niggas," or "gangstas"—all terms taken from American rap vernacular—revealed beliefs about language use that work into the ongoing formation of young Malawians' social identities. These radically recontextualized terms take on new sets of meanings, partially based in an American inner-city gang culture provenance (or, rather, Malawian interpretation of that world) and partially based on the contemporary social experiences of Malawian youth.

These terms are multivalent markers of identity shared by Malawian hip hop fans and performers, but there is not always a consensus about what they mean. Moreover, the immediate social context of language—the "here and now" of Malawian youth in relation to the rest of the world—figures into the interpretation of such terms. For example, Van Nyasulu, a nineteen-year-old Form 4 student at the time of this fieldwork, based his self-identification as a gangsta, or "G," on his fluent command of English. In addition to being a dedicated student in school, Nyasulu worked as a woodcarver in the tourist town of Nkhata Bay, talking to and negotiating with many English-speaking travelers on a daily basis, especially during the tourist season. He made good money selling woodcarvings and attributed his success to hard work in both carving and school. During discussions with Fenn, Nyasulu qualified his status as a "real G" by attaching it to his knowledge of English and his willingness to work. He believed these two factors distanced him from the others in town who were "lazy" and unwilling to learn English or work hard. Linking his status as a serious "G" to his ability to comprehend lyrics of songs by American stars like Snoop Doggy Dogg or Notorious B.I.G., Nyasulu indicated that he found messages in those lyrics that helped shape his lifestyle. A major lifestyle component that set Nyasulu apart from his peers in town was his material possessions (portable stereo system, compact discs, rap posters, trendy clothing), all status-laden items that he gained through hard work.

What is interesting about Nyasulu is the degree to which he linked his command of English to his economic success and social status as a "real G." As far as violence or crime is concerned, he had no interest in living the lifestyle of a "gangsta" in the United States; being a "tough guy" did not appeal to him. Nyasulu acknowledged that in comparison to "G's" from the United States—which he knows about primarily through lyrics—he and his cohorts were not truly "real." After all, they did not have cars or guns, so how could they measure up to those in the United States? But on more local ground—Nkhata Bay—Nyasulu's command of English grew out of his valuation of that language as important and status-granting. He set himself apart from his local social group via his use of English, turning to a more abstract social world that, for him, the lyrics of Notorious B.I.G. or Snoop Doggy Dogg embodied. He yearned to be independent and respected, just as his favorite artists were—at least in their lyrics. The core value of being a "G" for Nyasulu was to stand on one's own, and he connected this value directly to competence in English. To be a "real G" meant economic and social independence. The disparity between these interpretations and the "meaning" of the term in the United States was not lost on Nyasulu, but neither did he place much significance on that semantic gap. The symbolic meaning of the English language and a speaker's competence with it were at least as significant as replicating any literal meanings of terms through social practice. Nyasulu posited an equation of competence in English with a type of social status; as a result, choosing one language over another was not as important as accurate or competent use of a particular language (English) that carries a significant social and political history in Malawi.

The preceding example illustrates how language choice and language ideology can be used by youth to make judgments about others and place them in different social categories. Another example illustrates how language choice can unify youth into groups and provide an individual with a way into a local scene. The youth in this case, Malenga Msiska, was born in Dar es Salaam to Malawian parents, and he completed his primary level education in Tanzania. In a 1998 interview, Msiska explained that he learned to rap while living in Dar es Salaam, honing his rhyming and composing skills in Swahili during his Standard 6 year of schooling (circa 1994). For two years he wrote rap songs and sang only in that language. Following his family's move to Lilongwe in 1996, he began to learn to rap in Chichewa but soon decided that people were not interested in hearing Chichewa rap. By then he had begun secondary-level education at a boarding school in the Nkhata Bay district, and friends there taught him to rap in English, the language in which he now composes and performs.

Through his narrative about the phases of his own language use in rap music, Msiska traversed a broad ideological and cultural space while fitting himself into different scenes. At the time of his family's return to Malawi, the country was undergoing significant political change. This was not coincidental, for many Malawians who had been living outside the country for political reasons returned when multiparty democracy took hold in 1994. Msiska negotiated his personal geographical relocation with a parallel linguistic shift; Swahili is not widely spoken in Malawi, so he began to rap in Chichewa. Changing locations and languages again shortly thereafter, he learned to rap in English at the Nkhata Bay Boys Secondary School, a prestigious boarding school that recruits students from all over the country. The environment of the school itself presented another level of language ideology, for posted in a central courtyard there was a hand-lettered sign that read: "Academic Grounds—English is the Official Language." When Fenn inquired about the sign, students of the school, including Msiska, confirmed that they were required to speak only English, both in and out of classes. Fully exploring the implications of this institutionalized ideology is beyond the immediate scope of this essay, but here we can observe yet another facet of the broader sociolinguistic landscape of Malawi.

A key aspect of Msiska's experience with language choices and practices is that his successive social identities flowed from contextualized language ideologies. For each living situation or scene in which he found himself, his choice of language in rapping was strongly influenced by his need to merge into the dominant patterns of language use. His desire to be part of a scene intersected with prominent language ideologies and practices, such that choices he made served as portals into each successive scene. Just as with Nyasulu, Msiska's language choices undergirded his social identity, but toward slightly different ends. Whereas Nyasulu relied on language to set himself apart from his peers, Msiska used language as a means to integrate into the local scene. The many different ways that language choice lends itself to the construction of social identities in Malawian rap scenes underscores the wide range of language ideologies that individuals can draw on in different situations to bolster or justify their social and musical practices. The multiplicity of such ideologies, then, comprises a rich and dynamic pool of cultural resources and serves as a bridge between global and local levels of rap musical practice.

Mimesis and embodied motivations, as manifested in the style of using a language such as English, represent a final angle for examining language choice in Malawian rap.[20] This more tacit realm of language choice finds expression in the appropriation or imitation of ways of talking, and these linguistic practices are not as readily acknowledged by Malawian youth in terms of the kinds of overt language ideologies (beliefs about language) seen in the preceding examples. Accents, vernacular terms and phrases, or aspects of nonverbal communication take on rich meanings and serve as status markers in rap musical culture, yet they do not necessarily involve explicit language choice. More important here is the style with which English is used rather than whether it is used and/or understood accurately. Talking in a certain accent or using key vernacular phrases entails a level of participation in rap music and its language that, unlike previous examples, does not necessitate or invite overt explanation in terms of intended audiences or the relaying of messages. The meaning of linguistic elements such as curse words or "American" accents stems from mimetic use, in the sense of "enacting" rather than "copying."[21] Use, rather than metalinguistic acknowledgment of use, undergirds these aspects of language choice, and a sense of aesthetic accomplishment arises through employing them. For example, on one of the national radio stations in Malawi, Radio 2 FM, Vic Smooth hosted a weekly program dedicated to "hip hop, R&B, and soul." This show was popular with youth throughout the country, and the days following any given broadcast were often filled with discussions about Smooth's play list or particular events in the show. His on-air announcing was in a highly affected "American" accent, complete with phrases Smooth extrapolated from hip hop culture—"Where's the party at, caller?" "enough respect," or "give a shout-out to ———." Many Malawian youth, including those Fenn met and worked with in Nkhata Bay, enjoyed imitating Smooth and incorporating his idiomatic phrases into their own daily speech. Knowledge of English was necessary to do this, but not the same kind as in the other cases presented earlier. Youth instead were concerned with the "doing" of speech acts and through this "doing" enacted membership in localized rap scenes. The meaning of language in these cases lies not in the semantic realm but in a participation-through-doing that is socially meaningful. As in the Tanzanian examples, some individuals here may not have known the literal meaning of some of the phrases they used; often, however, ignorance of such meanings did not matter to them. It was more important to be able to replicate the phrase, incorporating it into the situation at hand and thus highlighting one's knowledge of rap vernacular. For example, greeting someone with "Where's the party at, caller?" signifies familiarity with Smooth and his speech in general, identifying the speaker as a hip hop supporter—even if there is no party and there is no caller. The language choice here lies in choosing to use English phrases at key moments. And this choice serves as a badge of belonging, a status symbol indicating that one knows a phrase and can employ it aesthetically, whether semantically it is totally grasped or even makes sense. This is not a false or incorrect meaning but an important, socially emergent one that is rooted at the intersection of linguistic, social, and musical practices.

Language use in Malawian rap musical practice spans the issues of choice between languages (generally English and Chichewa) and styles of speaking a language (mainly with English). The former entails more explicit explanations or rationalizations, whereas the latter encompasses a more mimetic dimension of language ideology. The two realms, however, constitute aspects of discursive and musical practice in Malawian rap culture that are conjoined via language ideologies and are not so easily separable in lived experience. It is at their intersection that youth formulate their places in the world and negotiate social identities, and it is here as well that language ideologies come into play as components of these identities. Like their Tanzanian counterparts, Malawian youth draw on beliefs about language when performing or talking about rap music. These beliefs stem from larger historical and social developments and connect rap musical practice to the issues and linguistic institutions that pervade contemporary Malawian life. The focus on "messages" and conveying or interpreting them through music exhibits the confluence of a global popular music (rap) with local youth concerns (HIV/AIDS, economic stability, and so forth). In all of this, language not only "means" in a referential or semantic fashion but in a social fashion as well and serves as a vehicle for conveying young Malawians' participation in a globalized musical culture that they enact daily as a localized identity phenomenon.

Conclusion

This essay has shown how a new popular music, hip hop, was linguistically localized into the music scenes of two countries in eastern Africa: Tanzania and Malawi. While the language practices and choices of youth drew on the predominant linguistic duality of their respective countries (Swahili/English or Chichewa/English), the reasons behind individual choices differed in terms of language ideologies as experienced and expressed in social contexts. In each country, colonial and postcolonial influences informed the broader social attitudes toward language, while the English of American hip hop—which youth in both countries initially considered to be the "authentic" language of the genre—influenced how youth learned to rap and compose lyrics. In Tanzania, English became less popular as Swahili gained recognition as more socially and culturally appropriate to the aims and goals of hip hop participants. Youth continued to adopt American vernacular into their music and into their identities as rappers, but they altered the language and the meaning of the musical culture that they borrowed to accommodate their unique social circumstances. In Malawi, English was the favored language, particularly in young people's mimetic enactment of American hip hop and their appropriation of American hip hop terminology in descriptions of themselves. Youth sometimes held Chichewa to be more important, believing that language would allow the messages of songs to reach the broadest possible audience. But multiple language ideologies existed, leading to differing perceptions of the "best" language to use in a given situation. These multiple language ideologies arose out of the varied social, economic, and demographic experiences of individual Malawian youth.

Larger social and economic forces—aspects of recent history in Tanzania and Malawi—also factored into language choice in each country. Some of these forces were the state of the music industry, commercialization, and the acceptance of hip hop among parents, elders, and others in Tanzania and Malawi. Other forces were broader and less specific to the two musical cultures. Patterns of language choice in Tanzanian and Malawian hip hop scenes are strongly tied to the time when hip hop musical culture began to flourish in each country. After Tanzania liberalized its economy in the late 1980s, hip hop music flooded local markets. At that time, the government was still trying to push socialism and maintain a strong, community-based society. Filtered through this socialist ideology, hip hop music changed from an imitation of North American styles to an educational and socially conscious music. Even though English still commanded a large presence among the many urban youth who identified linguistically with African American culture, Tanzanian hip hop was now delivered in Swahili, the most widely spoken and accepted language in the country. Malawi, on the other hand, did not see a surge of hip hop until 1994, when massive political change and economic deregulation resulted in social and cultural liberalization. Malawi was then a country reeling from years of repression under a semidictatorial government that had influenced everything from musical preferences to language use and beyond. Chichewa—a forced national language under Banda's government—maintained its status as an official language and lingua franca, but because of politics, it did not command unilateral usage or support. The choice of language in Malawian hip hop scenes has been based in individuals' ideologies regarding English and Chichewa, which in turn are tied to broader debates and practices of language use. While English has been the dominant language of Malawian rap musical culture up to this point, changes similar to those seen in Tanzanian rap may be on the horizon (that is, a shift toward Chichewa or other regional languages).

The cases of rap music in Tanzania and Malawi illustrate the complex intersection of language ideologies, larger historical shifts (political, social, economic), and popular musics. In either country, the choice of language both in performing rap and talking about it reveals the constant negotiations between individuals and larger groups, whether these are local or transnational, physical or conceptual. It would be erroneous to assume that the use of English in either Tanzanian or Malawian rap musical practice simply reflects a global influence and the use of Swahili or Chichewa a local influence, for in both countries more general linguistic histories serve as backdrops that continuously anchor language usage at the local level. Though English is not indigenous in either country, it has a strong local presence, mainly due to colonial forces that have been partially internalized and have resulted in particular structures of valuation and evaluation. Subsequently, the choice to use English or another language in rap musical practice is not always couched in terms of "foreign" versus "indigenous" by performers or enthusiasts. Usage often entails more of a choice between two (or more) locally viable alternatives that carry different meanings, depending on the language ideologies invoked by youth to justify or explain their choices.

Our research has sought to highlight the processes through which musicians in Tanzania and Malawi engage a "global" popular music and incorporate it into their own experiences as youth. But inquiry into this area has only just started. Much more in-depth study of performance practices, discursive fields, and language ideologies needs to be done by scholars working with popular musics. It is by talking to people about what they are hearing in music, and what they are trying to communicate through music, that we can move closer to understanding the role of musical practices in social economic, political, and cultural life.

Notes

All translations of interviews from Swahili to English are by Alex Perullo.

1. Some examples of differences in Swahili dialects are sound differences—for instance, "*jicho*" (eye) in standard Swahili is "*dito*" on the island Mvita; morphology—such as "*nyumba hii ni yangu*" (this house is mine) in standard Swahili is "*nyumba hii ndangu*" in

Lamu; and vocabulary differences—"*soko*" (market) in standard Swahili is "*marikiti*" in Zanzibar (Deo Ngonyani, pers. comm. 11 Jan. 2002).

2. After Ali Hassan Mwinyi became president in 1985, he made changes over his ten years in office that dramatically altered the economic and political state of the country, such as allowing for private business, the importation of luxury goods, and the opening of the country's airwaves. When the government allowed independent broadcasting companies to operate in Tanzania in 1994, radio and television became extremely important for disseminating rap music. However, these stations preferred to play English rap music, as discussed later in this section. Swahili rap grew with live performances and later with cassettes (see Haas and Gesthuizen 284) until the late 1990s, when radio started to play local Swahili rap.

3. *Swahili Rap* appeared in Tanzania in 1992, though Saleh J's version of "Ice Ice Baby" was released a year earlier as a single.

4. Mr. II even refers to himself as the "*Nyerere wa* [of] rap" (Remes, "Global," 1).

5. Violence does appear in some Tanzanian rap lyrics, such as Hashim's song "I Smoked a Deejay," but in general, violent themes are uncommon.

6. For many fans and older rappers, however, Kwanza Unit is recognized as an important innovator in the Tanzanian hip hop scene. Their production quality, vocal techniques, and the flow of their lyrics serve as guidelines for young rappers and remind experienced rappers of the ability of one of the older Tanzanian groups.

7. Rap lyrics and the widespread sale of rap tapes have created a quick way for new words to develop. Pieter Remes points out, for instance, that the word "*msela*" came into common usage in Tanzania after Kwanza Unit released a song by that name on cassette ("Global" 1).

8. The word "*ngangari*" originally was an ideophone, and no exact translation exists in English for its original meaning. Yet the image portrayed by the word, which is now used as a noun, is that of a strong, unwavering person.

9. In 2001, Tanzanian rappers released approximately fifteen albums and more than a hundred singles, though hundreds of groups and artists throughout the country were never able to make recordings, despite their desire to do so.

10. Several other Swahili rap albums appeared between 1992 and 1998, including two more by Mr. II. After 1998, however, the market for Swahili albums grew tremendously.

11. Even in the international music industry, many musicians see Swahili as being the more important language for Tanzanian hip hop music. In a telephone interview, Mr. II spoke with Perullo at length about the importance of Swahili in selling Tanzanian music to Western audiences. Having traveled to Europe and the United States, Mr. II realized that Western audiences desire to hear African languages, like Swahili, in African music. He explained that most Tanzanian artists realize this as well and switched from English to Swahili in an effort to sell their music internationally.

12. For instance, in 2000, the R&B artist Lady JD switched from English to Swahili because her new manager decided that she would be able to draw larger audiences and sell more albums in that language.

13. In the Malawian school system, which is based on the British system, primary school starts in Standard 1 and ends in Standard 8. At that point, students move on to the secondary levels, Forms 1 to 4.

14. The three main political parties in Malawi are based in the three different geographic regions of the country, and the bulk of their support follows those divisions. Alliance for Democracy (AFORD) is from the north; Malawi Congress Party (MCP) is from the central region; and United Democratic Front (UDF) is from the south. Ethnic identities are also regionally based, and even after many years, a family from the north that has been living in the south will refer to the northern regional culture, rather than the southern one, as "theirs."

15. Under Banda, there was only one legal political party, the Malawi Congress Party. All politicians were members of that party, and all citizens were required to become members and pay for a party card. Banda was both president of the party and "president for life" of Malawi.

16. Mzuzu Crew is not the actual name of the group. The name has been changed here for ethical reasons.

17. Situated in a traditionally Chitumbuka-speaking area, Mzuzu is in the north of Malawi. Given the recent history of the country and the ongoing tensions over regional identities, Mzuzu's northern locale is particularly important to the language politics of rap in that city. No performers sang in Chitumbuka, but the pattern of language choice is constantly changing and more research is needed to explore the unfolding situation.

18. The notion of "differential identity" refers to the ways in which people structure their identities as individuals and members of social groups according to both shared and nonshared characteristics. In Malawi, "rural" and "urban" are important identity markers, and individuals frequently identify with (or distance themselves from) one or the other term to achieve material and social goals. See Bauman for a general folkloristic examination of the concept.

19. See Turino for a recent examination of "cosmopolitanism" in relation to African popular musics. While he looks specifically at Zimbabwean musical culture, his development of the concept speaks to the situation of Malawian rap in numerous ways.

20. See Hymes for an expanded discussion of the concept of style, especially his notion of style as a "way of doing something."

21. See Winn (42–43) for an expansive discussion of mimesis that takes into account gesture, performance, and enactment.

Works Cited

Abrahams, Roger. "Black Talking on the Streets." *Explorations in the Ethnography of Speaking.* Ed. Richard Bauman and Joel Scherzer. London: Cambridge UP, 1974. 240–62, 461.

Bauman, Richard. "Differential Identity and the Social Base of Folklore." *Toward New Perspectives in Folklore.* Ed. Américo Paredes and Richard Bauman. 1972. Bloomington, IN: Trickster Press, 2000. 40–53.

Chimombo, Steve, and Moira Chimombo. *The Culture of Democracy: Language, Literature, the Arts and Politics in Malawi, 1992–1994.* Limbe, Malawi: WASI Publications, 1996.

Cohen, Sara. "Scenes." *Key Terms in Popular Music and Culture.* Ed. Bruce Horner and Thomas Swiss. Malden, MA: Blackwell, 1999. 239–50.

Dolasoul. Letter to Perullo. 3 Nov. 1999.

———. Personal interview (Perullo). 22 June 1999.

Haas, Peter Jan, and Thomas Gesthuizen. "*Ndani ya Bongo*: KiSwahili Rap Keeping It Real." *Mashindano!: Competitive Music Performance in East Africa.* Dar es Salaam: Mkuki wa Nyota Publishers, 2000.

Harun, Inspecta. Personal interview (Perullo). 28 May 2001.

Hymes, Dell. "Ways of Speaking." *Explorations in the Ethnography of Speaking.* Ed. Richard Bauman and Joel Scherzer. London: Cambridge UP, 1974. 433–52.

Ice II. Personal interview (Perullo). 15 July 1999.

Iliffe, John. *A Modern History of Tanganyika.* Cambridge: Cambridge UP, 1999.

Kayambazinthu, Edrinnie Lora. "I Just Mix: Codeswitching and Codemixing among Bilingual Malawians." *Journal of Humanities* 12 (1998): 19–43.

Kishindo, Pascal J. "Politics of Language in Contemporary Malawi." *Democratization in Malawi: A Stocktaking.* Kachere Book No. 4. Ed. Kings M. Phiri and Kenneth R. Ross.

Blantyre, Malawi: CLAIM, 1998. 252–82.

Kroskrity, Paul, ed. *Regimes of Language*. Santa Fe, NM: School of American Research, 2000.

Kwanza Unit. *Kwanzanians*. Madunia/RAHH. 2000.

Liundi, Taji. Personal interview (Perullo). 23 Oct. 2000.

Lwanda, John LC. *Promises, Power, Politics, and Poverty: Democratic Transition in Malawi (1961–1999)*. Glasgow: Dudu Nsomba, 1996.

Msiska, Malenga. Personal interview (Fenn). 18 March 1998.

Mutahaba, Ruge. Personal interview (Perullo). 24 June 1999.

Nigga J. Personal interview (Perullo). 19 Jan. 2001.

Phiri, Kings M. "Dr. Banda's Cultural Legacy and Its Implications for a Democratic Malawi." *Democratization in Malawi: A Stocktaking*. Kachere Book No. 4. Ed. Kings M. Phiri and Kenneth R. Ross. Blantyre, Malawi: CLAIM, 1998. 147–67.

Polayni, Michael. *The Tacit Dimension*. Garden City, NJ: Anchor/Doubleday, 1967.

Remes, Pieter Walter. "Global Popular Musics and Changing Awareness of Urban Tanzanian Youth." *Yearbook of Traditional Music* 31 (1999): 1–26.

———. "'Karibu Geto Langu/Welcome to My Ghetto': Urban Youth, Popular Culture, and Language in 1990s Tanzania." Diss. Northwestern U, 1998.

Spitulnik, Debra. "Mediating Unity and Diversity: The Production of Language Ideologies in Zambian Radio." *Language Ideologies: Practice and Theory*. Ed. Bambi B. Schieffelin, Kathryn A. Woolard, and Paul V. Kroskrity. New York: Oxford UP, 1998. 163–88.

Temu, A. J. "The Rise and Triumph of Nationalism." *A History of Tanzania*. Ed. I. N. Kimambo and A. J. Temu. Nairobi, Kenya: East African Publishing House, 1969. 189–213.

Turino, Thomas. *Nationalists, Cosmopolitans, and Popular Music in Zimbabwe*. Chicago: U of Chicago P, 2000.

II Proud. "Hali Halisi." *Niite Mr. II*. Dar es Salaam, Tanzania: FM Music Bank. 1998.

———. Personal interview (Perullo). 29 July 1999.

———. Telephone interview (Perullo). 28 Jan. 2000.

Winn, James Anderson. *The Pale of Words: Reflections on the Humanities and Performance*. New Haven, CT: Yale UP, 1998.

Yahya-Othman, Saida. "Kiswahili, la consecration d'une langue nationale africaine." *La Tanzanie contemporaine*. Ed. Catherine Baroin and Francois Constantin. Paris: Karthala, 1999. 77–86.

"Goodbye My Blind Majesty"

Music, Language, and Politics in the Indonesian Underground

—*Jeremy Wallach*

Much of the currently fashionable discourse on "global English" predicts that the English language will have a progressively greater presence in the popular cultures of nations subjected to globalizing forces. While demonstrably true in some cases, such a claim underestimates continuing attachments to national and local languages, as well as the semiautonomous creative development of imported cultural forms once they take root in new settings. In this essay, I discuss issues of language choice in Indonesian "underground" rock music and document a remarkable shift over the last decade that defies the global English thesis: once the dominant language of Indonesian underground rock, English has given way to Indonesian as the preferred language for underground song lyrics.

Keeping in mind that musicians are social agents whose practices must be understood in the context of their larger creative and social purposes (Berger), I will examine the social, historical, and political forces that helped motivate Indonesian underground musicians to sing their songs in the national vernacular instead of in English and the rewards and creative challenges they faced in doing so. Specifically, I will argue that the remarkable growth of an indigenous underground music movement in Indonesia precipitated a shift in consciousness among its participants, such that they began to imagine their primary audience not as an abstract, English-speaking global music subculture but as a national, Indonesian-speaking musical community composed of active local scenes distributed throughout the country. This growing underground music movement was strengthened by the proliferation of Indonesian-language underground songs, which made the music accessible to a larger segment of the national audience. In this context, underground musicians switched to Indonesian not out of a desire to "indigenize" the music but with the aim of making their music resemble more closely underground music in the West, which they viewed as using everyday language to convey urgent and powerful messages to its listeners.

The following discussion focuses on a small number of musical innovators in the underground who consciously refashioned the Indonesian language to make it compatible with underground music's poetics of vernacular speech, emotional directness, and sonic aggression. My arguments are based on interviews and ethnographic participant observation conducted in Jakarta, Bandung, Yogyakarta, Surabaya, and Denpasar in 1997 and 1999–2000; E-mail correspondence with interviewees since then; and the contents of a variety of Indonesian-language Internet sites devoted to underground music.

After a brief introduction to the underground music movement in Indonesia and a description of the social and political context in which it developed, I review the linguistic options potentially available to under-ground lyricists and summarize the advantages and disadvantages of each in the opinions of underground scene members. I then investigate reasons behind the growing popularity of Indonesian- versus English-language underground music and discuss possible future developments in the under-ground during the current period of chaotic political and social transition in Indonesia.

The Poetics of Musical Translation

What difference does language choice really make in popular music lyrics? A satisfactory response to this question must address the complex interplay of form and meaning that is fundamental to all musical expres-sions. A language's iconicities and sonorities, essential to what Roman Jakobson terms its "poetic" function, can be very difficult indeed to "translate," based as they are on the material specificity of a particular linguistic code and the sensorial effects of its material presence. This is not to say that one language may be more "poetic" than another; rather, my aim is to draw attention to the different formal properties of languages, which are exploited poetically in diverse ways by their speakers.

Song, of course, highlights language's poetic aspect. Shifting from one language to another in a musical genre is therefore not a simple, straightforward process, since songs in that genre may exploit poetically significant features characteristic of the first language but absent in the second. This alone can constitute a formidable creative challenge to musical translation, but there is a further complicating factor beyond differences in formal properties: the weight of each language's prior history of utterances tends to condition its expressive possibilities in different ways. For instance, in their attempt to adapt their language to the stylistic parameters of English-language underground rock music, Indonesian musicians had to confront a long history of Indonesian-language popular song lyrics characterized by "elevated" literary expression, poetic indirection, and sentimentality, all of which were anathema to the styles they wished to emulate.

It is not surprising, then, that many Indonesian underground music fans in the early years of the movement were skeptical about whether their national language could ever become a satisfying vehicle for underground rock music lyrics. Despite the fact that few were proficient in the language, many scene members viewed English favorably, not only as an "international" language but also as the most sonically appropriate linguistic option for underground music. In this sense, their attitude resembled that of American opera enthusiasts who prefer to hear arias sung in Italian or German even though they may not completely understand the meaning of the words.

Underground Rock in Indonesia

In order to grasp what was at stake in the language games of the Indonesian underground, it is necessary to provide a historical and ethnographic sketch of this largely undocumented youth music movement. In contemporary Indonesia, "*underground*" (the English term is used) is an umbrella term that encompasses a variety of imported rock music genres on the loud side of the spectrum.[1] These genres, called *aliran* (streams), include hardcore, punk, death metal, "Oi!" (skinhead music), grindcore, ska, gothic, grunge, and black metal.[2] These musics arrived in Indonesia in the late 1980s and began to attract an enthusiastic audience of predominantly male, middle-class, urban youth. Some of these fans formed bands dedicated to "covering" the songs of their favorite underground groups, with vocalists approximating the sounds of the English lyrics they contained. Later, some groups began to create and record their own songs. Since 1991 or so, a loose network of bands, small record labels, fanzines, and performance venues dedicated to underground music has existed in Indonesia, with full-blown local scenes emerging in most major cities by the end of the decade.

Indonesian underground bands usually choose English monikers that stylistically resemble those of Western groups; examples include Burger Kill, Vindictive Emperor, Corporation of Bleeding, Full of Hate, Kill I Can, Hellgods, Betrayer, Death Vomit, Virus Kingdom, and Purgatory. Occasionally band monikers are in other nonindigenous languages, such as Grausig, (German for "scary"), Puppen (Dutch for "shit"), and Arrigato (Japanese for "thank-you"). A small number of groups choose Indonesian names: Tengkorak (skull), Restu Ibu (mother's blessing), Tumbal (an object used to ward off evil), Kremasi (cremation), and Trauma (trauma). Musically, Indonesian underground bands do not differ markedly from their Western counterparts, and nearly all musicians begin their careers playing songs by Western groups. Most bands attempt to stay within the stylistic parameters of their chosen genre with regard to instrumentation, performance practice, and sonic approach, though many experienced groups have developed their own distinctive sounds within these parameters by which they are identified in the scene.

Urban, middle-class, male university and high school students remain the primary consumers and producers of Indonesian underground music. Female students are involved in smaller but significant numbers, and some join bands as both vocalists and instrumentalists. In a developing country where higher education is a privilege of the very few, these students form a miniscule percentage of Indonesia's relatively youthful population, yet their musical and cultural influence is substantial.[3] The underground community increasingly has begun to expand beyond its original constituency as larger numbers of rural and working-class youth (once again, mostly, but not exclusively, male) embrace the music. This is particularly the case within the black metal and punk communities, perhaps because these genres rely more on performative spectacle than lyric-focused genres like death metal and hardcore.[4] The latter two genres seem to have their largest constituencies in the capital city of Jakarta, while black metal tends to be popular in provincial capitals and rural areas.

The Indonesian underground music movement appears to have developed relatively autonomously, guided by indigenous interpretations of imported media (fanzines, recordings, and videos, among others) without much direct contact with Westerners. This distinguishes it from rock music phenomena in other Asian countries such as mainland China, where foreigners have played an important role in local scene developments as advisers, performers, and audience members (Cynthia Wong, pers. comm.). In general, the growth of Indonesian underground music can be viewed as a creative response by Indonesian youth to two recent macrosocial developments: first, the increased globalization of Western popular music; second, the dramatic political and social upheavals that have characterized Indonesian society in the last decade. These two contextualizing factors are central to any examination of language choice issues in underground music.

Musical Globalization and Indonesian Pop

Many studies of cultural globalization focus on the impact of global culture on conservative or formerly isolated societies; in contrast, Indonesia (and Southeast Asia in general) has been characterized by "patterns, going back millennia, of creatively assimilating or absorbing the influences and peoples emanating from outside . . . [into] indigenous structures and values, and creating out of them a new synthesis" (Lockard xiv).[5] Such patterns of assimilation and appropriation are readily apparent in the development of Indonesian recorded popular music in the twentieth century. Though it is best known in the West for Javanese *gamelan* and other indigenous performance traditions, Indonesia has had a long and distinguished history of producing Western-influenced popular musics sung in the national vernacular and currently enjoys one of the liveliest and most diverse pop music markets in the world.[6] Indonesian popular music genres range from the Indian- and Arab-influenced *dangdut* to melodramatic pop ballads to sophisticated jazz and jazz/rock fusion. Indonesian rock music enjoys tremendous popularity, and groups like Slank, Gong 2000, and Boomerang—influenced by bands such as the Rolling Stones, Aerosmith, Nirvana, and Metallica—have large and loyal followings. In the midst of this hybridic diversity, the underground music movement represented a departure from the typical ways in which foreign popular musics were assimilated into Indonesian life and was symptomatic of globalizing processes in music in which technological advances empower the global and the local at the expense of the once-dominant national level of cultural production.

The underground arose during a period when urban, middle-class Indonesians had unprecedented direct access to the products of the global entertainment industry. This access was the result of new communications technologies (notably satellite television and the Internet) and the aggressively expansionist marketing strategies of transnational multimedia conglomerates. The arrival of MTV Indonesia in November 1994 had a particularly dramatic impact on local music-making, increasing Indonesians' familiarity with Western recording artists and with global youth-oriented genres such as rap, R&B, alternative rock, and metal.

The increased access to Western popular culture enabled Indonesian youth to explore musics that were produced outside of corporate media control. Indonesian fans learned about nonmainstream rock genres, first from commercial crossovers promoted in the global media and later from their own forays into the direct-mail-order world of small, independent recording labels and low-budget fanzines. In the West Javanese city of Bandung, the location of one of the earliest and most influential scenes, the underground community began with a small group of teenaged skateboarding enthusiasts who, through exposure to the media of the international skateboarding subculture, learned about the aggressive metal and punk music hybrids that formed the soundtrack to their chosen hobby in Western countries. In this manner—beginning with the products of global corporate media and then searching beyond them—Indonesian young people gradually gained access to the grassroots networks that had sustained nonmainstream and sometimes anticommercial rock genres since the late 1970s (Azerrad). These networks connected local scenes around the world that valorized autonomous creative expression over business profits and that preferred to work outside the official channels of the music business (Goshert 90–92). From these networks and the flows of knowledge they channeled, Indonesian scene members learned about the cultural context and philosophical underpinnings of independently produced underground music, and, most important, they learned of a new approach to musical production and distribution that would permit the exercise of creative freedoms that the mainstream Indonesian music industry denied them.

The D.I.Y. Philosophy

Musik underground could have merely been the most recent of a long series of Western popular music styles to become fashionable among Indonesian youth were it not for the fact that the music carried with it an ethos of "D.I.Y." (Do It Yourself).[7] This ethos encouraged bands performing underground music to record and release albums on their own, with whatever resources were available to them, instead of waiting to obtain a recording contract with a large record company. Aspiring underground musicians in Indonesia were able to take advantage of an abundance of inexpensive recording studios located in urban areas. Local rock and pop bands originally used these facilities to record promotional "demo tapes"— rough recorded versions of songs that groups would use to obtain live engagements and, for a lucky few, a recording contract. For underground bands, however, these homemade recordings became the finished product and were duplicated and sold through mostly informal channels. As veteran members of the scene grew older and more concerned with making a living, many opened small rehearsal and recording studios specializing in the production of underground cassettes. Local bands could rent these studios at reasonable rates. While modestly equipped by professional standards, many of these facilities have produced recordings of surprisingly high sound quality.[8]

The D.I.Y. ethos, coupled with the increasing availability of inexpensive recording and rehearsal facilities, contributed to a dramatic and unprecedented upsurge of independent cassette releases between 1991 and 2001. Significantly, bands that created these cassettes were not constrained by the rules of the music business in Indonesia, including the nearly compulsory use of the national vernacular in song lyrics. They could record songs in English that lacked catchy melodies or even pitched vocals and write lyrics that addressed topics considered too controversial by the mainstream.

The majority of underground groups still release cassettes on small independent labels, though the number of bands with "major label" contracts is increasing as some underground styles become more popular.[9] Even these major label releases show the traces of a musical style that developed outside the official channels of the national recording industry, and in one case, a punk group called Rage Generation Brothers released an album on a large national label, Aquarius Musikindo, with almost all of the songs in English (eleven out of twelve tracks). Thus the rise of the underground, spurred on by globalizing musical and technological forces, eventually transformed the Indonesian musical mainstream—a case of local appropriations of global cultural forms influencing cultural production on a national level. This may well become a common pattern in an increasingly globalized world.

Indonesian Politics and the Underground

The second key context for understanding the Indonesian underground movement is Indonesia's political situation in the 1990s. The growth of local underground music scenes began in the final years of former President Soeharto's rapacious and repressive New Order regime, which lasted from 1966 until 1998. In the wake of the 1997–98 Asian economic crisis, the New Order was toppled through the efforts of student protesters (many of whom were underground rock enthusiasts), factions in the military, and political opposition leaders. In Indonesia's current postdictatorship climate of free expression and incipient democratization, the musical underground has continued to develop and expand, in spite of the country's continuing economic crisis and political instability.

Everyone I spoke with agreed that underground musicians had far greater freedom in the post–New Order era of *Reformasi* (reform) than they had under Soeharto. As in the West, however, opinion in the Indonesian underground community was divided on the appropriateness of mixing music and explicit political messages and whether a coherent progressive politics is, can, or should be articulated by underground music. A group of university student fans in Jakarta once told me the only ideology the underground movement possessed was an "*ideologi pembebasan*"—an ideology of liberation. But such an ideology has significant political ramifications under a military dictatorship. Indeed, the artistic and social freedoms celebrated in the underground scene were fundamentally at odds with the practices of a totalitarian government. While the regime never cracked down on underground artists, most scene members adopted an oppositional stance toward Soeharto's rule, and many with whom I spoke suggested that the anger and negativity of underground music resonated with many young Indonesians who grew up under an oppressive regime prone to violence against its own citizens.[10] However, underground opposition to the Soeharto regime was not commonly extended to include an opposition to the regime's overseas supporters, the United States prominently among them. Therefore, underground scene members did not, for the most part, perceive any contradiction between embracing elements from global popular culture and opposing a dictatorship propped up by global capitalist interests.

Expressions of political protest in the underground increased in the months before the New Order's downfall. Some scene members, like Puppen's Arian Tigabelas, were active in the student movement that helped topple Soeharto, and locally produced fanzines covering underground scenes often contained articles explaining, in plainspoken Indonesian, various streams of leftist thought, from feminism to anarchism to animal liberation. Dominant political themes in the underground included opposition to capitalism, racism, and militarism; many scene members were also familiar with the ideological movements that emerged from within Western underground subcultures, such as "straight edge" (a punk-based movement for voluntary abstention from promiscuity and substance abuse) and the antiracist skinhead movement. In contemporary post–New Order Indonesia, where left-of-center thought is still routinely equated with reviled Communism, the active presence of leftist political discourse in Indonesian student culture stems in part from such discourse's association with underground rock music.

Political lyrics have been especially prevalent in Indonesian punk, hardcore, and grindcore songs—all genres that tend to take on political and social themes in the West as well. Despite a general tendency toward a nonpolitical, music-for-music's sake orientation in the international metal subculture (Roccor 83), Indonesian metal bands of various subgenres have also been among the most politically outspoken. In fact, impassioned and courageous indictments of the Soeharto regime and the military were common in underground music well before the regime was toppled. For example, on a song entitled "The Pain Remains the Same" released in 1997, the Surabaya-based death metal band Slowdeath sang (in English), "*There is no difference between Dutch colonialism and the New Order!*"—a statement that could have landed the band members in prison. The often violent imagery in the songs of many Indonesian underground bands was frequently supplemented by cover art and album graphics that incorporated press photographs of atrocities committed by the Indonesian army or police. While examples such as these may interest popular music researchers preoccupied with the relationship between music and social change, underground scene members themselves do not attribute an active political role to the music, perhaps because they view it more as an expressive form than an instrument for coordinating group action.

Arian Tigabelas from Puppen explained to me that he writes lyrics about his feelings (*perasaan*), and sometimes these feelings are reactions to political matters. For the most part, underground songwriters claim they write for themselves first, and secondly for anyone who feels the music "represents" him or her. They tend not to connect their music to larger political or social goals; as perhaps in the majority of world popular musics, politics follows from affect, not vice versa, and affective rather than didactic language dominates in song lyrics. Thus the emotional impact of language conjoined with music is essential to the underground phenomenon and to any sociopolitical consequences of its presence in Indonesia.

Unity across Difference: The Underground's Political Project

The connections between underground music and political activism are in the end perhaps less important than the internal politics of the local scenes. "Unity" is an important slogan in underground scenes across Indonesia and the subject of countless fanzine editorials. These view cooperation between the *aliran* as crucial if not wholly unproblematic, and much of the rhetoric of scene unity bears a striking resemblance to Indonesian nationalism's rhetoric of "unity in diversity." While tensions exist between followers of different genres, sometimes resulting in violent incidents at concerts, punk, death metal, black metal, and hardcore fans continue to share space and recognize their shared allegiances to the underground ethos of independence and self-expression.

It is striking that commentators in the underground scene regard the divisions between followers of different genres to be the most problematic social difference in a musical movement that, like Indonesia as a whole, is deeply divided along ethnic, religious, linguistic, and class lines. During a late-night rap session in Surabaya, an underground scene veteran pointed out to me that everyone in the room came from a different class background, from very rich to middle-class to poor, but that everyone got along because such distinctions "are not mentioned" (*tidak diungkap*). He added that the same held true for ethnicity: the half-dozen young men hanging out that night included ethnic Javanese, Chinese, and one Surabayan of Arab descent. It is not at all unusual for underground bands to include members from different ethnic groups and to contain both Christians and Muslims who thank Jesus or Allah, respectively, in the liner notes of their cassettes at the beginning of their individual "thank-you" lists.

The concern with "unity" in the underground is consistent with both Indonesian nationalist discourse and Indonesian social norms that emphasize tolerance and social harmony. Similarly, the antisocial, nihilistic tendencies of some underground music in the West are far less apparent in Indonesia, where social relationships are generally cooperative and supportive and where Western-style, individualistic competition is a new and unpopular notion. One underground fanzine from Pare, East Java, *Dysphonic Newsletter*, even stamps the English slogan "*Be United & Fuck Individualism*" on the back of stickers they produce. Indeed, rather than name social alienation, their families, or existential angst as the cause of their musically expressed anger, many underground fans asserted that the sonic and affective extremism of underground music is a reaction to years of being oppressed by the Indonesian government and the military. To them, a unified underground community appears to constitute a utopian analogue to the old nationalist dream of a unified, multiethnic, harmonious Indonesian nation-state, a dream that for many Indonesian youth had been brutally extinguished by the corruption, social injustice, and state violence of the Soeharto regime and the chaos of its aftermath.

Whether or not underground music contributed decisively to the New Order's downfall, the growth of the Indonesian underground scene illustrates how globally circulating popular cultural artifacts can provide a vehicle for the aspirations, desires, and identity projects of youth in developing countries, particularly those who are urban and educated and have access to electronic media (Greene). While international artists such as Rage Against the Machine, Korn, the Dead Kennedys, Napalm Death, Cannibal Corpse, Sepultura, the Ramones, and Biohazard are still respected and celebrated as "influences," Indonesian underground fans increasingly listen to underground music created by and for Indonesians. In addition to being easier to obtain and much less expensive to purchase, these homegrown sounds often are better able to address the concerns and aspirations of their audience than those that originate outside of the national context, though this is not necessarily because they are sung in an indigenous language instead of English.

The question every Indonesian underground musician faces is whether to sing songs in the same language as his or her influences or sing in a language more accessible to a local audience. The next section will examine the various linguistic options available to Indonesian underground lyricists and the complexities and risks involved in choosing between them. As we shall see, the allure of the global ecumene, the rhetoric of scene unity, the drive for self-expression, and a politically oppositional consciousness all play important roles in this choice, as do the poetic features of the languages in question.

Linguistic Options in the Underground

Indonesia is well known in the ethnographic literature as a nation containing hundreds of indigenous languages and dialects that coexist in complex ways. Aspiring Indonesian songwriters thus face a number of choices when deciding in what language they will sing. The official national vernacular, Indonesian, is based on the Malay lingua franca of the Dutch East Indies and is now spoken nearly everywhere in the country; it is the language of the mass media, government, and education.[11] Indonesian is also the obvious choice for mainstream recording artists seeking a national audience. Throughout Indonesia's history, speaking (and singing) in Indonesian has been an expression of patriotism, upward mobility, and a commitment to the vision of Indonesia as a modern, forward-looking nation (Anderson 139–51; Oetomo).

On the other hand, very few young Indonesians speak Indonesian as a first language, and even fewer regularly speak the stilted, poetic Indonesian that is employed in nearly all popular song lyrics, regardless of genre. In Bandung, for instance, underground musicians will sing songs in Indonesian or English, but offstage with their friends they speak Sundanese, the language of the dominant ethnic group of West Java province. In Surabaya and other cities in East and Central Java, local punks and metal enthusiasts speak a dialect of *ngoko*, Low Javanese, with their friends but use Indonesian when speaking from the concert stage. Even in multiethnic Jakarta, when socializing with peers most young people do not speak the Standard Indonesian (*bahasa Indonesia baku*) used in the classroom but instead speak Jakartanese, a slang-filled, pithy urban dialect based on *bahasa Betawi*, the Malay variant spoken by the city's original native inhabitants.[12]

Despite the centrality of the so-called regional languages (*bahasa daerah*) in the everyday social life of underground fans (and Indonesians in general), they are generally not used for underground song lyrics. Disadvantages of using local languages include their provincialism and their association with "backward" village life. With the exception of Jakartanese, which is the basis for hip youth slang throughout the archipelago, the speech communities for regional languages are usually confined to the inhabitants of a particular area and/or members of a specific ethnic group, thus limiting the audience for songs in these languages. Another drawback is that the language used in everyday speech among intimates, including Jakartanese, is often seen as rather coarse and vulgar (*kasar*) and considered inappropriate for public expressions. It is the language of joking and laughing and gossip, of informal socializing, but not profound artistic expression.[13] Moreover, according to one Bandung artist, using Jakartanese constructions in a song makes the singer seem "arrogant" (*sombong*) and presumptuous, since his or her intended addressees include nonintimates.

More refined registers of regional languages are also inappropriate for rock song lyrics as they are strongly associated with elders and traditional culture, neither of which is very compatible with modern, youth-oriented music. The florid language of Javanese court culture, for example, is inextricably associated with *gamelan* and other traditional genres and would be an unlikely candidate indeed for the language of a punk song. Additionally, regional languages of any register are often considered inseparable from regional musical traditions. When I asked the Sundanese members of one underground group why they never tried singing in Sundanese, they laughed and said they didn't sing "ethnic" music.

A final disadvantage of regional languages as an option for underground music lyrics is that the underground community in Indonesia is self-consciously national in scope. The frequent interactions between, for example, scenes in Javanese-speaking Surabaya and Yogyakarta, Sundanese-speaking Bandung, Indonesian/Jakartanese-speaking Jakarta, and Balinese-speaking Denpasar in the form of letters, E-mail messages, Web sites, and guest appearances at concert events reinforce the use of the national language as the main medium of communication in the underground. This is why even during the underground's early years, when most groups sang in English, fanzines were always written in Indonesian. Thus the transregional networks that sustain the Indonesian underground strengthen a sense of national belonging among its members, though this is perhaps not what one would expect from a cultural form that originated from elsewhere and would appear to encourage supranational allegiances.

In fact, most young Indonesians possess overlapping allegiances to local, national, and global entities. This is apparent in their everyday language use, which is characterized by frequent code switching between English, Indonesian, and regional languages in informal speech and writing (especially in E-mail messages). Yet underground rock songs that combine one or more languages are exceedingly rare, perhaps because code switching in publicly circulating discourse is usually viewed as overly informal, even frivolous. Therefore, songwriters face a difficult either/or decision when contemplating what language to sing in, and, given the aforementioned disadvantages of singing in regional tongues, the choice is most often between English and Indonesian.

English in Indonesia

English is a language both ubiquitous and poorly understood in contemporary Indonesian society. In a study of commercial popular music in West Java, Sean Williams writes

English usage was and still is a very prestigious matter in Indonesian society, and the Sundanese are no exception. Inserting catchy English phrases into the conversation (such as "to the point" and "up to you") is considered stylish and educated and worldly, in much the same way that an American's use of French (*laissez faire* or *je ne sais quoi*) could be. (109)

Williams's analogy to French expressions in English is illuminating, since an English speaker's use of particular French words and phrases does not necessarily suggest that he or she can actually *speak* French—the aura of sophistication created by these expressions does not require speakers to demonstrate fluency or even competence in the language being quoted. In a similar way, "catchy English phrases" appear frequently in the Indonesian mass media, particularly in advertising, to add an aura of cosmopolitanism and sophistication to Indonesian-language texts, and in the underground scene itself English expressions such as *"old school," "straight ahead,"* and *"sell out"* are common-place in spoken and written (Web site and fanzine) discourse. These instances of English use do not carry with them the expectation that readers and listeners know much English beyond these particular words and phrases—in many cases, they do not. Regardless of their level of fluency, however, many Indonesians regard English as *the* language of global power and prestige, and many consider international English-language pop music to be superior to Indonesia's indigenous versions.

Virtually every pop, rock, and underground musician I interviewed in Indonesia listed Western rather than Indonesian groups as primary influences. For decades Indonesian rock and pop bands learned to play together by covering English-language songs, and English-language cover bands have long been ubiquitous in nightclubs, malls, and other venues (as they are in most of Southeast Asia). However, prior to the proliferation of D.I.Y. productions, mass-produced music recordings were nearly always sung in Indonesian, since music business personnel did not think songs in a foreign language would be commercially successful in the national market. The underground's relative autonomy from the mainstream music industry allowed bands the freedom to choose what language in which to sing. Indeed, for many the choice *not* to sing in Indonesian was one indication of their music's separation from the mainstream music business. While Indonesian record companies discouraged English-language songs because their potential national audience was limited, members of the underground scene were less interested in their music reaching the undifferentiated mass public outside their specialized subculture. The majority of early groups therefore chose to write songs in a language that not only enjoyed great prestige in their own country but would also, at least in theory, make their musical accessible to an international audience of cultural insiders.

The Advantages of English

The use of English in lyrics by Indonesian underground musicians cannot be entirely dismissed as mere mimicry of foreign influences, an example of the pursuit of trendiness and sophistication, or even an attempt to garner a global audience's attention. While the use of English remains a compelling index of cultural capital in Indonesia, Indonesians, particularly educated youth, also use English to express deeply personal thoughts and emotions. Many young urban Indonesians use English words and phrases in courtship and romance, for example, and employ English expletives to express anger and disgust, since these are considered safer than indigenous obscenities.

The connection between English and direct, uninhibited emotional expressions of love and particularly of anger has implications for the role of English in underground music. When asked why they liked underground music, scene members often emphasized the genre's emotional power. Underground musicians were said to *"mengeluarkan suara hati"* (release the voice of the heart) through their music. One fan answered my question concerning his enthusiasm for underground music with a single English cognate: *"ekspresi"* (expressiveness). Thus the use of English by an Indonesian band does not detract from their music's authenticity of expression and can even augment it. This leads to an unsurprising conclusion: much like other pop music fans all over the world, Indonesian fans are moved by and locate authenticity in powerful music, even when they cannot understand the meaning of all the lyrics.[14] Furthermore, for some Indonesians, conveying certain types of strong emotions in English may be considered safer, more suitable, or both compared to using Indonesian.

As mentioned above, early underground bands sang primarily in English. The English these groups employed varied considerably with regard to what a native speaker would recognize as correct grammar and syntax and was often incomprehensible to its audience. As the previous discussion indicates, the reasons why many Indonesian underground groups would choose to laboriously piece together lyrics with a dictionary rather than sing in a language they and their audience could easily understand are complex. Here in summarized form are the main arguments for choosing English, according to my conversations and interviews with scene members.

1. *Influences.* The bands that exerted a formative influence on the early scene (and continue to do so) were from Great Britain and America and sang in English. Thus English was the natural choice for music intended to iconically resemble as much as possible the songs performed by these bands.

2. *Phonology and Syntax.* Many participants in the underground scene complained that Indonesian is "stiff" (*kaku*) compared to English as a language for underground song lyrics. According to Yukie, lead singer of

veteran rock group Pas, one of Bandung's first underground bands, Indonesian is less "flexible" (*fleksibel*) than English in that Indonesian songs tend to be soft (*lembut*), romantic, and melancholy and tend not to vary rhythmically. In contrast, he said, English-language underground music is characterized by sudden and dramatic timbral and rhythmic transitions. Yukie originally thought these transitions would be impossible to replicate in Indonesian.

In fact, Indonesian and English are not very distant phonologically. One significant difference, however, with regard to how the spoken languages sound is the tendency in English for speakers (and singers) to shorten unstressed syllables and replace their vowel sounds with neutral vowels. For example, "anthropology" is often pronounced by English speakers as "anth-ruh-PAH-luh-gee." Nonneutral vowel sounds are always fully enunciated in Indonesian whether or not they are part of stressed syllables, as they are in Spanish. Thus "*perjalanan*" (journey) is always pronounced "per-jah-LAH-nahn," never "per-juh-LAH-nun," and the Indonesian word for "anthropology", "*antropologi*," is always pronounced "an-tro-PO-lo-ghee." (The significance of this difference between English and Indonesian was underscored for me when I once ordered a well-known global brand of soft drink and was surprised when the drink stand's proprietor corrected my American pronunciation. In Indonesia, the correct pronunciation is "koke-ah-KOLE-ah.") This feature of pronunciation may be one cause of Indonesian's relative "stiffness" to which Yukie refers, as it tends to create a smoother, more uniform rhythmic cadence when sung.

Another significant phonological dissimilarity is the absence of aspirated consonants in Indonesian. To many Indonesian underground fans, the percussive, harsh sounds of English consonants are constitutive of fierce, powerful hardcore/metal vocals, and Indonesian lacks any ready phonological equivalent. In fact, consonant sounds are often elided in rapid speech. Thus many supporters of English in the underground scene claim that Indonesian just doesn't "fit" or "sound right" in the context of underground music. The material differences between the two languages extend to the level of syntax; many singers contend Indonesian does not lend itself to direct expression because what takes very few words to express in English requires many more in Indonesian. I was frequently told that one line of verse in the former language was equivalent to two in the latter.

3. *Disassociation from Indonesian Pop Music.* Using English avoids the problems of trying to create convincing underground songs in Indonesian. For many, Indonesian is inextricably associated with Indonesian popular music styles, and therefore underground lyricists must take care to avoid the clichés and poetic devices used in commercial Indonesian pop, lest their music sound overly sentimental, hackneyed, and mainstream. One Bandung group, Cherry Bombshell, proudly claimed to me that none of their songs contained the word "*cinta*" (love), a word ubiquitous in Indonesian popular music lyrics. Many in the underground regarded Indonesian popular music, particularly those genres that appeal to the working class, as overly fatalistic, bathetic, and backward. In the disparaging words of one university student punk musician, "Indonesian is only good for *dangdut*"—the working-class-identified, syncretic popular music genre that for many in the scene constituted the mass-culture antithesis of *musik underground*.

4. *Politics.* Writing songs in English allows greater freedom of political expression. Government censors were far less likely to notice the lyrics of songs sung in a foreign language, and although now the threat of censorship and government intervention is less severe, many songwriters still admit that they feel more comfortable expressing political convictions in English than in Indonesian. In the words of Yukie, from Pas, "If you say '*fuck the government*,' no one cares. But if you say the same thing in Indonesian you get in real trouble!" Arian Tigabelas commented that an English-language T-shirt slogan, "*Fuck Your God*," found in a Jakarta underground boutique could never be translated into Indonesian, since antireligious sentiment is unacceptable in Indonesian society. He laughed, saying that anyone foolish enough to wear a shirt with the slogan "*Persetan dengan Tuhanmu*" "would be chased by the *Laskar Jihad* [Holy War Militia, a radical Indonesian Islamic organization that became infamous for its threats against Americans]!" English is thus a vehicle for transgressive statements in the underground that would be far more dangerous if rendered in Indonesian (see Sen and Hill 177).

Political messages in English are also found in album liner notes. For example, included in the notes of metal band Purgatory's cassette *Ambang Kepunahan* (Threshold of Extinction) is the following statement: "*No Thank To: Political Clowns Who Gots The Double Face and also To Indonesian Army Who Repressing The Students and Indonesian People since 30 years ago until*

NOW!!!" Sentiments such as these, particularly when the target is unambiguous, are almost always rendered in English, regardless of the language
used in the rest of the liner notes and in the lyrics.

To conclude, underground rock fans view English both as a link to
the world outside Indonesia and as an outlet for direct emotional expression
and unfettered political commentary. Like Western popular music itself, the
English language is simultaneously exotic and intimate to members of the
Indonesian underground movement. However, it is important to reiterate
that despite its popularity, English is a language relatively few Indonesians
have mastered (Mulder 174). Although most begin studying the language
starting in middle school, the method of instruction tends to center around
memorizing English's complex and often senseless grammatical conventions,
which many Indonesians find baffling, and tends to underemphasize conversational and communication skills. As a result, even Indonesians who interact
frequently with English-speaking foreigners may feel uncomfortable speaking
English with them, and Indonesian students who are not inclined or who are
unable to study hard in school often know very little English, including many
of those who continue their education beyond high school. There are of
course exceptions to this rule. Jill Jennifer, the Manadonese lead singer of
the Jakarta hardcore group Step Forward, speaks fluent, idiomatic American
English, a skill she claims to have learned *"from the TV."* Significantly, even
Jill, who has no trouble writing lyrics in English, has recently begun writing
songs in Indonesian, even though she admits this is more difficult for her.

The Advantages of Indonesian

Despite the cosmopolitan attractions of English, an increasing
number of underground groups have begun writing songs in Indonesian.
This has occurred for a number of reasons that relate to the desire for comprehensibility, the drive for uniqueness, commercial pressures, and, most of
all, the consciousness of a national underground community. Significantly,
the shift has not occurred as a result of any pressure exerted by other scene
members. The bands' choice of which language to employ in their lyrics is
their decision alone, according to underground's ideology of freedom and
self-expression, and the topic does not appear to be a subject of much debate
in fanzines or discussions among scene members. The rise of Indonesian and

the decline of English therefore appear to have resulted from voluntary decisions by individual songwriters. According to my interlocutors, there are a number of reasons for choosing Indonesian over English. They include:

1. *Comprehensibility.* The meaning of Indonesian lyrics and the messages they contain are more accessible to the listener, and the meaning of the lyrics is "easier to catch" (*lebih gampang ditangkap*). The use of Indonesian lyrics facilitates communication between musician and listener and shows greater consideration for the Indonesian audience. As one hardcore musician put it, "It's a pity (*kasihan*) if they have to go running to a dictionary just to understand the lyrics!" As the imagined "underground community" in Indonesia became more of a phenomenological reality for its participants, musicians became increasingly sensitive to the needs of their national audience and increasingly sought to communicate with them despite the difficulties of forging a new linguistic register adequate to the task. Moreover, the increasing number of rural and working-class fans of underground music meant a greater percentage of the audience had very limited English comprehension.

2. *Uniqueness.* A few underground artists told me that singing in Indonesian makes their songs sound distinctive and unique compared to those of their Anglo-American counterparts. This realization was an ironic result of Indonesian bands successfully making contact—first through letters and later through the Internet—with underground scenes overseas. To their surprise, foreign underground scene members were often more interested in Indonesian underground music that sounded "Indonesian" in some way than they were in English-language songs. This reaction was a relevant factor for only a small number of artists who were able to establish substantive contacts with scenes in the United States and other countries, but the encouragement by outsiders to "sound Indonesian" was a key catalyst for early experiments with Indonesian-language underground songs.

3. *Commercial Pressures.* The larger recording companies strongly prefer to record songs in Indonesian and limit the number of English songs on albums they release because they believe songs sung in a foreign language are not commercially viable. As more underground groups are signed to larger independent and major labels, they increasingly find themselves under pressure to sing in the national language.

The cassette liner notes for the *Metalik Klinik 3* compilation contain the slogan (in English): "*UNDERGROUND MUSIC IS NO LONGER BEYOND*

YOUR VISION." This collection is the third volume of a successful series released by Rotorcorp, a subsidiary of one of Indonesia's largest national recording companies, Musica. All the songs on the compilation, which contains bands from various metal *aliran*, are in Indonesian. Due to efforts like this one by large commercial record labels, underground Indonesian metal is indeed "no longer beyond [the] vision" and grasp of many potential fans, but it is certainly no coincidence that the songs chosen for the compilation are sung in a language most likely to attract a large national audience. Even groups such as Slowdeath that normally sing in English contributed Indonesian-language songs to the album. Similarly, recordings by metal bands on "major labels" such as Purgatory, Grausig, and Tengkorak are all or mostly in Indonesian, which appears to be a major factor in the rapid expansion of the Indonesian underground metal audience beyond the urban student population.

4. *Community.* Ultimately, the most important factor in the rise of Indonesian-language underground music was that underground musicians' perceived audience became less an imagined global (and English-speaking) underground audience than a national community of Indonesian speakers. This shift led to the drive for greater comprehensibility described previously and to efforts to promote the Indonesian underground movement as a proudly indigenous enterprise.

Making Indonesian-Language Underground Music: Hazards and Innovation

Pride in the accomplishments of local scenes grew as more and more independently produced cassettes were released and concert events attracted ever-larger crowds. Nevertheless, a university student once commented to me that the group Pas was "brave" (*berani*) in their later albums because they recorded more songs in Indonesian than in English. Singing underground songs in Indonesian was still considered risky in 1997, when that comment was made. Beyond the fact that Indonesian lyrics were far more likely to attract the attention of New Order government censors, singing in Indonesian ran the risk of forfeiting the prestige that came from singing in English and having one's work rejected because it too closely resembled Indonesian pop music. The Soeharto regime's lionization of Western knowledge and

Western modernity rendered indigenous popular music inferior and suspect; by singing in Indonesian, one abandoned the pretense that one's music transcended its "backward" national context.

In order to create convincing underground songs in Indonesian, early underground groups had to overcome several obstacles, among them finding the appropriate linguistic register for lyrics. Over the last seven years, a small number of well-known underground bands, including Suckerhead, Pas, and Puppen, have successfully provided models for Indonesian-language underground music composition. These models then became available for other musicians to follow. In particular, the lead singers of these groups excelled in the type of vocal transitions—chants to growls, melodic singing to screaming—that Yukie from Pas identified as initially difficult to execute in Indonesian due to the language's association with less dynamic, slower music. A raspy underground singing style compatible with Indonesian phonology also evolved and was adopted by newer groups.

By 2000, almost all underground bands still recorded at least one English song per cassette, but while these songs once dominated, they were increasingly in the minority. One reason cited by scene participants was that the underground had existed long enough to attract a younger generation of fans, now in high school or college, for whom Indonesian-language underground music was no longer "strange" (*aneh*) and problematic but rather a normal part of the scene.

Post-New Order Politics, Language Choice, and the Underground

In addition to poetic innovation, political changes have also encouraged the rise of Indonesian-language underground music. The veritable explosion of periodicals, slogans, and other publicly circulating discursive forms in the post-Soeharto era representing a range of opinions and orientations from Islamic fundamentalism to feminism has freed the Indonesian language from serving as a mere mouthpiece for an authoritarian regime and from the banal popular culture it encouraged. The post-New Order growth of Indonesian civil society thus contributed to the linguistic indigenization of the musical underground, making the language more available as a language of critique and dissension.

Many bands are still hesitant, however, to write potentially controversial songs in Indonesian. Pas's farewell/good riddance song to ex-president Soeharto, "Blind Majesty," is the only song in English on their fourth album, which was released shortly after the New Order's downfall. The final verse of the song is:

You turn the page / You wrote the lines / Your book is out / With a bitter end / Anger
goodbye / Is your farewell / Cry my majesty / You will got no time / Goodbye my majesty

While the meaning of some of the stanzas is somewhat obscure, this song is one of the few examples of a rock text that addresses Soeharto directly (in the second person, no less), and such brazenness is still difficult to imagine in an Indonesian-language song.

Despite a continuing preference for English in some particularly sensitive contexts, it is apparent that the recent democratic transition, in combination with greater mainstream acceptance of underground music, has given greater incentive for Indonesian underground bands to write increasingly bold songs in the national vernacular. A few bands such as Puppen have written aggressive political lyrics in Indonesian. The band's antimilitary song "Hijau" (Green) contains the refrain, *"Hijau seharusnya sejuk"* (Green is supposed to feel cool).[15] According to Arian Tigabelas, Puppen's lead singer and lyricist, "green" is a reference to the Indonesian army, which wears green uniforms.[16] He explained that while green things like leaves and plants are cool and calming to the touch, the army's hot tempers and violent acts during student demonstrations were quite the opposite.

Hijau
Hijau menindas menekan secara represif / Rebut hak yang terampas, cukup sudah
ketakutan / Hijau menekan, korban pun berjatuhan / Takkah sadar t'lah menuai
bibit-bibit perlawanan? / Rebut, rengkuh, hijau seharusnya sejuk (2x) / Hijau
membungkam, membungkam tanya alasan / Menyebar ketakutan, membangun
penjajahan / Hijau menindas, semua ditenggelamkan / Rebut hak yang terampas,
cukup sudah kita tertindas / Rebut, rengkuh, hijau seharusnya sejuk (2x) / Tolak
kehadiranmu, terlampau banyak sakitku / Luka dan derita: hijau seharusnya sejuk
(2x) / Cukup sudah kita tertindas!

[Green oppresses, pressuring repressively / Snatching away rights that have been trashed, fear is already enough / Green represses, victims too fall / Aren't they aware that they have grown the seeds of resistance? / Seizing, tearing, green is supposed to feel cool / Green silences, silences questions why / Spreading fear, developing colonization / Green oppresses, all has been drowned / Snatching rights that have been trashed, we've been oppressed long enough / Seizing, tearing, green is supposed to feel cool / Reject your presence, too great is my pain / Wounds and suffering: green is supposed to feel cool / We have been oppressed long enough!

The lyrics of this song were inspired by the poetry of Arian's classmate and fellow political activist Ade Irawan, and the language employed is indeed poetic, almost literary, despite its strong content. Describing his Indonesian lyrics as a combination of *"puisi"* (poetic) and *"straight to the point,"* Arian explained that in "Eastern culture" (*kebudayaan timur*), there exists a greater need for politeness and subtlety, and thus harsh statements must be balanced with poetic indirection. While Puppen songs used to be sung primarily in English, Arian, a university student who speaks English well, asserted that, at present, writing in Indonesian is much easier for him.

Another political song, "Agresi" (Aggression), by Jakartan thrash metal band Suckerhead, expresses the political disillusionment now felt among many Indonesian middle-class youth and exemplifies heavy metal's general preoccupation with condemning official hypocrisy:

Integrasi dalam negeri / Kepentingan diri sendiri / Kontribusi ideologi / Kenyataan hanya teori / Refrain: *Hey—katanya demokrasi / Hey—munafik! / Hey—katanya konstitusi / Hey–agresi! / Transformasi informasi / Transparasi diamputasi / Sikut sana sikut sini / Semuanya tidak terkendali / Kompensasi regenerasi / Birokrasi tidak terjadi / Janji-janji, mimpi-mimpi / Halusinasi politisi.*

[Integration in the nation / Selfish priorities / Contribution of ideology / Turns out it's only a theory / *Refrain:* Hey—they say democracy / Hey—hypocrite! / Hey—they say constitution / Hey—aggression! / Transformation, information / Transparency amputated / Deceiving here, deceiving there / It's all out of control / Compensation, regeneration / Bureaucracy nothing happens / Promises, dreams / Hallucinations of politicians.]

The lyrics to "Agresi" exemplify a more direct lyrical style. Suckerhead's use of Latinate/English cognates (*demokrasi, politisi, amputasi, halusinasi*) allows the song to sound much like those of many Western thrash metal bands, who also string together multisyllabic words for dramatic effect. Suckerhead was one of Indonesia's pioneering thrash metal bands, and its career resembles that of other veteran groups like Puppen and Pas in that the band began recording songs in English aimed at an international audience but then decided to concentrate on the domestic market. Over the years, Suckerhead's lyrics increasingly addressed specifically Indonesian topics with social commentary and even occasional humor, as in the metal-ska song "Pegawai Negeri" about the difficult life of underpaid, underworked Indonesian civil servants.

Obscenities and Language Choice

Bands have not only started to address political subjects in Indonesian but have also begun to incorporate Standard Indonesian expletives and relatively coarse language into their songs in an attempt to match the vulgarity and shock value of English-language underground music. One of Puppen's most popular songs, "Atur Aku" (Regulate Me), is a defiant statement of personal autonomy and resistance to authority that contains the lines:

Aku tak akan berubah ini / Aku kuatur jalan hidupku, / Keparaaaaaaaaaaaat!

[I will not change this / I, I regulate the way I live my life, / Bastaaaaaaaaaaaaaaard!]

"Atur Aku" is a popular song in concert, and fans sing along with the lyrics with gusto, particularly the transgressive final line of the preceding stanza.

Moel, lead singer of the Balinese "*lunatic ethnic grind death metal*" band Eternal Madness, claims he was the first songwriter "brave" enough to use the Indonesian obscenities *bangsat* (scoundrel, SOB) and *brengsek* (worthless, good-for-nothing) in song lyrics.[17] Again we see that courage is required for introducing novel and potentially transgressive language into publicly circulating forms. There remains, however, a significant gap between the language of everyday speech and the elevated language of song lyrics. Even the obscene words quoted above are Standard Indonesian—it is difficult to imagine Jakartanese, Sundanese, or Javanese obscenities used in the same fashion, since they are even more vulgar and definitely not intended for public circulation.

The Future of the Underground

The underground scene began in Indonesia with groups of middle school and high school students playing the songs of their Western idols.

This was followed by the formation of bands that wrote their own songs and recorded them. In the most recent phase of the underground's development, the recording of "cover songs" exemplifies the growing self-confidence of veteran Indonesian underground groups. Rather than mimicking the style of their influences, versions of Western songs are recorded in the bands' own distinctive style. Puppen's most recent EP contains a fiery cover of M.O.D.'s "Get a Real Job," while Bandung hardcore group Burger Kill's newest cassette includes a version of 1980s American hardcore group Minor Threat's "Guilty of Being White," the lyrics of which attack white skin privilege in U.S. society. I commented to Arian once that this was an interesting song for an Indonesian band to cover. He laughed and said perhaps the title should be "Guilty of Being Melayu [Malay]!" but added that it was likely the members of Burger Kill just wanted to play their favorite Minor Threat song and weren't terribly concerned about the meaning of the lyrics.

Balcony's 1999 album *Terkarbonasi* (Carbonated) represents a watershed of sorts in the history of the Indonesian underground. Balcony is an "emo-core" (short for "emotional hardcore") group from Bandung that has released three cassettes on Harder Records, an independent label co-owned by members of the band. *Terkarbonasi*, the second of these releases, is extraordinary in several respects. One cover song on the album, a collaboration with Bandung punk group Turtles Jr., is in Sundanese. There are also seven songs in Indonesian and three in English, including a musical collaboration with Ucok from the underground rap group Homicide, entitled "Politics Is Sceptical Hypocrite Imbicilic Trust [*sic*]."

Significantly, the album credits in *Terkarbonasi* are written almost entirely in formal, grammatically correct Indonesian, unusual even in the mainstream Indonesian music business. Instead of the usual "arranged by" or "produced by" credits, the Indonesian words "*diaransir*" and "*diproduseri*" appear in the text. These Indonesian words are of course English cognates, but they are nonetheless recognized terms in Standard Indonesian, and their use in the liner notes conforms to proper Indonesian usage.

The album is extraordinary for reasons other than language: the cassette resembles Puppen's albums more than those of any Western group with regard to production values, musical approach, album graphics, and even the presence of a musical collaboration with Homicide. (Puppen and Homicide together recorded the hardcore/rap/metal song "United Fist" in 1998.) This may indicate that future Indonesian underground bands will some day acknowledge their peers, rather than Western artists, as their most important influence.

Musical Shifts

While the lyrics and social context of underground music have been indigenized to some extent, musically it tends to stay within the stylistic parameters set by Western artists. This is consistent with the thesis that the writing of lyrics in Indonesian was more an attempt to approximate the Western underground ideal of a music capable of unmediated communication than a desire to "Indonesianize" underground rock. However, many members of rock and underground bands I spoke with did express a willingness to combine Indonesian traditional genres with their music. Despite this, they were generally hesitant about attempting to do so, saying it "had not yet been tried."

Robin Malau, Puppen's guitarist, once mentioned an idea he had for a side project involving the merging of ethnic traditions from all over Indonesia with underground rock. In an E-mail message responding to my query about this project, Robin wrote:

Untuk rekaman mix sama musik etnik ngga tau juga euy, itu kayak mixing chemical kalau salah bisa blow up jadi saya masih belum tahu approach yang ideal buat saya seperti apa, yang pasti saya ngga mau terlalu repot kalau manggung bawain lagu-lagunya, pakai sample kurang keren sedangkan bawa alat-alat musiknya bakalan repot banget, tahu sendiri keadaan gigging di Indonesia seperti apa . . . jadi saya masih belum tahu.

[As for the recording of the *mix* with ethnic music I don't know *euy* (untranslatable colloquial Sundanese particle), it's like *mixing chemicals*, if you make a mistake it can *blow up*, so I don't know yet what the ideal *approach* is. What's certain is I don't want it to be too much of a hassle when playing the songs live, (but) using samples isn't very cool while bringing (traditional) musical instruments (to concerts) would really be a hassle—you yourself know what *gigging* is like in Indonesia . . . so I still don't know yet.]

While most bands seem to have a similarly cautious attitude, at least two underground metal groups, Kremush from Central Java and Eternal Madness from Bali, have successfully blended death and black metal with elements of traditional music. Whether these groups become trendsetters or remain anomalous remains to be seen.

Most transgressive of all, perhaps, are the handful of campus-based groups that creatively combine underground music (death metal, ska, punk, and others) with *dangdut*, the lowbrow popular music genre that, despite scattered elements of social commentary in the music, middle-class Indonesians consider the epitome of mindless mass entertainment. In a sense, the handful of underground *dangdut* groups are rebelling against underground orthodoxy and its elevation of Western, English-language music over indigenous popular styles. By combining *dangdut* with underground rock, these bands playfully deconstruct the class hierarchy that lies behind such value judgments and begin to confront the elitism of the underground scene. These groups sing in Indonesian, with occasional songs in regional languages.

The Indonesian underground seems quite a long way off from achieving any kind of grand synthesis between "Indonesian" and "Western" music, as genres continue to fragment (newly introduced *aliran* include crustcore, brutal death, and hyperblast) and musical approaches ranging from syncretism to austere purism coexist and compete. At present, each underground band addresses the issue of language choice in its own way—subject, of course, to certain social and artistic constraints, such as the unspoken but strict rule against code switching in underground song lyrics. One veteran Jakarta hardcore group, Straight Answer, recently released a cassette entitled *Straight Answer Is Your Friend* that contains both Indonesian and English songs and includes Indonesian translations of the latter in the liner notes. In the words of one reviewer from a Jakarta-based online underground fanzine:

Sementara bagi mereka yang boten ngertos bahasa Inggris, STRAIGHT ANSWER keliatannya nggak rela juga mempersulit kalian dengan membuka kamus untuk memahami pesan-pesan yang terkandung dalam lagunya. Mereka menyelipkan selembaran fotokopian yang merupakan terjemahan lagu-lagu bahasa Inggris mereka. Cool action, guys.

[Meanwhile for those who *boten ngertos* ("don't understand" in High Javanese) English, it looks like STRAIGHT ANSWER is not willing to trouble you with opening a dictionary to understand the messages contained in their songs. They've slipped in a photocopied page of translations of their English songs. *Cool action, guys.*]
(http://www.bisik.com/underground/RilisAlbumdetail.asp?idw=20)

The author's use of High Javanese in this passage is very unusual. While code switching from Indonesian to regional languages is common in fanzine prose, usually more familiar linguistic registers are used. But instead of the Low Javanese *ora ngerti*, the author uses the more refined, polite register in a sentence about the inability to understand a foreign language. This particular instance of code switching appears to be a humorous metacommentary on the relativity of linguistic competence. While the members of Straight Answer and some of their audience may understand English, this is no guarantee they have also mastered the intricacies of High Javanese, which a Solonese or Yogyanese aristocrat is likely to know much better than a Jakartan. Perhaps the reviewer is reminding readers that there is no shame in not understanding English, since it is not the only language of prestige and power for Indonesians. Nevertheless, the entirely predictable use of an English phrase at the end of the passage ("*Cool action, guys*") underscores the importance of that language in the underground scene, even as it voices the author's approval of a strategy that allows Indonesian listeners to hear singing in English but also to understand the meaning of the song.

Significantly, the reviewer of Straight Answer's cassette also questions why the group chose not to include his favorite Straight Answer song, "*Tentara Anjing*" (Dog Troops). The word for "dog," "*anjing*," is one of Indonesian's most powerful obscenities, akin to the English "motherfucker," and it is likely the band was reluctant to include such a harsh and obscene political song in Indonesian on the album.

Conclusion: Language, Politics, and D.I.Y. Nationalism

The linguistic indigenization of underground music in Indonesia has larger historical ramifications. Indonesian underground artists are participating in a continual and recently renewed debate over the nature of modern Indonesian culture that has gone on since before independence, first in the writings of early nationalists and later, on a much larger scale, on the semiotic battlefield of popular culture (Frederick). As *musik underground* gains popularity in the post-Soeharto era, its influence on how Indonesian youth envision their country and their place in the contemporary world is likely to increase. As this essay has demonstrated, members of the Indonesian underground value openness to global influences, but they also stress the importance of a unified local and national community. The ability of underground musicians, writers, and fans to reconcile these two ethical imperatives through the creation and reception of aesthetically compelling cultural forms is a considerable achievement.

Furthermore, the case of Indonesian underground music demonstrates that cultural globalization is not merely the play of scapes and the diffusion of Western cultural forms; it is also a series of intimate transformative processes that shape publicly recognized identities and privately felt subjectivities. Current researchers often allude to the link between global media incursions and the transformation of subjectivities, but this link and how it develops are rarely explored in depth with attention to experiential context. Through examining the aesthetic, social, political, economic, and cultural factors that conditioned the shift from English to predominantly Indonesian lyrics in Indonesian underground songs, I have attempted to elucidate how globally circulating cultural forms enter the consciousness of social actors and how actors changed by such encounters may create novel yet related cultural forms that subsequently alter consciousness further, giving rise to new social formations and allegiances (see Urban).

By adapting Indonesian to suit their musical purposes, Indonesian underground musicians created a new voice to enunciate the existential condition of Indonesian youth during a time of social change and political uncertainty. The hybrid musical forms they produced have been sufficiently powerful to consolidate new interpretive communities of Indonesian youth that often transcend deep social, religious, and regional divisions in their society. The emergence of Indonesian-language underground rock music therefore has implications for our understanding of the formation of community and subjectivity in the contemporary world, as it demonstrates not only the creative agency of social actors confronting a changing reality but also the crucial role popular music plays as a site of reconciliation between conflicting cultural and communal allegiances. Rather than disrupt the sense of an integrated modern Indonesian identity, the emergence of a proudly indigenous underground music scene has paradoxically given the concept more credibility in the eyes of its participants in an uncertain and challenging time. Could this then be a case of cultural globalization actually strengthening the hold of the nation-state on the imagination of its citizens?

Acknowledgments

This essay is based on ethnographic research conducted in Indonesia in 1997 and 1999–2000, as well as on Internet research and continuing conversations conducted over E-mail with some of the principal interviewees. I would like especially to thank Wendi Putranto and the members of Cherry Bombshell, Eternal Madness, Step Forward, Slowdeath, Puppen, and Pas for their hospitality, patience, and input. I am also grateful to the Department of Anthropology, University of Pennsylvania, for funding the 1997 research and the United States–Indonesia Society for funding my travel to Indonesia in 1999–2000. Thanks are also due to Paul D. Greene, Benedict Anderson, and Sharon Wallach for their helpful feedback on earlier drafts of this essay.

Notes

1. Throughout the article I italicize all Indonesian terms and commonly used English loanwords. In quoted passages, words and sentences that originally appeared in English are reproduced in italics; English translations from the original Indonesian, Javanese, or other non-English languages are not italicized.

2. According to Clifford Geertz in his classic ethnography *The Religion of Java, aliran* was the term Javanese used to describe the different "streams" of Islamic practice in 1950s East Java. The quasi-religious overtones of the underground movement are also apparent in the use of the word "*kiblat*" (literally, toward the direction of Mecca) to describe the musical orientations of underground bands. So a grindcore group like Tengkorak, strongly influenced by the British band Napalm Death, is said "have a *kiblat* toward" (*berkiblat ke*) Napalm Death. One Indonesian fanzine even refers to Ian MacKaye, a punk musician based in Washington, D.C., who became the inspiration for the "straight edge" hardcore movement, as *Nabi* (prophet), a title usually reserved for figures like Jesus, Moses, and Muhammad. More could certainly be said about the similarities between the spread of world religions and the spread of music subcultures to Indonesia, but such a topic lies beyond the scope of this essay.

3. Students have also historically played a crucial role in national politics. Student demonstrations in Jakarta helped bring down the New Order regime, just as they had pushed nationalist leaders to declare independence from Holland in 1945 and hastened the removal of Indonesia's first president Soekarno from power in the wake of a 1965 coup attempt. Thus, while numerically few and occasionally the object of envy by the impoverished majority, students in Indonesia have long been at the vanguard of social and political change.

4. As in many other underground contexts, "hardcore" and "punk" are considered separate genres, despite their historical connection. The former genre tends to be more musically complex and eclectic, while the latter adheres closely to the musical template created by bands such as the Exploited and the Sex Pistols. Death metal and black metal also differ with regard to songs' subject matter, stage presentation, and musical approach, the latter far more likely to incorporate mythological and occult themes.

5. According to Waters, "A globalized culture admits a continuous flow of ideas, information, commitment, values, and tastes mediated through mobile individuals, symbolic tokens, and electronic simulations" (126). He defines cultural globalization as the processes by which the world is brought closer to this idealized state. The globalizing processes that brought underground music to Indonesia have not eliminated long-standing asymmetries in cultural flows but certainly have contributed to the rise of a borderless underground music community that now includes many parts of the world far from the geographical origins of the music, including Indonesia.

6. Useful accounts of the history and development of Indonesian national popular musics can be found in Hatch, Lockard, Lysloff, Manuel, and Piper and Jabo. For an account of the cultural dynamics of the 1980s mainstream pop music scene that discusses the importance of incorporating Western influences, see Siegel (201–31). Sen and Hill discuss the burgeoning popularity in the 1990s of "disorderly" rock music, including underground genres, in their study of media and politics in Indonesia. They state erroneously, however, that English lyrics are "increasingly common among underground bands" (177), an assertion that most likely results from their failure to distinguish older commercial Indonesian rock bands like Boomerang and Slank (which for commercial reasons have always recorded songs in Indonesian) from the true underground, indie label bands that constitute the subject of this essay.

7. In fact, the term "*underground*" had been in use in Indonesia since the 1970s to refer to locally performed Western-style hard rock music (Franki Raden, pers. comm.). There is no evidence, however, that the music of this period became the basis for an extensive grassroots network dedicated to the independent production and distribution of recordings, as occurred in the 1990s.

8. One of the most celebrated of these is 40.1.24 Studio located in the Sukasenang neighborhood in Bandung, where nearly every local band has recorded at one time or another. For most of its history, the studio's main tape machine was an eight-track cassette recorder.

9. Some clarification about my use of the phrase "major label" is in order here. In Indonesian underground discourse, "major label" refers to any large for-profit record company. This includes those companies that, in American terminology, would be classified as "independent" labels because they are not owned and operated by transnational multimedia giants such as Sony or BMG. Branches of these conglomerates do operate in Indonesia, but national recording companies like Musica, Virgo Ramayana, and Aquarius remain important players in the Indonesian music market. Underground scene members generally do not distinguish between national and transnational recording companies. They reserve the term "*independent*" or "*indie*" for the small, grassroots, D.I.Y. labels run by their peers.

10. Why this crackdown never occurred is unclear, given the New Order's history of suppressing dissent and censoring popular culture (see Yampolsky). Most likely, the underground scene was too small to attract the government's attention, and, as will be discussed, the preponderance of English lyrics in underground songs appeared to limit the reach of the music's politically subversive aspects to a small, and elite, minority.

11. The Indonesian language is closely related to the Malay dialects spoken in Malaysia, Brunei, and Singapore and by large minority populations in neighboring Southeast Asian nations. Combined with these speech communities, Indonesian Malay is part of a world language with more than 200 million speakers (Collins xxi). Addressing the increasing influence of English in the Malay-speaking world, linguist James Collins writes:

> It is a curious artifact of history that Malay and English, languages which are about
> the same age and which have a documented history of literacy also roughly parallel in
> age, now meet in Southeast Asia as competitors. But, then, Malay has competed

before with major languages and has emerged enriched and more powerful from the experience. (86)

12. The multiregistered nature of language use in Indonesian is exemplified by its array of pronominal options. Indonesian speakers have a choice between at least three different first person singular pronouns when referring to themselves; which is chosen depends on a number of contextual factors. The polite, neutral pronoun *"saya"* is normally used when speaking with older people and persons whom one does not know well. The informal, confessional, and poetic pronoun *"aku"* is used in somewhat more relaxed settings, but with intimates one usually either uses a "low" register of a regional language or the Jakartanese *"gua"* or *"gue."* Almost all Indonesian songwriters, including those in the underground, use *"aku"* or the shortened literary form *"ku"* in their lyrics.

Second person singular pronouns are even more complex: the Jakartanese *"lu"* is considered very coarse; the informal *"kamu"* and *"kau"* are used more often. The latter two pronouns, along with the poetic form *"engkau,"* appear most often in song lyrics. The use of the capitalized formal second person pronoun *"Anda"* is usually restricted to highly formal situations and impersonal forms of communication such as signs and advertisements; in most polite speech between nonintimates, second person pronouns are avoided as much as possible.

13. The fact that underground rock musicians tend to aspire to certain level of musical seriousness and profundity is one reason why they rarely use regional languages in their songs. Indonesian hip hop lyrics, in contrast, are often comical and lighthearted in tone and frequently contain Betawi, Javanese, and Sundanese expressions. Nonstandard Indonesian and codeswitching in song lyrics therefore generally signals humorous or satirical intent, which is relatively unusual in Indonesian underground rock.

14. Any doubts I may have had about the possibility of investing emotionally in music sung in a foreign language were dispelled as I found myself becoming an ardent fan of several Indonesian popular music groups during the course of my research.

15. The phrase literally means "green should be cool." The gloss used here is based on Arian's own suggestion when I E-mailed him a draft of my translation of the song.

16. The Bandung hardcore band Injected recorded a similar song entitled *Coklat* (Brown), a reference to the color of the uniforms of the national police. The lyrics (originally in Indonesian) are somewhat less "poetic" than Puppen's and include the lines:

> *Coklat, coklat* oppresses people / Although sweet, what's sweet is still hated / Coklat, coklat is pigfaaaaaaced [*bermuka babiiiiiiiiiiiii*]!

17. For more on the music of Eternal Madness, see Wallach.

Works Cited

Anderson, Benedict R. O'G. *Language and Power: Exploring Political Cultures in Indonesia.* Ithaca, NY: Cornell UP, 1990.

Azerrad, Michael. *Our Band Could Be Your Life: Scenes from the American Indie Underground 1981–1991.* New York: Little, Brown, 2001.

Berger, Harris. *Metal, Rock, and Jazz: Perception and the Phenomenology of Musical Experience.* Hanover, NH: Wesleyan UP/UP of New England, 1999.

Collins, James. *Malay, World Language: A Short History.* The History of Malay Monograph Series. Kuala Lumpur: Dewan Bahasa dan Pustaka, 1998.

Frederick, William. "Dreams of Freedom, Moments of Despair: Armijn Pané and the Imagining of Modern Indonesian Culture." *Imagining Indonesia: Cultural Politics and Political Culture.* Ed. Jim Schiller and Barbara Martin-Schiller. Ohio University Center for International Studies Monographs in International Studies, Southeast Asian Series, No. 97. Athens: Ohio UP, 1997. 54–89.

Geertz, Clifford. *The Religion of Java*. Glencoe: Free Press, 1960.

Goshert, John Charles. " 'Punk' after the Pistols: American Music, Economics, and Politics in the 1980s and 1990s." *Popular Music and Society* 24.1 (2000): 85–106.

Greene, Paul. "Mixed Messages: Unsettled Cosmopolitanisms in Nepali Pop." *Popular Music* 20.2 (2001): 169–88.

Hatch, Martin. "Popular Music in Indonesia." *World Music, Politics, and Social Change*. Ed. Simon Frith. New York: Manchester UP, 1989. 47–68.

Jakobson, Roman. "Closing Statement: Linguistics and Poetics." *Style in Language*. Ed. Thomas Sebeok. Cambridge: MIT, 1960.

Lockard, Craig. *Dance of Life: Popular Music and Politics in Southeast Asia*. Honolulu: U of Hawaii P, 1998.

Lysloff, René T. A. "Popular Music and the Mass Media in Indonesia." *The Garland Encyclopedia of World Music Volume 4: Southeast Asia*. Ed. Terry Miller and Sean Williams. New York: Garland, 1998. 101–12.

Manuel, Peter. *Popular Musics of the Non-Western World: An Introductory Survey*. New York: Oxford UP, 1988.

Mulder, Niels. *Indonesian Images: The Culture of the Public World*. Yogyakarta: Kanisius, 2000.

Oetomo, Dede. "The Bahasa Indonesia of the Middle Class." *Prisma* 50 (1990): 68–79.

Piper, Susan, and Sawung Jabo. "Indonesian Music from the 50's to the 80's." *Prisma* 43 (1987): 25–37.

Roccor, Betina. "Heavy Metal: Forces of Unification and Fragmentation within a Musical Subculture." *World of Music* 42.1 (2000): 83–94.

Sen, Krishna, and David Hill. *Media, Culture, and Politics in Indonesia*. Melbourne: Oxford UP, 2000.

Siegel, James. *Solo in the New Order: Language and Hierarchy in an Indonesian City*. Princeton, NJ: Princeton UP, 1986.

Urban, Greg. *Metaculture: How Culture Moves through the World*. Minneapolis: U of Minnesota P, 2001.

Wallach, Jeremy. "Engineering Techno-Hybrid Grooves in Two Indonesian Sound Studios." *Wired for Sound: Engineering and Technologies in Sonic Cultures*. Ed. Paul D. Greene and Thomas Porcello. Hanover, NH: Wesleyan UP/UP of New England, forthcoming.

Waters, Malcolm. *Globalization*. New York: Routledge, 1995.

Williams, Sean. "Current Developments in Sundanese Popular Music." *Asian Music* 21.1 (1989/90): 105–36.

Yampolsky, Philip. " '*Hati yang luka*,' an Indonesian Hit." *Indonesia* 47 (1989): 1–10.

At the Crossroads of Languages, Musics, and Emotions in Kathmandu

—Paul D. Greene and David R. Henderson

Westernization is not a term with which we are especially comfortable. Neither is modernization.[1] Yet in discussing the connections between music, language, and social change in Kathmandu, Nepal, we are unable to ignore these terms, for versions of them have been traced out time and again for us in conversations and interviews with Nepali pop musicians and their audiences.[2] How do the sounds and senses of Nepali pop, rock, and "sentimental" music index particular kinds of social change? We take one emotional register—which we can loosely denote as one which encompasses romantic love, longing, and desire—and examine how the linguistic and musical choices that Nepali pop musicians make articulate particular ways of loving, longing, and desiring.[3] Language choice—by which we mean not just the languages people choose, but the ways people choose to use language—also implies an ideology of emotion in which some ways of expressing feeling are privileged over others. Sung expressions of love and desire likewise inspire listeners to imagine this emotional register, and their own experiences with it, in novel ways. Moreover, the ways young musicians and listeners in the Kathmandu Valley express sentiments like love and desire can be turned into broader critiques of what they perceive as typically Nepali ways of doing things.

Kathmandu is a city of remarkable cultural diversity and vitality. Once situated at a lucrative intersection of trade between India and Tibet, it has in recent decades become a busy crossroads of world tourism. While the ethnographies of the 1800s and early 1900s often represented the intersections of Newars, Tamangs, Sherpas, Gurungs, and other groups of Nepal with Indians, Tibetans, and other foreigners as a vibrant cultural mix of diverse peoples, contemporary portrayals of the Kathmandu Valley often focus on the difficulties of diversity. Newspaper writers, government officials, music critics, and others frequently engage in a form of cultural critique in which they repeatedly weigh the values of local cultural practices and technologies against the potential benefits of practices and technologies which appear to originate outside Nepal.

Of these outside practices, Western popular music[4] has been part of Nepal's soundscapes since the 1950s, when the hundred-year reign of the Rana prime ministers came to an end and this remote mountain kingdom cautiously increased its traffic in Western goods, styles, and peoples. Beginning with the advent of Radio Nepal in 1951, the most prominent composers in Nepal gradually and intentionally incorporated elements of Western pop into the country's two developing popular musics, *ādhunik gīt* (modern song) and *lok gīt* (folk song, which could be called Nepal's "country music"); in the 1970s some composers turned their attention to *philmi gīt* (film song), as Nepali-language films began to compete with the Indian imports that had monopolized the market. Meanwhile, a massive tourism industry emerged to capitalize on a perceived Western desire for all things Eastern. Along Kathmandu's Freak Street in the 1960s and 1970s, and in Thamel's "no-star hotel" district in the 1980s and 1990s, foreigners flocked to stay in hotels, dine in restaurants, buy Nepali goods, and plan treks (cf. Henderson, "Sound"). Yet while these foreigners were busy observing Nepalis in their natural environment, Nepalis were also observing Western tourists, developing their own impressions of Western culture, and listening to Western pop. With the expansion of the cassette industry in the late 1970s and the availability of international music television in the 1990s, Western pop became an even more important presence in the Kathmandu Valley. Many young Nepalis began to make music with electric guitars, synthesizers, and amplifiers. Informal schools emerged, offering training in the instruments, chord progressions, and technologies of Western pop. Bands like Wrathchild, Crisscross, Chimpanzees, the Elegance, and Next performed Western pop, rock, and heavy metal songs in English in school auditoriums, restaurants, and large, public festivals (cf. Greene and Rajkarnikar). Young Nepalis were now dressing like Western musicians and performing Western musical forms complete with stylized emotional expressions and stage personae. By the late 1980s, a veritable "pop craze" was well under way (Sharma and Sharma), as bands like the Influence, recognizing that a teenage audience for Nepali language songs was emerging, had moved away from doing covers and toward singing songs in the Nepali language. The Western influence in Nepali music no longer was limited to composers of intentionally hybrid genres like *ādhunik git*, *lok git*, and *philmi git*; young Nepali pop musicians were now regularly experimenting with musical and linguistic styles drawn from Western popular music.

Perhaps a greater change, also attributed to Western influence, is the rise of dating as a common teenage activity in the 1990s. When Paul Greene, in structured interviews at three Kathmandu schools, asked, "What new freedoms do young people have today?" the single most common response was the freedom to date. "We can sit with girls and talk with them," said one teenage boy. "We can roam about [the city] with girls," said another. The significance of this should not be underestimated, for certainly youth perceive that the Nepali *chalan* (practice) is to have an arranged marriage, while the Western *chalan* is to "do a love marriage."⁵ As one youth put it, "we are free to choose our own spouse and avoid the dangers of arranged marriage." The social climate is changing such that not only is it acceptable for Nepalis to choose a spouse for themselves, but also marriages across castes, social classes, and ethnic groups are becoming more common. Young Nepalis, in the absence of conventional ways to frame their new experiences of dating, sometimes reflect on the images of and ideas about dating they encounter in films, music, and other elements of popular culture. Since the practice of dating in Nepal is generally considered to be the result of Western influence, it is not surprising that Western-influenced pop music should become an expressive space in which young Nepalis feel their way through the new experiences of dating. As one teenage student said, "[Western pop music] is the right music for songs about love, isn't it?"

Songs about love, though, aren't just songs about romantic longing. They also implicate other desires: to modernize, to Westernize, and to be or to be with a very different kind of person. In general, the "Western influence" that young Nepalis feel in Nepali pop music is something that is very tantalizing, sensual, emotional, and even at times irresistible, like romantic attraction. Under the spell of this influence, they desire the freedom to experience and express longings for the kind of romantic and erotic experiences Westerners seem to be having, as well as the freedom to explore other Western ways of being. If the "West" appears in Nepali pop in the form of deeply romantic and at times erotic sentiments, young Nepalis also associate the "West" with flashy images and sounds, empowering technologies, fantastic wealth and influence, and teeming business. The urge to be connected to this imaginary and undeniably exotic modern world, however, also recognizes Nepal's disconnectedness from it. Nepali pop singers frequently express the pain of detachment from a *māyālu* (lover), yet such a lover is often a ghostly presence attached not to the real world but to the modern and Westernized dream worlds of singers and listeners; if the distance between a singer and his (or occasionally her)[6] *māyālu* seems large in Nepali pop songs, the gap between the everday worlds of the Kathmandu Valley and the worlds in which imagined lovers reside can appear even larger.

In this article, we investigate what we call "grammars of sentiment" (Henderson, "Collected Voices" 294) found in the Nepali pop music of the 1980s and 1990s. By "grammar" we mean a kind of opportunity structure for the expression and exploration of emotion. We do not wish to imply that either music or words are self-contained systems of meaning, analytically separable from context. Rather, we examine ways that young Nepalis, driven by longings to forge new kinds of selves and new social patterns in Nepal, explore and create new means of self-expression at the crossroads of several musics and languages. Young Nepalis, often fluent in several musics and languages, express themselves within musical and linguistic conventions that shift as they develop the expressive power of Nepali pop. First, we examine how the Western musical grammar of a pioneering band, the Influence, parallels the lyrical intent of their songs, bringing Nepalis into closer alignment with ways of articulating longing and desire common in Western pop and rock. Then, we lend an ear to the verbal grammar of Nepali pop musicians, who supplement conventional Nepali ways of expressing love and desire with novel syntactic structures and thematic devices which mimic, transform, and comment upon the verbal styles of English-language pop and rock. In the last section, we focus on the stylistic grammar of "mix music," a practice which emerged in the mid-1990s, and explore uses of the English language in these elaborate sonic montages of linguistic and musical styles. In layering these three kinds of analysis, we argue that an exploration of the ideology of emotion must attend not only to pragmatic and metapragmatic sense, but also to musical and verbal sound and style.[7]

The Influence of Western Pop

Starting in 1983, a band called the Influence pioneered Nepali pop by singing thoroughly Western pop music in Nepali rather than English.[8] Bhim Tuladhar, leader and vocalist of the band, explains, "We started off the Influence as the symbol of the Western influence upon us, and to influence Nepali audiences with a completely new taste" (Phuyal 36). Nepali pop emerged as a new expressive space in which the forms and styles of Western pop were more thoroughly incorporated than in any earlier Nepali music. But the "Western influence" in it is not just musical or lyrical; it is also emotional, affecting expressions of intense longing both for romantic love (*māyā*) and for progress (*bikās*), longings which begin to merge in Nepali experience. Both longings are "Western": longing for *māyā* emerges through Western-inspired practices of dating, while desire for *bikās* is cultivated in urban schools through the intensive study of engineering, business, English, and other subjects associated with the West. In this section we examine how American rhythm and blues, Western verse-chorus patterns, and Beatles-inspired melodies shape Nepali explorations of love, desire, and longing in Influence songs. We find that Nepali pop bands and audiences do more than merely perform and listen to Western sounds: they explore, reflect on, and express these new feelings within what we call a Western "musical grammar."

Although youth culture in the Kathmandu Valley is "Western-influenced," young Nepalis are not trying to recreate a Western society. Rather, "Western influence" involves selectively internalizing and refunctioning various Western elements, including music, films, fashion, gang warfare (cf. "Tuff Turf" Parts 1 and 2), and drug use (Liechty 181–83). As new expressive spaces emerged in which young people could tentatively explore new terrains of desire, the Influence emerged to voice some of these desires. To examine Nepali notions of "Western influence," we turn to "Yubā Āwāj" (Youth voice), a song which the Influence offers as a kind of anthem of youth culture:

Our life is the city's, / Our youthfulness is joy's, / Far, far from the purity of the countryside. // In this we are happy. / We don't need / The artificial rubbish that fills [us] in the company of anyone else. // Our eyes well up with tears. / Our souls scream. / [We] are bound to our situations by obligation. // We have to fulfill our wishes. / We have to realize our dreams. / We have to rise up above the ocean of mirages.[9]

In addition to singing in the first-person plural, *hāmi* (we), the band reinforces a communal spirit by having three different vocalists sing the first
three stanzas alone and having all three join together for the final one. The
melody is repetitive and memorable, and the rhythm is lively and inviting.
The singers distinguish their urban youth community from rural communities in the first verse, and from more "old-fashioned" Nepali family structures, in which people seem to be bound by the artificiality of tradition, in
the second.[10]

In the third verse, the Influence expresses a sense of the difficulties of love,
longing, and desire in the new youth culture. The love given by one's parents,
described as "artificial rubbish" in the previous verse, seems to turn sour in
teenage years as youths find themselves pushed away from many of their burgeoning desires and wishes. Young Nepalis often express their contempt for
their "obligations," and chafe against the compulsion to adhere strictly to
traditional ways. These are common themes in talk about romantic feelings
and in Nepali pop lyrics as well. In fact, the Influence primarily sings about
romantic longing. Of the thirty-two Influence songs we have analyzed,
50 percent are songs of heartache. An additional 41 percent express sentiments
of more hopeful romantic longing.[11] In almost all their heartache and hopeful longing songs, the singer's attraction to his *māyālu* (his real or imagined
lover) is irresistible, often leading to unsatisfied urges and obsessions. Such
sentiments are not at all uncommon in Western pop. Yet in Nepal, where
sexual desire must often be kept relatively secret, it is remarkable that there
is such a strong emphasis on longing—often to the exclusion of other
sentiments—in pop songs.

In the fourth verse, the Influence expresses a concern for *bikās* (development or progress),[12] a desire to rise above the false security of traditional
ways. They articulate a position commonly voiced by young Nepalis: that
Nepal is underdeveloped, impoverished, even backward. Such opinions are
not hard to find, for the "West," to many Nepalis, signifies fantastic wealth
and indulgence: "we are not rich, like you," one teenage boy told Paul
Greene. Further, "Western influence" is believed to be a key to economic
progress, both for the country and for the individual studying in school.
By contrast, "old-fashioned" or "backward" cultural practices sometimes
become constraints that make it difficult to "rise up," forces that make it feel
as if one is drowning in an "ocean" of continually unfulfilled desires. Bhim

Fig. 1.

Tuladhar of the Influence told Paul Greene that this struggle is what he intended to show in the cover image (see Fig. 1) of *Jijibiṣā* (Will to survive). The image of Bhim, struggling to escape from an enveloping net, on one level represents his own struggles to pioneer Nepali-language pop despite the constraining inertia of earlier music traditions; on another, it is an allegory of the struggle in which young Nepalis find themselves as they fight against the constraints of "old-fashioned" Nepal.

"Western influence" is aurally evident in the Influence's music. They feature a standard rock lineup (lead singer, bluesy lead guitar, riff-playing rhythm guitar, bass, drums, and synthesizer) and use the scales of American and British pop. Occasionally, they even borrow melodies from Western pop songs: "Sapanimā . . . " (In dreams . . .) uses the tune of the Beatles' "And I Love Her," "Masaṅga" (With me) uses the melody of Ben E. King's "Stand By Me," and "Chhāyā Bani" (Shadow) employs chord progressions and melodic fragments reminiscent of the Turtles' "Happy Together." As Bhim Tuladhar has remarked, the Western melodies that the band has incorporated were irresistible: "we couldn't remain unaffected by the intoxicating melodies and exceptionally beautiful musical performances of popular western bands like the Beatles and Pink Floyd" (Phuyal 36). But regardless of the melodic source, Nepali listeners immediately identify the Influence's singing style as Western, particularly when vocal harmonies in thirds are included. To be sure, Western instrumentation had been incorporated into *ādhunik git* before (Grandin 120–21) and Western scales and melodies had been employed in Nepali film songs.[13] But in no earlier music were Western elements used so consistently and thoroughly as in Nepali pop.

A compelling reason for Nepalis hearing the Influence as "Western-influenced" is that Western pop forms and expressive styles guide and shape their Nepali lyrics, functioning as a kind of expressive grammar. For example, in 13 percent of the songs we analyzed, the twelve-bar blues form is adopted, and with it one often finds the typical lyrical organization of three-line stanzas in which the first two lines are similar. In other songs, such as "Bhani Deu Māyālu" (Tell me, my love) a Western-style alternation of verses and refrains is used to structure a contrast in the lyrics. The singer makes pledges of his love in the verses: "if you become the river, then I will become the banks," or "if you become the flower, then I will become the scent." He then repeatedly poses a question in the musically contrasting refrain: "tell me, my love, to whom do you belong?" In "Sapanimā . . ." the band borrows the contrasting verse and bridge music from the Beatles' "And I Love Her" to structure a contrast in the lyrics. The singer recounts dream experiences in the verses: "I see her always in my dreams," and "my heart beats faster as I feel that she is coming." To the bridge music, he steps back and asks, "Is it my madness, or the recalling of a past life?" Thus the Influence not only borrows Western pop elements; they also are guided by them as they write their lyrics. In this important sense, the Influence parts ways with *ādhunik git* (cf. Grandin 119), *lok git*, and Nepali film song. In Nepali pop, musicians are feeling and expressing themselves in a thoroughly Western musical grammar.[14]

The following musical analysis shows how Western rhythm and blues functions as a musical vehicle for Nepali sentiments of love, desire, and longing in "Juneli Rock 'n' Roll" (Moonlit rock 'n' roll), a rockabilly-like piece featuring several dynamic guitar solos. Throughout most of the song, with minor variations, a hard-driving rhythm is provided by a bass guitar, which plays on each of the four fast-tempo quarter-note beats, and by high-hat and organ sounds, which subdivide this four-beat rhythm into eighths.

As in many blues songs, the stanzas are each comprised of three lines, and the music is structured around a contrast between the first two lines on the one hand, and the last line on the other. For the opening two lines there is a momentary break in the insistent motor-like rhythm: the organ and high-hat drop out, and the bass and drums perform attacks on the first beat only. In the closing line of each stanza, the full rhythm section returns. Our experience in listening to stanzas like these is that the sudden reduction of the rhythm section in the first two lines not only draws attention to the lyrics, but also puts the listener in a kind of suspense, awaiting the return of the full rhythmic articulation in the closing line. Performers like Chuck Berry and Carl Perkins—two of the obvious influences on the musical style of "Juneli Rock 'n' Roll"—used this structure to similar effect.

The musical contrast maps onto a distinction between cause and effect, or between reflection and response, in the lyrics. The opening two lines are expressions of the singer's attraction to his *māyālu*, sometimes phrased as questions:

Are you the moon of the moonlit night? / Are you the pupil of the long-lashed eye?[15]

and sometimes as descriptions of her features:

There is black eyeliner [*kājalko koś*] around yearning eyes. / Those lips are thirsting to break into a smile.

In the last line of each stanza, the singer begs for a response from his *māyālu* (or, here, his *priyasi*)—"Talk [to me], my lover, give [me] my life"—or describes his own physical responses to her—"This look [you give me], how [it] makes my heart beat faster."

A synergy emerges between lyrics and music. As the singer's amorous reflections inspire responses in him, so music with a suddenly reduced rhythm section calls for the return of the song's dominant rhythmic pattern. The music reinforces a sense that the first two lines call for—perhaps compel—the response in the third. In both music and words, "Juneli Rock 'n' Roll" performs some of the romantic compulsions Nepalis are experiencing as they internalize "Western influence."

By formulating lyrics of love, desire, and longing within a Western musical grammar, the Influence carves out an altogether new expressive space in Nepali pop. Much as Nepalis train themselves in school to tackle engineering and business problems through Western methods, so the Influence and their fans grapple with new feelings through a musical grammar derived from their diligent study of Western pop styles. Accompanying this musical development are shifts in patterns of Nepali language use that allow for a more direct engagement with issues of love, desire, and longing in Nepali pop lyrics.

New Modes of Language Use in Nepali Pop

It is impossible to overstate the importance of the words of Nepali song genres. Whereas it is not at all uncommon for Western pop listeners to mistake or even ignore the lyrics of some pop songs (e.g., "Louie Louie"), this listening mode seems much less prevalent in Nepal. In numerous contexts, musicians, engineers, and listeners have told us repeatedly that the words of a song are primary. Krishna Narayan Shrestha, an exceptional musician who had worked for Radio Nepal from its inception in 1950 until his retirement in 1987, remarked in an interview that "tunes are developed from words and sounds"—words and sounds are the starting point, not melodies (Nyachhyon 19).[16] And Dilip Kumar Kapali, a singer with whom David Henderson studied, insisted time and again on the need for clarity of *swar* (voice) with both musical and lyrical implications. Likewise, the sound engineers with whom Paul Greene worked go to great lengths to ensure that the words are audible in mixdown. And listeners, too, emphasize the importance of words for their understanding of musical style. Often, in interviews, this took the form of a negative evaluation. Gopāl, a Nepali man in his twenties, said he had no desire to listen to English-language songs because he didn't understand them. When questioned on this point later in the interview, he retorted, "English *ta kina sunne?*" ("Why [should I] listen to [songs in]

English?"). Hasinā, a twenty-four-year-old Newar woman, said that despite liking many kinds of music, she didn't like *śāstriya saṅgit* (classical music) because she didn't understand its words. "*Tyasko bol nai bujhidaina. Kasari man parne?*" ("That [kind of music's] words really aren't understood [by me]. How [would I] like it?") she explained. "*Sabai musicharu mātra hunchha*" ("[It] is all only musics"). And Bijay, a teenage Tibetan boy, remarked that he didn't like "American rock" because "*tyo kuireharule gāeko hunchha—ke ke bhanchha, ke ke bhanchha?—fast bhanchha bujhdaina*" ("those white people are singing—what do they say, what do they say?—[because they're] saying fast, [I] don't understand").[17]

Given a widespread concern for the intelligibility of lyrics, then, we now turn to grammatical styles for the expression of love, longing, and desire in Nepali pop songs. What new linguistic spaces for imagining romantic attachment have emerged alongside more conventional modes of expression? Especially prominent is a shift toward the direct, assertive, and immediate expression of love and desire. This is accompanied by a tendency to emphasize both the internal and external agency of the singer—or of the listeners, if we grant for the moment that part of the pleasure of listening comes in imagining the subject of a song to be oneself. Here, the singer, much more than in previous genres, becomes the subject of the song, producing affectivity in specific others, rather than experiencing the effects of others' actions.

In contrast to Nepali pop songs, *ādhunik git* (modern songs) often draw upon an expressive tradition of ambiguity: while singers express the dimensions of emotional states with devastating clarity, it is left to the listener to decide how to identify the object of desire. Kathmandu youth, in interviews, comment on the pleasure they take in this genre, and sometimes even consider Nepali pop to be a part of *ādhunik git*. While the dynamism of Nepali pop fits with the sense of development or progress (*bikās*) characteristic of *ādhunik git*, though, the specificity of grammatical reference in Nepali pop is different, as we will discuss below. *Lok git* (folk songs)—or at least the versions produced by Radio Nepal since the 1950s—also speak very differently about love and desire. Although the Nepali-language lyrics (often written in Kathmandu to replace lyrics in Sherpa, Tamang, Gurung, or other languages) sometimes celebrate other aspects of village life in Nepal, those songs that do speak of love often narrate the flirting that occurs especially on festive occasions, and people use these songs themselves, both during festivals and in everyday life, as stylized expressions of flirtatious love. However, this is a clearly public discourse that is full of innocent suggestion and possibility but empty of the sense of yearning and deep-seated desire that proliferates in pop and rock songs. While Kathmandu youth suggest, in interviews, that *lok git* is important because it preserves a sense of the *Nepālipana* (Nepaliness) of the nation, they by and large express a disdain for it except perhaps as background music; urban listeners tend to interpret the sentiments expressed in *lok git*, like the actions that are narrated, as quaintly typical of *gāūle* (villagers or "hicks").

Nepali pop musicians and lyricists often do build upon the work of other musicians in Nepal, and particularly the work of famous *ādhunik git* singers like Narayan Gopal, Nati Kazi, and Ambar Gurung. However, they also articulate a distinction between their styles and other popular music styles, experimenting with new ways of placing themselves, and their listeners, within the emotional states of song. One way they align sentiments differently is through the use of active grammatical structures rather than passive structures. This helps emphasize the sense that the singer is the locus of sentiment, rather than allowing the singer to be a captive audience in his (or, infrequently, her) own emotional theater. In the Nepali language, emotions as well as bodily states usually take on the role of agents grammatically, while the one doing the experiencing becomes the indirect object in a sentence. "*Malāi thirka lāgyo*" (I'm thirsty) could be translated literally as "To me thirst adhered." "*Timilāi dukha lāgyo*" (you're sad) literally means "To you sadness adhered." Expressions of love often make use of the noun "*māyā*," which Nepalis usually translate as "love" even though the range of referents is somewhat different. "*Malāi timro māyā lāgchha*" (I love you) might be translated as "To me your love adheres." Indeed, this is a common form of expression in Nepali pop songs. Yet in Nepali pop and rock *māyā* is also more and more frequently detached from this conventional phrasing and used as an object for contemplation or use, while grammatical action resides elsewhere in the sentence. "*Ma timrai māyāmā chhu*," sings Babin Pradhan in the first song on his album *1994*—literally, "I am in your love." Grammatical action here resides in the verb form "*chhu*," expressing a locative state of being. Likewise, in the title track of Sushil Shrestha's album *Anjulimā*, the first line— "*Anjulimā rākhchhu māyā timrai*" (I place your love in my cupped hands)— clearly objectifies *māyā* as something with which to do something. No longer is *māyā* most frequently an elusive state that overtakes or overpowers the passive recipient of it in song. Emotional action takes the place of emotional experience (cf. Henderson, "Emotion and Devotion" 461–62).

A second way to reframe love and desire as sentiments that demand immediate attention is to use language that requests specific action. Rather than using indirect expressions of one's plight in the hope that such expressions will cultivate a feeling of *māyā*, singers plead their cause directly. Babin Pradhan, in another song from his album *1994*, pleads, "*sajāu yo jivan*" (mend this life). In this small phrase are embedded three common practices of Nepali pop and rock songs. First, singers frequently use imperative forms of verbs (here, "*sajāu*," or "mend") to request specific actions from their imagined lovers. Second, the form of the verb indexes the pronoun, "*timi*," a medium honorific form of "you" that implies close familiarity and the existence of a longstanding relationship with the "you" in question; while singers of other song genres in Nepal use "*timi*" to refer to wives, childhood friends, or even gods, in Nepali pop the presence of a lover as the *timi* in question is almost always made explicit somewhere in the song, usually through the use of terms like "*māyālu*" or "*priyasi*," which unambiguously translate as "lover." And third, singers often use the definite article, "*yo*" (this), to index a part of themselves: "*yo jivan*" (this life), "*yo man*" (this heart-mind),[18] and "*yo muṭu*" (this heart) are all common expressions. The effect of this is both to generalize and to particularize the possession of such emotion-laden objects: "this heart" can become any heart, such as that of a listener, but it also can be that part of the song's "me" that demands attention. Through these grammatical choices, singers and lyricists clarify the actors, the actions, and the objects to be acted upon in ways that both parallel and depart from the conventions of other Nepali song genres.

A third way by which love is expressed directly in Nepali-language pop and rock song is through foregrounding the medium of song itself. Many songs function as vehicles for confessing one's desire—laying out a lopsided attachment to another in the hope that this revelation will prompt a response. The Influence's "Juneli Rock 'n' Roll," discussed in the previous section, is one such song. Crossroads, a band that began in the early 1990s with five members, often uses this lyrical strategy as well. On the album, *Nayā Mode* (New mode), Sanjay Shrestha and Sharad Singh Mahat, the lyricists and singers for most of the songs (as well as the instrumentalists for later albums), refer to the song itself in three of ten songs. The second song of the album, for example, begins, "*Timi deu jawāph mero prem gitko*" (You, give [the] answer to my love song's [question]). By highlighting the context of song itself, this song becomes not only an expression of a desire for someone else, but also an expression of desire for someone immediately present and listening. As an on-the-spot confession of love, this song also later highlights the importance of music for the emotions expressed in the lyrics: "*Mero manko rahar*" (My heart-mind's desire), sings Sanjay, "*gitārsanga jhumechha*" (will sway with [my] guitar). Yet even though these songs and others like it refigure song as a dialogue between the singer and a lover, the lyrics consist primarily of a monologue about one's own desire and imagination.

Certainly, a shift in song toward the subject who desires is predicated on an assumption of being alone. Remaining detached from the object of desire, the singer removes himself from the everyday social world, preferring instead to explore a private terrain of memory and desire. Lovers appear in dreams (*sapanā*) and memories (*yād* or *samjhanā*) of lovers saturate the discursive space of Nepali pop. Often, lyricists make use of the word "*sunyatā*," a markedly poetic term suggesting a solitary space where one can leave behind the worries of everyday life and take solace in contemplation. Conventional expressions of solitude like this, when attached specifically to youth culture in the Kathmandu Valley, suggest that a novel space for thinking about memory and desire exists, and it is often in this developing leisure space that new possibilities for expression take hold alongside new senses of loss. If one oft-remarked aspect of Nepali *samāj* (society) is the intense sociability that saturates public space, one way of articulating a resistance to this and stating a desire for a contradictory form of modernity is through the intense privatization of social space. In Nepali-language pop, the subject often decides to be lonely or decides to remain separate from other Nepali social worlds; implicit in this is a desire for a connection to a distant world—one in which the exotic pleasures of modernity are immediately accessible.

The connections between desire, distance, and modernity become clear in the occasional uses of English-language phrases within Nepali-language pop, which heighten a sense of distance and draw upon the exoticism and novelty of love and desire. Uma Gurung, one of the few female pop singers in Nepal, contributed one track to the 1990s compilation album, *Billboard*. "*Timro manko khāli kāgajmā*" (On the empty page of your heart), she sings. This line is then repeated, setting up a greater sense of expectation for the conclusion of the action: "*lekhidiẽ maile* [I wrote], 'I love you.'" The phrase, "I love you," is then repeated twice. While it is quite possible that she could have written a tender phrase in the Nepali language on this empty page, she chooses instead to write in English, suggesting a sense of the novelty of this desire, a sense of the exoticism of this modern love—and these senses are heightened by the musical articulation of the lyrics. The occasional use of English-language snippets is both iconic of an occasional unfamiliarity with the desires being expressed as well as indexical of the pleasure that such unfamiliarity itself holds.

With the emergence of Nepali-language rap and mix music in the mid-1990s, the use of the English language within a predominantly Nepali context became much more frequent. We now need to mix in some observations on how separate musical styles index the existence of different linguistic terrains and show how language as well as music can be symbolic on the level of sound, as well as on the levels of sense that we've traced out so far.

A Mega-Mix of Languages and Musics

As one teenage listener put it, 1990s Nepali pop is "very mix." Urban soundscapes have been infiltrated by a high-tech sound known generally as "mix music": a sonic montage of heavy metal, rap, Nepali folk song, jazz, reggae, and rhythm and blues, sung in a mix of English and Nepali, commonly with a disco-styled dance beat. It is inspired by Indian remixes, American rap, and Western dance music (cf. Greene and Rajkarnikar). Typical of the sound is the *remix*, a studio-produced reworking of a familiar song.[19]

Since the mix aesthetic and new Nepali cosmopolitanisms are already treated elsewhere (Greene, "Mixed Messages"), we focus here on language choices and emotional expressiveness in a leading album, *Mega Mix*. An assertive, attention-grabbing idiom, mix music reflects a new, more outgoing spirit in youth culture in the Kathmandu Valley. In the preceding section we argued that singers and lyricists use linguistic means to engage with their object of desire more actively and directly; with mix music, we find that musicians use musical and stylistic means to draw even more attention to their expressions of desire and to themselves as subjects who desire, almost demanding their *māyālu*'s engagement.

Young urban Nepalis say that it is more important than ever before to develop skills and confidence in social interaction. "You must socialize more! . . . Socializing is essential to face the competitive world," a young woman told Paul Greene. A teenage boy offered, "We can now have intercaste marriage, love marriage. Nepali culture is not good for us. . . . We have to change our mind, to develop the country. To fit into world community." Again, desires for *māyā* and *bikās* merge in Nepalis' experience, but here, perhaps, with a heightened sense of urgency. Young Nepalis also say it is important to be "forward" today. This English word, used in different language contexts, has different nuances in Nepal. A middle-aged Newar office manager explains:

"Backward" means sticking close to tradition. Also, hesitating to talk to a stranger. "Forward" is developed [*bikās*], and also Western. It also means never hesitating to talk to a stranger. You have to be a *little* forward: don't hesitate to learn something that is useful to you. But *very* forward is vulgar. A girl staying out without telling her parents for several nights is considered too forward, vulgar. Should be more back. So, backward is a bad thing, but too forward is also bad. Should have a balance between backward and forward.

Thus, "forward" commonly not only means outgoing, but also is opposed to backward or undeveloped (*abikāsit*) practices. In many educational contexts, young Nepalis study "forward" (developed) Western technologies and business practices, and as aspiring urban professionals they are preparing themselves for careers in which they will interact more with Westerners and Westernized people, whom they identify as characteristically outgoing.

To use English is to be "forward" in both senses. A Newar father said:

If you don't use any English words in your speech, it means you're not standing in the present context. You are still backward. If you use English words, and have some modern equipment you are using, you are forward, well-off. Even when people don't know the ABC's, they teach their kids to use "Mummy" and "Daddy". . . Using "*āmā*" and "*bā*" ["Mother" and "Father"] might mark you as backward. I don't feel comfortable with this. I get my kids to say "*bā*".

Also evident in this quote is a tension that urban Nepalis increasingly feel, a struggle between the competing claims of Nepali, English, and often other languages, to be the appropriate language for a given social context. This point is taken up below.

Discussing music, a teenage boy told Paul Greene, "The purpose [of English words] is to make the listener to want to listen. Also to make the girl [in the song] to want to listen." In Nepali mixes, short English words and phrases primarily serve phatic or listener-engaging functions, drawing attention. Inspired by American rap, mix music includes recurring sound samples of English words and non-linguistic vocal sounds but never of Nepali words or phrases. Samples of "Hey! . . . Hey! . . . Hey! . . ." are sometimes employed as part of a rhythm track, and samples of "Uh!" are used as periodic interjections. Phrases such as "Come on!" and "Everybody!" are directed at the listener, perhaps even calling for her or his involvement. Many mix songs begin with an introduction in English. For example, on the *Mega Mix* album, the song "Ghās Kāṭne" opens with the line, "In my dream last night I was in a Spanish village where *macarena* was invented,"[20] and in "Badha Parun Jati Nai" the singer intones, "This is a romantic love story." As such opening narratives draw the listener into the song, they sometimes include phrases directed at the listener (e.g., "You want to hear it?"). In contrast, the Nepali language is rarely used in these ways.[21]

Inspired by Western rap and dance music, young Nepalis have developed a more outgoing, "forward" expressive idiom that draws the listener's attention to the song and to the singer, a process begun in the linguistic shifts discussed in the preceding section. Moreover, obviously high-tech sounds, like sound effects and identical, recurring speech samples, are most commonly reserved for passages in English, suggesting that these passages are "forward" in both senses: attention-grabbing (outgoing), and technologically sophisticated (developed, *bikāsit*). In very fast rap and in samples of electronically sped-up speech, the sounds of verbal communication are increasingly used not only to communicate messages, but also as bravura, inspiring an "exhilaration of surfaces" (Manuel 233). As one teenager told Paul Greene, "I like the rap. It's fast. It's good. He's able to sing fast. It's impressive and fun."

But attention-grabbing devices do more than draw the listener into the song. They also suggest a more confident, "forward" style of engaging one's *māyālu*. One Nepali teenage boy said:

As the singer is singing the song for his girlfriend, and as the girlfriend doesn't want to listen, the music is suitable for the lyrics. Music makes the lyrics sound great. There is a fast beat because . . . the music is attention-grabbing, just as boy wants to be, to have her hear his words.

The new mix music thus embodies a more confident, "forward" mode of flirting. Not only are musicians performing for a *māyālu* who is immediately present and listening, as we argued in the previous section; the music also has the persuasive power to reach her even if she is reluctant to listen.

As the Newar father quoted above suggests, urban Nepalis find themselves in something of a tug-of-war to determine the appropriate language to use in any given circumstance. This linguistic tension becomes patent in mix music, which abruptly juxtaposes passages in Nepali and English. We find that mix music offers no easy answers to the growing linguistic conundrum Nepalis face every day. Following the work of Tricia Rose, we have examined moments of musical disrupture or interruption in mix music,[22] and we find that it is almost invariably English-language lyrics which interrupt Nepali ones, and Western musical styles which interrupt Nepali ones. But we are not certain what to conclude from this. Clearly, moments of disruption draw the listener's attention, thus reinforcing the assertive tone of the "forward" English passages. But it is also possible that being or becoming "forward" is a disruptive, disjointed, and confusing practice. By making these disruptions central in mix music, perhaps, some Nepalis are seeking ways to find pleasure rather than frustration in the new Nepal.

We've focused here on different grammatical aspects of Nepali pop in order to highlight the ways singers and lyricists have opened up the exploration of love, longing, and desire through music. At a crossroads of possibilities, bands look both toward and away from Nepal for stylistic help, drawing upon the lyrical styles of older Nepali song genres as well as figuring out ways in which to fit their interpretations of the emotions of Western pop and rock music into the context of Nepali-language songs.

Working at an intersection of linguistic and musical styles, youths in the Kathmandu Valley have been imagining and performing deeply felt and indisputably novel sentiments. It is, of course, not the sentiments themselves which are novel, but the ways in which they are expressed and the ways in which they are connected with a range of other desires. In Nepali pop, romantic love spills over into a desire for Westernization, a plea for modernization. This is evident in the ways people use language in song, the ways musicians use sound to highlight the senses of song, and the ways musicians and their listeners speak about what song does. The increasing assertiveness and directness of musical and linguistic styles in Nepali pop parallel a desire that male youths in particular express: a desire to be more assertive, to be more direct, to exert greater control and command over their lives and lifestyles. Part of the pleasure of rock music in Kathmandu since the 1970s has come from its power to express a sense of individuality that is clearly distinct from a way of doing things that is marked and remarked as distinctly Nepali, a way of privileging the sphere of the social over the realm of the individual. And part of the pleasure of Nepali-language pop since the 1980s has come from how it helps map previously unexplored geographies of love and desire, how it lends sound and sense to feelings that previously seemed to have been reserved for the West. Yet in this unfamiliar terrain of sentiment, singers and lyricists have also explored the process of detachment, the process of becoming lonely in order to feel more deeply. If the kinds of love expressed in Nepali pop music often remain unrequited, it is equally possible that the overtures to modernity apparent in the linguistic ideologies of Nepali pop will fall on deaf ears.

Acknowledgments

Thanks especially to Shamsher B. Nhuchhen-Pradhan, who facilitated dozens of interviews; Sarmila Maharjan, who transcribed over 700 pages of interviews she conducted in Nepali and Newari; Suresh Ranjit, who transcribed the lyrics of some of the Nepali-language cassettes discussed here; and Nanda Chhetri (Kulu), who answered many last-minute questions on translation.

Notes

1. See Pigg's "Disenchanting Shamans" and Leichty's "Media, Markets, and Modernization" for more thorough discussions of Nepali engagements with modernity. While debates on the dialectic between tradition and modernity have flourished particularly since the 1960s, we wish mainly to highlight the use of the term "modern" in Nepali-language contexts to signify certain kinds of *bikās* (development), as well as the desire for *bikās*. This use parallels that articulated in Appadurai's *Modernity at Large* and Appadurai and Breckenridge's "Public Modernity in India."

2. This article is based primarily on Henderson's field research in Kathmandu, Nepal, in 1987, 1994, and 1995 and Greene's work there in 1994, 1998, and 1999.

3. While Judith Irvine makes use of Michael Halliday's work on linguistic registers, this isn't exactly the sense of "register" that we mean to engage here. By "register" we simply mean to suggest that the recognizable range of terms associated with love, longing, and desire in the

Nepali language map closely, but not directly, onto similar terms in the English-language lexicon. "Register," then, implies a cross-culturally similar, but not identical, range of meanings for the terms used, as well as (in Halliday's sense) distinct contexts of use.

4. Much music popular in the U.S. or U.K. has been available in Kathmandu since the 1970s. Pop music from other European countries has generally not been represented. Rhythm and blues, disco, reggae, Latin dance fusions, heavy metal, and rap have been particularly popular. Especially popular bands and musicians include the Beatles, Jimi Hendrix, the Doors, Michael Jackson, Madonna, Pink Floyd, Deep Purple, and Nirvana.

5. "Love marriage" is a common English-language phrase used in Nepali-language contexts, often in conjunction with a form of the verb "*garnu*" (do). For more on the meaning of "*chalan*," which comes from a verb stem meaning "move," see Henderson's "What the Drums Had to Say."

6. Nepali pop, like most forms of public culture in Nepal, has always been a male-dominated expressive space. Girls and women, however, participate as listeners and sometimes as performers.

7. For more on language in and about music, see Feld and Fox. For more on language and emotion, see Abu-Lughod and Lutz; Lutz and White 417–27; Urban 172–92; and, specifically on South Asia, Greene ("Professional Weeping"). For more on language ideology, see Schieffelin, Woolard, and Kroskrity.

8. With their album *Newabeatles*, the Influence also innovated the merging of Western pop with Newari, the primary language of the Newars of the Kathmandu Valley. Other bands also produce Western pop songs in some of Nepal's other languages.

9. All translations and transliterations from the Devanāgari script throughout this article are ours.

10. "Old-fashioned" is a common English-language term young Nepalis use in interviews.

11. Heartache is most frequently caused by the loss of a loved one (44 percent) and occasionally by the inconstant ways of a moody lover (6 percent). The remaining 9 percent of our analytic sample is comprised of songs celebrating joyful, requited love (3 percent) or songs voicing social concerns and desires for *bikās* (6 percent).

12. The meanings and implications of "*bikās*" are traced out further in Pigg's "Disenchanting Shamans" and "Inventing Social Categories Through Place."

13. This parallels a Western influence in Hindi film songs (cf. Arnold).

14. This is not to say that the Influence (or any Nepali pop band) always structures its songs in the same ways that Western bands do. Inspired by Western pop, they sometimes structure their music in idiosyncratic ways. The Influence cultivates an emphasis on melody, which is highly valued in South Asia generally, and Bhim has been described as the "renowned melody prince" (Phuyal 36). Moreover, the Influence is eclectic and selective, incorporating elements of rhythm and blues and the Beatles, but not soul, country, or jazz.

15. There is a common notion in Nepal (and South Asia generally) that eyes are especially powerful vehicles of sexual attraction, and expressions including reference to them are considered quite alluring and typically Nepali.

16. Sadly, neither of us was able to interview Krishna Narayan Shrestha. When David Henderson met him in 1995 he was on his deathbed, and he died a month later.

17. These quotes come from interviews conducted by research assistant Sarmila Maharjan, June 1995.

18. The Nepali word, "*man*," is considered the locus of both feeling and thinking (cf. March; Jacobson).

19. Although mix music is commonly associated with dancing, dance halls are relatively new to Nepal, and the music still functions primarily as listening music.

20. Actually, the *macarena* seems to have originated in Roma (or "gypsy") culture, and was popularized in Europe in 1993 with the hit song "Hey! Macarena" (by the Spanish flamenco duo Los Del Rio). This song was reworked into a Hindi-language song in the 1997 Indian hit film, *Auzaar*, which was also screened in Nepal.

21. An exception on the *Mega Mix* album is the "Deusi Re Extended Mix," in which the opening narrative, most of the song samples, and many of the interjected phrases are in Nepali.

22. Although records were never a fully-developed musical mass medium in Nepal, Nepali sound engineers imitate the sounds of record scratching that they hear in moments of disrupture in Western rap. At the RRC Recording Centre, an engineer explained to Paul Greene that he produced his record scratching sounds by sampling his jacket zipper as it was zipped up.

Works Cited

Abu-Lughod, Lila, and Catherine A. Lutz, eds. *Language and the Politics of Emotion*. Cambridge: Cambridge UP, 1990.

Appadurai, Arjun. *Modernity at Large: Cultural Dimensions of Globalization*. Minneapolis: U of Minnesota P, 1996.

Appadurai, Arjun, and Carol A. Breckenridge. "Public Modernity in India." *Consuming Modernity: Public Culture in a South Asian World*. Ed. Carol A. Breckenridge. Minneapolis: U of Minnesota P, 1995. 1–20.

Arnold, Alison. "Popular Film Song in India—A Case of Mass Market Eclecticism." *Popular Music* 7.2 (1988): 177–88.

Feld, Steven, and Aaron A. Fox. "Music and Language." *Annual Review of Anthropology* 23 (1994): 25–53.

Grandin, Ingemar. *Music and Media in Local Life: Music Practice in a Newar Neighbourhood in Nepal*. Linköping, Sweden: Linköping U Dept. of Communication Studies, 1989.

Greene, Paul. "Mixed Messages: Unsettled Cosmopolitanisms in Nepali Pop." *Popular Music* 20.2 (2001): 169–87.

———. "Professional Weeping: Music, Affect, and Hierarchy in a South Indian Performance Art." *EOL: Ethnomusicology OnLine* 5 (1999). http://www.research.umbc.edu/eol/5/greene/.

Greene, Paul, and Yubakar Raj Rajkarnikar. "Echoes in the Valleys: A Social History of Nepali Pop, 1985–2000." *Wave Online* 50 (2000). http://www.wavemag.com.np/wave/echoes/Echoes.html. Reprinted in *Wave* 63 (2001): 16–18, 21.

Halliday, Michael A. K. "The Users and Uses of Language." *The Linguistic Sciences and Language Teaching*. Ed. M. A. K. Halliday, A. McIntosh, and P. Strevens. London: Longmans, 1964. 75–110.

Henderson, David. "Collected Voices: Echoes of Harmony and Discontent in the Music of the Kathmandu Valley." Diss. U of Texas, 1998.

———. "Emotion and Devotion, Lingering and Longing in Some Nepali Songs." *Ethnomusicology* 40.3 (1996): 440–68.

———. "The Sound of the City (Kathmandu Remix)." Asian Studies on the Pacific Coast conference. San Diego, California, 18 June 1999.

———. "What the Drums Had to Say—And What We Wrote About Them." *Creativity in Performance*. Ed. R. Keith Sawyer. London: Ablex Publishing Corporation, 1997. 67–93.

Irvine, Judith T. "Registering Affect: Heteroglossia in the Linguistic Expression of Emotion." *Language and the Politics of Emotion*. Ed. Lila Abu-Lughod and Catherine A. Lutz. Cambridge: Cambridge UP, 1990. 126–61.

Jacobson, Calla. "Ambiguities of Agency: Grammar, Self, and Feeling in Nepali Language, Speech, and Song." Unpublished manuscript, 1992.

Liechty, Mark. "Media, Markets, and Modernization: Youth Identities and the Experience of Modernity in Kathmandu, Nepal." *Youth Cultures: A Cross-Cultural Perspective.* Ed. Vered Amit-Talai and Helena Wulff. New York: Routledge, 1995. 166–201.

Lutz, Catherine, and Geoffrey M. White. "The Anthropology of Emotions." *Annual Review of Anthropology* 15 (1986): 405–36.

Manuel, Peter. "Music as Symbol, Music as Simulacrum: Postmodern, Pre-Modern, and Modern Aesthetics in Subcultural Popular Musics." *Popular Music* 14.2 (1995): 227–39.

March, Kathryn S. "Engendered Bodies, Embodied Genders." South Asian Seminar. U of Texas. Austin, 1 Oct. 1992.

Nyachhyon, Mohan Gopal. "A Life of Music." *Himal* 6.6 (1993): 18–19.

Phuyal, Surendra S. "The Influence: It's in the Name." *Wave* 28 (1998): 36.

Pigg, Stacy. "Disenchanting Shamans: Representations of Modernity and the Transformation of Healing in Nepal." Diss. Cornell U, 1990.

———. "Inventing Social Categories through Place: Social Representations and Development in Nepal." *Comparative Studies in Society and History* 34.3 (1992): 491–513.

Rose, Tricia. *Black Noise: Rap Music and Black Culture in Contemporary America.* Hannover, NH: UP of New England, 1994.

Schieffelin, Bambi B., Kathryn A. Woolard, and Paul V. Kroskrity, eds. *Language Ideologies: Practice and Theory.* New York: Oxford UP, 1998.

Sharma, Rajendra, and Robin Sharma. "A Study of the Current Pop Craze and Its Implications." Unpublished manuscript, n.d.

"Tuff Turf: Reminisces of a Lost Childhood—Part 1." *Wave* 20 (1997): 11–14.

"Tuff Turf: Reminisces of a Lost Childhood—Part 2." *Wave* 21 (1997): 18–22.

Urban, Greg. *A Discourse-Centered Approach to Culture: Native South American Myths and Rituals.* Austin: U of Texas P, 1991.

Discography

Crossroads. *Nayã Mode.* Tape. Kathmandu, Nepal: SSS 83, n.d.

The Influence. *Again.* Tape. Kathmandu, Nepal: RRC TI 003, 1992.

———. *Jijibiṣā.* Tape. Kathmandu: Annapurna Cassette Centre ACCA 007, 1991.

———. *Newabeatles.* Tape. Kathmandu, Nepal: RRC, 1994.

———. *Sapanimā. . . .* Tape. Kathmandu, Nepal: Annapurna Cassette Centre ACCA 002, 1985.

Mega Mix. CD. Kathmandu, Nepal: New Media, 1998.

Pradhan, Babin. *1994.* Tape. Kathmandu, Nepal: Nova Studios, 1994.

Pradhan, Sanjeep. *Naśā Bhitra.* Tape. Kathmandu, Nepal: Square Audio Centre SAC 004, n.d.

Shrestha, Sushil. *Anjulimā.* Tape. Kathmandu, Nepal: Freak Street Music Point 002, n.d.

Nation,

REGIO

ETHN

in the

POLITICS

and

LANG

and
CITY
OF Music

Part Two

Mucho Loco for Ricky Martin; or The Politics of Chronology, Crossover, and Language within the Latin(o) Music "Boom"[1]

—María Elena Cepeda

African-American comedian Chris Rock's remarks, made in reference to Puerto Rican Ricky Martin's performance of his recent hit "Livin' La Vida Loca"[2] at the 1999 MTV Video Music Awards, neatly summarize the contradictions embodied in mainstream U.S. attitudes towards Spanish: "Livin' *la vida loca*, man—I'm gonna write me some Spanish jokes or somethin'. . . . Can't make no money speakin' English no more. . . . There ain't no money in English, man, c'mon—no money in English. . . . *Vida loca*, you know." As Rock's remarks suggest, while Spanish is the target of much popular media jocularity and scorn in the form of what linguistic anthropologist Jane Hill terms "mock Spanish," it is simultaneously considered an essential tool in corporate strategies to target the bilingual, bicultural U.S. Latina/o youth market. Indeed, the Latina/o population's youth (more than one-third of the thirty-one million U.S. Latinas/os are under eighteen years of age) combined with its spending power (Latinos funnel more than 300 billion dollars yearly into the economy, more per capita than any other U.S. consumer group) render them the latest object of the popular music industry's attentions (Larmer 48–49; Negus 134). Industry efforts to attract the key Latina/o youth audience have paid off handsomely thus far, in the form of Latin music sales that are up fifty four percent in the first six months of 1999 as compared to the same period in 1998. This Latino music boom, however, cannot be attributed solely to increased spending on the part of Latina/o consumers; rather, industry sources are noting that a majority of the current growth in Latin(o) music sales is taking place in "American" (read: Anglo/white) music stores (Lannert 8). And as Robert Walser reminds us, analyzing popular culture—in this case, popular music—solely in terms of "units sold" masks the identity politics and power struggles at hand (xi). The questions then emerge: beyond signaling industry recognition of the obvious shifts in U.S. demographics, does the recent craze for "Latin" music offer any alternative representations of U.S. *latinidad*? How do the U.S. popular media construct—and in some cases, contest—a historical chronology of the boom? What do labels like "crossover" signify in this context? And how is Spanish, as a principal marker of U.S. Latina/o identity, depicted within popular musical texts—by non-Latinos and Latinos alike—as per current industry trends?

The mere presence of Spanish language and other cultural markers typically associated with U.S. Latina/o communities does not necessarily guarantee that mainstream audiences are being educated with regard to the multiple, and often conflicting, realities of U.S. Latina/o experiences, or moreover, that these realities are relayed by Latina/o voices. Therefore, via an examination of representations of "crossover," historical chronologies, and Spanish, this essay problematizes the prevailing and largely superficial depictions of the Latin/o/ music boom extant in the popular media. In particular, I underscore the de-contexualized, de-historicized language and subject matter of various recordings, television programs, and popular print media produced, written, and/or performed by non-Latinos (and, in some cases, U.S. Latina/o performers themselves). Thus, within the context of the current Latin/o/ music boom, this essay probes the larger questions of agency, identity, and, ultimately, economic and cultural capital, which arise upon closer examination of the politics of Latina/o representation in the current U.S. popular music industry.

The motivations underlying the Latin(o) boom are indeed multifaceted, and they encompass possibilities for economic gain as well as the increasing consumer influence and visibility of U.S. Latinas/os within the public sphere. During approximately the past two years, a majority, if not all, of the numerous popular publications that have devoted space to the discussion of Latin(o) (or what is often referred to as "Latin-tinged") music's rising popularity among non-Latino audiences have offered their interpretations of the "boom's" appeal to mainstream audiences. Recent magazine cover stories with titles like "The Making of Christina Aguilera," index the self-conscious nature of the boom's media construction, while its accompanying photo illustration of singer Aguilera in a half-human, half-cyborg pose—created with the aid of digital mesh computer graphics—exemplifies the industry's mindful recipe for "[t]he [b]uilding of a 21st [c]entury [s]tar" (Farley with Thigpen 71). Such self-reflexivity, however, does not routinely materialize, as media representations more often than not uncritically mirror existing stereotypes regarding U.S Latina/o and Latin American performers' locations with respect to mainstream audiences.

For example, in the June 27, 1999, *New York Times* article "A Country Now Ready to Listen," journalist Peter Watrous describes Latin American nations as "places that only a few years ago saw the world through virtually pre-Columbian eyes." He then hypothesizes that "Americans [are] longing for music more rooted in a certain place and produced more honestly" (27), hinting at the latent Anglo attraction to the "primitivistic Other" that also permeates the narrative of Jennifer López's video for the single "Waiting for Tonight," whose action takes place in a jungle setting, as well as Ricky Martin's performance at the February 2000 Grammys, during which, surrounded by "African tribal drummers," he danced and sang from within a ring of fire. An analogous echo of the dominant gaze surfaces in the one-hour September 1999 television special "Latin Beat," a chronicle of the current popularity of Latina/o musicians hosted by ABC news correspondent John Quiñones, a Chicano journalist, whose presence, along with the program's "news" format, provides an air of credibility. Rife with euphemisms and stereotypical references (Quiñones cites, among other descriptors, the "heat," "intoxication," and "spice" embodied in Latin(o) music), and apparently oblivious to the historic presence of many Latina/o communities in what is now U.S. territory, "Latin Beat" characterizes Latin(o) music as "hitting the States like a tropical storm," in a coded reference to the supposedly ephemeral, "dangerous" element of the music. Throughout the broadcast U.S. Latina/o performers are presented to viewers as museum pieces and labeled accordingly (Ricky Martin, Jennifer López, and Enrique Iglesias are respectively introduced as "Exhibit A," "Exhibit B," and the "Third Exhibit"). Thus in retrospect, "Latin Beat" could be interpreted as an hour-long promotion for U.S. Cuban producer/performers Gloria and Emilio Estefan's "crossover acts," as all the artists profiled, with scant exception, have already released or are in the processing of preparing English-language albums in collaboration with the Estefans.

The industry dominance exercised by Gloria and Emilio Estefan's Crescent Moon Studios, a Miami-based Sony affiliate that grosses 200 million dollars yearly (Drummond 78), is also evident in prevailing popular media constructions of the historical chronology of Latin(o) music in the United States. Said chronologies cede a disproportionate amount of credit for current crossover successes to the Estefan's company, as well as to Ricky Martin's live performance at the 1999 Grammys. In fact, Martin's performance is often depicted as the "beginning" of the current Latin(o) music "boom," as was apparent during the televised ceremony for the 2000 Grammy Awards. Indeed, in a paternalistic gaze that permeated the duration of the 2000 Grammys broadcast, each time a Latina/o took the stage to perform, present, or accept an award, ceremony cameras panned to the Estefan's seats in the audience in order to capture their reactions. Thus, the camera's gaze established an unspoken visual economy in which less established and powerful Latin(o) music industry figures were rendered subject to the "approval" of Emilio and Gloria Estefan—most notably registering Gloria Estefan's apparent shock upon viewing Jennifer López's now infamous Versace gown.

During the portion of the same broadcast dedicated to showcasing musicians of the year's Latin(o) boom, Gloria Estefan was recognized by actor Jimmy Smits as the "notable exception" among the U.S. Latina/o artists who had struggled for Anglo acceptance in preceding years. As Levin notes, the Estefan's view themselves as the "*first* people to combine the two [U.S. and Latin American] cultures" to produce what Emilio Estefan calls a musical blend of "hamburger with rice and beans," and they fervently embrace this role (Levin, "Miami's" 49, emph. mine; E. Estefan ctd. Levin, "Grammy-winning" 56). Ricky Martin's ongoing representation as the central figure of the current Latin(o) boom made possible by the Estefan's efforts was further reinforced in a later comment by singer Christina Aguilera. Aguilera cited Martin's February 24, 1999, Grammys performance as the watershed moment that had facilitated the signing of more Latina/o recording artists than ever before to major contracts in the year that followed ("Grammys").

Such widely held assumptions overwhelmingly fail to acknowledge the echoes of previously well-known Latina/o entertainers at work in both music industry constructions and Anglo receptions of current performers like Martin. Mainstream interpretations of today's Ricky are inevitably informed by the collective memory of that "other Ricky": Ricky Ricardo, Cuban actor/musician Desi Arnaz' alter ego on the television sitcom *I Love Lucy* (1951–1957). While rarely recognized, Arnaz' underlying presence in media depictions of Martin—despite the several decades between them—testifies not only to the general dearth of Latina/o performers occupying the mainstream historical consciousness, but more significantly, to the effectiveness of efforts to render the long, complex web of Latina/o contributions to "official" music histories short and simplistic. In addition, as Garofalo aptly notes with regard to long-standing industry notions of "crossover," "the identification of music with race, which has tended to exclude African-American artists and others from certain marketing structures in the music industry, makes the task of unearthing an accurate history of U.S. popular music quite difficult and encourages serious underestimates of the degree of cross-cultural collaboration that has taken place" (11–12). Thus, as chronological gaps that disproportionately privilege the Estefan's and Martin's roles within U.S. Latin(o) musical history—while simultaneously erasing those of others—the hegemonic silences constructed in popular media representations of the Latin(o) music boom could well be interpreted as "structural silencings," or the ongoing presence of institutional frameworks that facilitate such prevailing chronologies, in spite of their anachronistic nature (Trouillot xix, 28).

These mainstream media chronologies directly conflict with the works of numerous scholars, such as John Storm Roberts, Ruth Glasser, Frances Aparicio, and Manuel Peña, among others, whose works on Latin(o) popular music in the U.S. and Latin America contest the discrete time frames imposed by widely viewed programs such as this year's Grammys. As such, Glasser's *My Music Is My Flag*, in which she states her intent to "reevaluate the structure of ethnic history in general and the place of ethnic cultural expression with in it" explores the interplay of power, history, and the silences imposed upon contestatory accounts (4; xix) and provides compelling evidence of the long-standing impact of Latina/o musicians on U.S. popular musical forms. And unlike Storm Roberts, whose widely cited text on Latin(o) popular music, *The Latin Tinge*, elides the role of female participation in twentieth century Latin(o) music industry, Glasser traces key Latinas' roles in the dissemination of Latin(o) popular forms. Most notably, she focuses on the role of Victoria Hernández, sister of famed Puerto Rican composer Rafael Hernández, thereby challenging prevailing mainstream histories that erase women's contributions, if not much of U.S. Latina/o musical production in general (the example of Gloria Estefan notwithstanding). Upon winning contracts with major English-language U.S. labels, most Latin American and U.S. Latina/o performers who perform primarily in Spanish are repackaged as "debut artists" and "discoveries" of mainstream record companies, in a reflection of what Wilson Valentín-Escobar terms the "Columbus effect." We see this phenomenon in the careers of many performers, including veterans like Peruvian Susana Baca, Cuban Rubén González, and Nuyorican (New York Puerto Rican) Marc Anthony. This ability to re-contextualize and in essence "resemanticize" Latina/o artists serves as a lesson in the importance of "discovery" and nomenclature:

The naming of the "fact" is itself a narrative of power disguised as innocence. Would anyone care to celebrate the "Castilian invasion of the Bahamas"? . . . Naming the fact thus already imposes a reading and many historical controversies boil down to who has the power to name what. . . . Once discovered by Europeans, the Other finally enters the human world. (Trouillot 114)

Furthermore, the same hegemony wielded upon "re-naming" Latin American and U.S. Latina/o artists is also embodied, as we shall see, in designators such as "crossover." As such, within the context of the current Latin(o) music boom, who defines "crossover"? And what remains unspoken in the often-invoked language of crossover, a politically loaded term that does not persist, however, without considerable protest from key figures in the U.S. Latin(o) music industry? And finally, what possibilities (if any) do mainstream definitions of crossover allow for the recognition of bicultural identities? In *Rockin' Out: Popular Music in the USA*, Reebee Garafalo delineates the roots of the term "crossover," and specifically its basis in the music industry's historical presumption that each musical genre corresponded to its own distinct consumer group, absent any overlap. (For example, folk music was designated for southern, rural whites, rhythm and blues for blacks, and pop for northern, urban whites from the middle/upper classes, otherwise known as the "mainstream"). "Crossover" thus "refers to that process whereby an artist or a recording from a secondary or specialty marketing category . . . achieves hit status in the mainstream market . . . historically it connoted movement from a marginal category to the mainstream" (9–10). As a result, the segregationist marketing ideologies and business practices propelling the notion of "crossover" as it refers to either particular artists and/or their recordings have sustained a lasting impact on public perceptions of musical production and history.

In this light, the case of popular music phenomenon Christina Aguilera, a singer of Irish/Ecuadorian descent whose 1999 English-language debut *Christina Aguilera* achieved multi-platinum status, raises crucial questions regarding the situational nature of identity and the politics of crossover within the male, Anglo-dominated U.S. recording industry. In the months immediately preceding her February 2000 Grammy win for Best New Artist of 1999, Aguilera's record company launched an aggressive campaign to re-situate Aguilera within the U.S. market not as a phenotypically Anglo singer with an ambiguously "foreign-sounding" last name, but rather as a teenaged U.S. Latina preparing to re-release a series of her previous hits plus some original tracks, recorded this time in her newly-acquired *español*. Targeted at U.S. Latina/o consumers, BMG/RCA's highly visible campaign to manipulate Aguilera's public persona included cover stories with accompanying photos in widely-read Latina/o publications like *Hispanic* and *Latina*, as well as the previously mentioned *Time* cover story.

While most of the press coverage regarding Aguilera's Spanish language album largely fails to address the questions of phenotype (i.e., an individual's physical make up resulting from genotypical and environmental factors), skin privilege, and language politics that many U.S. Latinas/os grapple with on a daily basis, her December 1999 interview with *Latina* magazine discloses a bit more with regard to the way in which she locates herself. In response to inquiries about her (dyed) platinum blonde, blue-eyed appearance, Aguilera asserts that "[Latinas] come in all shapes, sizes, and colors." And while the rationales dictating her foray into Spanish-language music are never explicitly expressed in the article, Aguilera shares that "A lot of my fans are young girls, and they go, 'You're someone young Latin women can look up to,' because there really aren't many. . . . It's not like I was *born* in Ecuador. . . . Still I have those roots" (Méndez 81, emph. mine). Foremost, Aguilera's response provokes multiple readings that on one hand display what might be termed an "insider's" sensitivity to the complexities of Latina/o phenotype ("[Latinas] come in all shapes, sizes, and colors"). On the other hand, in the statement "It's not like I was *born* in Ecuador," she reveals her own lack of awareness regarding the very nature of U.S. Latina/o identity. Here, Aguilera's limited concept of *latinidad* is predicated upon national/territorial, as opposed to primarily political/cultural/historical factors, and sharply contrasts with a more politicized vision of U.S. Latina/o identity as "imbued with social, cultural, and political values that are resilient against the homogenizing impulses of the economically and politically dominant society" (Cabán 203–04). (It is also interesting to note that Aguilera self-identifies here as a role model for "Latin" girls, as opposed to young Latin*as*). While many Latina/o music fans do profess a certain amount of skepticism regarding the motives underlying this very abrupt shift in marketing strategy, questions of agency must be taken into account. Not only is the public not privy to the particulars of Aguilera's contract with BMG/RCA: we are also kept from knowing all but the barest details regarding her personal experience with Spanish, which raises questions regarding linguistic colonialism and unequal access to Spanish for many U.S.-educated Latinas/os. We are also left wondering about her relationship with her Ecuadorian father (Aguilera's parents divorced when she was very young, and she and her younger sister subsequently lived exclusively with their mother).

As their repeated representation as *fin de siècle* fad artists attests, Latina/o performers and other performers of color have had to contend with an industry that has historically and systematically categorized their music in opposition to an unmarked, white pop norm. (Incidentally, the March 2000 cover of *Hispanic* magazine featured Aguilera bearing the caption "Latin Pop: Just a Fad?"). As Suzanne E. Smith notes in her cultural history of Motown, shifts in the way in which industry designators such as "pop" and "rhythm and blues" were applied to the recordings of Motown artists directly reflected the amount of crossover success a particular group had achieved. However, as far as the media and industry were concerned, the race of Motown performers ultimately overrode any consideration of musical styles: "The Motown sound was always 'brown,' regardless of the company's diverse musical output and its popularity with multiracial audiences" (88, 163–64, 167). As evidenced by the title of *Time*'s May 24, 1999, cover story on the Latin(o) music boom ("Latin Music Goes Pop!"), during the Motown era as now, the label "pop music" functions as a euphemism for "Anglo" or "white" music, which in turn affords artists greater access to larger and ostensibly more affluent white audiences and thus higher sales. And while consumers and music executives no longer employ the term, constructions of categories of "race music" persist, re-packaged in Rhythm and Blues, Hip Hop, and Latin(o) forms, among others. Racial gatekeeping within the U.S. popular music industry, however, extends beyond the subtext legible in *Billboard*'s market categories or the pretenses visible in the layout of music stores; as Puerto Rican author Esmeralda Santiago observes with regard to Latina/o artists with large Anglo followings, "this is still the white face of the Caribbean" (Farley 78). As within the music industry, phenotypical considerations have not escaped the media's notice, as the following comments describing Ricky Martin suggest: "His voice isn't great. But he's got the looks, he's got the energy, and he's got the backing . . . And he's not *too* Latin" (Pellegrini).

In other words, the popular media recognizes that part of Martin's (and López, Marc Anthony, and Aguilera's) appeal to mainstream audiences is their *appearance* of "whiteness." Furthermore, mainstream media representations of the Latin(o) music boom as a crossover phenomenon rely on the assumption that "crossing-over" to pop music is the ultimate goal of all Latina/o artists, and a status, once achieved, which they should gratefully and passively accept: "Latinos are the fastest-growing demographic in the U.S., and as a rule, they tend not to complain too loudly when one of their own crosses over" (Pellegrini). This presumption that "America" is synonymous with the English language and whiteness is illustrated in a recent article about Nuyorican artist Marc Anthony: "It's good to be the king . . . of salsa. But it's taken some fancy crossover moves and an English-language hit to get America talking about Marc Anthony" (Willman). Thus, the question emerges: to just *which* America is Anthony's interviewer referring?

Such representations, however, do not go uncontested within the Latina/o community. For his part, Anthony has, in both print and television interviews, repeatedly rejected the crossover label on the grounds that it fails to encompass the bicultural nature of U.S. Latina/o identity (*Latin Beat*; Willman; Farley 79). Demonstrating a parallel line of reasoning, actor and *salsero* Rubén Blades has been more openly critical of the concept of crossover, stating: "I hate the word 'crossover' with a passion because it is a racist term for people who can't accept the mixture that has already taken place" (García 27). In more covert fashion, popular magazines aimed at U.S. Latinas/os have responded to the assumptions posed in more mainstream publications, establishing a kind of dialectics of contestation. The Latina/o-produced magazine *Mía*, for example, "answered" *Time*'s May 24, 1999, "Latin Music Goes Pop!" cover story with its own cover bearing the phrase "Música Latina: Did It Really Go 'Pop'!?", a title that simultaneously questions the profundity of pop music's influence on "traditional" Latin(o) musical forms, as well as the sincerity underlying Latin(o) music's appeal to Anglo audiences.

As the preceding discussion regarding the chronologies of Latin(o) music and the dynamics of crossover suggests, media representations of the Latin(o) music boom are rife with contradictions, the most apparent of which are those surrounding the increased use of Spanish in the popular musical texts of the Latin(o) boom. As Aparicio observes, language exists as a "site of social contestation" ("Whose Spanish" 8), and therefore, an examination of the complex ways in which Spanish is employed in U.S. popular music by both Latinas/os, non-Latinas/os, and media outlets alike underscores not only prevailing mainstream consumer attitudes towards Spanish, but also—and perhaps more importantly—dominant attitudes towards the Latina/o cultural "invasion" that many of these performers embody. Indeed, a not-so-subtle form of xenophobia emerges upon closer examination of the various textual representations of the Latin(o) music boom and the growing U.S. Latina/o population's predicted impact on the monoracial, monocultural "America" encoded within them, as titles such as "*¿Se Habla* Rock and Roll? You Will Soon: A Musical Invasion from South of the Border" (Hayden and Schoemer) and "Watch Out: The Rhythm Is Gonna Get You, Too" (Robinson) suggest. (The latter title ironically refers to Gloria Estefan's 1987 hit "The Rhythm Is Gonna Get You," a connection that leads one to wonder just how uptempo the rhythm in question could possibly be, as it took twelve years to arrive).

Given the Spanish language's increasing public presence in the U.S., in combination with (or perhaps in part engendered by) the recent Latin(o) music boom, examples of what linguistic anthropologist Jane Hill terms "mock Spanish" abound in mainstream press coverage, as the article title "America Goes *Mucho Loco* for Ricky" illustrates. As such, here I seek to highlight the presence and functions of various representations of the Spanish language, and by extension, U.S. Latinas/os, in a few representative texts. Hill defines "mock Spanish" as a variety of Anglo Spanish that "has been incorporated into English primarily as a form of parody, where the 'Mexican' voice is sharply opposed to the English one . . . Spanish [that] is filled with 'boldness' in the form of exaggeration, and with 'impossibility', manifested in hyperanglicizations and absurd grammatical constructions." The sub-register of mock Spanish known as "parodic pejoration," in which "Spanish loan-words and expressions are given an ironic spin or subjected to semantic 'pejoration' to adopt them for usage in jocular registers, especially as insults," is widespread in contemporary U.S. popular culture. These include the use of hyperanglicizations (such as "hasta banana" for "*hasta mañana*"), the Spanish syntactic frame "*el . . . -o*" to form English pejoratives (i.e., phrases like "el greaso"), and borrowed fixed phrases (such as the ubiquitous "Hasta la vista, baby"). Mock Spanish also exhibits elements of what Hill terms "distancing," or the willful phonetic, orthographic, and syntactic distortion of Spanish by non-native speakers as a form of contempt for the Spanish language and the population with which it is traditionally associated ("Hasta la vista" 149, 163–63, 167).[3] In contrast to assertions that many linguistic practices deemed offensive within certain contexts could actually function as part of an anti-racist/sexist/homophobic social agenda, Hill asserts that in many contexts, these "subversive" speech acts are often merely another means by which some Anglos permit themselves—while simultaneously denying others the same privileges—a type of linguistic "disorder" which serves to further delineate the larger "white public space" ("Language"). Here, as Trouillot suggests, "wordview wins over the facts: white hegemony is natural and taken for granted; any alternative is still in the domain of the unthinkable" (93).

With respect to the use of Spanish by those who exhibit limited to no competence in the language, both Hill ("Language" 44) and Urciuoli (45) note substantial mistrust and resentment on the part of native Spanish speakers for those who attempt to encroach upon their "linguistic territory." These reactions range from the mere awareness of mock Spanish as an exclusively Anglo public gesture (Hill, "Language" 46) to more explicit statements such as the following conversation between a Nuyorican individual ("FC") and an outside interviewer ("I") regarding the use of Spanish by U.S. Anglos in positions of authority over Puerto Ricans:

FC: When you do that [speak Spanish] you threaten us. When you go into somebody else's language, you're threatening their—how will I describe it?
I: Security?
FC: Yeah, security, their life. That's where it becomes racist. (Urciuoli 47)

Far more public examples of the (sub)conscious enactment of power differentials include remarks by 2000 Grammys host Rosie O'Donnell, who introduced singer Marc Anthony with the words: "*Su música me encanta en mi corazón. Lo amo mucho. Quiero Taco Bell. ¡Mi amiga, Marc Anthony!*" ("Grammys"). (While O'Donnell's attempt at Spanish is so error-laden that it is difficult to translate, I would venture to guess that she was trying to communicate the following: "I love your music with all my heart. I love it very much. I want some Taco Bell. My friend, Marc Anthony!")

For many viewers, O'Donnell's use of Spanish could be superficially read as a benign cross-cultural gesture; by the same token, however, the combination of the tremendous industry authority that O'Donnell enjoys, in conjunction with her use of the phrase "*Quiero Taco Bell*" (and the audience laughter that ensued), testifies to the effectiveness of media attempts to reduce dominant notions of "Latin American culture" to a single, universally recognized punch line. In this context, the usage of mock Spanish encompasses the enactment of societal power differentials, as Spanish speakers serve not as the agents of but rather as the (in)direct objects within an elite discourse. Thus, the problem for the cultural critic is to discern how certain speech acts cease to even "superficially indicate speakers' high regard for the donor language" and become, as in the case of mock Spanish, "a racist distancing strategy that reduce[s] complex Latino experience to a subordinated, commodity identity" (Woolard and Schieffelin 62).

While examples of mock Spanish employed as a tool of linguistic hegemony proliferate, the works of numerous U.S. Latina/o recording artists serve as compelling proof of the redemptive powers of Spanish and English-Spanish code-switching among U.S. Latina/o communities, as well as the formidable challenges that their communicative realities pose to narrow definitions of linguistic competence. A case in point is Nuyorican Jennifer López's 1999 album *On the 6*, which, while predominantly recorded in English, does incorporate various sections in Spanish, as in the tracks "It's Not that Serious" and "Should've Never." In both songs, Spanish functions as a primary contributor to their overriding themes; as a result, much of these tracks escape the comprehension of monolingual English listeners.

As Aparicio and Chávez-Silverman state, "to *tropicalize* . . . means to trope, to imbue a particular space, geography, group, or nation with a set of traits, images, and values" (8, emph. in original). And notably, in the track "Should've Never," López performs what could be interpreted as an ambiguous act of self-tropicalization, as she provokes predominant stereotypes linking Spanish to sex, sexuality, and romance:

A veces tengo miedo / . . . que nunca más voy a sentir tus manos / Sobre mi piel /
(moan) *. . . ¿Qué voy a hacer? /* (moan) / (moan) / *Este amor que es cruel / Y tan dulce*

a la misma vez / Tócame / Una vez más / Así, así / (moan) */ Bésame/ . . . Como si fuera la
última vez . . . /* (moan) */ Devórame, devórame /* (moan).

[Sometimes I'm afraid / . . . that I'll never feel your hands on me again / on my skin /
(moan) / . . . What am I going to do? / (moan) / (moan) / This love is cruel / And at the
same time so sweet / (moan) / Touch me / (moan) / One more time / Like that, like
that / (moan) / Kiss me / . . . As if it were for the last time . . . / (moan) / Devour me,
devour me / (moan).] (tr. Cepeda)

This passage, taken from the final, whispered portion of the track and
punctuated by López's multiple moans, functions as the reenactment of a
sexual encounter as it simultaneously reifies the traditional vision of the
"Latin lover," who, seized by passion, is drawn back to the "primordial"
Spanish. Ambiguous instances of self-tropicalization aside, however, López's
ad-lib could also be construed as resistance to the hegemonic linguistic par-
adigms that portray U.S. Latinas/os as semi- or a-lingual and as a re(butt)al
to industry executives who, upon completion of her original demo in Spanish, allegedly insisted that she record the final product in English (Freydkin).

López's presence as a highly visible icon of U.S. *latinidad* also provokes
multiple, complex readings of Latina corporality. As Negrón-Muntaner
insightfully observes, López's body, racialized in media representation, and
more specifically her celebrated *culo puertorriqueño*, serve as an discomfiting
reminder to many of the "Africa in(side) America" (185): "A big *culo* does not
only upset hegemonic (white) notions of beauty and good taste, it is a sign for
the dark, incomprehensible excess of 'Latino' and other African diaspora cultures. Excess of food (unrestrained), excess of shitting (dirty), and excess of sex
(heathen) are its three vital signs" (189). Ever aware of the media focus on her
body, during the publicity tour surrounding the 1997 release of *Selena*, López
herself overtly acknowledged the plight of her Latina show business forerun-
ners such as Rita Hayworth and Raquel Welch, who "could only become stars
after they disguised themselves" (Vincet qtd. in Negrón Muntaner 186–87). In
contrast to Anglo feminist interpretations that tend to monolithically interpret
media attention to López's rear end as merely another sexist, racist display,
Latina scholars like Negrón-Muntaner and Casillas offer alternative, U.S.
Latina-centric readings of López in which "the big rear end acts both as an
identification site for Latinas to reclaim their beauty and a 'compensatory fantasy' for a whole community" (Negrón-Muntaner 189, 192; cf. Casillas).

In comparison, the rap group Cypress Hill demonstrates the limitless political and artistic potential of code-switching in their music. The track "Latino Lingo," from their album *Los Grandes Éxitos en Español*, exhibits the group's considerable code-switching skills as self-proclaimed "biolinguals" based on their deft usage of *pachuco* Spanish.[4] The presence of *pachuco* Spanish in "Latino Lingo" performs various functions: while it serves as a marker of Cypress Hill's Los Angeles base, it also underlines the group's pan-Latina/o, pan-ethnic origins, as the trio is made up of a U.S. Cuban, a Chicano-Cubano, and an Italian-American, and performs a musical genre traditionally associated with urban African-Americans. Their acute awareness of the financial and cultural stakes at hand also surfaces in "Latino Lingo" as they declare: "they're clowning on me 'cause of my language / .... / I have to tell them straight up it's called Spanglish / Now who's the pinga[5] the gringo / Trying to get paid from the funky biolinguals." Moreover, the fact that "Latino Lingo" appears as the "Spanish language" remake of the "Latin Lingo" track from the group's debut album neatly conveys Cypress Hill's linguistic positioning as a uniquely U.S. hybrid whose lyrical messages literally resist the complete comprehension of all but community insiders. As such, groups like Cypress Hill epitomize not only the opportunity to contest linguistic hegemony and display one's competence in the community code, but also the possibilities for self-affirmation and community-building via audience identification with a particular linguistic repertoire.

In this essay, I hope to have problematized the largely de-contexualized, de-historicized nature of the Latin(o) music boom's numerous representations, as well as its prevailing depictions of Spanish and Spanish-speakers. As Richard Ruiz notes in an important distinction between the functions of language and those of voice, "*Language* has a life of its own—it exists even when it is suppressed; when voice is suppressed it is not heard-it does not exist" (321). This reminds us that inclusion means little without representations in which U.S. Latina/o communities are empowered to act as subjects as opposed to mere objects. A statement of similar tone in the December 1999 issue of *Hispanic* clearly captures the frustrations of many U.S. Latinas/os in the face of the current "boom": "Of course, invading pop culture is no substitute for real political power" ("The Best"). However, I would dispute *Hispanic*'s assessment on the grounds that "pop culture power," while not analogous to more overt and traditionally recognized forms of political power, *does* encompass not only the opportunities for resistance and revision but also the possibilities for oppositional praxis. As performers such as Cypress Hill and Jennifer López, among others, attest, the words of these artists, as well as the language(s) in which they choose to speak them in, emerge as a very public testament to the political power and possibilities embodied not only in music, but in the linguistic repertoires of U.S. Latinas/os as well.

Notes

1. As in most examples of what Hill labels "mock Spanish," the title "America Goes *Mucho Loco* for Ricky" displays incorrect usage of basic Spanish. (It should read: "America Goes *Muy Loco* for Ricky.") Also, I employ the term "Latin(o)" music in this essay because it foregrounds the tensions between the designators "Latin" (the label that much mainstream media employs) and "Latina/o" (a grassroots term used by U.S. Latinas/os themselves), without erasing either (Aparicio and Jáquez). Also, *gracias mil* to the following people for their insights and assistance with this essay: Annette Alonso, Frances Aparicio, Mike Carroll, Holly Cashman, Dolores Inés Casillas, Patricia Cepeda, Kathy Jurado, and Wilson Valentín-Escobar.

2. The 1999 release of Martin's "Livin' La Vida Loca" has resulted in the resematicization of the phrase "*la vida loca*"; no longer primarily associated with Chicana/o gang life, it has now come to signify U.S. Latina/o life in general. As articles like "Puerto Rican Singer Damages Perfectly Good Chicano Phrase" attest, this shift in meaning has not gone unnoticed by the Chicana/o and Latina/o communities.

3. I would add that distancing strategies also serve to protect the individual by allowing one to forgo the experience—however momentary or superficial—of what it is to function as an ethnolinguistic minority.

4. *Pachuco* Spanish (also known as *caló*) is a variety of Spanish most often associated with Southwest Chicanas/os, particularly males. According to Rosaura Sánchez, *caló* "incorporates standard Spanish, loanwords from English and even code-switching. It is primarily characterized by its penchant for innovativeness in its expansion of the lexicon to produce an argot" (128–34).

5. In many Spanish-speaking nations, "pinga" is slang for "penis"; similar to "dick" in English.

Works Cited

Aparicio, Frances R. "Whose Spanish, Whose Language, Whose Power?: An Ethnographic Inquiry into Differential Bilingualism." *Indiana Journal of Hispanic Literatures* 12 (1998): 5–23.

———, and Cándida Jáquez. Introduction. *Musical Migrations: Transnationalism and Cultural Hybridity in Latin/o America.* Ed. Frances R. Aparicio and Cándida Jáquez with María Elena Cepeda. New York: St. Martin's Press, 2002.

———, and Susana Chávez-Silverman. Introduction. *Tropicalizations: Transcultural Representations of Latinidad.* Hanover, NH: Dartmouth College/UP New England, 1997.

"The Best & Worst of 1999." *Hispanic* Dec. 1999. 18 Feb. 2000; also at http:// www.hisp. com/dec99/the.htm.

Cabán, Pedro. "The New Synthesis of Latin American and Latino Studies." *Borderless Borders: U.S. Latinos, Latin Americans, and the Paradox of Interdependence.* Ed. Frank Bonilla, Edwin Meléndez, Rebecca Morales, and María de los Angeles Torres. Philadelphia: Temple UP, 1998. 195–215.

Casillas, Dolores Inés. "From Colonial Hottentot to Post-Colonial 'Hottie': Jennifer López' Re(butt)als to White America." SCOR (Students of Color of Rackham) Conference. U of Michigan, Ann Arbor. 13 Feb. 2000.

Drummond, Tammerlin. "Godfather of the Miami Sound." *Time* 24 May 1999: 78.

Farley, Christopher John. "Latin Music Pops." *Time* 24 May 1999: 74–79.

Farley, Christopher John, with David E. Thigpen. "Christina Aguilera: Building a 21st Century Star." *Time* 6 March 2000: 71–72.

Freydkin, Donna. "Biography: Jennifer López." *People.com.* 28 May 1999. http://people.aol.com/people/pprofiles/jlopez/bio.html.

García, Guy. "Another Latin Boom, But Different." *New York Times* 27 June 1999: 25+.

Garofalo, Reebee. *Rockin' Out: Popular Music in the USA.* Boston: Allyn and Bacon, 1997.

Glasser, Ruth. *My Music Is My Flag: Puerto Rican Musicians and Their New York Communities, 1917–1940.* Berkeley: U of California P, 1995.

Grammy Awards. CBS. 23 Feb. 2000.

Hayden, Thomas, and Karen Schoemer. "¿Se Habla Rock and Roll? You Will Soon: A Musical Invasion from South of the Border." *Newsweek* 8 Sept. 1997: 70–71.

Hill, Jane H. "Hasta La Vista, Baby: Anglo Spanish in the American Southwest." *Critique of Anthropology* 13 (1993): 145–76.

———. "Language, Race, and White Space." *American Anthropologist* 100 (1998): 680–89.

Lannert, John. "Latin Sales Swell in First Half of '99." *Billboard* 21 Aug. 1999: 8.

Larmer, Brook. "Latino America." *Newsweek* 12 July 1999: 48–58.

Latin Beat. ABC. 7 Sept. 1999.

Levin, Jordan. "Grammy-winning Producer Touts Heart Over High-tech." *Variety* 10–16 June 1996: 56.

———. "Miami's Potent Musical Mix." *Variety* 10–16 June 1996: 49.

Méndez, Juan M. "Unbottled and Unleashed: Christina Aguilera." *Latina* Dec. 1999: 78–81.

MTV Video Music Awards. MTV. 9 Sept. 1999.

Negrón-Muntaner, Frances. "Jennifer's Butt." *Atzlán* 22 (Fall 1997): 181–94.

Negus, Keith. *Music Genres and Corporate Cultures.* London and New York: Routledge, 1999.

Pellegrini, Frank. "America Goes Mucho Loco for Ricky." *Time Daily* 13 May 1999: 14 Nov. 1999. <http://www.pathfinder.com/time/daily/0,2960,24750,00.htm>.

———. "Puerto Rican Singer Damages Perfectly Good Chicano Phrase." *Pocho.com Archives* 24 Mar. 2000. <http://www.pocho.com/news/APN-RickyM41999.html>.

Robinson, Linda. "Watch Out: The Rhythm Is Gonna Get You, Too." *U.S. News & World Report.* 24 May 1999: 61.

Ruiz, Richard. "The Empowerment of Language-Minority Students." *Latinos and Education: A Critical Reader.* Ed. Antonia Darder, Rodolfo O. Torres, and Henry Gutiérrez. New York and London: Routledge, 1997. 319–28.

Sánchez, Rosaura. *Chicano Discourse: Socio-historic Perspectives.* Houston: Arte Público P, 1983.

Smith, Suzanne E. *Dancing in the Street: Motown and the Cultural Politics of Detroit.* Cambridge, MA: Harvard UP, 1999.

Storm Roberts, John. *The Latin Tinge: The Impact of Latin American Music on the United States.* 2nd ed. New York and Oxford: Oxford UP, 1999.

Trouillot, Michel-Rolph. *Silencing the Past: Power and the Production of History.* Boston: Beacon P, 1995.

Urcuioli, Bonnie. "The Political Topography of Spanish and English: The View from a New York Puerto Rican Neighborhood." *American Ethnologist* 18 (1991): 295–310.

Valentín-Escobar, Wilson. "Between Salsa and Jazz: The Latin Scene in New York." Center for African and African-American Studies conference. University of Michigan, Ann Arbor. Fall 1998.

Walser, Robert. *Running With the Devil: Power Gender, and Madness in Heavy Metal Music.* Hanover, NH: Wesleyan UP/UP of New England, 1993.

Watrous, Peter. "A Country Now Ready to Listen." *New York Times* 27 June 1999: 25+.

Willman, Chris. "Marque Marc." *EW Magazine* 8 Oct. 1999. 14 Nov. 1999. http://www.pathfinder.com/ . . . r_ref+ON&mtype=0&list_size=25&direction.htm.

Woolard, Kathryn A., and Bambi Schieffelin. "Language Ideology." *Annual Review of Anthropology* 23 (1994): 55–82.

Discography

Cypress Hill. "Latino Lingo." *Los Grandes Éxitos en Español.* CD, Ruffhouse Records, CK 63712. 1999.

López, Jennifer. "Should've Never." *On the 6.* CD, Sony. OK 69351. 1999.

Just for Fun? Language Choice in German Popular Music

—Edward Larkey

After World War II, West Germany, in its search for a post-Nazi identity, encountered the emerging hegemony of the United States, the political and military leader of the Western world whose culture industry challenged the weakened German cultural elite with a powerful combination of unbridled and unrepentant commercialism, populism, and consumerism. Americanization became a looming threat to conservatives competing for legitimacy in a national-cultural marketplace that was severely discredited by the Nazi-tainted popular culture of the recent past. Some conservatives rallied around pre-Nazi cultural ideals rooted in a romanticized folk culture, seeking a mythical German *Heimat* (homeland) untouched by the polluting influences of industrialization, massification, and standardization. Other critics, both conservative and liberal, drew upon Theodor Adorno and Max Horkheimer's critique of the "culture industry" (60–150), arguing that mass entertainment discouraged rational contemplation and infected the unsuspecting masses with the virus of unrestrained emotional stimulation and Dionysian excess for which the recent Nazi atrocities seemed to offer the most perfidious examples.

The crisis of German culture in the years following World War II would lead to changes in popular music in terms of language choice and lyric content. At this time German popular music was dominated by three genres: *Schlager*, *volkstümliche*, and *Volksmusik*. *Schlager*, rooted in nineteenth-century operetta and dance traditions, blossomed into a vibrant form of cultural expression in the 1920s and 1930s, and after World War II served as a vehicle for expressing a variety of feelings—loss, abandonment, loneliness, disillusionment, and hope. Because *Schlager* is a historically syncretized genre capable of adapting various influences and traditions, it is difficult to pin down its specific characteristics

131

(see Wicke 445–54); in general, however, it employs 4/4 time, orchestral or pop arrangements, and, some exceptions aside, African-American musical characteristics like syncopation and blue-notes are not used. During this same period, an industry producing the *volkstümliche* (folk-like) genre (i.e., commercialized folk music) evolved from a vast number of *Heimat*-movies, a good example of which is *Der Förster vom Silberwald* (1954). Popular in the 1950s, these movies are generally characterized by a romantic plot, an idyllic and unspoiled alpine setting, and a hero who saves the country folk from encroaching industrial civilization and falls in love with a country girl while so doing. Like the scores for these movies, *volkstümliche* employs the melodies, instrumentation (accordion, clarinet and other woodwinds), and vocal patterns of traditional folk music while being distinguishable from *Volksmusik* ("authentic" folk music) (cf. von Schoenebeck 279–92). To many critics, *volkstümliche* seemed both polluted by the post-war commercial recording industry and too uncritical of the recent past in the form of the politically manipulated folk songs produced under Nazi rule. Contesting that heritage was a folk music movement with roots in the pre-Nazi youth movement, which re-emerged in the early 1950s with affinities to the concurrent folk movement in the United States.

These three genres—*Schlager*, *volkstümliche*, and *Volksmusik*—generally used German lyrics; however, by the late 1960s and continuing into the post-unification period successive waves of popular music from the United States and Great Britain brought new genres (rock, and later, rap) into the German popular music scene; this set the stage for continuous competition, contestation, and accommodation of English language use in German popular music. At the same time, influences from within the German-speaking countries, combined with the contestatory impulses of the rock and rap genres, would lead to the increasing use of German dialects, and later, the use of Turkish (a significant minority language in some major German urban areas), resulting in a complex, multiglossic approach to language in several sectors of the German popular music market. Relatedly, in terms of both language practices and lyric content, German pop would turn to more controversial expression, particularly in relation to sexuality, all of which has resulted in extraordinarily ironic and linguistically complex forms of popular music. This paper will examine these developments, and in the concluding section, we will consider how these developments relate to audiences, the culture industry, and the process of globalization.

German Popular Genres and Language Choice

At various stages in the history German pop, musicians have employed non-standard dialects in lyrics to reinforce a sense of regional (in the case of Germany) and even national (in the case of Swiss and Austrian) identities on the defensive because of the dominance of either Standard German (in the *Schlager*) or English-language pop (distributed by the global, Anglo-American-dominated industry). Considering first the relationship between Standard German and regional dialects: the historical lack of a politically unified center for German culture and language has meant that regional dialects—distinguished from the Standard by lexical, phonological, and syntactical differences (Clyne 4ff.) and based on centuries-old tribal divisions (Alemannic in the southwest, Bavarian in the Southeast, Franconian in the West and East Central regions)—have persisted and achieved political and cultural legitimacy.

In addition to the linguistic vestiges of ancient tribal distinctions, a further distinction exists between *Niederdeutsch* (Low German; i.e., the northern German plains) varieties, which are related to Dutch and Frisian, and *Oberdeutsch* (High or Upper German, spoken in the southern regions and equivalent to Standard German, though linguists often avoid the term and its implication that *Niederdeutsch* varieties are somehow sub-standard). The differences in the two are based on gradually dissipating consonants and other differences stemming from the High German Sound Shift between the sixth and eighth centuries in southern German regions and moving north (Clyne 6–7) (e.g., the German word for "I" is sounded as "ich" in High German and "ik" in Low German). This difference is geographically delineated by the "Benrather Line," a linguistic border running West to East through the Düsseldorf suburb of Benrath. The Standard pronunciation is derived from northern German varieties combined with standardization that was the result of Lutheran reforms incorporating East Franconian varieties from the central German provinces of Thuringia and Saxony.

For many speakers of German language varieties, particularly in Switzerland and Austria, the written form of the language represents the official standard against which the Alemannic or the Bavarian dialects are considered regional varieties in Germany proper. For speakers in the north of

Germany, many of these southern varieties are barely intelligible, and in Switzerland and Austria, specific terms are used to denote the linguistic differences between the spoken varieties and the official ones—in Switzerland, Standard German is "*Schriftdeutsch*" ("written German"); in Austria it is "*Bühnendeutsch*" ("stage German") or "*Binnendeutsch*" ("Internal German").

The "nationalization" of dialects in Austria and Switzerland led to their use in rock and pop songs. Many people, especially among the youth, sought greater legitimacy for dialect as a way to achieve more adequate expression for feelings of alienation, solidarity, intimacy and identity with their linguistic community. Even within Germany, the use of Bavarian, Swabian, or even Franconian dialect in lyrics signaled increased regional self-awareness in the face of linguistic homogenization. For pop bands, vocal artists, songwriters, and audiences, skillful use of dialect lyrics usually plays with and against linguistic knowledge, experience, and expertise with both Standard and dialect, and thus serves to reinforce the in-group solidarity, as well as demonstrating an additional layer of linguistic and artistic expertise and creativity (Ammon 161–78; cf. Woolard 53–76).

Singers in Bavarian dialect in Germany and Austria encounter what is jokingly referred to by musicians as the "White Sausage Line," an indistinct border in Germany (generally north of the Main River) above which Bavarian lyrics are nearly unintelligible. Viennese groups like Ostbahn-Kurti und die Chefpartie and vocalists like Wolfgang Ambros and blues singer Heli Deinboek encounter this phenomenon, as do singers from the Styrian city of Graz, an important center for pop music in southeastern Austria. Many Austrian bands use dialect-colored Standard German to mark their heritage on the German linguistic periphery while increasing their comprehensibility, and in so doing, their chances for success, on the German-language market (110 million pop.) beyond the narrow confines of Austria (7.8 million pop.). (This interest in negotiating various audiences is also evident in the way the dialect lyrics are placed in relation to the recorded music and the printed information on the covers or in CD-booklets. In order to facilitate lyric comprehensibility, many bands include either translations of their dialect lyrics into the Standard, or provide glossaries for equivalent Standard terms on their CD booklets or album covers.). In Switzerland, however, many bands do not use this strategy: some prefer to use the Bernese dialect, and as a result go largely unnoticed in other German-speaking countries where their dialect is incomprehensible, whereas within Switzerland, Bernese is considered the most artistically expressive dialect, even more so than the Zurich or Basel varieties, the two other major dialect areas of Swiss-German. However, some Swiss-Germans seeking wider commercial success on the international market may employ either French lyrics (like Stephan Eicher) or, to move to our next topic, English lyrics (like the techno duo Yello).

The introduction of the rock genre forced a realignment of attitudes regarding musical genres and language use: *Schlager* (the lyrics of which generally refrain from social criticism, and countercultural or oppositional content or attitude) came to denote conservative, obsolete, orthodoxy with regard to musical taste and social/cultural behaviors, whereas "rock" signified the rebellious, insurrectional aspect of avant-garde or heterodoxic aspects of popular music. At this time, while a number of German lyric writers used English fragments to poke fun at its usage, it increasingly became a sign of artistic prowess and intent, demonstrating global competitiveness and legitimacy, particularly in the rock genre, where its use dominated. Indeed, the introduction of the rock genre and the influence of popular British bands like The Beatles and The Rolling Stones entailed an imitative phase for German rock bands, which included the use of English lyrics based on these British, as well as American, models.

While *Schlager* and *volkstümliche* continued to use Standard German, its use in rock lyrics (as opposed to English) would evolve as a contested form for student and countercultural youth in the German-speaking countries, and, following the imitative phase, bands began to introduce German lyrics. They gained performance experience, cultivated audiences, and were recruited by major record companies, a development beginning in earnest around 1970–1971. Standard German is now the language preferred by nationally visible artists in the *Schlager, volkstümliche, Volkmusik,* and now the rock and contemporary pop genres (in the rock sector, this includes, among others, Udo Lindenberg, early Nina Hagen, and Herbert Grönemeyer; in the *Schlager* and pop sector, Udo Jürgens, Roland Kaiser, and Peter Maffay). The new German rock music lyric aesthetic evolved throughout the 1970s and into the 1980s based on the peculiarities of language use in Germany among the three variants (i.e., Standard German, various regional dialects, and English). The use of German lyrics signaled the expectation that a substantial political or social commentary or critique would be forthcoming. Playfulness, experimentation, and irony were qualities developed under the influence of the dialect movement among German, Swiss, and Austrian songwriters; these qualities were later imported into songs using Standard German. This was true for the productions of Udo Lindenberg and Nina Hagen, who started using Standard German in the 1970s. These artists influenced the subsequent punk-influenced *Neue Deutsche Welle* (German New Wave) in the late 1970s and into the 1980s, who continued to exploit the particular rhythmic and prosodic qualities of the German language to convey humorous, ironic, yet socially critical messages, all of which contributed to a broad rejuvenation of German popular song in the 1980s and subsequent decades.

We have been primarily concerned with West Germany, but the use of English in German pop also occurred in the former East Germany (GDR), where such a practice was, at times, a highly-charged political issue. The East German government attempted to create an alternative to the Western popular music in the hopes of counteracting the English and American influence found in the West German music that was favored by most East German youths. As part of this attempt, they banned English for *original* productions, though they did allow its use in cover versions. Songs using German lyrics were closely scrutinized by the *Lektorate* (editorial boards), the censorship offices of radio and television stations, and by the state's monopoly record company. This led to the practice of avoiding censorship through the use of figurative language that allowed nature imagery and personal relationship narratives to represent dissatisfaction with political, economic, and cultural affairs (later we'll provide a specific example). Also, East German bands from the independent scene increasingly used English as an oppositional identity-marker in order to subvert censorship aimed at achieving conformity to socialist ideology and as a way to repudiate and actively withdraw from the official institutionalized context and discourse of what the government popularized as "GDR Rock." In effect, these musicians announced that the GDR was an irrelevant context for making music.

The presence of this broad variety of language choice in German popular music has influenced the composition process in several other ways as well. As with song writing in general, sometimes writers and composers will first establish a melody before attempting the lyrics; likewise, a rhyme scheme may precede the lyrics, and certain vocalizations will be needed, regardless of lyric content, in order to complete the rhyme. These vocalizations (referred to as "*Schimmeltexte*" in Germany and "*Schmähtexte*" in Austria—are idiomatic terms with no precise English translation) are usually derived from English-sounding words and are generally nonsense sounds. The lyric writer finds the suitable German words to correspond with the English-sounding vocalizations in order to shape German rhymes to relate a particular narrative and/or to construct a refrain. This procedure is to some extent influenced by the historical tradition of German pop: often kitschy and clichéd, *Schlager's* stereotypical rhyme schemes even have a specific label—"*Herz-Schmerz*" (heart-pain) lyrics. The Austrian State Broadcasting Service (ORF) even went so far in the 1970s as to ban what were called "*Schnulzen*," sentimental songs that seemed to embody the worst of German song tradition (however, English lyrics with the similar shortcomings were not subjected to the same critique, and the ban could probably be construed as a means of promoting songs in English at the expense of German ones).

Another interesting development regarding English and American influence is found in the way in which many German and Austrian artists have used the cultural legitimacy of well-known pop songwriters from the United States or Great Britain to produce German language cover versions. One prominent U.S. singer/songwriter chosen for this type of reinterpretation is Bob Dylan. Wolfgang Ambros (Austria) recorded cover versions of Dylan songs in 1978 employing Austrian dialect lyrics; Wolfgang Niedecken, lead singer of the band BAP, also recorded covers of Dylan, using the Cologne dialect, in a 1995 recording. Both singers cover "It Ain't Me, Babe," but while the Ambros version's dialect lyrics are included on the inner sleeve of the album, those for the Niedecken version are *sung* in the Cologne dialect, but *printed* in the CD booklet in Standard German, with the exception of the title, which is printed as an approximate Cologne dialect translation of the English: "Dat benn ich nit." Both songs are close in content to the original: the male rejection of a female partner because of his inability to embody her utopian ideal partner and his unwillingness to "settle down" and become that ideal.

But these cover versions may also be done in a way that relates to the particular regional, socio-cultural, and historical context of a given audience, employing interpretations that diverge substantially from the lyrics employed with the original melody. This practice also helps to identify a band with a particular tradition. For example, the Austrian singer Willi Resetarits has built his reputation as the fictitious figure "Ostbahn-Kurti" (his band is Ostbahn-Kurti und die Chefpartie) by reworking songs by U.S. artists like Bruce Springsteen, Lynyrd Skynyrd, and even Frank Zappa into Viennese dialect. The familiarity of both audience and artist with the melody of the original often becomes a complementing common referent for the acceptance of the new interpretation, which, as in the Dylan examples, may either be a faithful translation of the original, or an approximate rendition of its meaning (within the confines allowed by individual copyright holders), or a more creative interpretation. One Resetaritis song reworks "I Heard It through the Grapevine" into a question—"*wo ham wir hier den Fahrschein?*" (where do we have the tram ticket?). This interpretation successfully and playfully transfers the feeling of bad luck in the original—learning about an unfaithful mate—into dismay at being caught in a tram without the required ticket (in Germany, one generally buys a tram ticket on good faith, though attendants will perform spot checks).

As with Dylan, Randy Newman's songs have likewise been a popular choice for German cover versions. Heli Deinboek (Vienna) recorded an entire album of his songs in 1995, including some of most commercially successful ones like "You Can Leave Your Hat On" ("Lass den Hut auf"), "Louisiana" ("Miese Männer"), and "Birmingham" ("Oberwart"). Deinboek's cover of "Birmingham" provides a strong example of the way in which a translated lyric can be creatively reworked in a way that relates to a particular regional situation. Newman's original version presents a satire of a dimwitted, white working man who glorifies life in the U.S. city of Birmingham, Alabama, while remaining blind to racism and other negative elements. Deinboek turns Birmingham into Oberwart, a small town in the Austrian countryside known for its racial prejudice and where four Gypsies were murdered by unknown assailants in the mid-1990s. Deinboek's protagonist is a small-town official who dislikes foreigners and sends in his dog "Tasso"—Newman's dog is "Dan"—to take care of law-breaking foreigners. In a similar manner, the East German band City transposed the decay and despair in Newman's song "Baltimore" into the East German industrial town of Rüdersdorf, a town outside of East Berlin in which the local, state-run cement factory completely ruined the environment. In both songs, the respective cities symbolize environmental and social decay for which there seems to be no solution other than escape: in the original the protagonist flees Baltimore for good; in the cover, the escape from Rüdersdorf means going to the West (the song was recorded before the unification) and never returning. In an earlier recording, Udo Lindenberg (West Germany) set "Baltimore" to German lyrics, but his version follows the original very closely, and thus in this case the audience interprets the song according to received ideas in Germany regarding the negative effects of capitalism and urban decay in the United States.

The influence of African-American hip hop culture, and rap music in particular, has in recent years added a new layer of complexity to the multiglossic strain within German popular music. In Germany, appropriated African-American rap and hip hop have provided a way in which African-Americans and African-Germans can become participants in German popular culture; rap also provides Germany's ethnic minorities (the Turks in particular, a subaltern group in Germany whose experience in some ways resembles that of African-Americans) a way to communicate with the rest of German society. Additionally, rap has allowed elements of African-American hip hop slang to enter German vocabulary, particularly among the youth, and now terms like "*dissen*" (to "diss," i.e., to show disrespect for), "bitch," "posse," "fucker," and "crew" are commonly used. The multi-ethnic rap group Fresh Familee, for instance, in a 1993 recording, calls on their audience, and German society in general, to "fuck the skins" (i.e., racist Skinheads); interestingly, the band decided to use this English phrase rather than a translation. Another Fresh Familee rap from a 1994 recording is entitled "Mothafucka," again borrowing from popular American slang, but with an interesting political twist, for here "mothafucka" refers to Germans who deface the environment, are racist, and pursue selfish goals at the expense of society as a whole.

Along with the use of sampled music from the African-American repertoire to provide rhythm and bass tracks, ethnic minority rap groups often use folk instruments (particularly Turkish) and Turkish and other languages in their rap narratives. Mixing German and other languages has the effect of signaling inclusion or exclusion of a particular group from its audience. The 1995 disc *Cartel*, which features a number of Turkish rappers, has only one track that uses German lyrics, and in the text accompanying the CD, those who didn't pay attention to Turkish lessons in school are told (in German) they can send in a postcard if they want to receive the lyrics in German translation. Not surprisingly, *Cartel* became a major hit in Turkey and helped establish Berlin as a center for Turkish hip hop culture in both Germany and Turkey. But other rappers take different approaches. Aziza-A, for instance, released a CD in 1997 that includes the German translations of her Turkish lyrics in the accompanying booklet, and she raps in German on several tracks and uses some German on others that are primarily in Turkish. Fresh Familee, to provide an example of yet another approach, address a primarily German-speaking audience, so that even a story about a Turkish worker, Ahmet Gündüz, though it includes Turkish-sounding instrumentation, is sung in broken ("foreigner" pidgin) German.

Middle-class Germans as well as members of ethnic minorities living in Germany have turned to rap and hip hop as a way of defining themselves vis-à-vis the majority society and as an innovative form of musical and linguistic expression. One of the most commercially successful of these groups is the Fantastische Vier (Fantastic Four), who, in their 1992 release, "Hip-Hop-Musik," directly address the question of language choice and image. They question the authenticity of those German rappers who in their view promote and idealize a ghetto image and lifestyle; they also attempt to delineate a space for a German, non-ghetto rap and hip hop. Rejecting what they call "Goldchain-motherfuckers" (in English) for being "*zu viel kitsch*" (too much kitsch), they urge German rappers to stop borrowing from the Americans and instead turn to "*deutscher Sprechgesang*" (German chanting speech), which, they concede, is a controversial means of expression. They proposed replacing English terms that call for audience response with German ones: "*heb die hand hoch*" instead of "put your hands in the air," and "*hey Leute, was geht ab?*" (Hey people, what's up?) instead of "say ho." Programmatically, they declared that "only in the mother tongue can the game of language-playing function in a fun way," and believe that "only then can the words be accentuated well," urging their fellow countrymen to maintain their linguistic self-confidence and self-awareness.

One means of mixing languages—either English and German or Turkish and German—is to intersperse single words (usually borrowing from hip hop) in the other language into a predominantly German text. Another manner of mixing the languages is practiced by Aziza-A in her song "Es ist Zeit" (It is time) urging her fellow German-Turkish countrywomen to assert their rights, and in so doing reject the patriarchal structures of Turkish society in Germany. While her rap narrative is in German, the refrain is adapted from the Turkish folksong "Daracik, Daracik sokaklar kizlar misket yuvarlar" (Narrow, narrow alleys, in which girls play marbles) and sung by a male chorus in Turkish. In

Cora E's 1998 recording, "Next Stop New York," the narrative is in German while the refrain is in English: "From East to West Heidelberg to New York / It's about where your Head is at / We're gonna lace this Track with some Rhymes that hit back / Next stop New York—rock on." This layering of lyric languages is an effective way of addressing several audiences at once, and serves to authenticate and legitimate the addressor to each different audience.

Sex in the Desert and Other Delights: Sex, Language Choice, and Narrative Stance

Sexuality has been a traditional topic of blues and rhythm and blues songs in the Afro-American traditions for many decades, forming the basis for double entendre and metaphor-laden lyrics; as a direct result of this influence, sexuality is one of the most prevalent topics in rock music, and indeed the very term rock and roll, as is well-known, has its origins in a rhythm and blues code term for sexual intercourse. Sex is a major topic in rock music not only because of its obvious inherent appeal, but as for its shock value— as a way to violate what is considered "good taste" and propriety and to signal a kind of rebelliousness that has characterized rock music in general. The sexual-political nexus of rock eventually evolved to encompass topics related to gender conflict, feminism's critique of patriarchal discourse, and gender identity and construction. These features of American and English lyrics have also found their way into German rock.

In terms of language choice, it is interesting that German popular lyrics show a preference for the English term "sex"; the formal German equivalents— *"Geschlecht"* (sex) and *"Geschlechtsverkehr"* "sexual intercourse"—are multi-syllabic mouthfuls almost never used in song lyrics (although Fantastische Vier makes ironic use of the abbreviation for *"Geschlechtsverkehr"—"g.v."*—in the song entitled "Saft" ["Juice"]). It would seem that the German term doesn't have the right semantic register for rock lyrics. The English term "sex" refers to intercourse, foreplay, caressing, and other related behaviors, and in this way is more comprehensive than either *"Geschlechtsverkehr"* or informal German terms like *"ficken"* (to fuck), *"vögeln"* (to screw), or *"bumsen"* (approx., to get laid). Using a foreign term instead of the more direct and narrow German ones allows a greater degree of emotional distanciation and ironic detachment. As a widely used loanword, "sex" may also denote a certain cultural perception, real or imagined, often connected with Anglo-American-derived consumer culture—assumedly more easy-going, relaxed, and fun.

Throughout its development, German rock has displayed a wide variety of representations regarding the physical and emotional dimensions of sex. Historically, these narratives are situated between a largely male-dominated sexual liberation movement in the late 1960s and the feminist reaction to that movement in the 1970s. In the course of this development, sexual roles have been blurred, and male and female homosexual behavior has become more accepted. To some extent, rock mythology is still dependent on (traditional heterosexual) sexist imagery and narratives regarding the exploits of the male rock-star hero with (largely female) fans, depictions which provide their audiences (both male and female) with mythical, utopian, and romantic illusions about fulfilling their own sexual fantasies. However, some rock or pop songs now challenge lyric conventions in innovative ways reflecting the changing attitudes about sexuality that may help audiences to negotiate new sexual identities and gender roles.

A good point of departure is Drafi Deutscher's "Marmor, Stein und Eisen bricht" (Marble, stone, and iron breaks), a song that is situated between the *Schlager* and rock genres and has remained, since it first topped the German charts in 1966, a favorite among audiences of all ages, most of whom now use it ironically, as it expresses a naive attitude with regard to sexual matters. The refrain of the song celebrates eternal faithfulness and the bonds of matrimony: "*Marmor, Stein, und Eisen bricht / aber unsere Liebe nicht / alles, alles geht vorbei / doch wir sind uns treu*" [marble, stone, and iron breaks / but not our love / everything, everything passes on / but we remain faithful to each other]. It is not surprising that subsequent audiences—with their experiences of marriage, divorce, and separation—should find lyrics like these comical or worthy of derisive trashing when sung in unison at parties, dances, and other gatherings.

Many German rock lyrics deal with sexual experience in terms of disillusionment, disappointment, and detachment. Udo Lindenberg's song "Bitte keine Love-Story" (Please, no love story) (1974), is a case in point. The song's male narrator tells a new-found female companion about his past disappointment in a previous relationship, and, after emphasizing how vulnerable and tentative he feels about pursuing a new relationship, he is surprised by her decision, revealed in the last verse, to pursue the relationship with him in spite of his questionable past.

Shortly after the release of "Marmor, Stein und Eisen bricht," the student movement and the sexual revolution led to radical social-sexual experiments like the notorious Commune I in Munich, as well as very explicit books explaining the techniques of (hetero-) sexual pleasure. While sexual pleasure first became a common theme in the lyrics of English rock bands, the Germans soon followed in the early 1970s.

Earlier we had noted the controversial use of English lyrics in East Germany; similarly, during this same period, sexuality became an important and controversial factor. One such example is provided by Puhdys, an East German band whose popular 1973 song "Geh zu Ihr" (Go to her) contains a thinly veiled sexual metaphor, i.e., "*Geh zu ihr und lass dein' Drachen steigen*" (go to her, and let your dragon climb). But the lyric also supports a more innocent interpretation—*Drachen* (dragon), but also, *Drachen* (to fly a kite). This kind of word-play is a good example of the way in which East German rock bands often eluded censorship. The song's notoriety was reinforced by its use in *Die Legende von Paul und Paula* (The Legend of Paul and Paula) (1974), a controversial East German film about a young male Party faithful who forsakes an unhappy marriage to pursue a relationship with a single mother with whom he feels a deep emotional connection. In this film, "Geh zu Ihr" is heard in the background during an almost surreal scene which takes place on a barge floating down the Spree River and in which Paul and Paula consummate their relationship before a gathering of friends and relatives. For a prudish Communist leadership, *Die Legende von Paul und Paula* and "Geh zu Ihr" represented not only sexual independence, but a declaration of liberation from orthodox cultural and political ideology as well.

The advent of the feminist movement in West Germany in the 1970s prompted women to critique male sexism and to assert their own sexuality. Some male vocalists like Herbert Grönemeyer reflected both the new male insecurity with conventional models of sexual behavior as well as a sensitivity to female sexuality, coupled with a desire to negotiate new gender models based on non-sexist thinking. Some of Grönemeyer's songs, as well as those by Udo Lindenberg and Wolfgang Niedecken, are characterized by male figures who show a heightened consciousness regarding female sexual pleasure. But a new female sexual assertiveness is best reflected in the work of Nina Hagen. Her 1976 album *Nina Hagen Band*, her first LP after leaving the GDR in 1976, contains several songs which break with the German

(*Schlager*) lyric tradition of avoiding explicitly sexual topics and language. In one of these, "Rangehen," (Go to it) the narrator tries to pick up a man at a party. In another, "Unbeschreiblich Weiblich" (Indescribably Female), sentimental notions about pregnancy are decisively rejected as the narrator describes the physical symptoms ("*mir ging's zum Kotzen*" [I feel wretched]) and rejects the traditional female role ("*ich hab' keine Lust meine Pflicht zu erfüllen*" [I don't want to fulfill my duty]). Ultimately, she declares that she wants to "*bevor die ersten Kinder schrein, muss ich mich selbst befreien*" (liberate myself before I hear the first children scream). Another song on the same LP ("Heiss" [Hot]) has her alone in the shower, masturbating while "talking" with a man of her fantasy, "Mr. Rub-Man" (*Herr Wichsmann*). When her "boyfriend" (another English loan word) enters, she greets him with "*Tach Herr Wichsmann / Wie man weiss, isses heiss / ich brauche Wasser, / denn ich schwitze in der Ritze*" [Hello Mr. Rub-Man / as you know, it is hot / I need water, / because I am sweating in my crack] (qtd. in Buhmann and Haeseler 150–51). The narrator has transferred her fantasy-object onto the boyfriend by referring to him with the same, as it were, term of endearment, and he then satisfies her, although it's not clear just how—possibly with a stream of water aimed at her vagina.

A 1981 release by the New Wave band Ideal called "Sex in the Desert" reflects a similar disillusionment and dissatisfaction with sex in the feminist era. The refrain (sung by the band's vocalist, Annette Humpe) points out the discrepancy between the desire for sex and the impossibility of satisfaction because of the heat in the desert: "*Der Horizont rückt näher und was keiner weiss / jeder denkt das eine / doch dafür ist's zu heiss / Sex—Sex in der Wüste*" (The horizon moves closer and what no one knows / everyone is thinking the same thing / but for that it is too hot / Sex—sex in the desert). Thus the attribute "hot" normally associated with sexual pleasure (as in the Hagen song) is rendered here as a negative attribute.

Yet another negative portrayal of sexuality comes from the band Rammstein; the first track from their CD *Herzeleid* (heartache, also, to suffer from heart disease) is "Wollt ihr das Bett in Flammen sehen?" (Do you want to see the bed in flames?), which portrays sex as "a battle," and equates the band's identity within a misogynist view of sex and love. In the song's refrain—"*Rammstein / Sex ist eine Schlacht / Liebe ist Krieg*" [Rammstein / Sex is a battle / Love is war]—"Rammstein" of course refers to the band, but could also refer to the "ramming" of phallic aggression. This belligerent stance is introduced by the questions of the protagonist addressing not the singular "you" as in many pop songs, but the plural "you" with insistent questions reminiscent of Nazi propaganda minister Josef Goebbels's question to the Germans in the late phases of the Second World War—"*Wollt ihr den totalen Krieg?*" (Do you want total war?). In the middle of the stanza it switches from this question to the narrator's insistent, rhetorical suggestion that he will "*den Dolch ins Laken stecken*" and "*das Blut vom Degen lecken*" (stick the knife into the sheets and lick the blood from the knife). By explicitly and metaphorically equating sex with war or death, the song questions the motivation of sex as a purely pleasurable and innocent practice, asking "*Ihr glaubt zu töten wäre schwer / doch wo kommen al die Toten her?*" (if you think killing is so difficult / where do all the dead come from?). Rammstein's darkly insistent music lends credibility to a reading of the song as a foreboding, misogynist diatribe. However, a reviewer for the *Berliner Zeitung* (in an article focused on Rammstein's lead singer Till Lindemann entitled "Till klopft sich auf die Brust" [Till pounds himself on his chest]), suggests a more cynical reading, observing that the band's video and CD *Live aus Berlin* was a "calculated" and "transparent" attempt at provocation with "seemingly controversial topics."

Both Rammstein CDs play ironically with romantic attitudes—the title *Sehnsucht* is a typical, even quintessential Romantic concept in German poetry and music, which combines the poetic sound of the word with a feeling of desire and sensuousness. Both titles would seem to represent the opposite of what the Romantic movement would be about. However, upon closer scrutiny, Rammstein shares some qualities of musical and aesthetic Romanticism. One of these is the "fantastically formed and generically ambiguous artwork" first theorized by the German philosopher Friedrich Schlegel (Daverio 4). Rammstein concerts aim, as do most rock concerts, at creating a musical experience "as a quasi-mystical event, where the listener gives in to the enigmatic, wondrous, and oracular accents of pure instrumental music" (Daverio 5). In addition, some aspects of the Romantic movement, which idealized artistic uniqueness and creativity, omnipotence of the poetic imagination, synthesizing disparate artistic entities, and others also included self-destructive and negative aspects as well, with writers like Heinrich von Kleist committing suicide and suffering, raised (by Nietzsche) to a necessary prerequesite to authentic artistic ephiphany and catharsis.

Language, Authenticity, and the Culture Industry

Two types of language use have informed this essay: the first concerns the way in which various artists in the German-speaking countries use various combinations of Standard German, German dialects, English, and Turkish in order to convey both specific lyric messages and a general cultural-linguistic stance within a given musical genre. Standard German lyrics are used by nationally renowned artists to convey meaningful messages across dialect areas, talk about intimate feelings as well as social and cultural issues in a language approaching everyday speech, and negotiate identities on the German regional market within the global marketplace. Dialects are used by German pop artists as a way to reinforce a regional identity among members of their immediate target audience and to represent that identity to audiences from the majority culture of which it, the regional culture, forms an integral part. On a larger level, these practices help situate the global styles of rock and pop music in regional and national space and time; specifically, the use of English lyrics in German pop signifies the intent to participate in the global music industry, reach audiences beyond national borders, and exhibit artistic expertise in the international language of rock-based pop music, though in a way that generally foregrounds the entertainment quality of the instrumental component rather than conveying a particularly meaningful lyric message. Finally, members of the Turkish minority employ their native language to establish their presence and identity in Germany. More generally, the practice of using regional dialect in lyrics reflects a political tension evidenced in all kind of ordinary speech practices—the tension between dominant and non-dominant languages in which the dominant often serves as the criterion for evaluating the minority language (Gal ctd. in Heller 249). Relatedly, the use of Standard German, dialects, and finally, the use of English, in popular songs in the German-speaking countries is governed by principles similar to those governing code-switching in the speech of bilingual communities based on "the ways in which the communities are differently situated within the regional political and economic system." In "code-switching," bilingual populations employ a specific language in specific situations, which may be used to "establish, cross, or destroy group boundaries; to create, evoke or change interpersonal relations with their accompanying rights and obligations" (Gal qtd. in Heller 247–48).

The second aspect of language choice centered on the ways in which German pop lyrics deal with the topic of sexuality, from the naively couched affirmation of heterosexual love and the institution of marriage in the popular *Schlager* "*Marmor, Stein und Eisen bricht*" to a period of Anglo-American influence, including the widespread use of the English loanword, "sex," to the insecurities of masculine gender roles in the face of feminist assertions of sexual identity and activity, to both East German artists' use of veiled metaphors and the new explict use of sexual language by artists like Nina Hagen and Rammstein to express anti-sentimental attitudes towards sexuality and relationships—indeed, a total reversal of the *Schlager* tradition.

Both of these aspects of language usage (language choice and the use of language to explore a controversial topic) are rooted in the performers' and audiences' need for credible and authentic expression. But authenticity is of course problematic, as we see in the example of German hip hop, which is constructed and contested by various audiences with various ideas as to what constitutes authenticity. For some, authenticity and credibility consist of projecting the hip hop lifestyle, mode of communication, and attitude onto the social reality of German society, while others, like Fantastische Vier, reject this as non-authentic imitation and appropriation of an alien subculture. While identifying "authentic authenticity" remains problematic, perhaps, in any case, the more important factor here is the way the authenticity problem allows the audience to actively participate in the construction of that authenticty—in pleasurable, playful collusion with the artists, regardless of the transparency of the undertaking or the influence or the audience's understandable cynicism regarding the possiblity of any product of the market-driven "culture industry" being truly authentic. The Austrian band Ostbahn-Kurti und die Chefpartie, for instance, was a completely fictional construction in which the pseudonymous band members were featured in narratives that were circulated about fictitous exploits in fictitious Viennese clubs. Interestingly, the audience actively participated in the construction of these narratives.

Here we see that irony undercuts the question of authenticity and contributes an element of play, allowing performers and audiences to willfully suspend the manifest character of the lyrics (although because verbal irony is founded on thorough linguistic competence, this kind of play usually takes place in the home language). Irony also allows performers and audiences to violate the boundaries of "good taste" while introducing an element of doubt about the seriousness of the violation or of the intended meaning, as in the case of Nina Hagen and Rammstein. One could argue, for instance, that Rammstein's "Wollt ihr das Bett in Flammen sehen?" does not promote an aggressive attitude towards sexuality but rather serves as a warning, pointing out the negative effect of looking at sex as a "battle" and warning the audience not to engage in the "total war" concept of the Nazi era. In any case, descriptions of the audience would indicate that Rammstein fans are not fanatical warmongers, but are instead "normal" people with a variety of different musical interests and cultural tastes.

We should also note the role played by genre in these interactions between audiences and performers. Song genres help create historically-grounded expectations about the cultural behavior associated with specific audiences and specific expectations about lyric content, as we saw in the case of German pop genres from *Schlager* to rock. Genres provide musical and cultural contexts, frames for the social and cultural positioning of the lyric message as well as the mood and the attitude transmitted by the lyrics. As Linda Hutcheon's discussion of genre suggests, song genres help cast the interpretative stance communicated to the listener by the artists and shape the position and attitude of the listener towards the music. But genre may also serve an ironic function, giving the interpreter a frame "in addition to and different from what is stated, together with an attitude toward both the said and the unsaid" (11). Popular music often partakes of this irony, acquiring a polysemic quality that "removes the security that words mean only what they say" (14) and giving it a particular power, as Hutcheon suggests in a more general discussion, to play a role in the negotiation and encoding of authority and power and in the general processes of social discourse (17).

While it is true that the bands may be manipulated by the culture industry into a certain manner of marketing, identity, visual and music presentation, it is also true that the audience, as suggested before, may see through this and collude in the effort at constructing the identity and ironic distance to the band's ostensible image and identity. Irony, ambiguity, ambivalence, and the use of non-standard dialects allow the bands to employ devices for negotiating and re-negotiating identities through the music with their audiences under continually changing circumstances. Thus we might be able to conceive of multiple and even conflicting identities in a late capitalist society.

The collusive nature of constructing credibility and authenticity by both audience and artist means, on the one hand, that the culture industry is the means for investing the artist with the legitimizing power of his audience, while on the other hand the artist expresses some of the ambivalent and multiple feelings of his diverse audience community. The audience projects its own utopian and/or dystopian desires on to the artist, and constructs itself as the empowering element of the equation enabling the popularity of the artist to be constructed. This is a part of the common knowledge of what Pierre Bourdieu calls the "cultural field," in which the participants are aware of the inherent and implicit set of rules and conditions constituting the field (97–250). The Frankfurt School critique of the cultural industries was aimed at enlightening the critical public about the inimical relationship of the industry to "culture," its manipulative manner with regard to cultural needs and processes, and indifference to the actual content of cultural commodities. To a certain extent, today's audiences have taken Horkheimer and Adorno's warnings to heart and are using this knowledge to their own advantage to construct multiple, and ever-changing identities whose material may be supplied by the global entertainment industry to subvert its intent.

In an era in which the global pop music industry has made selected popular musics available on a world-wide basis, the use of lyrics, the particular mixture of languages and images used in popular music on various regional and local markets is an important mechanism for negotiating the changing "global-local nexus" in which global space becomes one of "flows, an electronic space, a decentered space, a space in which frontiers and boundaries have become permeable" and in which "economies and cultures are thrown into intense and immediate contact with each other" (Morley and Robins 115). Within this context, the "local" becomes a "struggle for a sense of place," in which life histories are embedded "within the boundaries of place, and with the continuities of identity and community through local memory and heritage" (Morley and Robins 116). In this view, the language of the lyrics in German popular music becomes a part of the "relation between globalizing and particularizing dynamics in the strategy of the global corporation" and a "local" that is "a fluid and relational space, constituted only in and through relation to the global" (Morley and Robins 117).

Note

All translations by Ed Larkey.

Works Cited

Ammon, Ulrich. "National-variety purism in the national centers of the German language." *Language Choices: Conditions, Constraints, and Consequences.* Ed. Martin Pütz. Amsterdam and Philadelphia: John Benjamins, 1997. 161–78.

Bourdieu, Pierre. *Distinction: A Social Critique of the Judgement of Taste.* Cambridge: Harvard UP, 1984.

Buhmann, Heide, and Hanspeter Haeseler, eds. *Zeitzeichen. Liederbuch der Rock- und Songpoesie. Band 2.* Schlüchtern: Verlag Buhmann und Haeseler, 1993.

Clyne, Michael. *Language and Society in the German-speaking Countries.* New York: Cambridge UP, 1984.

Daverio, John. *Nineteenth-Century Music and the German Romantic Ideology.* New York: Schirmer Books, 1993.

Der Förster vom Silberwald (aka *Echo der Berge*). Dir. Alfons Stummer. Screenplay, Alfred Solm, Alfons Stummer. Austria/West Germany, 1954.

Gal, Susan. *Codeswitching. Anthropological and Sociolinguistic Perspectives.* Ed. Monica Heller. Berlin, New York, Amsterdam: Mouton de Gruyter, 1988.

Hagen, Nina. "Heiss." *Zeitzeichen. Liederbuch der Rock- und Songpoesie. Band 2.* Ed. Buhmann, Heide, and Hanspeter Haeseler. Schlüchtern: Verlag Buhmann und Haeseler, 1993. 150–51.

Horkheimer, Max, and Theodor W. Adorno. "Kulturindustrie. Aufklärung als Massenbetrug." *Dialektik der Aufklärung.* Frankfurt: M. Fischer Taschenbuch Verlag, 1969. 108–50.

Hutcheon, Linda. *Irony's Edge: The Theory and Politics of Irony.* London, NY: Routledge, 1994.

Die Legende von Paul und Paula. Dir. Heiner Carow. Screenplay by Heiner Carow and Ulrich Plenzdorf. East Germany, 1974.

Morley, David, and Kevin Robins. *Spaces of Identity: Global Media, Electronic Landscapes and Cultural Boundaries.* London, NY: Routledge, 1995.

"Till klopft sich auf die Brust" (Till pounds himself on his chest). 15 Sept. 1999. http://www.BerlinOnline.de/wissen/berliner_zeitung/archiv/1999/0915/feuilliton/0012/index.html.

von Schoenebeck, Mechtild. "The New German Folk-like Song and Its Hidden Political Messages." *Popular Music* Volume 17.3 (1998): 279–92.

Wicke, Peter. *Wieland Ziegenrücker, Rock, Pop, Jazz, Folk. Sachlexikon Populäre Musik.* Berlin: Berlin Lied der Zeit Musikverlag, 1985.

Woolard, Kathryn A. "Codeswitching and Comedy in Catalonia." *Codeswitching. Anthropological and Sociolinguistic Perspectives.* Ed. Monica Heller. Berlin, New York, Amsterdam: Mouton de Gruyter, 1988. 53–76.

Discography

Ambros, Wolfgang. *Wie im Schlaf. Lieder von Bob Dylan gesungen von W. Ambros.* Bellaphon 27001028, 1978.

Aziza-A. *Es ist Zeit.* BMG. OX001.43215 08082 4. 1997.

Cartel. Karakan, Erci E. Da Crime Posse. Various Artists. Spyce 526 914-2. 1995.

Cora E. *Cora E. Corage*. EMI/Electrola-Crucial. 7243 4 94483 2 2. 1998.

Heli Deinboek. *Schuldig. Heli Deinboek singt Randy Newman*. Gig Records. 660 218. 1995.

Fantastische Vier. *Vier Gewinnt* (CD). COL 12-472263-10. 1992.

Fresh Familee. "Fuck the Skins." *Falsche Politik*. Mercury (Universal Vertreib), 1993.

———. "Mothafucka." *Alles Frisch*. Mercury (Universal Vertreib), 1994.

Ideal. *Der Ernst des Lebens*. Track 3. WEA/EitelImperial K58471.

Niedecken, Wolfgang. "Dat benn ich nit." Track 13. Leopardenfell, EMI Electrola, 7243 8 32473 2 5, 1995.

Puhdys. "Geh zu Ihr." 1969-1999. BMG 74321636152, 1999.

Rammstein. *Herzeleid*. Motor Music 7314 529160-2. 1995.

Drafi Deutscher. "Marmor, Stein und Eisen bricht" ("Marble, Stone, and Iron Breaks"). 1966.

The Choices and Challenges of Local Distinction

Regional Attachments and Dialect in Chinese Music

—Sue Tuohy

A very long time ago, the Jade Emperor Pavilion was constructed on Lianhua Mountain. . . . Although the people wanted to commemorate the temple's completion, they argued about which activity was best suited for the celebration: some wanted to perform opera, some wanted to chant scripture. Since members of several ethnic groups were participating and their languages differed, some people thought opera and scripture were inadequate for expressing their common sentiments. In the midst of this argument, two goddesses floated down from the sky singing "*hua'er*, two leaves" (*hua'er liang ye'er*). . . . The beauty of their song amazed . . . [and] filled the hearts of the people who then could not help but sing the songs together.

This excerpt comes from one of many legends told about the song form called *hua'er*. The legends locate the origins of *hua'er* songs sometime in the distant past and someplace in Northwest China. This version tells us that, in this multilinguistic environment, the people wanted to sing in a language capable of communicating their shared feelings. They chose songs coming from heaven that were sung in Chinese. But this decision did not settle the language issue permanently. In contemporary China, people continue to make decisions about which languages to use when singing and talking about *hua'er* songs.

Hua'er is a type of folk song native to Northwest China that is performed by men and women from different ethnic groups. Although popular today, historically the songs were marginal to mainstream public life in the Northwest and were virtually unknown outside the region. Institutions that exerted political and religious power in the area at best ignored the songs and at worst banned them as vulgar and obscene. Beginning in the late 1940s, official support for *hua'er* songs increased, knowledge of the songs spread

153

beyond the region, and the contemporary definition of the genre began to solidify in the scholarship. The current configuration of the genre encompasses a mix of song styles sung by a mix of people in a mix of languages. The heterogeneity of the genre and of its performance contexts in the Northwest, coupled with its promotion in the national cultural arena, offers many choices to people attached to *hua'er* songs today.[1]

In this essay, I examine the language choices that people make when they sing, talk, and write about *hua'er* songs. I argue that many decisions about language are shaped by the fact that the genre is promoted as a distinctive local musical form and that this local distinction is defined by, and in relation to, the Chinese nation.[2] The process of local distinction thus has a dual nature. The local is defined internally, by identifying the shared characteristics that make it recognizable as a form, and externally, by distinguishing the unique characteristics that differentiate it from other forms. Local legends show little concern for explaining how *hua'er* songs differ from those performed in other parts of China. The delineation of characteristics that distinguish *hua'er* from other genres is carried out primarily in the Chinese scholarly and public discourse.

Publications illustrate the various ways in which the genre of *hua'er* is attached to its locale. In the Northwest, we find the area commonly referred to as the "sea of *hua'er*" (*hua'er de haiyang*), the place where *hua'er* songs are concentrated, and the songs are said to express the spirit of the region and of its people. Through the use of local dialects and references to local places and people, song lyrics further strengthen the local attachments. The duality of local distinction presents a double bind, however. *Hua'er*'s local attachments are the basis for the genre's local popularity and distinction; they are also among the very factors that make it difficult to popularize the songs beyond their locale, and issues of language choice are among the most challenging aspects in national promotion. The dialect used in sung *hua'er* combines the vocabulary and linguistic structures of local Northwest Chinese spoken dialects with a linguistic aesthetic that emphasizes ambiguity, metaphor, and innuendo. Not surprisingly, people outside the region find the lyrics difficult to understand and appreciate.

In spite of such challenges, efforts to expand the popularity of *hua'er* songs have been extensive. Through print and live performance, *hua'er* songs have been presented to a national audience. These efforts to introduce local forms to the nation and to encourage the nation to become attached to its local manifestations are part of a larger governmental agenda of strengthening national unity. Government rhetoric seeks to display China as a diverse yet harmonious country, and the genre of *hua'er*—a musical form created jointly by different ethnic groups in China—is used as a concrete symbol of the principle of unity within in diversity. *Hua'er* thus is made to serve as a symbol of the unity of the "Chinese nationality" (*Zhonghua minzu*), an ethnically diverse family of citizens within the People's Republic of China (PRC) that includes Han Chinese (the dominant ethnic group) and a large number of minority nationalities.

Because the government supervises those institutions capable of the mass dissemination of ideas and music, it stands in a privileged position to represent the local. Backed by powerful institutions, *hua'er* is promoted as a local genre within the nation and as a Chinese national folk music genre internationally. Through its rhetoric, funding, and institutional structures, the state determines the value of having local products and the means by which they can be publicized across the country. It not only defines the local but also mediates its relationship with the nation and the rest of the world.

Language choices in *hua'er* songs are made within broader linguistic, cultural, and regional frameworks. I place these frameworks within the context of the national discourse on local distinctions, the structure and rhetoric of the Chinese cultural bureaucracy, and the Northwest as a region of China and of *hua'er* songs. After an overview of the genre, I discuss both the language choices made within musical performances and those found in the promotion of *hua'er* songs. In all of this, I seek to reveal the practices, challenges, and debates involved in the efforts both to maintain and to make widely comprehensible the characteristics of *hua'er*'s local distinction.

The National Contexts of Local Distinctions

In the legend, the people celebrating on Lianhua Mountain needed a shared language to express their common feelings. In China, this same need is extended to the members of the Chinese nationality (the ethnically diverse family of PRC citizens), and the language chosen in the twentieth century has been Chinese. The idea of a Chinese language not only indicates a language spoken by the Chinese people, but it also unifies the variety of languages they speak under the concept of "Chinese dialects."³ That these spoken languages may be mutually incomprehensible is less salient than that they belong to the Chinese-language family, can be written in Chinese characters, and have been historically associated with ethnic Han Chinese. These Chinese languages are contrasted with languages spoken by minority nationalities (*shaoshu minzu*), and both are contrasted with foreign languages. The version of Chinese that dominates—the "common language" (*putonghua*), or Mandarin—was promoted by twentieth-century politicians and educators as a means of unifying the nation, and it has become the national language of the PRC. Along with spoken Mandarin, the government also has championed a standard written Chinese.⁴ Regardless of their ethnicity, a majority of the country's population can speak some version of the Chinese language, read Chinese characters, and at least understand Mandarin.

Five or six mutually incomprehensible dialects of Chinese, sometimes called languages, are distinguished at the broadest level; these dialect-languages correlate with large geographical regions. Subdialects within Mandarin and the other dialect-languages are spoken in more geographically limited areas. Linguists consider the Chinese language spoken in the Northwest to be a part of the Mandarin dialect-language, and Leo Moser refers to it as Northwestern Mandarin, one of five dialect divisions within Mandarin. Subdialects within Northwestern Mandarin are differentiated locally, but they do not constitute officially classified dialects. Aspects of the Northwest dialects will be discussed later in relation to *hua'er* songs, but here the point is that the local dialect is variable and that it differs from standard Mandarin Chinese and from minority nationality languages spoken in the region.

Members of nearly all fifty-six officially designated minority-nationality groups live in the Northwest, with some groups dominating in terms of population size and some considered unique to the region. The groups known for singing *hua'er* are Han Chinese; Hui (Chinese-speaking Muslims); Bao'an, Dongxiang, and Salar (predominantly Muslim groups); Tibetans; and Tu peoples. These simple designations belie the complexities of these groups and their languages. In small pockets in the Northwest, new languages have arisen from the interaction of other languages historically spoken in the region (Ekvall). In some cases, only a portion of the members of a minority group can speak their "own" languages; in other cases, such as that of the Tibetans, the members of an ethnic group speak local dialects of their ethnically identified language. Some Salars speak the Salar language, a Turkic language, but others speak Tibetan.

The linguistic complexity of China and of the Northwest can be summarized through two basic binary distinctions: national Chinese (Mandarin) versus local Chinese dialect and Chinese as a whole versus the minority languages. Mandarin dominates the national mass media, but in areas in which particular minorities are concentrated, television and radio stations also broadcast in the relevant minority languages.[5] These same binary distinctions operate within the context of *hua'er*; *hua'er* singers choose between Mandarin or Northwest dialects of Chinese and between Chinese and Northwest minority languages. In print, however, standard Chinese is used for published *hua'er* texts and articles about *hua'er*.

Distinctions are made as well between national and local musical forms. Among the primary criteria for identifying local musics are that they are popular within geographically limited regions and, in the case of folk songs, that they are sung in local dialects. Based on her research in southern Jiangsu province (an area in which the Wu dialect-language dominates), Antoinet Schimmelpenninck specifies local dialect as the "single most important aspect in which one can distinguish the lyrics of Wu songs from folk song repertoires in other parts of China" (203). Dialect singing also can be a mark of distinction in contrast to the national folk song (*min'ge*) style, a style used to sing folk songs from any region of China or to perform new songs designed to resemble traditional songs. This style is heard throughout China in popular music disseminated through the mass media (Brace; Tuohy, "Social"). Many singers of this genre are professionally trained; nearly all sing in Mandarin Chinese and use a vocal quality called *meisheng*, a term that loosely refers to the Western-trained voice.

While the details of a national language have been worked out through official programs and textbooks, no similar standards are in place for music. "National Music" (*minzu yinyue*) comes closest, although it is not publicized as a nationwide standard per se. It encompasses different styles developed primarily by professional musicians in Chinese conservatories in the twentieth century. Chinese National Music often combines sonic elements historically associated with China with features of Western music, including instruments, tonal harmony, formal structures, and vocal and instrumental ensembles.[6]

Aspects of Chinese National Music and the national folk-song style, along with their foreign influences, have been incorporated into local music forms. For example, some *hua'er* performances are accompanied by the "national music ensemble," which includes both Chinese and Western musical instruments. A portion of local *hua'er* singers have accepted influences from beyond China, including the electric guitar, tonal harmony, and rock music as a whole. When performing rock and roll style *hua'er*, however, Northwest musicians are responding less to global popular music than to Chinese popular music; in other words, foreign influences on local styles are mediated through national music forms.

The Cultural Bureaucracy

Since the establishment of the PRC in 1949, the government and the Chinese Communist Party (CCP) have taken primary responsibility for coordinated programs that promote and develop local music. The government has managed a cultural bureaucracy that is organized through a structure that moves vertically (from national offices at the top to those in villages at the bottom) and horizontally (between the same levels and across the national territory). It involves many of the same organizations that have promoted Mandarin—the Ministries of Education and Culture, those offices charged with the dissemination of information (formerly called departments of propaganda), and the National Tourism Administration.

The cultural bureaucracy determines many of the options open to singers and promoters, including the contexts in which they work. For example, the offices of the Cultural Ministry organize performance troupes that train amateur and professional singers, and the Gansu and Qinghai provincial cultural bureaus sponsor local folk-song competitions and send the winners to the national contests in Beijing. Furthermore, the cultural bureaucracy organizes scholars in folklore, music, and minority studies who conduct research on *hua'er* songs. Beginning in the late 1980s, the opening of a market economy was accompanied by the loosening of state controls and a decreased government interest in local folk music. Such structural changes have brought new possibilities for musicians. For instance, singers such as Ma Jun in Qinghai province have become local entrepreneurs and have formed their own nonstate performance troupes. However, *hua'er* singers who formerly were subsidized or rewarded through government programs have seen a decrease in opportunities.

The efforts of the post-1949 cultural bureaucracy have expanded public performance of *hua'er* songs in the Northwest and have raised the genre's national profile. Yet much of what is known today about *hua'er* has been processed through the cultural bureaucracy in the context of a government-sponsored production of national knowledge. In her article on the politics of world music, Jocelyne Guilbault encourages us to examine not only "how the status of the 'local' has been transformed within contemporary societies, but also why and for whom it has been vitally important to redefine it today" (33). Theoretically, anyone can define and represent the local, but in practice, those in control of the broader discourse have a greater chance to frame the terms and parameters of cultural debate, often through the use of rhetorical language.

The cultural bureaucracy has articulated several reasons for promoting *hua'er*, all of which derive from the ideological principles and national policies of the government and the CCP. As an expressive genre associated with the "people" (that is, the workers and the peasants), *hua'er* is, the government asserts, a style that should be elevated and extolled. As an example of the government's claim of unity among the different ethnic groups in the PRC, the official rhetoric points to the multiethnic origins of *hua'er*. This idea has been repeated so often in publications that, within local *hua'er* research circles, scholars such as Ke Yang have criticized as "superficial and vague" the common description of *hua'er* as "that [which is] created by all the nationalities together" (54).

The government discourse presents a historical narrative that describes why *hua'er* is in need of support. The product of people who historically had been forced by feudalism into a subordinate position, *hua'er* had been excluded from the Chinese artistic canon. Histories of *hua'er* cite a variety of political, religious, and social institutions that tried to ban *hua'er* singing and examples of Chinese intellectuals who looked down upon the songs. As a mimeographed introduction to the 1985 Lianhua Mountain festival states, rulers in the "feudal past . . . tried in vain to seal off the people's entertainment."[7] Again, in local *hua'er* research circles, scholars advocate going beyond this common trope, called the "struggle theory" (Ma Guihua, 229). Yet general introductions to *hua'er* repeatedly describe the songs as symbols of the endurance of the working people of the Northwest and their resistance to oppression prior to 1949. The historical narrative continues by declaring that, under the policies of the PRC, the status of *hua'er* and its producers has been elevated, and Chinese literary anthologies celebrate the inclusion of *hua'er* after centuries of neglect and silence. No longer underrepresented, *hua'er* has become a "flower in the garden of Chinese culture."

The Northwest as a Region of China and of *Hua'er* Songs

Hua'er songs are popular in a region that has been called by different names throughout history, and the term used today, "Northwest China," locates that region as an area within the PRC. Here, it usually refers to Qinghai and Gansu provinces and the Xinjiang-Uighur and Ningxia-Hui autonomous regions.[8] Its vast deserts and high mountains, sparse population, and large concentration of minority nationalities are among the factors that distinguish it, geographically and culturally, from China's dominant regions, the East and the South. Chinese central authorities have frequently viewed the Northwest as a frontier zone on the periphery of the Chinese cultural center and as an area in need of special treatment. While remote in terms of a Chinese center, the ancient Silk Road crossed through the region, bringing people and goods from as far away as Rome on their way to Chinese metropolitan areas.

The region's history and its current linguistic and ethnic diversity have been represented in a variety of ways in the Chinese mass media. The region is alternatively portrayed as a beautiful natural treasure or a barren area in need of settlement. A border zone rich in minorities and folk traditions, it is seen as either more backward or more authentic than the metropolitan east coast. The media frequently emphasize the bountiful natural resources that the area offers and depict it is a land of vast open spaces. And, paradoxically, it may be portrayed as either an isolated territory or a crossroads of inter-national culture. National literary anthologies and tourist guidebooks alike present *hua'er* songs as products of the multicultural context of the region. Indeed, the *hua'er* song region is a complex land of many distinctions.

Chinese control over the Northwest has waxed and waned over the last 2,000 years and often has been confined to particular locales within the region. Through military expansion, settlement, and trade, the Chinese

Empire was involved in the area since at least 100 BCE. In the twentieth century, the national government added to these practices, sending large numbers of officials, educators, and immigrants from other parts of China to the Northwest. The region also has been a target for immigration from other nations and empires, including various Islamic groups such as the Salar from Central Asia and Mongolians and Xianbei from the north. Southwest portions of the region have long been part of Tibet. At one time or another, some of these groups controlled vast expanses of territory, and most held at least small pockets of local authority (Lipman). In the Hezhou area of what is today called Gansu province, for instance, Muslim officials held power in several towns; indeed, the area was called "Little Mecca." Only thirty miles away from the Hezhou area, a large Tibetan monastery governed the populace in the area around the town now known as Xiahe. Not far away, Chinese imperial forces controlled the garrison city of Xining.

The mix of peoples often resulted in periods of intense warfare, but it also produced a wide assortment of languages and artistic traditions. Some traditions, such as *hua'er*, were shared between the groups that interacted within the region, and itinerant workers, primarily Muslim, often are credited with spreading *hua'er* songs. Local sacred sites attracted travelers from throughout the region, and such sites, along with the annual temple and trade fairs, served as mechanisms for the exchange of musical traditions. As suggested in the legend referred to earlier, Northwest inhabitants encountered tremendous diversity, possibility, and choice in these events, including the choice of a common language for intergroup communication (Ekvall).

Today, the most common languages for communication between groups are the local Chinese dialects that together form Northwestern Mandarin. Ning Wenhuan calls them dialect "branches" and explains that the formation of the Taozhou dialect branch was bound up with the mix of ethnic groups and languages brought about through five or more centuries of immigration:

Although a border region, it was integrally linked with the Chinese culture of the central plains. . . . In this area, with its historical multinational origins, . . . Chinese gradually became the language of common use of the different nationalities. (50)

According to Ning, Han Chinese already living in the area mixed with newer Han immigrants from southern China during the Ming dynasty (1368–1644). Together, these northwestern and southern Chinese dialects mixed with the linguistic structures and vocabulary of local Qiang and Tibetan peoples to create local Taozhou speech (50–51).[9] Other dialect branches in the *hua'er* song region also are explained in terms of historical mixing, although the influence of particular languages varies in relation to the mix of people in those areas. For instance, in areas where Salar people are concentrated, the Salar language, rather than that of Qiang people, is more apparent in local Chinese speech.

These dialect branches generally are mutually comprehensible to people growing up in the area. But because of the PRC policy of moving people from other parts of China into the Northwest to develop the region, many of the more recent inhabitants are not able to speak Northwest local dialect, and in public they tend to use Mandarin. Most people growing up in the area can understand Mandarin, but a significant number of them cannot speak it, at least without a strong local accent. While conducting fieldwork, I frequently encountered situations in which one person would speak in local dialect, another in Mandarin with a local accent, and a third in standard Mandarin. Difficulties in comprehension certainly were not insurmountable; as a foreigner unable to speak Northwest local dialect, I still was able to participate in such conversations. People accustomed to interacting in mixed groups accommodate each other by reducing the speed of their speech, increasing redundancy, and explaining their use of words. Although Northwest dialect speakers are encouraged by the public education system to aspire to greater competence in standard Mandarin, I did not get the sense that most felt a need to do so.

Hua'er as a Genre

Like Northwest China and Northwest languages, the genre of *hua'er* is a blend of different local styles that developed over time. Some Chinese scholars claim the songs date back to the Tang dynasty (CE 618–907) or earlier, but theories of the origins of *hua'er* vary substantially. Only after the 1940s did scholars began to construct *hua'er* as a single genre, one that has subsumed a variety of styles previously considered to be distinct (Tuohy, "Social"). Many songs included in the genre today were not called *hua'er* even in the 1930s and 1940s, and several local historians say certain scholars have confused *hua'er* songs with those of other styles. For instance, they contend that a large portion of songs called *hua'er* actually are *shaonian*, which they consider to be a different genre (Du Yaxiong). Others argue that, prior to the 1940 publication of Zhang Yaxiong's influential *Hua'er Collection* (*Hua'erji*, reprinted in 1986), only a small portion of these songs were called *hua'er* by the local populace.

Even the simplest definitions of *hua'er* are based on multiple factors, such as who sings the songs, how they sing them, and in what contexts. The two most often cited characteristics of *hua'er* songs are that they are folk songs performed in the Northwest and that they are sung by several different ethnic groups. Sung primarily in Chinese, they are an orally transmitted form of linguistic and musical artistry. Most are lyric songs that rely on the juxtaposition of images and metaphors rather than on a linear narrative. The songs' words cover nearly any topic conceivable, but many focus on love and sex, descriptions of local scenery, current events, or, reflexively, the songs themselves. Many songs are topical, because singers compose lyrics to respond to contemporary concerns, the context of performance, or other singers.

Hua'er songs are a type of "mountain song" (*shan'ge*), a higher-level category used in Chinese folk-song scholarship to refer to pieces sung outdoors and usually outside the village or city. In practice, however, people sing *hua'er* while working in the fields and herding sheep as well as in concert halls, schools, city parks, and *hua'er* song festivals. Approximately seventy *hua'er* festivals occur annually throughout the Gansu-Qinghai region, with attendance ranging from 5,000 to 50,000 people. Performances are classified loosely into two types: organized (*zuzhi*) events, which include staged concerts, song competitions, and the portions of festival events put on by the cultural bureaucracy; and spontaneous (*zifa*) events, which include any situation where people gather to sing and listen to *hua'er* songs without the formality and official involvement of organized events.

The songs may be sung by soloists or by groups, a cappella or with instrumental accompaniment. The vocal qualities of singers vary, but most people distinguish between the local vocal quality and one similar to that of the Western-influenced *meisheng* technique used in the national folk-song style. When performing in the local singing style, men and women tend to sing in the same range, with no vibrato, and using a nasal timbre; the term "piercing tone" is often employed to describe the male falsetto in this style. When amplified, singers perform in a loud voice that many see as a characteristic of *hua'er* singing. Terms used to describe this local vocal quality are "resounding and resonant," "forceful and straightforward," and "intense and far reaching." There also is a correlation between vocal quality and language: those performers who employ a local style also use a local dialect, while those who employ the *meisheng* style sing in Mandarin.

Singers perform *hua'er* songs using basic tunes called *ling*. In each performance, they improvise on a *ling* tune, making variations to fit the lyrics and their individual styles. There are over a hundred recognized and named *ling* tunes, although based on my experience and the scholarly literature, I estimate that only about thirty are in common use. Many *ling* tunes are named after short, formulaic textual phrases associated with them, although the tunes are recognizable by the melody alone.[10] In staged performances and in published transcriptions of songs, the name of the *ling* tune is given rather than the song title. Most *hua'er* songs consist of a series of at least partially improvised verses brought together spontaneously in the moment of performance, often through a dialogic process. As a result, most *hua'er* are not thought of as "songs" per se, and apart from *xinbian hua'er* ("newly composed *hua'er*," pieces composed by named individuals and thought of as songs), *hua'er* songs do not have titles. Dialogue singing (*duige*) is one of the most common performance styles, with men and women, either as soloists or in groups, alternating verses. In this form of performance, a performer must sing lyrics that respond to those of the singer who precedes him or her, and this conversational exchange is competitive.

The timbre of a singer's voice and other musical factors are important in the evaluation of singing, but they generally are considered to be secondary to the lyrics; first and foremost, these elements must contribute to the effective delivery of the words. Artistic language play, metaphor, and ambiguity are key criteria in evaluating lyrics, and this linguistic artistry begins with the word "*hua'er*" itself. The "first" meaning of the term is "flower," but it has other meanings as well, such as "bloom," "pattern," or "design." In *hua'er* songs, the term is most often used metaphorically to refer to women, and women also may be symbolized by specific flowers, such as the peony or the crimson flower.[11] When knowledgeable listeners hear lyrics such as "There is a peony; looking at it is easy; picking it is difficult. Not picking it is even more painful," they understand that the reference is to a woman rather than to a flower.

Metaphor also organizes the line structure in many *hua'er* songs. In a common form, the first one or two lines of the verse present an image or idea, while the remaining two lines state the primary topic—a topic that often seems to be at quite a remove from the earlier images. Here, metaphor is the link that connects the two halves of the verse.[12] The relations between the parts of the verse are complex and subtle, and one of the key criteria by which singers are judged is by their ability to evoke suggestive and equivocal metaphoric connections rather than clear, explicit meanings.

Equivocation extends to the identities of the presumed speaker and the subject to which he or she speaks. When sung by a woman, the word "*gamei*" (little sister) can be used by the singer to refer to herself.[13] When sung by a man, it can refer to a potential, imagined, or current lover, and the same is true for the term "Elder Brother." As in the Nepali pop songs discussed by Henderson and Green's essay in this volume, both the subject and object of desire in these songs are ambiguous. Here, innuendo is valued over transparent language, and this aesthetic is made clear in informal performances of *hua'er*. Singing partners and audiences alike do not respond to, and may often criticize, singers who are unable to play with the ambiguity of words and images. On several occasions, I witnessed singers who abandoned their dialogue singing because of the straightforward, and thus inferior, lyrics of their partners.

In their attempts to bring some type of order to the diversity within the *hua'er* song genre, researchers have devised a number of classification systems. One of the most commonly accepted systems divides *hua'er* songs into Hezhou *hua'er* and Taomin (or Taozhou) *hua'er*.[14] The Hezhou *hua'er* style is more varied in terms of its *ling* tunes, is more broadly popular, and is sung by all of the ethnic groups; conversely, Taomin *hua'er* has a more limited range of popularity and is sung primarily by Han Chinese and Hui (Chinese-speaking Muslims) in southern Gansu province. Taomin *hua'er* songs typically are improvised, sung as dialogues between two groups, and set to one of two *ling* tunes, each associated with an area within the Taomin region.

Both the Hezhou and Taomin *hua'er* styles are called by other names, often depending on the local affiliation of the person doing the naming. Some call Hezhou *hua'er* "Qinghai *hua'er*," naming it after the province, but Xi Huimin says that this is "an opinion primarily held by researchers from Qinghai"; others call it "Linxia *hua'er*," after a place-name in Gansu, "a view held primarily by Gansu researchers, especially those in Linxia" (11). *Hua'er* researcher Gao Jingye told me that "because regional feelings in this area are strong and *hua'er* has received national and international attention, every area calls *hua'er* its own" (pers. comm.). One person I interviewed from Gansu province told me that only peasants sing *hua'er* songs. Not a peasant himself, he thought that *hua'er* lyrics were aesthetically inferior, and he did not like the melodies or singers' voices either. When I mentioned the names of Qinghai *hua'er* singers I enjoyed, he quickly came to the defense of his province, saying proudly that "while many good singers do come from Qinghai province, it is actually our province [Gansu] that is rich in *hua'er* songs."

Outside of scholarly circles, listeners seem less concerned with classification systems. Some listeners are only familiar with songs from their local area and consider only these to be *hua'er*; others listen to a wider range of songs and accept them all as part of the genre. Listeners thus have different senses of what constitutes a *hua'er* song and different responses to *hua'er* singers. At a 1995 *hua'er* festival in Qinghai province, I witnessed staged performances of singers invited from the Ningxia-Hui Autonomous Region. With audience members and cultural workers (people working within the cultural bureaucracy), I discussed the lack of audience response to some of these singers. Some people told me that Qinghai audiences were not familiar with the Ningxia style and therefore didn't like it or didn't consider it to be *hua'er*. Vocalist Ma Jun told me that Ningxia singers "mix some of the styles sung in Qinghai with Taomin *hua'er* and *xintianyou* [a different folk-song genre associated with Inner Mongolia] and sing with a Hehuang *hua'er* flavor." Regardless of whether particular audience members thought the Ningxia songs were *hua'er*, it was obvious that audience response was more favorable toward the male singer I observed who sang in a local dialect (even though the dialect was from a different region) than toward the female singer who sang in Mandarin with a *meisheng* vocal quality.

Though most local singers in Qinghai and Gansu provinces grew up listening to *hua'er* and began singing at a young age, few were formally trained. Cultural workers selected some of these singers to enter state-sponsored song troupes. Other song troupe members, however, received a music-school education and did not grow up singing *hua'er*. A formally trained female singer from the Ningxia Regional Cultural Literature and Art Troupe told me that because Ningxia is a "nationality minority region," she now primarily sings "national/nationality music" in the troupe—usually folk songs. Because the song troupes tour widely, many local listeners are familiar with their music. Yet outside the formal organizations, few local singers have taken up the *meisheng* vocal style used by the troupes or have incorporated Mandarin into their music.

The Languages of *Hua'er*

The different linguistic styles are complex, but the everyday discourse on *hua'er* boils them down to a basic three-part language choice: *hua'er* may be sung in some version of Northwest Chinese dialect, in Mandarin, or in local minority languages; they are not sung in Chinese dialects or in minority languages from other Chinese regions. A small portion of *hua'er* songs incorporate a few English-language words, but foreign-language *hua'er* are virtually nonexistent.[15] Of the three choices, local-dialect singing dominates in the Northwest, especially in spontaneous events. Mandarin singing, which developed only in the last four or five decades, tends to be associated with organized events in the Northwest and with promotional activities on the national level. Little consensus exists about the prevalence of minority-language *hua'er*.[16] Minority-language *hua'er* songs may be performed in small pockets in the region, but they are rarely heard at large festivals or included in published Chinese-language *hua'er* collections. One subtype of Hezhou *hua'er*, *Fengjuexue*, is a mixture of Chinese and Tibetan and is sung in areas where the two groups live in close proximity; Bao'an people sing *hua'er* in local Chinese dialect Chinese but use Bao'an and Salar languages in formulaic phrases.

The vast majority of *hua'er* performers sing in local versions of Northwest Chinese dialect, many of which incorporate minority-language terms and grammatical structures. *Hua'er* vocalists tend to sing in the local dialect that they use in everyday life, just as they tend to employ the song style(s) popular in their locales. While selection among different local dialects for *hua'er* singing causes little debate, singers and local scholars are often in disagreement about whether the genre should be sung in Mandarin and in what context such a language choice might be appropriate. Both scholars and singers agree, however, that the local dialects are important to the character of *hua'er*. Ning Wenhuan writes that "the unique linguistic style is the life force of *hua'er* artistry. . . . [It] is a linguistic art, and first and foremost a dialect art" (52). Writing specifically about Taozhou [Taomin] *hua'er*, Ning claims that the *hua'er* songs and "local dialect and local language have an intrinsic and inseparable relation. The tonal construction and rhythm of traditional *hua'er* music have been conditioned and influenced by Taozhou dialect" (54). Some scholars think these local characteristics must be preserved even when marketing the songs nationally. Others argue that Mandarin-language *hua'er* songs have a place even within the Northwest as a means of increasing the audience base for the songs.

The language of *hua'er* songs constitutes yet another type of dialect—a sung dialect that differs from both everyday speech and written poetry. As Liu Kai remarks, "*hua'er* is a type of folksongs improvised and created orally by the masses. They differ substantially from the written poetry of literati; they are created from the mouth rather than from the pen" (66). Apart from being set to music, *hua'er* songs go beyond regular speech with their characteristic vocal qualities and linguistic artistry, such as rhyme schemes and metaphoric language. Although it varies from place to place and from singer to singer, *hua'er* sung dialect is easily distinguishable from spoken languages. No one in the area speaks the way they sing, no matter what song style they use.

Formulaic language is an important feature that sets *hua'er* sung dialect apart from spoken language. Such language involves stock phrases and "padding words" (syllables without specific semantic meaning). Tacked on to the end of individual words or inserted into the middle or the end of phrases, padding words may make up over half of the song, as measured in terms of total syllables or performance time. Padding words fill in linguistic, rhythmic, or melodic patterns (Wei Quanming, "Groundbreaking," 84), and many are associated with specific *ling* tunes. Performers say that singing the padding words gives them time to compose the text of the next line they will sing, while *hua'er* listeners add that these words contribute to the "flavor" of *hua'er* and are central to its aesthetics. Unique to *hua'er* sung dialect, padding words are not used in everyday speech.

The difficulties involved with transcribing the lyrics of *hua'er* songs illustrate the difference between sung and spoken dialects. At the 1985 festival in Gansu, for instance, I participated in a session in which local *hua'er* researchers worked with a singer to transcribe song lyrics. They asked him to recite rather than sing the lyrics so that they could clear up confusion created by the sung dialect. Transcribing the spoken words, however, did not prove an easy task for the singer or the researchers. The singer spoke rapidly, and with the melody missing he often forgot the lyrics and had to hum through portions of the tune to refresh his memory. Accustomed to singing the lyrics, he recited them using musical intonations rather than the tones used in speech. Separating the lyrics from their melody was as difficult for this singer as understanding the sung lyrics had been for the scholars.

Both musicians and scholars praise *hua'er* as an artistic form of communication and extol the symbolic richness of its language. According to Li Lin, a local *hua'er* researcher, "*hua'er* is a language with a special flavor; it is used by all the nationalities [in the area] as a vehicle to exchange their thoughts and to express their feelings" (118). The songs also communicate love between men and women and friendship among people meeting at *hua'er* festivals. To underscore the emotional attachment to *hua'er* in the area, publications repeatedly quote the following lines from a song:

Hua'er songs are words of the heart, / Not to sing them, would be beyond my control. / Take a knife and cut off my head, / If I don't die, I'll keep singing like this.

Hua'er discourse emphasizes the improvisatory nature of composition and the creativity of singers who "make up words on the spot" to communicate their "innermost feelings" to listeners (Lin Cao, 84). Yet these discursive ideals are not always met in practice. Many song lyrics are composed prior to performance, and at least a portion of them are not understood by listeners.

Understanding *Hua'er* in Northwest Performance Contexts

The comprehensibility of a given song performance does not rest solely on the clarity of the lyrics but varies in relation to the composition of the audience and the sonic features of the performance environment. Although performance contexts vary widely, the distinction between spontaneous and organized events is most salient to understanding the implications of situated context for language choice and comprehension. Spontaneous and organized events differ in terms of scale, expectations, and types of audiences. The people most familiar with the genre are *hua'er* singers and committed *hua'er* listeners, the latter a group generally consisting of people who not only grew up in the *hua'er* region but who also regularly listen to these songs. They are the primary audience for the spontaneous events. Organized *hua'er* events, which are much larger, draw a broader range of people but also include the committed *hua'er* devotees. Though many attend the festivals in the Northwest, a large portion of the region's population does not listen to *hua'er* frequently. Audience members also may include immigrants and "outsiders" (*waidiren* as opposed to locals/natives, *bendiren*) visiting from other parts of China.

Spontaneous Performance Contexts

Spontaneous events are held in the countryside, in parks, and off the stage at *hua'er* festivals. These events are not advertised, but because they occur regularly, experienced listeners know when and where *hua'er* singers will gather. These are small group events, without MCs or preplanned programs, and most audience members are *hua'er* devotees—knowledgeable listeners who are most likely to understand lyrics sung in local dialects. In nearly every spontaneous performance I observed, singers sang in local Chinese dialect. Because singers perform without electronic amplification and must compete with ambient noise, the ability to sing in a loud voice is important. Listeners gather closely around singers, usually in a loose circle, to better hear them. In the city of Xining, for example, *hua'er* singers and listeners gather daily in a section of a small park adjacent to the area where retirees dance to amplified popular music tapes. Other challenges were presented by the spontaneous singing events that emerged in the evenings at the Lianhua Mountain festival. Here, groups of *hua'er* singers would engage in musical dialogue while walking down the mountain lanes. Two or more different groups would often sing in close proximity to one another, and they would further compete for the aural space with the large trucks that rumbled down the lanes. Spontaneous events are seldom quiet affairs, and at times even hearing the lyrics is difficult.

Singers nearly always perform in dialogue, and to participate effectively, they must be able to understand each other's lyrics. Zhu Zhonglu, a famous singer since the early 1950s, quotes a song text in which a singer complains that he or she cannot understand the words sung by his or her partner:

The black crow lifts up half a rib, gua, gua, gua [an onomatopoeic]; / The ancient tree is propped up by its branches. / Singing Elder brother, what are you singing about? [I/we] can't hear the words. / Please give your singing to me/us.

This example also illustrates the metaphoric structure of *hua'er* verses discussed earlier. The first two lines evoke images of the crow, which raises only one of its two ribs and caws meaningless syllables, and a tree that lacks solid support. These images of incompleteness provide the metaphor that introduces the main topic of the verse: because the singer's words are unclear, his or her singing partner is unable to respond.

Experienced singers usually have little trouble understanding each other, and problems arise instead with inexperienced singers. During the Lianhua Mountain festival in 1985, I asked one man to sing a *hua'er*, but he said that he had no one with whom he could dialogue. He suggested I sing a song, and his friend could then sing in response. When I told him I could not sing *hua'er* songs, he said, "That's all right; sing one from your nationality." I sang an Irish drinking song in English. After some hesitation, the man sang in local Chinese dialect a verse meaning, "I don't understand your speech; I want to sing a *hua'er*, but there is no way to answer you."

In spontaneous dialogue performance, a singer alternates verses with another singer. When he or she stops, the second singer steps in to take the previous singer's place. Anyone may sing, but those who cannot competently maintain a musical dialogue are moved out of the circle. Audience members are not reticent about making their opinions known. When they appreciate a singer, they laugh, make noises, and offer small gifts, such as bottles of orange soda or of alcohol. When they don't appreciate a singer, they are silent. If an incompetent singer does not stop soon enough, audience members become more vocal and may tell the individual to let another singer take over.

Singers cater to informed audience members and do not try to accommodate or win over outsiders who may not understand *hua'er* sung dialect. Part of the aesthetics of *hua'er* song lyrics in these contexts is that they should not be too easy to understand. The ability to interpret ambiguous lyrics and their references is a mark of a local *hua'er* connoisseur. However, ambient noise, variations in local dialect, and the intentional ambiguity of the lyrics may cause even experienced listeners to have trouble understanding the words. My field recordings of dialogue singing in the Xining park are filled with the sounds of people singing *hua'er* and of listeners discussing the lyrics just performed. During the portion of the song in which padding words are sung, a listener may turn to the person next to him or her and ask for clarification; others seem eager to explain the words, in part as a way of demonstrating their competence as listeners. No one appears annoyed by these discussions, which are done in spoken local dialects and take place in the midst of performance.

Organized Performance Contexts

The cultural bureaucracy has organized public events new to the area since the early 1950s, including concerts in theaters, sports arenas, and schools; staged performances at *hua'er* festivals; and music competitions. All of these are formal events replete with advertisements, official MCs, and, often, printed programs. Attendance ranges from a hundred people up to tens of thousands, and the audiences are diverse. Local cultural bureaus take responsibility for organizing these events as a part of their mission to "raise the level of culture" in the area and foster entertainment and educational activities. The events are centrally coordinated, and they follow policies put forth by the national Ministry of Culture.

The Riyue Mountain *hua'er* festival has been held since the 1980s, and the 1995 festival was conducted on a grand scale. Lasting over a week, festival events took place at multiple venues throughout Huangyuan county in Qinghai and included performances of *hua'er* and other musical forms, *hua'er* song competitions, shopping, games of skill, and smaller temple fairs. The festival began with a formal opening ceremony in a sports arena, during which the direction of the cultural bureaucracy was in clear view. A mimeographed program printed in Chinese articulated the festival's purpose:

Following . . . Comrade Deng Xiaoping's theory of constructing socialism with Chinese characteristics and the guiding principles of the CCP's fundamental line, the purpose of this *hua'er* festival is to help achieve the healthy development of enterprises aimed at promoting Huangyuan county and Qinghai province. It is meant to introduce enterprises, invigorate the market, and boost the economy and culture through activities such as cultural entertainment, cooperation between organizations, . . . [and] the exchange of commodities.

The program summarized the gist of speeches to be read at the ceremony (in either Mandarin or local dialect), printed the song lyrics (all in Chinese), and listed the names of all the sponsoring organizations, with the provincial Cultural Bureau on top. It also introduced the main themes of the 1995 *hua'er* festival: unity, friendship, prosperity, and development.

These themes were repeated in speeches made at organized events held in parks, concert halls, and in temporary performance arenas in the rural countryside. Outdoor staged concerts with audiences of thousands of people used electronic amplification, but the quality of the sound systems was quite poor, and the lyrics were often distorted. Singers for these events were selected by auditions, invitations, and/or a simple registration process. Most sang solo songs, but several concerts included a performance form called the "challenge arena" (*leitai*); this form resembles the dialogue singing of spontaneous events but with precomposed, rather than improvised, lyrics. At formal staged concerts, either the MC or the singers first read the lyrics (without padding words) before they were sung.[17] Lyrics were spoken in local dialect, except in those cases where the singers planned to sing in Mandarin. When MCs made announcements, however, they used Mandarin.

Many of the staged concerts were also part of formal competitions and were accompanied by a small national music ensemble. Singers rehearsed with the musicians prior to the performances, and the MC was present at the rehearsals I attended. Singers either gave the MC the printed lyrics to their songs or said them to her orally in local dialect while she wrote them down on slips of paper. This MC grew up in the area, was familiar with *hua'er* songs, and seemed to encounter only a few problems when writing down the words, problems that were solved through repetition and conversations with the singer and other people standing in the vicinity. During the concerts, the MC announced the singers and then read from the lyrics in the local dialect. The competitions employed official judges. A number of these were immigrants from other parts of China, and they told me that, in spite of living in the region for several decades, they still had some difficulty understanding *hua'er* sung dialect. Many times during performances, judges asked the MC to repeat or clarify the song lyrics. When they still did not understand all the lyrics clearly, they asked to see the printed words.

In organizing these events, cultural bureau officials balance different goals. For these events to be successful, the local populace, including *hua'er* devotees, must be satisfied. However, the officials also want to increase the number of *hua'er* listeners and to promote their own work. Thus concerts include *hua'er* songs in Mandarin and the local dialects as well as singers from professional troupes and amateurs from all the different locales.

Promoting *Hua'er*

Although some promotional efforts are directed internationally, the bulk of the work is targeted at two basic constituencies, the local and the national. This work overlaps considerably in terms of the people involved and the music and promotional materials produced. Singers who participate in national folk-song festivals also perform in local *hua'er* festivals; books distributed nationally also are sold in the Northwest. Yet the national dissemination of *hua'er* poses special problems because people in the primary target audience know little about the Northwest and often have never heard of *hua'er*. Since language artistry is considered among *hua'er*'s unique contributions and special challenges, decisions about the treatment of languages in printing *hua'er* lyrics are among the most frequently discussed. *Hua'er* is an oral form, and the difficulty faced by its transcribers is to represent the words in such a way that they can be understood by people unaccustomed to the songs and the local area to which they often allude. Even in live performance, language remains a difficult issue, since virtually no one outside the region can understand the songs when performed in *hua'er* sung dialect.

Printing *Hua'er*

Since the early 1950s, the majority of national anthologies of Chinese folk songs and minority literature have included *hua'er* songs. Published anthologies usually follow a standardized model devised by national committees, and many are released as part of nationally coordinated series organized by genre and province. Song lyrics are printed in Chinese characters, sometimes with cipher notation of the basic melody. Anthologies intended for the public omit padding words and treat the songs as written poems. Original lyrics often are revised to conform to standard written and literary Chinese.

In more academic publications, words and place-names peculiar to *hua'er* sung dialect are annotated. Annotations explain dialect terms in standard Chinese and often indicate their provenance with phrases such as "in the Salar language" and "in the Qinghai local dialect." Such annotations may be quite extensive. It is not unusual for four lines of text with a total of thirty-five characters to be followed by fifty or more characters of explanation. When padding words are printed, they are marked as different from the main text by changing the font size or by putting them in parentheses. Some minority-language and local-dialect words are pronounced using sounds unavailable in Mandarin, such as the padding word "*besh*," whose suffix "sh" is not found in Mandarin. These terms may be omitted, printed in Chinese characters without reference to the special pronunciation, or, less often, printed using other orthographic forms such as the Latin alphabet.

Local *hua'er* scholars and cultural workers do not accept uncritically the practices used in the past to print *hua'er* songs. Commenting on these practices, Li Fu states that some researchers "delete words conveying mood and auxiliary words of oral performance when they collect and edit *hua'er* songs." Those who do so, Li argues, "think those function words are not important or are even vulgar. They do not realize that dialect and local language words are actually the characteristic linguistic aspects of *hua'er*; eliminating them reduces the splendor [of the songs]" (159). Criticisms of experiments in national promotion have not been mild, particularly criticisms of publications that have the broadest readership and exposure. Commenting on a Bao'an nationality *hua'er* published in the national *People's Daily* newspaper, Lu Shimo charges that "this *hua'er* runs counter to stylistic rules; the rhyme is mixed up; it is not singable and is difficult to read aloud; moreover, it is not a *hua'er*" (86).

Lamenting the lack of original, unrevised materials, many scholars advocate the meticulous transcription of *hua'er* songs as originally performed. But this type of publication primarily exists in mimeograph form and is accessible only to researchers and local singers in the Northwest. Others suggest more careful revision of texts for public consumption. Ning Wenhuan agrees that people in the Taozhou (Taomin) *hua'er* region use dialect to sing Taozhou *hua'er*, but

to broaden the reach of *hua'er*, [the song texts] must be refined properly and with discrimination; they must be easy to understand when read and easy to speak. In relation to the popularization of Mandarin, good dialect words should continue to live. However, those words that are hard to understand . . . can fall into disuse through the selection process. Without such changes, it is impossible to disseminate and popularize Taozhou *hua'er*. (57)

Local scholars and cultural workers attempt to balance the retention of local characteristics of *hua'er* language with the need for song texts that a wider audience can understand and appreciate. Because they work primarily within government-sponsored institutions, they must deal with a variety of restrictions, one of which is to eliminate any expression that does not contribute to the cultural elevation of Chinese society, such as lyrics containing sexual innuendo or "superstitious elements."

Recording *Hua'er*

State-run and commercial recording companies have released many recordings of *hua'er* songs, particularly since the late 1980s. A few are produced by large commercial companies on the east coast, but the vast majority are produced by companies based in the Northwest. They have limited geographic distribution, and most are sold to regular *hua'er* audiences in the Northwest, although some recordings may reach a broader audience. The recordings and their liner notes illustrate some of the linguistic choices made in light of the uncertainty that the producers might have about their audience. The recordings I examined were all made in the 1990s.

While the name of the recording company and a few of the performers may be translated into English, the rest of the text printed on the covers and inserts of these cassette tapes is in Chinese. Nearly all cassette covers print the word "*hua'er*." Those with a national target audience also give explanatory glosses, such as "folk songs from the Northwest," and descriptive phrases pointing to the characteristics of *hua'er*'s local distinction, such as this passage from the cassette *Rapeseed Hua'er* (*Caizi hua'er huang*), "atmosphere of the high plateau, sweet and beautiful expressions, and the charm of the wild mountains."

Those recordings geared toward *hua'er* devotees in the Northwest are often labeled with terms that would be unfamiliar to outsiders, such as "*chumenren*" (travelers), a term related to a Hezhou *hua'er* substyle (see Ke Yang). Cassette covers and inserts provide little information to potential buyers who do not already know *hua'er* songs, singers, and practices. The most prominent features of the covers of regional recordings are the names or photographs of singers. The cover of the recording *Zhang Haikui and Hua Songlan in Concert: Hua'er* features a photograph of a red peony. Avid *hua'er* listeners would know not only the two singers but also that the picture of the flower is a visual representation of the word "*hua'er*." *Hua'er in the "Challenge Arena"* (*Hua'er "leitai" teji*) similarly seems directed toward local audiences and *hua'er* devotees. It was recorded live during a concert in which singers performed in the dialogic "challenge arena" form. As in the Zhang Haikui recording, all four singers on this tape use local dialects. Following practices used in organized events, the lyrics of several songs are spoken in local dialect by the singers before the pieces are sung. This is one of very few commercially produced tapes without instrumental accompaniment.

Qinghai Hua'er is an example of a locally produced recording that incorporates musical elements from Chinese national popular music with singing in both local dialect and in Mandarin. Its subtitle is "rock and roll; wild nature." (The character for "wild," "*ye*," can also be translated as undomesticated, untamed, rough, or unrestrained.) "Rock and roll" in this case is a generic term referring to a variety of popular styles current in the PRC in the late 1980s and early 1990s. The photographs of the singers, Ma Jun and "Rose," are prominent against a backdrop of the regional countryside. Several factors distinguish the two performers. One of the most famous singers in the Northwest, Ma Jun would have face recognition within the region but not in the rest of the country. Although a member of an organized song troupe, Ma Jun grew up singing *hua'er* and was trained by local *hua'er* singers. He nearly always sings in local dialect but is able to speak both Northwest-dialect Chinese and Mandarin. "Rose," on the other hand, is a professionally trained singer who sings in Mandarin and uses the *meisheng* vocal quality characteristic of the national folk-song style. Both modify their accents, but not their languages, on some songs. At times Ma Jun makes some words "clearer" by introducing more national-standard Chinese pronunciations, but his overall pronunciation and use of padding words still fall within the range of local and sung dialect. Rose occasionally attempts to give some "local flavor" to her songs by adding characteristics of local dialect to her national-standard Chinese, but her singing remains squarely within the range of standard Mandarin.

On the insert to this tape, the printed lyrics include nearly all padding words as well as annotations to several terms and phrases particular to local and sung dialect. The mixing of styles on this recording extends to the level of musical genres. Several songs are from other local genres, such as Salar nationality tunes sung and printed in Chinese. From traditional a cappella singing to accompanied performance with national music ensembles, Ma Jun produces a wide variety of other types of *hua'er* recordings, and these reflect his musical range and desire for experimentation. I have heard *hua'er* scholars complain that Ma often strays too far from the traditional aesthetics of *hua'er*; based on my observations, however, I can say that he is extremely well received by local audiences, no matter what style he uses.

Produced by the Shanghai branch of the China Record Company, *Su Ping: Honest and Sincere, Folksongs of Gansu and Qinghai* is a recording intended for national distribution. Su Ping is a member of the Salar nationality who grew up in Gansu. She sings here in Mandarin Chinese with a local Northwest dialect accent, accompanied by a large national music orchestra. The musical and linguistic style in which she performs on this tape reflects her carefully crafted agenda for the broader promotion of *hua'er*. As she wrote in her résumé, which she gave to me in 1995, her artistic goal is "to explore a new and original performance style that will be well received by a broad audience, a style created on the fundamental principle of preserving and carrying on the local style and nationality characteristics of Northwest *hua'er*." She believes that such a style is best accomplished through Mandarin-language singing. The recording illustrates one of the ways that local musical forms are modified for and marketed to a national audience; it also shows how such recordings may be returned to the Northwest by the national music industry. Only a few weeks after its release, the tape was sold in stores in Qinghai and Gansu provinces, and bootleg copies were available in the Xining city park.

Su Ping has several decades of experience singing *hua'er* in national sites. She has produced more than twenty recordings and has performed in national folk-song festivals and on the celebrated New Year's galas broadcast by the Chinese Central Television network. As an officially designated "level-one national performer," she has sung in Zimbabwe, Japan, Romania, and North Korea. She also has continued to perform regularly in the Northwest and to train local singers. Accompanied by a popular music ensemble (electric guitars, synthesizer, and drum set), she gave a concert during the 1995 Qutan Monastery *hua'er* festival in Ledu that employed a singing style similar to that heard on *Su Ping: Honest and Sincere*. The local singers she was mentoring at that time, however—three Bao'an nationality women—sang in local Chinese dialect. With her long experience, Su Ping recognizes the need for a variety of singing styles to suit the diverse contexts available for today's *hua'er* song performance. Although I heard several Northwest *hua'er* scholars and singers criticize her style as not local (*tu*) enough, she continues to draw large, appreciative audiences at her local concerts.

National Distinctions

Singers who have participated in national festivals, performed on national television programs, and been part of Chinese National Music ensembles touring abroad are celebrated locally. When these singers are introduced at local concerts, their achievements are announced as marks of national and international distinction. When Su Ping performed at the Qutan monastery *hua'er* festival, the posters advertising her concert featured a photograph from the cover of *Su Ping: Honest and Sincere*, a testament to the national attention given to both her and *hua'er* songs. The concept of the national is maintained by the central government and by local agencies that struggle to bring wider attention to "their" music.

Many singers speak of their desire to tour all of China and to release recordings that are nationally successful, often indicating these as sources of potential wealth. Aware that the Northwest still offers the best potential for large audiences, however, nearly all singers have decided to stay at home in the *hua'er* region. This is a wise decision, because efforts to popularize the songs beyond the region have not met with overwhelming success. Indeed, *hua'er* songs are not well known nationally.

In meetings and conferences, scholars, singers, and cultural workers come together to examine methods for promoting *hua'er*. I was able to attend many such events and hear debates about past practices and the future development of the genre. The published literature also contains anecdotal evidence on *hua'er* and its promotion. For example, in his 1991 book, *New Theories about Hua'er*, Wei Quanming describes the small audiences, "cold atmosphere," and lack of applause that he observed at *hua'er* concert in Beijing (35–36). Wei thinks that solving the problem of *hua'er*'s low national profile lies not in selecting the appropriate language or dialect for singing but in recognizing the importance of context. "As a product of a particular region and situation, the special character of *hua'er* determines that it must be performed in contexts in which it is easy for people to receive, . . . or the results will be disappointing" (34). For Wei, those contexts are associated with Northwest *hua'er* festivals rather than with staged concerts in Beijing, which he says entail a different set of aesthetic expectations.

While acknowledging that broadening *hua'er*'s listenership may require some accommodation to mainstream tastes, many involved in promotion of the music say that, even when the songs are stripped of their distinctive features, they cannot compete in the national popular music arena. Local *hua'er* scholars in particular argue that most attempts to promote the songs beyond the region have diluted the very aspects that distinguish *hua'er* from other Chinese song genres. And these national practices have had at least some local impact. For instance, *hua'er* songs taught in local music schools are sung in national rather than local styles. I attended an impromptu concert at the Northwest Teachers' College in which several students performed *hua'er* songs in Mandarin using the same vocal style used to perform other Chinese folk songs on the program. After the concert, a *hua'er* scholar commented that these voice students sang with a "flavor not typical" (*wei'er bu didao*) of *hua'er* songs.

Many *hua'er* promoters have operated under the assumption that language comprehension was a major obstacle in disseminating the songs, and they have advocated Mandarin-language singing. Yet Mandarin-language *hua'er* has not received national acclaim, nor does comprehension alone account for the lack of national attention given to the local-dialect singing. Other song genres, including English-language genres from the United States and Cantonese-language genres from Hong Kong, have become popular, in spite of the fact that their lyrics are incomprehensible to most Chinese. Promoted through the commercial popular music industry, often with international backing, these genres are represented in their accompanying discourses as modern and international. In contrast, the dominant image of *hua'er* is that of a regional folk-song form that is by definition limited in scope its of dissemination and sung by working-class people from the "backward" frontier region of Northwest China.

Conclusion

Local, national, and international distinctions are defined in relation to each other and in particular contexts. *Hua'er*'s opportunity for national fame seems to rest on its distinction as a local genre. Indeed, the cultural bureaucracy has highlighted local characteristics of *hua'er* to display the ethnic and regional diversity of the country and present an idealized version of the "voice of the people." When taken abroad, local characteristics recede further as *hua'er* songs are rhetorically recontextualized as Chinese folk songs, becoming just one of many examples of Chinese music. Ironically, the centrally directed and standardized practices of the cultural bureaucracy—along with experiments to make *hua'er* more comprehensible and acceptable nationally—have muted the very characteristics that make *hua'er* distinctive.

In spite of repeated statements in the public discourse that *hua'er* is beloved by the Chinese people, that it is a beautiful flower growing in the garden of Chinese music, and that it contributes to world culture, *hua'er* certainly has not become a nationally significant expressive form, nor has it become a factor within the global popular music industry. Outside its native region, *hua'er*, its singers, and its promoters are dependent on the institutions of the cultural bureaucracy and media. Inside the *hua'er* song region, the effects of the cultural bureaucracy can also be seen in the organized events that it sponsors.

Within spontaneous events, however, audiences expect to hear this music performed in *hua'er* sung dialect, and singers continue to do so. The popularity of *hua'er* sung dialect remains undisputed in its traditional spontaneous performance contexts, perhaps because their participants are not concerned about the broader dissemination of *hua'er* songs or with its externally defined characteristics of local distinction. The histories of *hua'er* cite resilience as a characteristic of the songs and their creators. Whether these local folk songs will be able to resist the cultural bureaucracy's efforts to promote the genre and the increased availability of other musical styles from the mass media remains a question for the future.

Acknowledgments

I would like to express my gratitude to the singers, listeners, and scholars who graciously devoted their time to helping me understand *hua'er* songs and their place in Chinese society.

Notes

Unless otherwise specified, English translations from the Chinese were done by the author. When citing Chinese names, I observe the Chinese order of surnames followed by given names.

1. This essay is based on field research conducted in Northwest China in 1984–85, 1990, 1993, and 1995 and on the scholarly literature. Extensive references to the Chinese-language scholarship are provided in Tuohy ("Imagining"; "Social") and Yang Mu.

2. I draw upon the concept of locally distinctive forms that is pervasive in contemporary Chinese society and is manifest in varied economic and critical practices. My theoretical approach also derives more generally from Pierre Bourdieu's writing on the process by which distinctions are characterized, classified, and ordered within an "economy of cultural goods . . . [that] has a specific logic" (1). Part of the analyst's task, therefore, is to understand the logic underlying the specific practices through which distinctions are made.

3. For further information on Chinese languages, dialects, linguistic practices, and ideologies, see DeFrancis, Lehmann, and Moser.

4. In the PRC, this written language is printed using simplified characters (*jiantizi*) as opposed to the complex characters (*fantizi*) used in Taiwan (the Republic of China) and in PRC publications intended for overseas Chinese.

5. Books are published in minority languages and, in the case of languages that have historically lacked a written orthography, in written languages developed after 1949. Based on my experience in the North and Northwest, there were no policies promoting local Chinese dialect broadcasting until at least the late 1990s.

6. For a discussion of Western music influences in twentieth-century China, see Mittler. Focusing primarily on musical style, Brace and Jones discuss popular music in relation to Chinese modern identity. Local, national, and transnational (particularly Asian) elements are discussed in Witzleben's article on the southern musical form, Cantopop.

7. After the conclusion of the Cultural Revolution in the late 1970s, more stories of bans on singing were published in official sources. These publications, however, criticized a more recent past and the mistaken policies of the PRC leadership. According to Li Zhang, "within the area in which *hua'er* songs are popular, [such bans] were nothing new. Historically, revolutionaries were all defiled in that way; those who attacked *hua'er* songs said they were heretical, licentious and base, and stirred up trouble" (15). Even today, some singers may still follow the customary restrictions on *hua'er* performance and refuse to sing this music in their homes, in their villages, or in front of family members of older generations. I never have heard of *hua'er* singing within the grounds of a mosque, and one well-known Muslim vocalist told me of Islamic religious leaders who scolded him for performing *hua'er* in public.

8. Ranging in size from small villages to provinces, the government-designated autonomous regions are geopolitical units in which one or more minority nationalities are concentrated. Lipman and Tuohy ("Imagining") discuss conceptual configurations of the Northwest, the autonomous regions, and the government policies related to minority nationalities.

9. Chen Ming follows a similar argument in relation to *hua'er* songs in the Taomin (Taozhou) dialect area, saying that when the Jiangsu immigrants came to this region in the Ming dynasty, they combined the performance styles of their native folksongs with song competitions popular among the Tibetans already living in the area. Together they "gradually created the new song form *hua'er*" (3).

10. I noticed people often called out the name of the *ling* tune when hearing the melody without the lyrics. Other instances demonstrate that *ling* tunes, and thus *hua'er*, are recognizable without lyrics. Instrumental versions of *hua'er*, in the style of light popular music performed nationally, can be heard on the audiotape *Hua'er Sentiments*.

11. The term "*shaonian*"—which some scholars consider to be a subgenre within *hua'er* and others consider to be an altogether different genre—is often used in the songs to refer to men. Both *hua'er* and *shaonian* can refer either to a genre of songs or to members of the opposite sex.

12. Liu Kai calls the opening phrases "leading" or "initiating" sentences. Apart from introducing metaphors related to the primary topic, these phrases may initiate a rhyme scheme that will be followed in the later phrases (67).

13. "*Ga*" is a Tibetan-language diminutive prefix. "*Mei*" is a Chinese-language term for younger sister; in local dialect it often is pronounced "*mi*."

14. There is some agreement about the primary classes, although the names used to designate them vary. Genre classification is the subject of intense debate and is described in detail in Tuohy "Imagining" (150–69, 306–13) and "Social."

15. Based on my experience, English words are rarely used and are limited to those that can be articulated with Chinese-language sounds. For instance, the term "*baibai*" is a transliteration of "bye-bye" and used in *hua'er* texts to refer to a couple slitting up.

16. Articles from the 1940s through 1990s discuss minority-language *hua'er* songs (Lu Shimo, Lu Tuo, Trippner, and Zhang Yaxiong), but scholars argue about how common the songs are and whether they have increased or decreased in the twentieth century. Some scholars conclude that minorities sing *hua'er* in their own languages when in minority-only contexts but use Chinese when at festivals (Lu Tuo 192). I have heard only a few minority-language *hua'er* songs in performance.

17. Audience members indicated their evaluations by laughter and other vocal cues. They often responded appreciatively upon hearing the spoken lyrics and reacted even more audibly when the lyrics were sung a moment later.

Works Cited

Bourdieu, Pierre. *Distinction: A Social Critique of the Judgment of Taste*. Trans. Richard Nice. Cambridge: Harvard UP, 1984.

Brace, Tim. "Popular Music in Contemporary Beijing: Modernism and Cultural Identity." *Asian Music* 22.2 (1991): 43–66.

Chen Ming. "Taomin hua'er chansheng de shehui jiqu ji minsu jiazhi" (The social basis of the production of Taomin *hua'er* and its folkloric value). Paper presented at the *Hua'er* Research Conference, 22–24 July 1985, Lanzhou, Gansu.

DeFrancis, John F. *Nationalism and Language Reform in China*. 1950. New York: Octagon, 1972.

Du Yaxiong. " 'Shaonian' yu 'hua'er' bianxi" (Discriminating between "*shaonian*" and "*hua'er*"). *Zhongguo yinyue* 2 (1983): 72–74.

Ekvall, Robert B. *Cultural Relations on the Kansu-Tibetan Border*. University of Chicago Publications in Anthropology, Occasional Papers, No. 1. Chicago: U of Chicago P, 1939.

Guilbault, Jocelyne. "On Redefining the 'Local' through World Music." *World of Music* 35.2 (1993): 33–47.

Jones, Andrew F. *Like a Knife: Ideology and Genre in Contemporary Chinese Popular Music*. Ithaca, NY: East Asian Program, Cornell U, 1992.

Ke Yang. "Juyou daibiaoxing de Huizu hua'er—'Chumenren de ge': Linxia 'hua'er' zushu wenti tantao zhiyi" (Representative Hui nationality *hua'er*—"Songs of the journeymen": An exploration of the issue of nationality categories in Linxia *hua'er*). In *Hua'er lunji*, ed. Zhongguo minjian wenyi yanjiuhui (Gansu fenhui), vol. 2. 53–62.

Lehmann, Winfred P., ed. *Language and Linguistics in the People's Republic of China*. Austin: U of Texas P, 1975.

Li Fu. "Shitan hua'er de gelu wenti" (A brief discussion of problems in the rules and form of *hua'er*). In *Hua'er lunji*, ed. Zhongguo minjian wenyi yanjiuhui (Gansu fenhui), vol. 2. 158–65.

Li Lin. "Hua'er yuanliu liangti" (Two issues in the origin and development of *hua'er*). In *Hua'er lunji*, ed. Zhongguo minjian wenyi yanjiuhui (Gansu fenhui), vol. 1. 116–25.

Li Zhang. "Huanjie hua'er de chuntian" [Welcome the springtime of *hua'er*]. *Qinghai wenyi* 5–6 (1977): 13–18.

Lin Cao. "Xinlihua huicheng kouzhong ge" (Words of the heart transformed into oral songs). *Gansu wenyi* 9 (1978): 84–88.

Lipman, Jonathan N. *Familiar Strangers: A History of Muslims in Northwest China*. Seattle: U of Washington P, 1997.

Liu Kai. "Xibei 'taoyu' lilun yu xibu 'hua'er' de koutou chuangzuo fangshi" (A theory of northwest formulaic language and the methods of oral composition in northwest "*hua'er*"). *Minzu wenxue yanjiu* 2 (1998): 66–74.

Lu Shimo. "Qiantan Bao'anzu hua'er de tese" (A brief discussion of Bao'an *hua'er* characteristics). In *Hua'er lunji*, ed. Zhongguo minjian wenyi yanjiuhui (Gansu fenhui), vol. 2. 80–86.

Lu Tuo. "Hezhou hua'er yu Hezhou hua" (Hezhou *hua'er* and Hezhou dialect). In *Hua'er lunji*, ed. Zhongguo minjian wenyi yanjiuhui (Gansu fenhui), vol. 2. 191–201.

Ma Guihua. *Zhongguo Xibu gewu lun* (Songs and dances of Northwest China). Xining: Qinghai renmin chubanshe, 1991.

Ma Tiancai. *Gansu luyou* (Tourism in Gansu). Lanzhou: Gansu renmin chubanshe, 1988.

Mittler, Barbara. *Dangerous Tunes: The Politics of Chinese Music in Hong Kong, Taiwan, and the People's Republic of China since 1949*. Wiesbaden: Harrassowitz Verlag, 1997.

Moser, Leo J. *The Chinese Mosaic: The Peoples and Provinces of China*. Boulder, CO: Westview, 1985.

Ning Wenhuan. *Taozhou hua'er sanlun* (Essays on Taozhou *hua'er*). Lanzhou: Gansu minzu chubanshe, 1992.

Schimmelpenninck, Antoinet. *Chinese Folk Songs and Folk Singers: Shan'ge Traditions in Southern Jiangsu*. Leiden: Chime Foundation, 1997.

Trippner, Josef. "Die Shaonien in Ch'ing-hai." *Folklore Studies*, supp. 1 (1952): 264–305.

Tuohy, Sue. "Imagining the Chinese Tradition: The Case of *Hua'er* Songs, Festivals, and Scholarship." Diss., Indiana U, 1988.

———. "The Social Life of Genre: The Dynamics of Folksong in China." *Asian Music* 30.2 (1999): 39–86.

Wei Quanming. "Biekai shengmian de min'ge yanchanghui: Gansusheng Lianhuashan hua'er hui diaocha baogao" (Groundbreaking folk song performances: An investigative report of the Lianhua Mountain *hua'er* festival in Gansu). In *Hua'er lunji*, ed. Zhongguo minjian wenyi yanjiuhui (Gansu fenhui), vol. 1. 72–85.

———. *Hua'er Xinlun* (New theories about *hua'er*). Lanzhou: Dunhuang wenyi chubanshe, 1991.

Witzleben, J. Lawrence. "Localism, Nationalism, and Transnationalism in Pre-Postcolonial Hong Kong Popular Song." *Popular Music: Intercultural Interpretations*. Ed. Mitsui Toru. Kanazawa, Japan: Graduate Program in Music, Kanazawa U, 1998. 469–75.

Xi Huimin. "Hua'er de leixing" (Types of *hua'er*). Paper presented at the *Hua'er* Research Conference, 22–24 July 1985, Lanzhou, Gansu.

Yang Ling. "China Recovers Her Past in Folk Songs." *Chinese Music* 6.1 (1982): 8–10.

Yang Mu. "On the *Hua'er* Songs of North-Western China." *Yearbook for Traditional Music* 26 (1994): 100–16.

Zhang Yaxiong. *Hua'erji* (*Hua'er* Collection). Revised ed. Beijing: Zhongguo wenyi chubanshe, 1940 (1986).

Zhongguo minjian wenyi yanjiuhui (Gansu fenhui), ed. *Hua'er lunji* (Anthology of writings on *hua'er*). 2 vols. Lanzhou: Gansu renmin chubanshe, 1983.

Zhu Zhonglu. "Hua'er yanchang jiqiao de tansu" (A talk on *hua'er* performance technique). Paper presented at the *Hua'er* Research Conference, 22–24 July 1985, Lanzhou, Gansu.

Selected Discography

Caizi hua'er huang (Rapeseed *hua'er*). Ma Jun and Na Jingcheng, performers. XBI-004. Xi'an: Shaanxisheng xibu yinxiang chubanshe, 1989.

Hua'er "leitai" teji, 2 (*Hua'er* in the "challenge arena," special issue, no. 2). Ma Jun, Zhao Jijin, Wei Guoying, Zhang Cunxiu, performers. ISRC CN-H09-93-0003-0/A.J6. Xining: Qinghai kunlun yinxiang chubanshe, 1993.

Hua'er qing: Xibei hua'er qing yinyue zhi yi (*Hua'er* sentiments: Northwest *hua'er* light music). ISRC CN-H07-93-302-00/A.J6. Lanzhou: Gansusheng yinxiang chubanshe, 1993.

Hua'er yu shaonian (*Hua'er* and *shaonian*). Video CD from the Collection of Famous Chinese Regional Songs. ISRC CN-C13-98-380-00/V.J6. Hebei: Hebei bailing yinxiang chubanshe, 1998.

Qinghai hua'er: Yaogun, yexing (Qinghai *hua'er*: Rock and roll, wild nature). Ma Jun and "Rose", performers. QK 1-08. Xining: Qinghai kunlun yinxiang chubanshe, n.d. (mid-1990s).

Su Ping: Handundun, Gan Qing min'ge (Su Ping: Honest and Sincere, Gansu and Qinghai folk songs). ISRC CN-E01-95-307-00/A.J6. Shanghai: Zhongguo changpian Shanghai gongsi, 1995.

Xibei min'ge (Northwest folk songs). Video CD no. 6 from the Collection of Famous Chinese Regional Songs. ISRC CN-C13-98-380-00/V.J6. Hebei: Hebei bailing yinxiang chubanshe, 1998.

Zhang Haikui, Hua Songlan tongli hezou: Hua'er (Zhang Haikui and Hua Songlan in concert: *Hua'er*). QK 1-014. Xining: Qinghai kunlun yinxiang chubanshe, n.d. (mid-1990s).

"Ordinary Words"

Sound, Symbolism, and Meaning in Belarusan-Language
Rock Music

—*Maria Paula Survilla*

[L]anguage itself contains sedimented layers of emotionally resonant
metaphors, knowledge and associations, which when paid attention to, can
be experienced as discoveries and revelations.
—Michael Fischer

Language embodies experience, triggers associations, and articulates
varied layers of significance.[1] Whether spoken, heard, read, or intimated, language can give voice to powerful meanings and encourage multiple responses
to the forms of expression in which it participates. As Michael M. J. Fischer's
remarks suggest, the sedimented and resonant allusions within language can
activate memory and cultural awareness. When combined with music, language's evocative power can go even further. Here, song texts move beyond
the referential meaning of their words to embrace metaphorics, rhyme,
rhythm, and other sonic dimensions of language. This "package" of potential
meaning can be read by different listeners in different ways according to
their competence and their predispositions as to the value and function of
the language at hand.

In popular music scholarship, both language and the listener's aesthetic
response have been objects of inquiry, although the two are not always connected. Media studies scholar Roy Shuker offers a brief history of the
approaches that have been taken to the analysis of song lyrics in Anglo-
American popular music studies since the 1950s (179–81). Initial attempts at
understanding pop music lyrics were based on the analysis of content, often
relating the meaning and structure of a song's words to their social context.
Such work, Shuker notes, rarely demonstrated musical expertise or any
awareness of non-Anglophone examples. It also failed to offer an exploration

of the impact of language and language choice on the music. Nevertheless, the interest in song texts has produced a variety of theoretical frameworks. Richard Middleton, for example, draws our attention to the role of affect (words as expression), story (words as narrative), and gesture (words as sound) in the analysis of lyrics (228–31). His work is consonant with that of Simon Frith, who, building on key trends in twentieth-century linguistics, sees the verbal dimension of song as a kind of "speech act" (*Rites* 158–59).

A central idea in Frith's work is that the listener's assignment of emotive power and meaning in music comes about through the interplay of individual, social, and cultural expectations about what music is—or what it can be. As a result, one of the central debates regarding aesthetic responses to popular music centers on the extent to which our preconceptions about a particular form of expression influence its aesthetic effect on us (Firth, *Rites*, 250–52).[2] Frith emphasizes that taste and the assignment of cultural value are not inherent in the text; rather, they come from an interpretive and social process. "For sounds to be music," he writes, "we need to know how to hear them" (249–50). In Frith's model, one's expectations about a musical package informs one's response to it, and both the expectations and the responses are influenced by social context. In those situations where the language itself announces a particular significance beyond the obvious, referential one, an affective response does not occur unless we know "how to hear" it. To this we should add that the individual and social dynamics that influence the listener's responses to the musical package resist reductionistic analyses. Ultimately, such reactions are elusive and complex. Nevertheless, we can discover much regarding the response to language in popular music if we consider some of the associations that influence the way in which it is heard.

These factors will be taken into consideration in this study of Belarusan-language rock in the 1990s. In this essay, I will analyze song lyrics from the genre and discuss excerpts from interviews with noted Belarusan rock musicians and writers. This material will illustrate how the Belarusan language has informed the music, serving as a strategic tool in the creative process and affecting the response of the primary audience in ways that go beyond basic, lexical meanings. Applying Frith's model, we will see how the use of the Belarusan language can resonate with a variety of contexts: social and political processes, cultural references, personal histories, and public battles. Here, the immediacy, intimacy, and comfort evoked by the sound of a familiar language can create a powerful act of recognition for the audience. The presence of the Belarusan language, as well as the quality of its use, can influence the audience's evaluation of the performers (in terms of their authenticity and creativity), the music (in terms of its political, cultural, social, and aesthetic value), and the genre itself.

In order to understand the complexity of language choice in Belarusan rock, we need at least briefly to consider the historical context. Bordered by Poland, Lithuania, Latvia, Russia, and Ukraine, Belarus is a country with a distinct ethnic history dating to medieval times. It is situated at the junction of trade routes that mark the threshold between eastern and western Europe and has continually been the target of the expansionist policies of its neighbor states. Such expansionism has often redefined Belarus's geographic borders, as well as its sense of national and cultural identity. Language has played a central role in the negotiation and manipulation of that identity.

At the end of the eighteenth century, the Russian Empire and the Kingdom of Poland began to vie for control of the Grand Duchy of Litva, precursor to Belarus. Russian domination continued throughout the nineteenth century with significant consequences to the indigenous culture and to the Belarusan language. Significant change came in 1905, when the revolution in Russia led to some democratic reforms both in Russia, such as the establishment of the parliament (the State Duma), and throughout the empire, as seen in the relaxation of certain policies against national minorities, such as the lifting of the ban on publication in non-Russian languages. At this juncture, restrictions placed on the use of Belarusan language in the previous century were temporarily lifted, the name Belarus was officially accepted, and Belarusan-language books and newspapers appeared in many cities, most notably *Nasha Niva* (Our Soil), published between 1906 and 1915 (see Zaprunik 63). In 1918, the instability created by World War I and the Bolshevik Revolution of the previous year led Belarus to declare its independence under the name Belarusan People's Republic. This independence was short-lived, however; in 1919 the Bolsheviks proclaimed the formation of the Byelorussian Socialist Soviet Republic (BSSR), and the Russian-Polish war (1919–1921) resulted in the partitioning of Belarus between BSSR and Poland. Some seventy years later, as the Soviet Union saw Mikhail Gorbachev's open policies fuel the sedition of many of its member states (see Brown), Belarus once again declared its independence, this time as the Republic of

Belarus.[3] The winds of political change were soon to blow again, though, and in 1994 Belarus came under the control of a government with Soviet-style policies led by President Alaksandar Lukashenka. Today, that regime is considered illegitimate by virtually every government in the world—with the exception of Russia.

Throughout the long period of Russian domination, Belarus has undergone aggressive attempts to assimilate the population and has endured the censorship of its indigenous culture. As Zaprunik's work reveals, the use of the Belarusan language persisted under the Russian Empire, in spite of efforts to stamp it out through conceptual and practical Russification. Such efforts included prohibitions against the use of Belarusan in education and in religious services, the Russification of the clergy, and the outlawing of Belarusan-language place-names (Zaprunik 35–44). In the twentieth century, similar policies were enacted by the Soviet Union. Most recently, the use of language for political control has been central to the platform of the post-1994 government. Lukashenka clearly recognizes a connection between the Belarusan language and political self-determination and has all but prohibited the use of Belarusan in the public sphere.

In times of relaxed cultural policy as well as in periods of heightened oppression, the Belarusan language has operated as a symbol of national identity and historical legitimacy. More recently, it has served as a means for postcolonial positioning. It was the Belarusan language that unified the late-nineteenth-century nationalist movements, serving as a muse for both poets and prose writers who examined the themes of identity, the Belarusan experience, independence, and nationality. With the systematic subjugation of Belarusan expression that occurred in this period, these writers found that the exploration of any Belarusan identity separate from a Russian-centered one required enormous determination. Belarusan-language newspapers were produced in the early twentieth century, and these publications fueled a growing intellectual movement that celebrated national identity. In the 1990s, questions about language choice were critical for those interested in the meaning of nation and the exploration of their pre-Soviet roots. Many in the country turned to the words of Franchisak Bahushevich (1840–1900), patriarch of the modern Belarusan literary movement, whose remarks on the importance of the national language became an oft-quoted maxim: "Do not abandon our Belarusan language lest you die" (Bahushevich 16–17).

Contemporary political activists associated the language with the preservation of culture and the forwarding of their goals; they have also allied the language itself to a specific iconography for the reemerging nation (see Rich). In all of this, we can see the interplay of cultural movements centered on language and political movements centered on independence; such alliances have strengthened the association between the Belarusan language and the quest for political self-determination—an alliance that has remained viable through the present day.

Like that of many post-Soviet states, Belarus's 1991 declaration of independence was not a spontaneous event. Grassroots intellectuals and those involved in the youth movements had been exploring the question of national identity since the early 1980s. Many of these movements, including Belarusan rock, were defined by a desire to reappropriate the national language. With independence, increased use of Belarusan in private and public spheres became an indicator of the new climate of exploration and, for many, symbolized the rebirth of the nation. The period from the beginning of independence in 1990 to the installation of the Lukashenka administration in 1994 is commonly regarded as a cultural renaissance (*adradzennie*). Language served as a practical means of expressing the desire for change and of exploring national histories that had been banned or reshaped in Soviet propaganda.

Because czarist, Stalinist, and Soviet cultural policies had left such a significant imprint on contemporary Belarusan identity, the Belarusan language became a locus of controversy as well as a symbol of rebirth. In the years of Russian domination, many urban Belarusans had lost the ability to speak their own language, and after 1990 a sizable group was perplexed by those who now embraced a culture and a language that had, in the past, been systematically devalued. The response to the Belarusan language was as much about its practical use as it was about its historically disparaged position. Debates about national language and identity played out in conjunction with the realities of a struggling market economy, new access to the West, and explorations of local democracy. Thus, while urban Belarusans were being asked to learn a new language for commerce, the media, and education, they were also being asked to simply and immediately forget the stigma that had been attached to Belarusan. As a result, many were uneasy with both the practical implications of change and the ideological adjustment regarding the value of Belarusan, and language became a hotly debated issue in the scholarship and the media of the early 1990s. In this context, the use of Belarusan often served as a powerful cultural and political signifier. Speaking Belarusan could confirm the speaker's position on political or social issues, advertise his or her regional and cultural identity, and mark him or her as an activist, intellectual, or rebel. In brief, language choice has so consistently been a barometer of the state of Belarusan culture that it is difficult to separate associations between language and cultural freedom, language and self-determination, or language and political awareness.

Given all of this, it is not surprising that language choice has been, and remains, a key aspect of Belarusan rock. In the early years of the movement, musicians who chose to produce rock in Belarusan faced several challenges. In addition to the absence of an independent national music industry, Belarusan rock musicians had to develop an audience that could accept their music and their language. This essay explores the ways in which language contributes to the aesthetics of the genre, the creative processes within that genre, and the experiences of the listeners. Five related issues are key here. First, there is the connection between three forms of cultural subordination: a subordinated language (Belarusan), a subordinated musical genre (rock), and a subordinated lifestyle (the lifestyle associated with the *rok muzykant* [rock musician]). Second, one must consider the fact that, unlike literary texts, rock lyrics are meant to be heard as part of the musical performance. Third, there is the question of aesthetics, both the aesthetics of language and the aesthetic issues that emerge in the relationship between language and music. Fourth, one must attend to the use of language as a basis for cultural critique. Fifth, there is the national symbolism associated with the language through borrowings from the Belarusan literary and scholarly canon. The last point is important because the texts of the nineteenth-century Belarusan literary movement have provided rock lyrics with a source of quotations, metaphors, and allusions.

The earliest roots of the Belarusan rock movement can be found in the urban music scenes of the Soviet era. During the 1960s, smuggled recordings of Western music saw an increasing popularity, and in response, the government tried to control nearly every aspect of popular music production, from musical style and textual content to the venues for performance and audience behavior. The government also created Vocal Instrumental Ensembles

(VIAs), which set nonpolitical lyrics to light musical accompaniments. In this climate of genre censorship, Belarusan audiences (and, eventually, other Soviet audiences) became receptive to a group called the Piesniary (Songsters), a VIA of conservatory-trained musicians who sang in the Belarusan language. The group managed to make a non-Russian language choice palatable to government officials, and, although they were criticized as "inauthentic" by some rock critics (for example, Troitsky), the Piesniary introduced the Belarusan language as a medium for contemporary music in the public sphere.

Though the Piesniary's (1969-present) early popularity was seminal to the emergence of a Belarusan contemporary music, the extraordinary events in the mid-1980s helped to shape the movement. The year 1986 is especially important to the political and cultural change that eventually defined the renaissance and Belarusan rock. First, the year is strongly associated with the emergence of rock in Belarus. Second, it marks the first aggressive appearance of the Belarusan renaissance, though at this point the movement faced official censorship and intimidation. Performers active during the early years of the movement attested to the difficulties of making music and performing (see Krauchanka). The forms of cultural and political criticism associated with these performers—and their treatment by government officials—forged an association in the public mind linking the Belarusan language, the rock musician, and rebellion. Finally, 1986 was the year of the disaster at the Chernobyl nuclear reactor in Ukraine, whose airborne radioactive fallout decimated many regions in Belarus. Historian David Marples has commented that the Soviet Union's inability to address the Chernobyl problem caused many to question the efficacy of the government and to consider the need for change.

During the late 1980s, Belarusan rock musicians saw their creative choices attacked on many fronts. In the minds of Soviet officials, any interest in rock music constituted a rejection of socialist ideals. Likewise, expressions of local cultural identity, such as the use of Belarusan in song, met with official disapproval. In addition to its "negative" association with the West and with what was often labeled "national chauvinism," rock musicians were officially seen as amoral individuals who led a lifestyle that was inappropriate for Soviet youth. This depiction has had a longstanding effect on public perceptions and, at least at the beginning of the 1990s, separated the power of youth movements from the aspirations of the Belarusan intelligentsia. Further, Belarusan rock was criticized for its alleged lack of artistic authenticity—the inevitable result, according to the official account, of its derivation from a highly commercialized form of Western popular music. In this view, rock music was inherently opposed to the "authentic" aesthetic values associated with "true" art, music, literature, and intellectual pursuits in general.

The dismissal of Belarusan rock on aesthetic grounds is ironic when one considers the high value that these musicians place on the quality of their lyrics. This goes beyond the issue of language choice. While the Belarusan language can be associated with political and cultural empowerment, language choice itself does not, of course, determine the quality of a song text. The literary history of modern Belarus, however, and the highly metaphoric and often stylized lyrics heard in folk repertoires have predisposed Belarusan rock critics to focus on lyrics when evaluating music.[4] The musicians and listeners also place a high value on the lyrics. Texts from Belarusan literary figures past and present, as well as lyrics from the folk repertoire, are often used in the music. It is common for Belarusan rock bands to have a lyricist as a nonperforming member of the group, and rock lyrics are frequently published as poetry.

In the mind of the public, Belarusan rock quickly became associated with the cultural renaissance. The burgeoning presence of these groups in the public sphere was due in part to the increased openness of the early 1990s. Veteran bands had asserted a connection with the Belarusan language even prior to independence, and Belarusan rock critics tended to foster the image of the rocker as a sincere, culturally conscious performer. This sincerity was tied to the rocker's language choice, use of folk metaphors and iconography, and direct quotation from literary sources and folk music. The use of musical, literary, and linguistic elements from Belarusan culture allowed the rockers to evoke complex aesthetic responses and multiple layers of meaning. Connected to issues of generation, gender, or nation, the songs are a key example of what Frith calls the "anthem response" to popular music ("Aesthetic" 137–49).

Although the early 1990s offered a more relaxed social and political climate for both established and newly emerging bands, recording opportunities and performance venues were few. As a result, bands that represented very different styles of rock would play at the same events. These performances emphasized the stylistic variety of the genre and shaped the public's perception of the music, which was seen as highly diverse. For example, during the early years of independence, the city of Miensk ("Minsk" had been the Russian spelling) could boast a roster of bands that included Krama (Store), a rhythm and blues band; Mroja (Dream), a heavy-metal outfit whose style expanded when they adopted the name NRM (Niezaleznaja Respublika Mroja [Free/National Republic of Dream]); Novaje Nieba (New Sky), an avant-garde/experimental group; Palac (Palace), a folk-modern group; and Ulis (Ulysses), an energetic, straight-ahead rock band.

Beyond their commitment to rock music and their shared use of the native language, Belarusan rock groups of the early 1990s did not articulate a unified political position. Despite the diversity of their politics and styles, however, their choice of language served as a powerful political statement and appealed both to young people interested in popular music and to those involved in the Belarusan cultural renaissance. Further, the use of Belarusan often became embedded in the material culture of rock music—album covers, posters, and publicity materials. Finally, the musicians' discourse outside the music itself (interviews, public statements, and so forth) had a powerful impact on the audience's interpretation of the genre and their vision of its ability to inform public opinion.

It is in these accompanying discourses that performers reveal the role of language in their music as well as their differing degrees of overt connection with political and social movements. In order to gather more direct information regarding the politics of language and nation in Belarusan rock, I conducted interviews in 1993 with some of the genre's most notable writers and performers: Kasia Kamockaja of Novaje Nieba, Lavon Volski of both NRM and Novaje Nieba, and all of the members of Ulis (Viachaslau Korjan, Siarhiej Krauchanka, Aleh Tumashau, Siarhiej Knysh, and lyricist Felix Aksentsev). While these interviews reveal the variety of perspectives that the musicians possess, they also illustrate the performers' shared understanding of the power that Belarusan language brings to their music.

The members of Ulis, considered an institution in Belarusan-language rock circles, were careful to differentiate the creative significance of the language from its social and political meanings. That is, while clearly inspired by the Belarusan language, they were more interested in the aesthetic rather than the political significance of their music. In the interviews, the musicians connected their intimate knowledge of the language and the power of the familiar to an instinctive approach to melody. Belarusan is often regarded as having a "melodic" character, not only because of the inflection used in everyday speech but also because of its diphthongs and the consonant sounds that affect its articulation. Lyricist Felix Aksentsev cited this melodic quality as critical for the band's music: "For me the use of Belarusan is very straightforward. Music, the melody, simply calls for Belarusan texts. It is more natural." Bassist Siarhiej Krauchanka commented that while English- and Russian-language rock were littered with clichéd expressions, Belarusan offered a fresh lexicon for the music. Placing familiar words into new contexts, the use of Belarusan brings original sounds to rock and shapes the melodic character of the songs as well. As Krauchanka remarked,

It [Belarusan] has not yet been fully explored in rock and roll. In English and in Russian there are already many words that have been overused, and from the point of view of understanding, of impact, Belarusan provides a wonderful language. You don't have to listen to it, it just comes to you.

The band's guitarist, Viachaslau Korjan, expressed similar views: "Traditional music is tied to the language of that people . . . if the language is such it will define the music . . . it is a question of intuition."

In their statements, both Kamockaja and Volski (who collaborated in the studio throughout the 1990s) revealed that, from the performer's point of view, the construction of the audience was both hampered and enhanced by prevailing attitudes toward the Belarusan language and rock music in general. They also said that the use of Belarusan could contribute to a heightened cultural self-awareness. Kamockaja commented that Belarusan bands who chose not to sing in Belarusan "don't feel their roots," and Volski said that "our music is seen as more original, partly because of language choice." Elsewhere (in remarks she made to the Belarusan newspaper *Svaboda*) Kamockaja stressed that Belarusan rock is a site for political and social critique: "rock and roll here, and especially Belarusan-language rock and roll, satisfies those functions that rock and roll used to have in the beginning of the movement."[5] Here, Kamockaja correlates the rise of rock music and social protest in Belarus with the limitations placed on freedom of expression by Lukashenka's administration. Further, she speculates that rock has shifted in its political significance in those places where repression has decreased: "The better a person lives, the less he wants to protest." Kamockaja's comments on the

social functions and political associations of Belarusan rock are partly connected to her early days as an urban bard. The bard movement uses a Pete
Seeger—esque delivery of poetic texts in order to make social and political
commentaries.[6] Following in this tradition, Novaje Nieba use their music to
explore the public's attitudes toward language and encourages Belarusans to
take a more proactive stance toward the explorations of their cultural identity.

In 1995, the Belarusan government banned Novaje Nieba's "Prezident idzi
damou" (President go home) from the airwaves because of the song's strong
and direct rejection of Lukashenka. The album title *GO Home* (on the album
cover "GO" is in upper case, and the title is in English) and the title song
draw attention to the fact that Lukashenka depended upon Russian support
in his political career and that he was not ratified through the Belarusan
political system. One manifestation of his non-Belarusan orientation is his
continuous attempt to suppress the Belarusan language and the renaissance
in general. It was Lukashenka who initiated the drive toward sovereignty
association (that is, political independence combined with some official connection) with Russia. He is therefore seen as an advocate for Russia who
belongs across the border rather than in Belarus.

The lyrics and musical gestures of "Prezident idzi damou" suggest the
stagnancy of the presidency as well as the populace's lack of political awareness and empowerment:

They don't know the word for "I" / They don't know the word for "word" / You and I,
we choose our words / But they don't hear them.

These lines clearly indicate the correlation between personal choice, cultural
awareness, political activism, and language. They also express the public's
ignorance in linguistic terms—their failure to embrace Belarusan. The music
supports these themes in several ways. The instrumental sections offer a
sequential riff with a wah-wah guitar that seems to parody the sound of inef-
fectual presidential rhetoric (see Survilla 136–37). Kamockaja's vocal sections
are lyrical by contrast—this contrast is typical of the band's overall style—
and these sections connect to the instrumental passages through the line
"Prezident idzi damou." The focus on language as a basis for critique is clear
in this song, and it is a consistent theme throughout Novaje Nieba's music.

Turning to the band Mroja, a related set of issues comes to light. This group emerged in the early days of the Belarusan rock movement with a guitar-driven, heavy-metal style and Belarusan-language lyrics infused with ironic commentaries and eloquent reflections. They also highlighted the importance of language choice, as seen on the cover of their album *28th Star* (produced in 1989, before the fall of the Soviet Union). The cover is in both English and in Belarusan and contains the statement "all songs in the Belarusan language." When the band changed their name in 1995, the new appellation, Niezaleznaja Respublika Mroja, set them up as a kind of political and cultural counterpoint to the real-world government of Lukashenka and its antirenaissance policies. The cover of their CD from that year, *Pashpart Hramadzianina NRM* (Passport for Citizenship of NRM), is a parody of a passport and pictures a vast, faceless crowd in front of a setting sun. The CD's accompanying insert contains passportlike gestures, most notably, a line that reads, "The holder of this passport is protected by NRM." The cover also sports a distorted Soviet-like logo of spiky sheaths of wheat around a skull and crossbones. In its title, imagery, and music, NRM's disc comments on the state of the Belarusan experience.

During the course of the 1990s, NRM maintained their lyrical excellence while shifting from their predominantly heavy-metal sound to one that can include quiet lyricism and an introspective, often meditative quality. Their ability to shift the style of their music is connected to the tendency within the scene toward collaboration between members of different bands. For example, NRM and Novaje Nieba have benefited from consistent collaboration since the early 1990s. Novaje Nieba, frequently described as an avant-garde band, has delved into a great variety of genres, with lyrics often borrowed from Belarusan poets.

In 1999, Novaje Nieba released a retrospective CD, as did a number of established bands.[7] *Piesni Roznych Hadou* (Songs from Various Years) offers cuts that range from the band's bard-influenced early songs to their more recent collaborations. The songs also employ a variety of genres and experimental techniques. One track in particular—"Ludzi na balocie" (People in the mud)—reflects an interest in the delivery of language. More than emphasizing the diction of the singers or the lyricism of the words/melody/performance, this cut illustrates how associations embedded within language can shape the listener's perception of the music and its meaning. The song's name is an allusion to a book of the same title. Part of a series called *Chronicles of Palessie*

(1961) by the noted Belarusan author Ivan Mielezh (1921–76), the book is a passionate rendering of human experience in the author's native region of Palessie in southern Belarus. The title is meant quite literally—Palessie as a place of vast marshlands. Volski's borrowing of the title, however, is metaphoric and draws on the audience's familiarity with Mielezh's text. Volski remarks that while the content of the book itself was not key to the narrative meaning of the words, the title was important because it could induce immediate associations for the audience:

As for the name of the book as a title and as a refrain: I chose it in order for the public to react to the habitual word association. This work is taught in schools and is the saga of life in Palessie, and in the context of the book it refers simply to the people who live in the marshes of Palessie. But in the context of the song the expression of these words refers to a definition of [a] people who are indifferent [careless; inert] to their fate.

Volski further explains his literal use of the words as "shock therapy, in order to activate emotion even if it is negative, in order to shake the ordinary careless thinking of the people" (Volski, E-mail) The shock he refers to results from employing a title that is in its original usage nonpejorative but which acquires a negative or critical meaning in Volski's application; the audience's familiarity with the original work produces the "shock." The words are an open critique of the political climate in Belarus; they offer a perception of a population willing to accept the state of the nation and the culture. This, too, is a source of the words' shock value. This poignant critique is delivered with constant linguistic rhythm—a controlled, almost monotonous inflection as performed by Kasia Kamockaja. The flow of the text (which represents a letter from the speaker to her sister) is punctuated by a unison refrain on the word "*balocie*" (mud):

Dear sister, I am writing you a letter,
*To tell you, that everything is fine [*narmalna—"fine," also "normal"*] here,*
Only the rain falls not one day, and not two,
And not a week, . . . but this is normal.
We live in mud, we like it.
About it we sing and paint canvases,
And that is why under the rain we are like fish in water,
And we really respect
Mud.

Here if you are sober, then you are dumb.
If you have a mind, then you must lose your conscience,
Every day in the mud we raise
For the mud new generations.

Dear sister, here everything is fine [kharasho—*Russian, meaning "fine"*]
Here Moscow is close, and Moscow is in our heads,
Moscow is on television and in the papers,
Here the children learn Muscovite [maskalskija—*pejorative term*] *songs.*
And this is normal, sister,
Because the winds don't bring freedom,
Because dirt will remain dirt
Because the fatherland is—mud,
Because there is no opposition,
Because no one is sober,
Because everyone has lost their minds,
They are all drugged.
People in the mud.

Dear sister, here some are screaming,
Others cry, and others dance,
And in this mess you can't hear a word.
And this means,
That rain will fall a few more years,
And there will be rain and there will be slush,
And **our** *mud will live on as usual,* [*understood now as "we"; the writer of "the letter" now includes himself or herself in the population*]
Mud.

We will raise high our flag of the mud,
Every morning we will go to work,
So everyone will know, in this century,
The feat [*heroic feats; progress*] *of the people of the*
Mud.

Dear sister. You lived here yourself,
You know the smell of moldy moss,
You know the taste of rotten water,
But that's all! Enough!
Enough words about our overcast country,
In rags, suffering, suffering, in rags [halecu, harotu, harkotu, halotu—*alliteration*]

Here you either choose or you don't choose,
But mud has chosen us
Mud
Everyday we sink in the mud deeper and deeper,
But it won't kill us, it won't suffocate us,
We will survive it all,
And in a few years we will learn to live in mud up to our ears.

People in the mud.

As the bracketed explanations indicate, the text contains many expressions and turns of phrase chosen for their associative power. The lyrics are a raw social and cultural critique that Volski remarks "continues to have relevance in contemporary Belarus" (Volski, E-mail). The meaning of the words and the choice of descriptors and of familiar turns of phrase illustrate Volski's use of "habitual word association" to direct the listener's response. The connection between rain and mud and the emphasis on rain imagery are particularly significant. The everyday usage "*shery dzien*" refers to a gray, overcast, and sad day; it is also used in everyday discourse to describe the state of the nation. The association between grayness and current political and social conditions has become a recurring metaphor in Belarusan rock, where the representation of positive change is symbolized by sunlight.[8] Volski frames the text of the song with the description of endless rain—playing on the popular recognition of this imagery as social and political commentary.

The artistic use of language in this song is supported by the music. Kamockaja's straight, controlled inflection produces a raplike delivery that Volski describes as being integral to the piece:

Indeed, the style of the music was deliberately intended to prevent the musical inventions from distracting the listener from the words. The text was, then, presented "nude" [*aholenym*] so that it was not burdened by melody [the suggestion is that the listener would not be distracted by the melody].

Volski explains that when this song was composed, rap was relatively new to the Belarusan rock scene. Subsequently, however, rap has become a common feature of Belarusan rock and is not considered an exotic option for rockers. As Volski explains, "It sounds natural. Presently many hard-core bands [understood here in terms of a level of activity and style but not suggesting the exclusive use of rap] use rap in order to reach clarity, 'read' [that is, 'speak'] their socially deep texts" (Volski, E-mail). In terms of narrative, choice of words, manipulation of language, and delivery, "Ludzi na balocie" exemplifies how language use—and the sedimented layers of meaning that language can activate—may heighten the relevance of music for the song-writer and the listener alike. An eloquent description of the process behind the creation of this song, Volski's remarks also emphasize that the intent to use language is as much instinctive and intuitive as it is conscious.

Belarusan rock offers performers the opportunity to use language and lan-guage choice as a vehicle for political commentary, allusion, and metaphor. Though politics are a key concept for this music, not all songs are charged with obvious political meanings. Many songs contain words and descrip-tions that allude to familiar experience, culturally relevant responses, per-sonal emotion, and community ritual. Members of the rock community are conscious of the potential that their songs have for signification; they know the canonical assumptions that have emerged about culture and language, and they respond to them as much as they explore them through their works. In the final analysis, the most important function of language choice is that it serves as a meta-frame that heightens the impact of the words and empow-ers the listener who is familiar with them.

The song "Prostyja Slovy" (Ordinary words) is such a good example of this that it borders on cliché. It celebrates the subtlety of language and suggests once again that Belarusan groups do not wield language casually. This song—which originally appeared as the final cut of the 1998 concept CD *Narodny Albom* (People's Album) and was later used on NRM's *Akustychnyia Piesni* (Acoustic Songs)—is a peaceful ballad. Volski's lead vocals are accompanied by steel string guitar, tambourine, and sparse backup vocals on the refrain. The text is a sim-ple expression of comfort through familiar words and imagery, a homecoming through language. Volski wrote the music for this song as well as most of the other pieces on the album. The lyrics were written by Mikhail Aniempadzistau, who Volski describes as a cult figure, poet, designer, and artist. Aniempadzistau conceptualized *Narodny Albom* and wrote all of the words to the original songs. The album itself is a statement on language. On the back cover and the insert of the disc is written "our language for us," emphasizing the ownership of lan-guage and the right to express it. "*Narodny*" can mean "traditional" as well as "of the people," and the authors of the CD played with the cultural authority afforded to tradition. Despite the fact that only two songs were truly folk-derived and that Aniempadzistau wrote all the others, the songs are referred to as "traditional" by the CD insert. As a result, some music writers have assumed that these songs were derived from folk sources. Volski even recounts that one critic who reviewed the disc positively assumed that Aniempadzistau had "collected" the songs on a cultural expedition in Western Belarus. In an E-mail message, Volski's explained that he believed that new songs can harbor the same depth of meaning and significance as traditional ones.

The recurring use of the word "*prostyja*" is crucial for the power of this song, and the word resists easy translation. No single English word is equivalent to "*prostyja*," which evokes something of all of the following terms: ordinary, straight, simple, truthful, understandable, immediate, sincere, unmistakable, and familiar. The simplicity of the words and the immediate images that are evoked are powerful because they suggest fundamental and common experiences—a welcome cliché that is relevant, so simple, and so ordinary:

Ordinary words, ordinary things
Bread on the table, fire in the stove
It is so simple, it is so good
Like putting your head under the covers

In the dusk blue of wintertime
In the house of your parents [forefathers] everything is so familiar
A place to get warm, a place to hide
In the house of your father and the home of your mother

Everything is so hopeful everything so deep
What could be added, maybe nothing
One can live longer, a new day will come
Goodnight ladies
Goodnight gents.

This brief example suggests a sensitivity to the expressive and poetic power of words: the sound of their pronunciation (their differentiation from Russian), their melodicity (as adding a lyrical quality), and the artistic and experiential sincerity of their combination and meaning.

Taken together, the examples considered in this essay demonstrate the significance of language for Belarusan rock. Here, the meanings of the music and the listeners' responses to them are informed by the content of the words, their delivery, the language used, and the simultaneity of associations and revelations that link language to its significance. Despite the variety of styles and intents represented by these examples, the bands presented here have one thing in common—they provide audiences with a consistent access to the Belarusan language and to the idea that both musical experience and social awareness are in some way about having a voice. This voice emphasizes an awareness of the power of oral expression as well as a consciousness of the possibility of being actively engaged in the political and social issues alive in Belarus. Belarusan rock music can generate responses according to a specific lexicon of cultural meaning:

- Language choice as the construction of meaning through association—an aural trigger that connects the idea of cultural rebellion with musical rebellion;
- Language choice as a basis for the definition of Belarusan rock as a genre, as well as the suggestion of links between the genre and social/cultural responsibility;
- The extension of the significance of language and genre, by informing other resources such as traditional and historical reference;
- The connections between language, aural qualities, and performance.

To borrow from Fischer once again, this lexicon represents some of the "sedimented layers of meaning" through which language contributes to the rock experience. For the Belarusan rock fan, the expectation is that the aesthetic experience of this music is bound up with the Belarusan language and the complex package of meanings that it entails, including the meaning of identity, history, experience, youth, and activism. Language can offer all of this, not only because it is about having a voice but also because in Belarusan rock it is about determining, using, and speaking the language in which that voice might be heard.

Acknowledgments

The excerpt from "Ludzi na balocie" (lyrics by Lavon Volski; performed by Novaje Nieba on their CD *Piesni roznykh hadou*) appears here with permission. English translation by Maria Paula Survilla. The excerpt from "Prostyja slovy" (lyrics by Mikhail Aniempadzistau, music by Lavon Volski, performed on the group project CD, *Narodny Albom*) appears here with permission. English translation by Maria Paula Survilla.

Notes

All interviews and song lyrics cited in this essay were originally in Belarusan unless otherwise noted. All translations are by Maria Paula Survilla.

1. The title of this essay is a reference to the song "Prostyja slovy" (Ordinary words, lyrics by Mikhail Aniempadzistau and music by Lavon Volski).

2. The concept of a "musical package" is also central to an intertextual model of popular song analysis (see Dettmar and Richey 3–5).

3. The official name change was decided by the Belarusan Parliament (Supreme Soviet) on 19 September 1991. The preferred adjective form for "Belarus" (pron. Be-la-rōōs') is *bielaruski*, rendered in English as "Belarusan" (pron. Be-la-rōōs'-an).

4. Geydar Jemal offers three criteria for judging the music of the amateur hero-rock musician of the former Soviet states. Good rock, he suggests, has a high energy level, values spontaneity and sincerity over professionalism, and emphasizes lyrics over music. Such lyrics are often heavy with introspection and the Slavic tragic-comedic worldview (12–14).

5. Qtd. in "Naviny," *Svaboda* 29.560 (1999).

6. Pete Seeger performed in Poland, Czechoslovakia, and the Soviet Union in the early 1960s. He provided a model of the socially aware musician as commentator and critic, and his style of delivery and the power of his social messages solidified the emergence of the modern urban bard in Eastern Europe (see Ryback 35–49).

7. At about this time, several other Belarusan bands also released retrospectives, including Palac's *Lepshvia* [The Best] (2000) and NRM's *Akustychnyia Piesni Kanca XX ST.* (Acoustic [Unplugged] Songs for the End of the Twentieth Century) (1999).

8. Most recently, the use of sun and cloud images as a metaphor for social and political conditions can be heard throughout the concept/collaborative CD *Ja Naradziusia Tut: Fotoalbom* (I Was Born Here: Photo Album).

Works Cited

Aksentsev, Felix. Personal interview. June 1993.

Bahushevich, Fracishak. *Tvory* (Works). Miensk: Mastackaja Litaratura, 1991.

Brown, J. F. *Surge to Freedom: The End of Communist Rule in Eastern Europe.* Durham, NC: Duke UP, 1991.

Dettmar, Kevin, and William Richey. *Reading Rock and Roll: Authenticity, Appropriation, and Aesthetics.* New York: Columbia UP, 1999.

Fischer, Michael M. J. "Ethnicity and the Post-Modern Arts of Memory." *Writing Culture: The Poetics and Politics of Ethnography.* Ed. James Clifford and George Marcus. Berkeley: U of California P, 1986. 194–233.

Frith, Simon. *Performing Rites: On the Value of Popular Music.* Cambridge: Harvard UP, 1997.

———. "Towards an Aesthetic of Popular Music." *Music and Society: The Politics of Composition, Performance, and Reception.* Ed. Richard Leppert and Susan McClary. London: Cambridge UP, 1987. 133–49.

Jemal, Geydar. "The Roots." *Soviet Rock.* Moscow: Progress, 1990. 11–28.
Kamockaja, Kasia. Personal interview (interviewed with Lavon Volski). May 1993.
Knysh, Siarhiej. Personal interview. June 1993.
Korjan, Viachaslau. Personal interview. June 1993.
Krauchanka, Siarhiej. Personal interview. June 1993.
Marples, David. *Belarus: From Soviet Rule to Nuclear Catastrophe.* Edmonton: U Alberta P, 1997.
Middleton, Richard. *Studying Popular Music.* Philadelphia: Open UP, 1990.
Rich, Vera. *Like Water Like Fire: An Anthology of Byelorussian Poetry from 1828 to the Present Day.* London: George Allen and Unwin, 1971.
Ryback, Timothy W. *Rock Around the Bloc: A History of Rock Music in Eastern Europe and the Soviet Union.* New York: Oxford UP, 1990.
Shuker, Roy. *Understanding Popular Music.* New York: Routledge, 1999.
Survilla, Maria Paula. *Of Mermaids and Rock Singers.* New York: Routledge, 2002.
Troitsky, Artemy. *Back in the U.S.S.R.: The True Story of Rock in Russia.* London: Omnibus, 1987.
Volski, Lavon. E-mail to the author. 9 June 2002.
———. Personal interview (interviewed with Kasia Kamockaja). May 1993.
Volski, Lavon, and Iura Chizin, eds. *Belaruski Rok-n-roll: Texty Bonda, Krama, Mroja, Novaje Nieba, Ulis.* Miensk: Kovcheg, 1994.
Zaprudnik, Jan. *Belarus at the Crossroads in History.* Oxford: Westview, 1993.

Discography

Ja Naradziusia Tut: Fotoalbom. Various Artists. Kovcheg, 2001.
Krama. *Hej Tam Nalivai.* Kovcheg, 1993.
———. *Kamendant.* Kovcheg, 1995.
———. *Xvory Na Rok-n-rol.* Kovcheg, 1994.
Mroja [NRM]. *Akustychnyia Kancerty Kanca XX ST.* Kovcheg, 1999.
———. *LaLaLaLa.* Kovcheg, 1995.
———. *Odzirdzidzina.* Kovcheg, 1996.
———. *Pashpart Hramadzianina NRM.* Kovcheg, 1995.
———. *28th Star.* Melodya, 1990.
———. *Vybranyja Piesni 1989–1993.* Minsk, 1993.*
Narodny Albom. Various Artists. Kovcheg, 1998.
Novaje Nieba. *Go Home.* Minsk: Novaje Nieba, 1995.
———. *Maja Kraina.* Kovcheg, 1996.
———. *Piesni Roznych Hadou.* Kovcheg, 1999.
———. *Son I Tramvai.* Kovcheg, 1994.
Ulis. *Blukannie.* Kovcheg, 1996.
———. *Dances on the Roof '93.* Dainova, 1993.
———. *Chuzanitsa.* Melodya, 1991
———. *Kraina Douhai Bielai Chmary.* Polskie Nagrania, 1991.

*While "Miensk" is the proper spelling in Belarusan, record publishing firms that operate primarily in Russia use the older, Russified spelling, "Minsk."

Cockney Rock

—Dave Laing

Since the global success in the 1960s of the Beatles, Rolling Stones, and other beat groups, it has been customary to refer to the dominant pop form as "Anglo American" music as if this was a homogenous bloc.[1] Indeed, there has been a convergence of generic style in forms such as progressive rock, blue-eyed soul, and heavy metal between musicians from North America and Britain over the past four decades. Associated with this musical convergence, however, has been a complex relation to American vocal styles by singers from Britain involving both imitation and resistance. This relation was discussed in technical detail in a 1984 essay by the sociolinguist Peter Trudgill.

Trudgill's essay first demonstrated through examination of recordings by the Beatles, the Stranglers, Dire Straits, and others that "British pop singers . . . are aiming at an American pronunciation" (Trudgill 145). However, Trudgill immediately qualified this statement with the proviso that "the end-product of this language modification is by no means entirely successful." He illustrated this contention with an analysis of the occurrence in British vocalization of the "non-prevocalic /r/," a linguistic feature of the American southern (soul/blues) speech, which British rock singers were eager to emulate. This feature occurs in words such as "car."

Trudgill was able to show both that British singers' misperception of the rules governing this usage led to their failure to imitate fully their American models such as Muddy Waters or Otis Redding and that the level of successful emulation declined in the 1970s compared with the mid-1960s. Trudgill attributed this decline to two factors. The first was the claimed dominance of British pop in the mid-1960s when the so-called British Invasion established a hegemonic position for a kind of hybrid pronunciation typified by the mid- and late-period Beatles. The second was the emergence a decade later of punk and new wave singers in Britain. These musicians' vocal styles involved a reduction in the use of American pronunciation features and

207

"an introduction of features associated with low-prestige south of England accents" (Trudgill 154).

Trudgill established the linguistic division between mainstream rock and punk by analyzing a range of albums issued in Britain in 1978–79 in terms of their use of features associated either with American pronunciation or with "low prestige south of England accents." Among these, the most "American" were the Rolling Stones's *Some Girls*, Dire Straits's *Dire Straits*, and the Stranglers's *Rattus Norvegicus*. The albums with the greatest provenance of English features were by the Clash (*The Clash*), Sham '69 (*Hersham Boys*), and Ian Dury (*Do It Yourself*). But while the Clash and Sham '69 used both American and British pronunciation features, Ian Dury's "single model was clearly that of the speech of working class London" (Trudgill 157). Trudgill further attributed Dury's vocal dialect to a combination of "the aggressive style of punk rockers . . . [and] the music-hall tradition which has often used Cockney pronunciation for comic effect" (158).

This essay discusses the use of "cockney pronunciation" and associated semantic and musical features in rock music since the 1950s with particular reference to its culmination in the work of Ian Dury. That discussion is preceded by an examination of the discursive construction of "cockney" in English popular culture and of the prehistory of cockney song.

The Cultural Construction of Cockney

Most popular culture accounts of the formation and representation of "identity" are celebratory of "hybrid," "diasporic," or "transgressive" identities and attendant subcultures. According to a recent essay on the "politics" of popular music published as part of an introductory textbook, "Black, Chicano and Asian cultural critics have shown that music and expressive culture are ways in which oppressed groups construct community, preserve collective memory, and narrate diaspora" (Balliger 62).

This canonical position reflects the conclusions of a number of recent studies of popular music, of which George Lipsitz's *Dangerous Crossroads* has been perhaps the most influential. Despite conflating the culture of two very different cities, Lipsitz has much to say about musical developments in Britain (among other countries).[2] With reference to "Afro-Caribbean and Southwest Asian immigrants to Britain," he claims that "popular music in Britain plays an important role in building solidarity within and across immigrant communities, while at the same time serving as a site for negotiation and contestation between groups" (Lipsitz 126).

This essay deals with the production of a very different music from those highlighted by Balliger and Lipsitz. Cockney is produced as the representation or trace of an identity that asserts itself as indigenous and regressive-nostalgic. Additionally, this claim to indigenous authenticity is distinct from those of, for example, Native Americans or the Australian aborigines. Indigenous cockney identity is presented as that of the original inhabitant of a city that has embodied both national and imperial power and oppression.

London has been the capital city of a nation-state and the metropolitan center of an empire, and it is now a leading cosmopolitan city in the era of postmodern globalization.[3] According to recent historians of the city, by 1851 half of London's population had been born elsewhere (Sheppard 289), while it now has almost two million citizens from "ethnic minorities" (Ackroyd 715). Between them, these citizens speak more than a hundred first languages. They comprise diasporas of cultures or nation states from the former British Empire in Asia, Africa, Australasia, and the Caribbean; political refugees from conflicts in Africa and Asia; economic migrants from Latin America and Eastern Europe; and citizens of other member countries of the European Union. To this must also be added the internal migrants from other parts of the nation-state, of which London is the principal center of administration and of finance.

According to an important political and cultural study of the cockney phenomenon, within this complex mosaic of multilingualism and multiculturalism, "the cockney has no legitimate place in the declassed and multiracial society that post-imperialism Britain has officially become" (Stedman-Jones 273). From this perspective, there should be no place for archaic fantasies of roots in the globalized city: in a society of hybridity and diaspora, the presentation of the cockney as an original, authentic population is doubly illegitimate, first, in its implicit assertion of a pure "nativism" but also in its primary existence not as community but as culture or as sound-and-image. The passage from Balliger quoted earlier uses a discourse of expressivity where there is a clear distinction between "oppressed groups" and the "expressive culture" that these groups can manipulate for purposes of identity construction. Leaving aside the extent to which this stark conceptualization is open to challenge at a theoretical level, it cannot be easily used as a template for mapping the operation of cockney popular culture.

In the case of cockney, any dialectic there might have been between a sociological "group" of plebeian Londoners and its expressive culture has long since collapsed. Indeed, the history of cockney since the mid-nineteenth century shows how the "group" has been constructed by representations emanating from the developing cultural industries. Stedman-Jones quotes a 1933 author who asserted that the cockney was "ruined by the knowledge that people have heard a lot about him [*sic*] and are interested in him . . . he is always, painfully and obviously, trying to live up to the idea of a stage cockney" (309).

There is no scholarly consensus as to the origin of the term "cockney" to describe native Londoners. The term is first documented in the sixteenth century, and one explanation was that it is connected to "Cockaigne," a mythical land of plenty in medieval English folklore. Francis Grose, the author of a collection of "popular superstitions" published in 1787, gave two further versions of the origin of this "very ancient nick-name for a citizen of London." Both had negative connotations. The first describes a person "delicately bred and brought up" but "unable to bear the least hardship." The second concerns a city-bred person so totally ignorant of rural life that

having been ridiculed for calling the neighing of a horse laughing, and told that it was called neighing, next morning, on hearing the cock crow, to shew instruction was not thrown away on him, exclaimed to his former instructor, how that cock neighs! Whence the citizens of London have ever since been called cock-neighs or cockneys. (Mullan and Reid 75)

The latter story introduces one of the central motifs attached to cockney identity—a certain insularity or ignorance of all but one's immediate surroundings. It is echoed, for example, in the opening of the novel *Alton Locke, Tailor and Poet* by the Victorian Christian socialist Charles Kingsley: "I am a Cockney born among Cockneys. Italy and the Tropics, the Highlands and Devonshire, I know only in dreams" (qtd. in Stedman-Jones 283).

The negative attributes of the cockney may possibly be traced to the long-established dominant position of London in British society as an administrative and trading center. For other regions of the country (and later the empire), London could be seen as a parasite, feeding off the productive industrial and agricultural areas. In this scenario, the cockney was a nonproductive trader and middleman with a propensity to exploit innocent country people. The "crafty cockney" was the nickname of Eric Bristow, a leading darts player of the 1980s when that sport was featured frequently on British television.

By the nineteenth century, the archetypal cockney was encapsulated in the figure of the "coster," or "costermonger," a street-trader who sold to the poorest sections of the community. The character-type of the coster has been traced by Pearl Binder to the seventeenth-century drama of Shakespeare and his contemporaries (Binder 12–14). Binder relates how the "native" costers faced an economic challenge from Irish immigrants and gives examples of cockney anti-Irish sentiments. In a revealing choice of verb, she writes of how "Cockney culture successfully weathered (even incorporated) successive waves of immigrants throughout the 19th century" (110). The suggestion is that cockney culture adopted a defensive posture whereby immigrants could be either fought off or "incorporated" in such a way that the culture itself remained essentially unchanged. This ideal of conservative assimilation emphasizes again the contrast with the radical hybridity celebrated by Lipsitz and others. In the twentieth century, this central feature of cockney culture made it an obvious vehicle for attempts to oppose and reject the perceived "Americanization" of Britain.

Gareth Stedman-Jones points out that this cultural conservatism was articulated with a subordinate sociopolitical position, a position constructed in part by the negative connotations of cockney dialect:

In the modern period, the "cockney" was one who could not wield political authority, above all because he or she could not speak with authority. He or she was thus always other, whether this other was to be repulsed and excluded, taught and improved or celebrated, encompassed and led. (278)

This conservative-subordinate position has been produced and reproduced in myriad representations of cockney in the sphere of popular culture and social commentary. The primary site of this process of reproduction has been the cultural industries of prose fiction, film, television, theater, and song. Cockney rock is just one aspect of this process.

The generative matrix for the production and reproduction of cockney identity through popular culture was set in motion in the mid-nineteenth century. In the 1850s, the journalist and protoethnographer Henry Mayhew compiled his extensive *Life and Labour of the London Poor*, while Charles Dickens began to create a gallery of low-life London characters. Literary researchers have suggested that Dickens used Mayhew's research to inform the settings of his fictions (Humpherys 163).

The cockney dialect was given a written, apparently phonetic, form in nineteenth-century literature, most famously in the work of Dickens, whose first cockney-speaking character was Sam Weller in the picaresque novel *Pickwick Papers* (1837). Weller is a manservant to the book's central figure, and Stedman-Jones argues that "by identifying this diction unilaterally with Weller, he [Dickens] left the way open to later equations between cockneyism and specifically lower-class patterns of speech and wit" (287).

The habits of diction and pronunciation attributed by Dickens to Weller form one of three dimensions that define the cockney dialect from this period onward. The others are two types of secret language: backslang and rhyming slang. Backslang involves the reversal of standard words (the most common survivor is "yob" for "boy"), while rhyming slang disguises meaning in a cumulative manner. The meaning is hidden behind a rhyme word that itself is the final part of a short phrase. In actual speech, the rhyme word itself is excluded, and only the first half of its phrase is articulated. Hence "stairs" is rendered as "apples" (the name chosen by Ian Dury for his only stage play), the remnant of the phrase "apples and pears," while "face" is "boat" from "boat race" and "eyes" are "minces" from "mince pies."

The cockney dialect was first codified in 1889 in a phonetic dictionary of "kaukneigh" compiled by Andrew Tuer (Stedman-Jones 295), and its perceived subordinate status motivated the plot of George Bernard Shaw's play *Pygmalion* (1913). In this drama, Professor Henry Higgins seeks to raise the status of flower-seller Eliza Doolittle by eradicating her cockney accent. That Higgins was not a reactionary eccentric is shown by the philosophy of the socialist educational reformer Margaret McMillan, a contemporary of Shaw. McMillan was an early advocate of universal nursery education, but she also believed that working-class children should receive elocution lessons as part of their schooling. She wrote that "the speech of the slums is not a dialect. It is the symptom of serious disorder, and is to be treated as a kind of deformity" (Steedman 219).

Beyond those linguistic features, the characterscape of the cockney was crystallized in the nineteenth century through repetition in fiction, comic writing, cartoon drawings, and songs. This characterscape included humor and wit (in part, an effect of the creativity of backslang and rhyming slang), a pretentious dandyism suitable for mockery, an antipathy toward the forces of law and order often articulated with criminality of various types, and an intense attachment to locality frequently articulated with jingoistic patriotism and conservatism. A further element, closely allied to the last of these, is an overpowering nostalgia for an era before the changes caused by such developments as town planning and the twentieth-century "Americanization" of English popular culture.

The reproduction of these cockney characteristics continued throughout the twentieth century and into the television era. In the 1950s, the first British national channel featured cockney policemen in the drama series *Dixon of Dock Green*; in the 1960s the coster reappeared as a rag-and-bone man in a situation comedy *Steptoe and Son* (shown in a U.S. version as *Sanford and Son*), to be updated in the 1980s in another comedy series, *Only Fools and Horses*. The cockney trope of caustic wit combined with pretension and excessive political conservatism was featured in *Till Death Do Us Part*, a 1960s series in which the principal character had verbal duels with the "Scouse git," his Liverpudlian son-in-law (the series was adapted for American audiences as *All in the Family*). And when the cockney character had seemed increasingly archaic and suitable only for broad comedy, BBC television created *Eastenders*, a soap opera set in the cockney heartland that has been one of British television's top-rated shows for twenty years. As Stedman-Jones points out, despite its veneer of contemporary "realism," "the physical setting and some of the central families in this drama hark back to a mythical time in the 1950s just before the traditional 'cockney' neighbourhood supposedly slid into terminal decline" (273).

The remarkable continuity of the characterization of the cockney is evidenced by a passing description of school students as "cockney wide-boys in the white jeans and the coloured shirts" in a very recent and critically acclaimed London novel by Zadie Smith (232). The appellation "wide-boys" might have been found at any time in the previous century and a half. The association of criminality with the cockney is equally vigorous through, for example, the films of Guy Ritchie and the pulp novels of Jeremy Cameron which are replete with stereotypical cockney wit and cockney villains.[4]

The Cockney Voice in Music to the 1950s

If there is a cockney discourse in popular culture whose primary tropes are centered on linguistic, occupational, and characterological features, how is this reproduced in music? There are several elements that could be defined as contributing to music recognized as "cockney." These include:

- the transposition of the cockney accent into vocalization;
- the prominence of dialect words in song lyrics;
- specifically cockney lyric themes, for example, certain types of references to London, especially nostalgic or comic ones;
- the persona of the singer—for example, his or her presentation as a stereotypical cockney through stage dress;
- a musical form or motif typical of earlier phases of cockney song.

In considering these features, three overlapping historical phases of popular music will be discussed. This section deals with the music hall era (approximately 1850–1910) and the age of Tin Pan Alley and musical theater to 1960. The final section considers the years from the arrival of rock and roll in the mid-1950s to the present.

The works of both Dickens and Mayhew were circulated in a growing mass market for cultural goods. Among the newest of the mass cultural industries of London at midcentury was the presentation of live entertainment aimed primarily at the more affluent sections of the working class. The venues for this entertainment were the rapidly increasing numbers of music halls. It was here that the most widely disseminated versions of cockney dialect and character in the nineteenth century were to be found.

Novelty songs dealing with cockney and coster themes were contemporaneous with the composition of *Pickwick Papers* and other early novels. The diaries of Charles Rice, a British Museum employee and semiprofessional singer, record that in 1840 a friend of his performed a song called "The Costermonger's Reminiscences." Rice's own repertoire included "Billy Taylor," a nautical ballad of a young woman who, disguised as a man, follows her lover by enlisting as a sailor. Rice's version included what his editor calls "a number of cockneyisms" (Senelick xxv). These included the substitution of *v* for *w* in the phrase "Vat vind has blown you here" and the vowel sound shift in pronouncing "discovery" as "diskivery."

Rice sang primarily in public houses where singers would gather to take turns in presenting current ballads. These events, known as glee clubs or "free and easies," were the direct precursor of the music halls that flourished in London in the 1860s, a decade of the extension of the franchise and the emergence of new forms of mass entertainment. These halls were roughly equivalent to the vaudeville theaters of the United States and served a similar lower-class audience. The most successful music hall entertainers not only performed comic or sentimental songs but did them in character, frequently acting out stereotypes of the cockney. According to music hall historian Peter Bailey, the contrasting but emblematic figures were two male singers, Gus Elen and Albert Chevalier, who took, respectively, a sardonic and sentimental stance in their "depictions of the costermonger in the 1890s" (Bailey 129).

Between them, Elen, Chevalier, and other singers established and embedded in the popular performing arts the first four of the five features of cockney music enumerated earlier. The feature common to all was the first: the emphasis on dialect pronunciation. One of the earlier music hall stars, the Great Vance, confirmed his "cockney" idiom by reversing *v* and *w* in such words as "werry" (very), while *h*'s were dropped liberally in " 'arf" (half), " 'e" (he), and many other words (Stedman-Jones 294). The singers were regarded by the intelligentsia as somehow the essence of cockneyism. George Bernard Shaw, the first to put the dialect into the serious theater, said that Albert Chevalier captured the cadences of modern cockney (299).

Vocabulary specific to the cockney dialect was sprinkled through the songs written for Chevalier, such as the sentimental "My Old Dutch," where "Dutch" means "wife," and the raucous "Any Old Iron." This comic song represented the street cry of the coster and was recorded as a novelty item by actor Peter Sellers in the 1950s. More recently, the song has been "outed" as a coded song of gay sexuality: "iron hoof" equals "poof" (male homosexual) in rhyming slang.[5]

Cockney themes and references were most often evident as geographical markers in such song titles as "Knocked 'Em in the Old Kent Road," popularized by Chevalier; "Pretty Little Villa Down at Barking"; and Elen's "Down the Dials." London's sheer size was evoked in Elen's hit "If It Wasn't for the 'Ouses in Between," a piece that typifies cockney music hall song:

It really is a werry pretty garden / And Chingford to the eastwards can be seen / Wiv a ladder and some glasses / You could see to 'Ackney Marshes / If it wasn't for the 'ouses in between.

Finally, the stage costumes of Elen, Chevalier, and others signified the stereo-typical cockney occupations and roles, including the costermonger and the "swell," "a lordly figure of resplendent dress and confident air, whose exploits centred on drink and women" (Bailey 101).

In the early years of the twentieth century, Britain's popular music business, centered in London, began to change under the impact of new trends imported from the United States. Ronald Pearsall has discussed the success of ragtime in England after 1910 in terms of a confrontation between cockney conservatism and American-inspired modernization. Pearsall contrasts ragtime's "thoroughly modern references appealing especially to young men and women" with the "pseudo-Cockney music-hall hits" that had "a Victorian veneer about them with stereotyped mother-in-law and disgruntled-husband situations" (186).

By the 1930s, however, London's Tin Pan Alley was reacting against the "friendly invasion" of American music and musical films. Its doyen was the music publisher Charles Armitage, who composed under the sobriquet Noel Gay. With lyricists Arthur Rose and Douglas Furber, Gay wrote the show *Me and My Girl*, which opened in London in 1937 and was successfully revived in the 1980s. The show's plot concerned a cockney coster who discovers that he is actually a member of the hereditary aristocracy, a powerful reiteration of cockney's subordinate conservatism. The hit of the show was "The Lambeth Walk" performed by Lupino Lane, a song that inspired a national dance craze.

Me and My Girl was the first of a line of musical shows and films that relied on variants of the cockney stereotype. The most commercially signifi-cant of these was *My Fair Lady*, the Broadway musical by Alan Jay Lerner and Frederick Loewe. First performed in 1956, it was one of the longest-running shows in both New York and London and was filmed in 1964. The original cast album sold over five million copies. *My Fair Lady* was based on Shaw's *Pygmalion*, and the stage production starred the middle-class English actress Julie Andrews as Eliza. Lerner and Loewe gave her songs for "before" and "after" her transformation from "yowling thick-headed cockney" to received-pronunciation speaker (Ganzl 289). "Wouldn't It Be Loverly" con-tinued the music hall tradition of emphasizing dialect features, and "I Could Have Danced All Night" was to be performed in a dialect much closer to that used by Noel Coward in his musical shows.

The representation of cockney speech was sometimes problematic in the history of *My Fair Lady*. In his autobiography, Alan Jay Lerner reported that

Andrews had problems in "learning how to speak Cockney. To assist her we found an American phoneticist who did in reverse offstage what Higgins was doing onstage" (Lerner 96). And in casting the part of Higgins for the film version, Lerner vetoed Cary Grant because "there is an unmistakable Cockney strain in his English and the role of Henry Higgins demanded the impeccable" (126).

My Fair Lady established a cockney stereotype for a global audience and led to the bathos of American television star Dick van Dyke's attempt at cockney pronunciation in the 1964 film version of P. L. Travers's children's fantasy *Mary Poppins*, where he appeared as a London chimney sweep opposite Julie Andrews as the middle-class governess of the film's title. The best that could be said of his rendition of the novelty number "Chim Chim Cheree" was that its attempt to capture cockney dialect was as unsuccessful as the efforts to replicate American southern speech by those British singers of the same era discussed by Peter Trudgill.

The impact in England of the internationalization of cockney represented by *My Fair Lady* can be shown through two examples. The determinedly modernist hero of Colin MacInnes's 1959 novel *Absolute Beginners* refers sarcastically to a London pub barman as speaking in an "authentic old-tyme My Fair Lady dialect" (MacInnes 12). Much later, in his 1997 composition "Had Away, Gan On," Jez Lowe, a singer and songwriter from the northeast of England, sings (in the Geordie dialect of his home region) of being misrecognized by "a Yankee on the aeroplane" who "smiled and said your humour tells me/you must be a cockney."[6]

Cockney Meets Rock

By 1951 an observer of the London scene could lament that "Cockney's decay has robbed the common tongue of vitality. American slang with all its vigour, has a juke-box rattle compared with the earthy freshness of the catchwords of the street boy of old" (Stedman-Jones 302). *My Fair Lady*'s projection of a cockney stereotype to an international audience coincided with a new stage in the American hegemony in Anglophone popular music. The play opened on Broadway in 1956, the year of Elvis Presley, Bill Haley, and rock and roll. For British popular music in general and cockney culture in particular, these events helped to precipitate a moment of crisis and fissure characterized by highly polarized reactions to the renewed transatlantic influence.

The complex and often contradictory British response to American culture became evident in two post-1945 movements that predated rock and roll. These were traditional jazz and skiffle. Traditional jazz (or trad) involved attempts at re-creating the supposed original sounds of New Orleans jazz in a reaction against both the commercialization of dance bands and the modernism of bebop. Skiffle had an equally authenticist and backward-looking momentum focused on American folk song of various kinds. In skiffle's earliest moments, its personnel overlapped with that of trad.[7]

While both trad and skiffle were inspired initially by a kind of purism, the two genres quickly became hybridized, with the introduction of elements from English popular culture, including some songs and vocabulary associated with cockney culture. In particular, the most commercially successful of skiffle performers, Lonnie Donegan, incorporated into his act music hall numbers like "My Old Man's a Dustman" and "Does Your Chewing Gum Lose Its Flavour on the Bedpost Overnight."

In contrast to the associations linking trad and skiffle with folk culture, rock and roll offered young English men and women a more or less unequivocal identification with the modernity of America. The lack of geographical mobility among the British working class meant that, initially, almost all the first generation rock and roll recording artists were recruited from the London region. Such figures as Tommy Steele, Adam Faith, Cliff Richard, Marty Wilde, Screaming Lord Sutch, and Johnny Kidd were all born or domiciled in London. None of them used their given name as their rock and roll name.

While most of these singers attempted to simulate the vocal sound of Elvis Presley, others, notably Steele and Faith, sang in a hybrid dialect that mingled American and London pronunciation. This hybridity was noted by Colin MacInnes in his 1961 essay "Young England, Half English," which astutely recognized that Tommy Steele represented a link between music hall and contemporary pop.

The complexity of British youth's response to rock and roll was also reflected in the formation of youth subcultures in London. The primary example was that of the Teddy Boys, or Teds, who "had grafted the shape of an American gangster's suit or zoot suit—with its exaggerated annexation of space—onto details stolen deliberately from a specialised Savile Row fashion of 1948: the

Edwardian look" (Savage 10). The Teds were associated with the first generation of rock and roll and its American stars, such as Bill Haley, Elvis Presley, Little Richard, and Jerry Lee Lewis, and they were much in evidence at several large "rock and roll revival" events in London in the late 1960s and early 1970s.

This apparently felicitous example of cultural hybridity had its darker side, however. As Phil Cohen showed in his pioneering theorization of youth subcultures, the Teds connoted the unmodernized, unskilled cockney working class, a designation also made in MacInnes's fictionalized ethnography *Absolute Beginners*. There, the speech of a character named Ed The Ted is rendered in comic cockney straight from the nineteenth century. In the novel's portrayal of the 1958 race riots in the West London district of Notting Hill, the Teds are shown as the instigators of violence against Afro-Caribbean immigrants. MacInnes has one of these (described by the narrator as a "yobbo") say, "So a few of ver blacks git chived. Why oll ver fuss?" (210). The trope of cockney chauvinism is reinforced when Ed (the follower of rock and roll) shouts at the London-born narrator, "go 'ome Yank," while MacInnes also cannot resist the parallel stereotype of the kindhearted cockney when one of the few whites to assist the beleaguered black community is "an old geezer with a cloth cap and choker" (48, 206).

The most pivotal musician in the complex negotiation between cockney and rock and roll was the songwriter Lionel Bart, who was born Lionel Begleiter in London's East End, the son of Latvian-born Jews. Prior to Ian Dury, Bart was the most important composer of the second half of the twentieth century to re-create the cockney stereotype. Unlike Dury, Bart had a deeply ambivalent relationship to American popular culture and in particular the new American music. As a young man, he declared after seeing the 1948 movie *Oliver Twist* that "one day, I'm going to write a musical based on that story and it will be better than any American musical" (Gorman 138).

During the 1950s, Bart had parallel musical careers in left-wing music theater and as a composer of pop hits. As a member of Unity Theatre, an amateur theater company, he imbibed the cultural anti-Americanism that was endemic in the Stalinist Communist movement. Bart's first broadcast song, "Oh for a Cup of Tea," a response to the arrival of American-style coffee bars, was written for a Unity satirical show (Gorman 192). Music hall was regarded by Unity Theatre as authentic English music, and Bart performed "Any Old Iron" during a tour of Poland in 1955 (Chambers 327).

In the mid-1950s, Bart's enthusiasm for the skiffle movement led him to cowrite Tommy Steele's first hit, "Rock with the Caveman." While musically this was an homage to Bill Haley, the lyrics betrayed ambivalence toward the latest cultural import from the United States. Bart's words portrayed a "prehistoric" scene where rock and roll was situated as the invention of our uncivilized ancestors.

While composing other pop hits such as Steele's "Handful of Songs" (1958) and Cliff Richard's "Living Doll" (1959), Bart maintained his links with Unity Theatre and another left-oriented group, Theatre Workshop, where he composed his first demotic musical show with the cockney author Frank Norman. *Fings Ain't Wot They Used T' Be* was a London equivalent of Damon Runyon's New York picaresque *Guys and Dolls*. The title song was a pastiche music hall number with a sing-along chorus and verses that portrayed the obliteration of the old London by the new transatlantic commercial leisure culture: "they changed our local palais [dance hall] / Into a bowling alley."

Bart's annus mirabilis was 1960 when his stage musical of Charles Dickens's *Oliver Twist* premiered. By now he had turned away from rock and pop modes to work with conventional music theater conventions, and though *Oliver!* contained many "London" songs, the most cockney of them was the semicomic "Gotta Pick a Pocket or Two" sung by the villainous master thief Fagin.

Elsewhere, too, the only traces of cockney in 1960s pop music were found in novelty or comic songs. In "What a Crazy World We're Living In," composer Alan Klein portrayed a caricature cockney family ("dad's gone down the dogtrack, mother's playing bingo / grandma's at the bottle, you should see the gin go!") while "Right! Said Fred," sung by the comedian Bernard Cribbins, told of incompetent removal men. The actor-singer Anthony Newley used a modified cockney accent to perform novelty versions of traditional songs like "Strawberry Fair" and "Pop Goes the Weasel." He was briefly imitated by Mike Sarne, whose "Come Outside" featured cockney vowel sounds from the actress Wendy Richard, later to star in the *Eastenders* soap opera, and by David Bowie who adopted the Newley mode for his first, self-titled album. Cockney interludes were also found on records by Cream and the Small Faces.[8] The Small Faces songwriters Steve Marriott and Ronnie Lane, like Ray Davies of the Kinks and Pete Townshend of the Who, nevertheless infused their music with a London element, but this was homologous with the modernity of Carnaby Street and "Swinging London" rather than with cockney.

Cockney Rebel, formed in 1973 in London by Steve Harley, was the first post rock and roll band to incorporate the word into its name. However, its music—a confection of currently modish styles, led by glam rock—bore no relation to cockney song, although critic Michael Bracewell thought that "Harley's gulps of caricatured intonation appear to cross Bob Dylan with Bob Cratchit" (Bracewell 20). There have been occasional incursions of cockney into British pop until the present day. These have ranged from deliberate significations like Blur's use of actor Phil Daniels on their *Parklife* album to the regular adjectival use of the word by music journalists. Chroniclers of British music in the 1990s write of Daniels's contribution to Blur as "cockerneee vocals" (Robb 130) and of "the cockney roughneck aspect" of vocal group East 17 (B. Thompson 57).

Aside from these occasional incursions, there have been three instances of a more substantial assertion of a nexus between cockney culture and rock music. These are punk, the cockney rock of Chas & Dave, and the oeuvre of Ian Dury.

In the mid-1970s, punk might have been expected to provide another option for the reinsertion of cockney into a popular music mainstream. Originating in London, the movement prided itself on its plebeian opposition to the dominant trends of progressive rock. However, the iconoclasm of early punk was at odds with the entrenched conservatism of cockney culture. The Clash, for instance, sang lyrics about London, but in terms of vocalization, as Trudgill pointed out, there was "a genuine split in motivation":

> The conflict is between a motivation towards a supposedly American model, and a motivation towards a supposedly British working-class model—which can be glossed as a conflict between "how to behave like a genuine pop singer" and "how to behave like a British urban working-class youth." The combination of linguistic forms that is typically found in punk-rock singing is an attempt to find a balance between the two. (159)

The most prominent figure in London punk, John Lydon (alias Johnny Rotten), had a different reason to avoid adding cockney to punk. Lydon grew up in an Irish immigrant family, and the title of his 1994 autobiography, *No Dogs, No Blacks, No Irish*, makes it clear that he refused an English (and cockney) identification. The title was taken from signs posted in the windows of London lodging-houses, and Lydon's use of it underlined an unpalatable fact about cockney's rejection of immigrant cultures that would not assimilate to it. While Lionel Bart, the child of Eastern European Jewish immigrants, found cockney a highly compatible inspiration for his music, it is notable that the considerable London Afro-Caribbean community has not adopted cockney traits to any significant degree. The difference may be due to first-language use as well as to racial discrimination. While Bart's parents had to learn English as a foreign language—and their children almost inevitably spoke with a cockney accent—sociolinguists have found that the younger generations of London's Afro-Caribbean community have created their own dialect as a variant of their parents' Caribbean English speech. The separation between London's black community and cockney was pinpointed in the 1984 hit record *Cockney Translation* by reggae sound system DJ Smiley Culture. Its lyrics played wittily with that gap by providing a London Caribbean gloss on cockney speech.

Among those who did enthusiastically combine cockney with punk, the most significant was Sham '69, a band led by Jimmy Pursey, which articulately and aggressively presented scenes from white working-class life. Although Pursey could not resist doing a comic cockney turn on his song "Sunday Morning Nightmare," "Hurry Up Harry" and "The Cockney Kids Are Innocent" ("why should we take shit? / everybody looks at us") were characterized by a banal naturalism. Pursey performed their lyrics with an energetic and imaginative singing style that nevertheless included American vocalization as well as the diction of working-class London (Trudgill 157). Pursey's songs also embodied a populist politics, whose ambiguity drew the enthusiastic support of skinhead followers of neo-fascist groups.

There was no such ambiguity in the political stance of subsequent groups that adhered to the Oi! genre. The genre's ethos of nostalgic white proletarian masculinity was exemplified by the Cockney Rejects, whose name indicates a mix of self-pity and masochism. Oi! bands, arising not only in London but in other regions of England and Scotland, were typified by their semiarticulate opposition to the state, "hippies," the "race relations industry," and even "Europe."[9] Oi! "gained a reputation as a music for racists, if not a music of racism" (Laing 112).

Chronologically coincident with punk but stylistically distant was the cockney rock and roll of Chas & Dave. This combination of cockney speech and rock music had a lone precedent in 1960s rock guitarist and singer

Joe Brown, who had recorded the hit version of "What a Crazy World We're Livin' In" and continued to insert a cockney element into his rock and roll persona. His backing group was named the Bruvvers (the spelling intended to indicate a cockney pronunciation).

Pianist Chas Hodges and guitarist Dave Peacock had played in rock and roll and country rock bands in the London area before writing and recording the albums *One Fing and Annuver* (1975) and *Rockney* (1977). Much of the lyric material was based on music hall comedy, but there were some original elements with specific contemporary references. Their later work mostly involved jingles for television commercials, songs celebrating soccer teams, and sing-along sequences. But the duo made one important instrumental advance by assimilating the 1950s piano style of Jerry Lee Lewis and Little Richard into the pub piano playing associated with "traditional" cockney music-making. After almost two decades, this aspect of rock and roll could be treated as material for nostalgia and added to the cockney musical repertoire.

The Case of Ian Dury

In many ways, the music of the late Ian Dury represents the apotheosis of cockney rock. It embodies many features that characterize cockney music, but at its best it transcends them, providing a kind of immanent cosmopolitan critique of the insularities of the ideological motifs that comprise the cockney stereotype.

Dury's career as a songwriter and singer began with the "pub rock" group Kilburn & the High Roads in 1971.[10] The band's name was taken from Kilburn High Road, a thoroughfare in a North London suburb associated with the Irish immigrant community. Its music was described by an early fan, Chris Foreman, later of Madness, as "reggae . . . [a]nd music hall type stuff, very English and the lyrics were very good" (Balls 129). Kilburn & the High Roads made one unsatisfactory album before dissolving in 1975. Ian Dury next concentrated on songwriting before forming the Blockheads with Chas Jankel, a guitarist who became Dury's most important songwriting partner. Jankel brought the vital funk and disco influence that powered Dury's most artistically and commercially successful work, featured on the albums *New Boots and Panties* (1977) and *Do It Yourself* (1979). Later albums such as *Laughter* (1980), *Lord Upminster* (1981), and *Apples* (1989)—based on a stage musical cowritten by Dury—were uneven in quality, although his final release, *Mr. Love Pants* (1998), was critically acclaimed. Ian Dury died in March 2000 of cancer.

Before some aspects of his work are examined in detail, three key biographical features must be mentioned. These features provide the subjective matrix from which Dury could evolve his complex and often contradictory relationship to cockney.

The first is the hybrid nature of Dury's family background. While his father was a working-class Londoner who drove buses and later became a chauffeur, Ian's mother was from a middle-class Protestant Irish family. This Irish background is an important but underacknowledged feature of English pop music—witness the roots of Shane McGowan, John Lydon, Morrissey, and the Gallagher brothers of Oasis among many others—and it emerges in Dury's music in two contrasting ways. First, there is a ferocious foregrounding of racist speech in the song "Blackmail Man," where the narrator refers to himself (among other sobriquets) as an "Irish cripple," a telling combination of national origin and physical disability. Second, and uniquely, he wrote and recorded a somewhat sentimental piece of Irish balladry, "O'Donegal," on his 1992 album *Bus Driver's Prayer*. The piece starts with a short solo on tin whistle, and the lyrics include stereotypical tributes to the beauty of the scenery and the friendliness of the people. Perhaps the superfluous inclusion of the prefix *O'* signifies Dury's own recognition of the conventional nature of the song.

Dury's biographer Richard Balls mistakenly regards his family origins and the fact that he was born in a lower-middle-class suburb of London as proof that "his roots were set firmly in middle England" (Balls 15), a phrase that has come to connote a particular social group of conservative-minded and narrowly patriotic English white-collar workers. This interpretation entirely misses the significance of Dury's Irish roots: as Lydon's book title confirms, the antipathy of the nineteenth-century costermongers to Irish immigrants lingered into the twentieth century so that to be Irish was to be excluded from "middle England."

The second aspect was his physical disability. Dury had contracted poliomyelitis at the age of seven in 1949, a time when the disease was not easily treatable. As a result, he had a withered left leg and arm. During his career as a musician, he deliberately drew attention to his condition, at first by dragging his leg across the stage in homage to one of his heroes, the American rock and roll singer Gene Vincent, who was also the subject of one of Dury's first major songs. More important, Dury referred both obliquely and directly to his disability in his lyrics. One early song was titled "Crippled with Nerves" while "Spasticus (Autisticus)," a song composed for the United Nations Year of the Disabled, was so full of direct description and controlled anger that it earned the accolade of being censored by the state broadcaster, the BBC, for being in bad taste.

The final aspect of Dury's formation to be mentioned is his education and work as an artist and illustrator. Prior to his debut as a singer with Kilburn & the High Roads in the early 1970s, he had trained with the renowned "pop artist" Peter Blake, the cocreator of the cover illustration for the Beatles's *Sgt. Pepper's Lonely Hearts Club Band.* Blake, who was to design the cover of the Ian Dury memorial tribute album, *Brand New Boots and Panties,* combined an affection for and obsession with popular culture with a painterly distance from it. This affection embraced American culture in particular, and Blake and his contemporaries were untouched by the anti-Americanism that had been featured in British cultural life (including cockney discourse) up to a few years earlier. The style Dury developed in his relatively brief career as a professional artist was distinctly similar to Blake's, and this combination of involvement and distance was transferred to his songwriting, notably in the creation of colorful narrators and third-person characters in such songs as "Billy Bentley," "Billericay Dickie," "Clever Trevor," and "Plaistow Patricia."

Blake's gathering together of numerous popular culture icons in the *Sgt. Pepper's* cover art is echoed in Dury's lyrics for his "list" songs whose lyrics pay similar homage to a heterogeneous range of musicians, objects, and places. These list songs include some of his biggest hits, such as "Reasons to Be Cheerful" and "Hit Me with Your Rhythm Stick," as well as "England's Glory" and "Common as Muck," the latter of which itemizes such stars beloved of pop art painters as Brigitte Bardot, Shirley Temple, and Fred Astaire.

If these biographical features tended to distance Dury from cockney, his music nevertheless contains many evocations of cockney motifs. In the following analysis, his music is considered in terms of the five dimensions of cockney music already discussed.

There is, first, a marked transposition of cockney pronunciation into vocalizations, as Trudgill's investigation shows. Trudgill's analysis found that

Dury's second solo album, *Do It Yourself* (1979), included an exceptionally high percentage of cockney elements (156). Over the whole Dury oeuvre, however, the cockney quotient varied significantly from album to album. His early work with Kilburn & the High Roads contained a significant amount of Anglo-American pronunciation in songs such as "Rough Kids" and "Crippled with Nerves," a song delivered in a sub-Elvis style. His early work also included an aberrant (and imprecise) Jamaican accent on "You're More Than Fair."

The cockney elements began to predominate on *New Boots and Panties*, in particular in Dury's most famous love song, "Wake Up and Make Love with Me." This contains dropped *h*'s ("'arfway," "'appens," "'ave") and other cockney features but, according to Jankel, Dury first sang it in an American accent. He shifted into cockney after the group's manager, Charlie Gillett, pointed out that this "sounded like Barry White" (Balls 158).

Another factor influencing the degree of cockney pronunciation used by Dury was the nature of a song's lyric statement. Cockney features predominated in songs that portrayed specific London characters (or caricatures), such as Billericay Dickie, Clever Trevor, and Plaistow Pam. Such broad cockney markers are less apparent in songs whose geographical and cultural references range more widely than the cockney coordinates of Billericay, Plaistow, and Ford Cortina. The vocal performances of the globetrotting multirhymed lyrics of "Hit Me with Your Rhythm Stick" (from "Bombay" to "Mandalay" to "Tiger Bay" and "Santa Fe") and the list of "Reasons to Be Cheerful Part 3" are still recognizably lower-class English (as opposed to Anglo-American) but contain few specifically cockney features.

A final characteristic of Dury's vocal style that distinctly affected his deployment of cockney speech is his widespread use of a semispoken delivery or recitative. Like rap, recitative need not conform to the contours of a melody line and thus can contain a wider range of word structures or local pronunciation elements than a fully sung lyric. It can also be used to foreground and emphasize particular words and pronunciations in contrast to the tendency for sung lyrics to be submerged by or subsumed into the melodic or instrumental dimension of a song. In Dury's work, recitative is closely linked to the use of funk rhythms and figures.

The second dimension of cockney music is the use of dialect words in lyrics. Dury's oeuvre offers numerous examples of rhyming slang and of other slang terms associated with cockney speech. The first and third verses of

"Billy Bentley," for instance, are composed mainly of a litany of contemporary "cries of London" from "how's yer father" and "fuckin' Ada" to "wot a carve-up." The male backing vocalists on "Clever Bastards" can be heard chanting "lucky bleeders" ("bleeder," according to one recent dictionary of slang, is "a person . . . often used with dislike or contempt. . . . Mainly Cockney. From around 1880") (Fergusson 18). "Blackmail Man" provides several instances where both the full rhyming slang phrase and the term to which it refers appear together. Dury sings, "I'm Greek . . . bubble and squeak," "Irish cripple . . . raspberry ripple," and "Scottish Jew . . . buckle my shoe."

More often, though, Dury's facility for rhyme exceeds the limits of the rhyming slang code and takes on a different, often surreal, resonance. In "Hit Me with Your Rhythm Stick," the rhyming logic is mainly geographical, as a sequence of lines ties together "Sudan . . . Japan . . . Milan . . . Yucatan" with "every woman, every man." The ferocious "Spasticus (Autisticus)" includes the rhyming sequence "I wiggle when I piddle 'cos my middle is a riddle" and elsewhere rhymes "dribble" with "nibble" and "quibble."

In some songs, Dury's excess of verbal invention produces phrases that are similar in structure to rhyming slang but lack the closure of the rhyme word. For example, "between her rum and her Ribena" (from "Billericay Dickie") is free of any denotative content but has a web of connotations from the alcoholic ("Ribena," a sweet fruit syrup used as a mixer) to the sexual, where "rum" and "Ribena" are double entendre—style gestures toward body parts. In these examples of carnivalesque excess, Dury's lyrics act to subvert and destabilize the established rigidities of cockney dialect vocabulary.

The third dimension of cockney concerns semantic markers in song lyrics that signify or connote cockneyism. Here, too, Dury's songs contain a plethora of local references. Some songs use these references as a marker of "authenticity" comparable to the use of place names in Bobby Troup's "Route 66" or Jimmy Webb's great sequence of Americana songs— "By the Time I Get to Phoenix," "Wichita Lineman," and "Galveston." "Thus What a Waste" has the line "I could be a ticket man at Fulham Broadway station," while a cautionary tale of drug addition is entitled "Plaistow Patricia" and ends with her rehabilitation in Mile End Road.

For the most part, though, Dury's use of London place-names is surreal rather than naturalistic. Several songs detach the place-names of districts and suburbs from their primary function as signifiers of geographical spaces and relocate these names through their potential for pun or rhyme. "The Bus Driver's Prayer," featured in the 1989 musical show *Apples*, is a reworking of the Lord's Prayer through syllabic similarities between, for example, "Wimbledon" and "will be done" and "Hendon" and "heaven." Elsewhere, the characters in the sequence of comic anecdotes of "This Is What We Find" include "Harold Hill of Harold Hill" and "Mrs. Elizabeth Wark of Lambeth Walk," the latter an intertextual reference showing Dury's awareness of the storehouse of cockney popular culture.

Although there was a considerable generation gap between Lionel Bart and Ian Dury—exemplified by very different responses to rock and roll—Dury, like Bart, was drawn to the musical theatre. In 1987, he composed songs for *Serious Money*, Caryl Churchill's satire on the greed and corruption associated with the "yuppies" of the Margaret Thatcher era in British politics. This was followed by his own musical play, *Apples*, presented at the Royal Court Theatre in London in 1989. Unlike *Serious Money*, *Apples* was not a commercial success. However, it presented a vision of contemporary London through a cast of character types similar to those created by Shakespeare's contemporary Ben Jonson in *Bartholomew Fair*. *Apples* is narrated by a tabloid newspaper journalist Byline Browne (played onstage by Dury himself) who is tracking down a political scandal. The plot line is loose, and the narrative moves fitfully to connect a dozen songs cowritten by Dury and keyboard player Mickey Gallagher. The characters include a classic cockney type—the street seller of fruit, a late twentieth-century costermonger: "Simpson from Harrow had fruit on his barrow, he sold it for love and for gain."

Outside the considerable number of songs with cockney and London coordinates are a number that confront other themes. There are some dealing with themes of love and sex, though in unconventional ways. "I'm Partial to Your Abracadabra" shows off an important element of Dury's idiolect: his ability to insert words from other discourses into rock song lyrics. In this lyric, Dury refers to an "unforeseen erogenous zone," while "Hit Me with Your Rhythm Stick" includes phrases from French and German.

Another powerful group of songs is focused on issues of disability and deviance, clearly inspired by Dury's outsider status as what he did not hesitate to call a "cripple." Apart from the controversial "Spasticus (Autisticus)," these include the comic "I Want to Be Straight" and "Dance of the Screamers," a surreal lyric that portrays life from "the last place in the queue" when "it's hard to be a hero when your helmet's cracked." A final extra-cockney lyric is "D'Orine," in which Dury portrays animals (reminiscent of George Orwell's *Animal Farm*) who speak in an eerily cheerful manner about their eventual fate as human food.

The fourth dimension of cockney music concerns the persona(e) adopted by Dury both as a stage presence and in the characters that populate his song lyrics. In his late-1970s heyday, Dury's stage costume was often inspired by cockney stereotypes. His biographer describes the range of clothes worn by Dury while on tour with Elvis Costello and others:

Sometimes he was Bill Sikes from *Oliver Twist* [more evidence of the continuing hold of the Dickensian paradigm, though now mediated by the stage and film versions of Bart's *Oliver!*], dressed in a tatty jacket, brown bowler hat and with black eye make-up. On other nights he was the Pearly King, glittering under the lights in a black sequinned jacket, or a cockney cabbie with chequered flat-cap or patched-up overcoat. (Balls 177)

As with his rhyme words, however, one feature of Dury's stage dress undermined his otherwise direct reproduction of cockney style: the razorblade worn as an earring in his left ear. This feature is often cited as an essential component of punk style in London. Sex Pistols's biographer Jon Savage noted in October 1976 that "razor-blade pendants" were among those things "in fashion at the moment" (Savage 230), but the Balls biography contains a photograph taken two years earlier of Dury wearing his razorblade earring. The issue of his influence on the transgressive character of punk deserves to be explored further.

The final dimension of cockney music is the employment of musical forms, sounds, or styles with strong cockney associations or connotations. The most frequently found are songs drawing on music hall forms, a tinkling pub piano and "sing-along" choruses. As mentioned earlier, Dury's contemporaries Chas & Dave had successfully incorporated rock and roll piano into their mellow, nostalgic sound-world, and Dury also uses rock and roll modes in two early songs. However, in these the rock mode is staged as a homology of the semantic world of the lyrics. In "Sweet Gene Vincent," the aim is to evoke the sound of Vincent's group, the Blue Caps, and "Upminster Kid" is a portrayal of Teddy Boys using the music of that subculture, the 1950s rock and roll song-shape, and a piano solo introduced by Dury with the words "come on Jerry Lee Hardy." Russell Hardy was Kilburn & the High Roads's first pianist.

The cockney music hall song form is almost entirely absent from Dury's work. One exception is the late piece "Poo Poo in the Prawn," where the nostalgic associations of the music are directly and rudely countermanded by the lyrics' graphic depictions of pollution and sewage. Generally, however, the musical bases of his songs range from ska, calypso, and rock in the early work to the triumphant funk rhythms devised by Chas Jankel for the most important and successful work of the late 1970s and early 1980s. Jankel's major influences included Sly and the Family Stone, War, Funkadelic, and the Ohio Players. The sophisticated polyrhythms derived from these sources and from jazz proved to be both a perfect foil for Dury's equally imaginative lyrics and served to give the songs a contemporary dance base lacking in the rock and roll and reggae backings of the Kilburn & the High Roads era.[11] To that extent, the funk rhythms acted as a counterforce to any lingering semantic or linguistic cockney nostalgia.

Conclusion

In his analysis of cultural formations, Raymond Williams distinguished between elements that were dominant, emergent, and residual. While cockney is not necessarily homogenous, its primary status in the contemporary English and international mediascape is incorrigibly residual. Its principal tropes and motifs were established in era of Dickens and Mayhew, and they were both continually re-created while remaining fundamentally unchanged throughout the era of high modernity and into postmodernity. During that long historical period, cockney has been more or less successfully applied as a style or mode of fiction, theater, music, film, and television production. Such applications have, however, increasingly taken the form of knowing or nostalgic pastiche or parody.

It is against this historical and ontological condition that Ian Dury's rendezvous with cockney took place. To some degree he, like many predecessors, reinvigorated the cockney stereotype by his witty and inventive variations on its linguistic modes and characterscapes.

But equally, his work at times exceeded the boundaries of the stereotype, principally by overflowing and deconstructing some of its linguistic and characterological features, notably rhyming slang and the lascivious, criminal, and "wide boy" male figures. An equally crucial feature was the articulation of the linguistic stereotype with funk and jazz. The resulting carnivalesque treatment of the stereotype had the momentary and dizzying effect of dislocating many of its elements and offering a vision of a cosmopolitan London culture in which a cockney accent could find its place.

At such times this surreal or utopian vision broke free of the conservative pull of a century and a half of sedimented and introverted cultural repetition. But it could not cause a fundamental disruption. Paradoxically, Ian Dury's final triumph may have been to demonstrate conclusively the impossibility of a truly contemporary cockney music in London, the global city.

Notes

1. See, for example, Frith.

2. Lipsitz confusingly entitles a chapter about the 1980s Birmingham-based group Musical Youth "London Calling: Pop Reggae and the Atlantic World" (95–116).

3. On the global city, see Sassen.

4. Ritchie's most acclaimed films are *Lock, Stock and Two Smoking Barrels* (1998) and *Snatch* (2000). Cameron's novels include *Vinnie Got Blown Away* (1995) and *Brown Bread in Wengen* (2000).

5. "Any Old Iron" was included in *Somebody Bin Usin' That Thing*, a revue produced by Howard Bradshaw consisting of "songs from the closet" and performed in England in March 2001. See W. Thompson (10).

6. Jez Lowe and the Bad Pennies, *The Parish Notices* (Green Linnet GLCD 1192, 1998).

7. On the history of skiffle, see Dewe and McDevitt.

8. Cream's album *Disraeli Gears* closed with a cockney novelty item "Mother's Lament," while comments are interpolated by cockney voices on "Lazy Sunday" by the Small Faces.

9. The riff for "Sex and Drugs and Rock 'n' Roll" was directly inspired by a bass line played by Charlie Haden on the Ornette Coleman album *Change of the Century* (Balls 150).

10. Ever the cockney loyalist, Pearl Binder wrote in 1975 that "cockney culture . . . has been unable to stand up so well against the American cultural invasion of the twentieth century. And it is now struggling for its life against Common Market conformity" (110).

11. On pub rock, see Birch and Laing (7–9).

Works Cited

Ackroyd, Peter. *London: The Biography*. London: Chatto and Windus, 2000.

Baily, Peter. *Popular Culture and Performance in the Victorian City*. Cambridge: Cambridge University Press, 1998.

Balliger, R. "Politics." *Key Terms in Popular Music and Culture*. Ed. B. Horner and T. Swiss. Oxford, Blackwell, 1999. 57–70.

Balls, Richard. *Sex, Drugs & Rock 'n Roll: The Life of Ian Dury*. London: Omnibus, 2000.

Binder, Pearl. *The Pearlies: A Social Record*. London: Jupiter, 1975.

Birch, Will. *No Sleep Till Canvey Island: The Great Pub Rock Revolution.* London: Virgin, 2000.

Bracewell, Michael. *England Is Mine: Pop Life in Albion from Wilde to Goldie.* London: HarperCollins, 1997.

Chambers, Colin. *The Story of Unity Theatre.* London: Lawrence and Wishart, 1989.

Cohen, Phil. "Subcultural Conflict and Working-Class Community." *Working Papers in Cultural Studies* 2 (1972).

Dewe, Mike. *The Skiffle Craze.* Aberystwyth: Planet, 1998.

Dury, Ian. *Apples: The Musical.* London: Faber and Faber, 1989.

Fergusson, Rosalind, comp. *Shorter Slang Dictionary: From the Work of Eric Partridge and Paul Beale.* London: Routledge, 1994.

Frith, Simon. "Anglo-America and Its Discontents." *Cultural Studies* 5.3 (Oct. 1991): 263–9.

Ganzl, Kurt. *The Musical: A Concise History.* Boston: Northeastern UP, 1999.

Gorman, John. *Knocking Down Ginger.* London: Caliban Books, 1995.

Humpherys, Anne. *Travels into the Poor Man's Country: The work of Henry Mayhew.* Athens: U of Georgia P, 1977.

Laing, Dave. *One Chord Wonders: Power and Meaning in Punk Rock.* Milton Keynes: Open UP, 1985.

Lerner, Allan Jay. *On the Street Where You Live.* London: Hodder and Stoughton, 1978.

Lipsitz, George. *Dangerous Crossroads: Popular Music, Postmodernism and the Poetics of Place.* New York: Verso, 1994.

Lydon, John, with Keith and Kent Zimmerman. *No Dogs, No Blacks, No Irish: The Authorised Autobiography of Johnny Rotten of the Sex Pistols.* London: Hodder and Stoughton, 1994.

MacInnes, Colin. *Absolute Beginners.* London: MacGibbon and Kee, 1959.

———. "Young England, Half English." *England, Half English.* London: McGibbon and Kee, 1961. 15–30.

McDevitt, Chas. *Skiffle: The Definitive Inside Story.* London: Robson, 1997.

Mullan, John, and Christopher Reid, eds. *Eighteenth Century Popular Culture, a Selection.* Oxford: Oxford UP, 2000.

Pearsall, Ronald. *Edwardian Popular Music.* Newton Abbot: David and Charles, 1975.

Robb, John. *The Nineties: What the F*** Was That All About?* London: Ebury Press, 1999.

Sassen, Saskia. *The Global City.* Princeton, NJ: Princeton UP, 2000.

Savage, Jon. *England's Dreaming: Sex Pistols and Punk Rock.* London: Faber, 1991.

Senelick, Charles, ed. *Tavern Singing in Early Victorian London: The Diaries of Charles Rice for 1840 and 1850.* London: Society for Theatre Research, 1994.

Sheppard, Francis. *London: A History.* London: Oxford University Press, 1998.

Smith, Zadie. *White Teeth.* London: Hamish Hamilton, 2000.

Stedman-Jones, Gareth. "The 'Cockney' and the Nation 1780–1988." *Metropolis: London Histories and Representations since 1800.* Ed. D. Feldman and G. Stedman-Jones. London, Routledge, 1989.

Steedman, Carolyn. *Childhood, Culture and Class in Britain: Margaret McMillan 1860–1931.* London: Virago, 1990.

Thompson, Ben. *Seven Years of Plenty.* London: Victor Gollancz, 1998.

Thompson, Warwick. "Have a Gay Old Time." *Guardian* (London), 9 March 2001.

Trudgill, Peter. "Acts of Conflicting Identity. The Socio-linguistics of British Pop-Song Pronunciation." *On Dialect, Social and Geographical Perspectives.* Ed. Peter Trudgill. Oxford: Basil Blackwell, 1984. 141–60.

Williams, Raymond. *Culture.* London: Fontana, 1981.

"Raising One Higher than the Other"

The Hierarchy of Tradition in Representations of Gaelic- and English-Language Song in Ireland

—Anthony McCann and Lillis Ó Laoire

At present, whatever might fit under the rubric of "Irish culture" is receiving widespread publicity and perhaps more recognition in international contexts than ever before. The discourses and social dynamics of development, consumerism, and tourism have become dominant forces in everyday life as Ireland has become "the place to be." Cultural "phenomena" such as the dance stage show *Riverdance* and Frank McCourt's best-selling novel *Angela's Ashes* have boosted this highly responsive climate for the commercial exploitation of Irish-related cultural marketables. The media-driven spectacle of celebration and "wonderlust" has not been without detractors. Crowley and MacLaughlin have drawn attention, for example, to exclusions and misrepresentations that could easily go unnoticed amid the clamor. Nevertheless, now at last, it seems to many, Ireland can identify itself as other than not-English as it takes pride of place within the European and global economies. The binary opposition of Irish and English is not so easily dismantled, however. Its long pedigree continues to color and structure life in Ireland. This is particularly the case in regard to the attitude of many toward language.

Speakers of the Irish language find themselves in a somewhat paradoxical situation. Within the bounds of the 1937 Irish Constitution, the Irish language is the "national" and "first official language." English is recognized as the "second official language." This in no way reflects the hegemonic status of the English language as the primary vernacular of Irish life, either at the time the constitution was drafted or now. The complexities of Irish-language practices in Ireland call for in-depth exploration that is beyond the scope of this essay. However, it can be said that the horizon of understandings and

233

expectations that encompasses Irish and English languages in Ireland has been deeply influenced by a radical discursive separation that, as Leersen would suggest, perhaps stretches back to the seventeenth century (173–86).

In this essay, we are not concerned with the interrogation of the term "language choice" as such. Rather, we explore this discursive operation of binary opposition, presented as a "choice of languages." The practice of what is commonly referred to as "traditional" or "unaccompanied" singing in Ireland is often represented as if singers have before them the "choice" of two radically distinct and symbolically disparate linguistic traditions. We might call this a "two-traditions hypothesis."[1] To summarize broadly, on the one hand, there is a Gaelic singing tradition—ancient in lineage, personal in character, lyrical in content, more ornamented in delivery, more authentic in essence.[2] On the other lies an English-language tradition—more recent in origin, more practical in character, more literal in content, more plain in delivery, less Irish in essence. Here, we explore the major ideological forces contributing to this opposition, in particular focusing on the gradual enclosure of unaccompanied singing in the Irish language within discourses of authenticity and otherness, which coalesce in the construction and perpetuation of the rubric of *sean-nós*.[3]

Drawing on our experience of ethnography and participant-observation fieldwork, we argue that the perception and representation of Irish- and English-language song traditions as radically separate prevents and indeed suppresses adequate understandings of the practices or experiences of singers themselves. Indeed, we will argue that the simplistic nature of the binary opposition accomplishes two things of note. First, it encourages structuralist and deterministic approaches to songs and texts and foregrounds a reified view of "tradition," thereby concealing important questions of social context and personal meaning. Second, as we have already noted, it leads us to understand the experiences of people who sing in terms of an either/or language choice between distinct, alternative entities. Considering these experiences in terms of "choice" leads us down theoretical roads that are inadequate to deal with the complexities disclosed by our research.

In response to the inadequacies of the two-traditions hypothesis, we celebrate the complexities of singers' experiences and make a plea for a methodological particularism. To be precise, we suggest the principles of social interactionism in order to work toward a clearer representation of the specificities of locally negotiated meanings. Invoking social interactionism may bring us closer to an understanding of the subtleties of the personal interactions of people who sing. To highlight the inadequacies of the two-traditions hypothesis, we briefly look at the lives of three singers, Elizabeth Cronin, Róisín White (Vallely), and Teresa McClafferty, whose experiences as singers disclose the nuances of social interaction. The complexity of their experience challenges the continuing representation of a strict dichotomy of Irish- and English-language song traditions and reasserts the importance, authority, and priority of personal experiences, as singers maneuver amid fundamentally quotidian considerations of courtesy, decency, friendship, and hospitality—values explicitly underlined by the dynamics of contexts for singing. We move, then, from generalization to particularism, from choice to expectation, from entrenched binarism to personalized, situational negotiation.

The two-traditions hypothesis is widely accepted as a valid representation of song, singing, and the experiences of singers in Irish life. Our essay attempts to challenge that validity, to unsettle the status quo, and to prompt a different approach to the subject. By doing this, we hope to contribute to what Shore and Wright refer to as an "anthropology of the present."[4] As Carrier argues, the issue is not that people reduce things to essences or establish dichotomies that lead to errors and misconceptions. Rather, it is that such reductions "become so entrenched that it becomes difficult to stand back from them and consider whether they help or hinder scholars in the pursuit of the questions that confront them" (Carrier 8).

The Binary Opposition of Irish and English Languages

The dominant ideological strains of cultural nationalism in Ireland during the nineteenth and twentieth centuries posited a binary opposition of Gaelic- and English-language worlds. This opposition has been explored in detail by O'Leary, particularly in relation to literature. In 1893, the Gaelic League was founded to preserve and extend the use of the Irish language. Scholars such as Ó Tuama and MacDonagh have shown that the Gaelic League explicitly viewed the true spirit of Ireland as the neglected and despised Irish-speaking one, to be found only among the poorest communities where the Irish language survived as an everyday vernacular. The world of the Irish-speaking *Gael*, then, was predominantly characterized as spiritual (and specifically Catholic), Irish-speaking, and rural, while the world of the English-speaking *Gall* was portrayed as secular, decadent (Anglicized and modern), and urban. The relationship was further complicated by the common attribution by cultural nationalists of the decline of the Irish language to systematic Anglicization, enacted by the British administration over hundreds of years of colonization.[5] This is clearly outlined in the entrenched political polarization that pervades every aspect of a Northern Irish life, as has been noted by McCoy (118). Couched in a simplistic binary of oppressor and oppressed, the Irish language contributed forcefully to an ideology of "national parallelism" in which Ireland was systematically portrayed as radically separate from the nefarious, socially decadent influences of modern English-speaking Britain. The work of Chapman and Ó Giolláin has shown that this binary opposition was informed, from the mid-nineteenth century onward, by anti-Enlightenment romantic nationalism, in particular by the works of German writers such as Johann Gottfried von Herder, and by a pervasive "Celticism" influenced by the writings of Ernest Renan and Matthew Arnold, among others. Together, these ideological supports legitimized the identification of the Irish language with the "personality" of the Irish nation while also allowing the essential qualities of this "Celtic" language to be idealized as exotic, ancient, pure, sensitive, spiritual, feminine, imaginative, poetic, passionate, and impractical (Ó Giolláin 26).

The Myth of the West

One of the most powerful themes elevated by the Gaelic Revival, the Gaelic League, and Irish cultural nationalism, and one that underpins the dichotomy of Gaelic and English languages, is the Myth of the West. Scholars such as Gibbons, Nash, and Byrne, Edmondson, and Fahy have shown how, in the nineteenth and early twentieth centuries, the West of Ireland became representative of an essentialized, "true" Irish identity. For others it became a "new frontier," drawing forth the act of "discovery." The West of Ireland proved a paragon of discursive closure, holding out the promise of a true language, folklore, and way of life. The West, generally, was also implicated in a process of marked temporal closure, achieving something of a transcendent value, "outside time, separated from normal temporal development" (Nash 187). It provided a model example for prevalent attitudes of cultural anachronism, critiqued by Chakrabarty, whereby the West was not quite of the present but magically peripheral, and contrasted with a mechanistic and rational urbanity redolent of colonial bureaucracies (Byrne, Edmondson, and Fahy 236). As noted by Ó Giolláin, such reification was undoubtedly exacerbated by the enormity of the social distance between the urban middle-class enthusiasts of the Gaelic Revival and the people in the West to whom they looked for spiritual nourishment. Where "Ireland" and "Irishness" had served (and continue to serve) as the convenient and primitive Other of colonial discourses, the West, and for some reason Connemara in particular, became something of an "internal other," a powerful symbolic manifestation of Ireland as not-England. As well as the foregrounded issues of language, folklore, and way of life, the West was at the furthest remove from the cultural influences of Anglicization, with a landscape in stark contrast to any that might be considered "English." The West became for the Gaelic Revival "a physical location for unpolluted Irishness" (Byrne, Edmondson, and Fahy 236).

The Gaeltacht

A crucial element in the persistence of the Myth of the West as an exotic Other is the symbolic, geographical, and legislative construction of the *Gaeltacht*, now most commonly understood as the areas in which Gaelic is deemed to be used as an everyday vernacular. The concept *Gaeltacht* itself needs some glossing. The first mention of the word in Ireland seems to be in a seventeenth-century poem, although its polar opposite, "*Galltacht*," from "*Gall*" (a "foreigner," is attested to from at least the sixteenth century in Ireland. As documented by Ó Torna, it is clear that, in contexts such as this, *Gaeltacht* does not represent a particular location but rather a group of people, the *Gaeil*, the "Gaels"—Irish or Scottish speakers of Gaelic and subscribers to a Gaelic worldview. By the nineteenth century, the concept of the Gaels had become a convenient Other for metropolitan culture, located at some distance from the urban "centers" in wild romantic locations. The term was appropriated by the revivalists to represent this Other in a sympathetic way, emphasizing the western location of the people and the region's importance as a container of pure, simple, cultural richness. In 1926, this spatial demarcation became enshrined in law, with districts where more than 80 percent of the people spoke Irish defined as *fíor-Ghaeltacht* (true/pure *Gaeltacht*), whereas those with between 25 and 79 percent became designated *breac-Ghaeltacht* (speckled/partial *Gaeltacht*). Subsequently, as Johnson has noted, the often extreme living conditions in these areas could be conveniently ignored by some, since the Other had been reified to represent the quintessential spiritual core of the nation. So, the *Gaeltacht* was imagined as an idyllic location of neatly thatched, whitewashed cottages, set against a romantic, mountainous landscape, where storytelling, singing, music, dancing, and other "traditions" were to be found in a state of linguistic purity, an image, indeed, that has stubbornly endured despite all the changes of the twentieth century. The construction, constitution, and enclosure of the *Gaeltacht* were perhaps the most visible political realization of the linguistic dichotomy of Gaelic and English.

We have seen, then, how a binary opposition between the Irish and English languages was established in the discourses of Irish cultural nationalism. This opposition was reinforced in four major ways: first, by the influence of the philosophies of romantic nationalism; second, by the rise of Celticism; third, by the Myth of the West; and fourth, by the constitution of the *Gaeltacht*. The radical cultural and linguistic separation between Gaelic and English was carried over into the way in which song was conceptualized. This is hardly surprising. Embodying both music and language, song in Gaelic was seen as something of a romantic synthesis within the cultural nationalist matrix of Irish identity.

The Two-Traditions Hypothesis

It is often the case that something is defined in terms of something else, that which is not itself. Rhetorician Kenneth Burke refers to this as contextual, or dialectical, definition and notes that this is at the heart of the very idea of definition (24). Many scholars have critiqued the process whereby "cultures," "traditions," or "societies" are presented as closed systems, essentialized, and reduced to a timeless essence. A key example is Said's *Orientalism*. Carrier acknowledges that in the process of dialectical definition, infinite complexities are reduced to the construction of an abstract, generalized entity; such an entity is then further reduced to a set of core features that are understood to express the essence of that entity but only as it stands in contrast to its Other (3). This is the key process in the construction of the two-traditions hypothesis.

Proponents of the two-traditions hypothesis construct an image of a Gaelic song tradition that is absolutely different and separate from an English-language counterpart. The Gaelic song tradition is constructed primarily as not-English (language).[6] To speak of a "song tradition" at all is usually to assume, albeit often implicitly, the persistence of a continuously existing entity that remains, in its essence, more or less identical through time. This entity is understood to undergo changes conceived as being more or less analogous to the changes that individual human beings experience. In many ways, then, supporters of the two-traditions hypothesis seek to outline the distinct and distinctive "personality" of a Gaelic song tradition as not-English.

A recent and illustrative statement of the two-traditions hypothesis can be found in Liam Mac Con Iomaire's definition of *sean-nós* in the encyclopedic *Companion to Irish Traditional Music*, in which he holds that

while there are similarities between traditional singing in English and traditional singing in Irish, they are two different traditions and are generally celebrated as such. The songs in Irish reflect an outlook on life and a view of the world that is quite different to the songs in English. (336)

The binary opposition is clearly established; the two traditions are presented as radically distinct, undoubtedly separate. Such an opposition is more developed in O'Rourke's description of Gaelic song:

In these songs, it seemed to me, they think differently, they look on the world with different eyes and minds, they fall in love differently—or at least express themselves differently about it; they grieve differently, they pray and curse differently. And they do all these things eloquently, imaginatively, impressively, attractively—more so, I thought, than in the [English-language] world with which I was already familiar. (13–14)

In this passage, Irish speakers are constructed as an exotic "other," a "they" whose proper medium of communication is song. We find an emotional, anti-rational, artistic, Gaelic worldview contrasted with a practical, rational, unimaginative English-language one. Highly redolent of the binary oppositions of cultural nationalism and Celticism mentioned earlier, this view reinforces the simplistic opposition of Gaelic- and English-language song traditions.

Gaelic song is understood to occupy the dominant pole of the binary opposition in its role as privileged "other." This dominance is consistent with

Jacques Derrida's observations on the relations of power within binary operations. As Derrida points out, there are very few neutral binary oppositions. The binary privilege, for example, is sometimes deployed within the two-traditions hypothesis to explain English-language song in terms of Gaelic-language loss. O'Sullivan, for example, writes,

We now turn to our popular songs in English, and here we come across an astonishing contrast. They differ enormously from their Irish counterparts, and the difference is indicative of the profound effect of the loss of their language on the psychology and character of the Irish people. (5)

English-language songs, then, are understood as degenerate in relation to Gaelic-language songs. This is reflected by O'Boyle, who presents the texts of English-language songs as the malformed attempts of a people to express themselves in a language not their own:

As for songs written in English by the Irish country folk themselves, it must be admitted that they are of much less merit than the Gaelic songs. They represent the attempt of people to express themselves in a language they knew imperfectly and had only recently acquired. (14)

The two-traditions hypothesis thus establishes a binary opposition between Gaelic- and English-language song traditions in Ireland. Each strand is constructed as an entity or "tradition" in itself, with a distinct and distinctive personality. Privilege is thereby asserted for the essential features of the Gaelic song tradition. Perhaps the most crucial element in the persistence of the two-traditions binary, though, is the social construction and maintenance of the discourse of *sean-nós*.

Sean-nós

Gaelic song served as a powerful unifying symbol of language, literature, and lore for Gaelic revivalists and Irish cultural nationalists at the end of the nineteenth and the beginning of the twentieth centuries, the epitome of Ireland as not-England. The term *"sean-nós"* has facilitated discourses of authenticity and identity that consolidate the privileged place of the Gaelic song tradition in the two-traditions hypothesis.[7] It is in and through the discourse of *sean-nós* that the "personality" of Gaelic song can be seen most clearly.

Over the years, *sean-nós* has been reduced to a set of core features that together are understood to express the essence of the Gaelic song tradition. Two factors in particular have contributed to the development, elaboration, and deployment of these core features. First, the adjudications of the annual *Oireachtas* competitive festival, the most important forum for unaccompanied singing in Gaelic today, have entrenched the radical separation of Irish- and English-language singing. Singers from the region of Connemara and the western islands have in the past been deemed by judges to be the possessors of the true and authentic art of *sean-nós*, and this perspective was profoundly influenced by the Myth of the West and the exoticization of the Western *Gaeltacht*. That the judges hold this view is reflected in the overwhelming number of national winners from Connemara and the islands and in the highly prescriptive pronouncements of adjudicators. Second, the analyses of academic scholarship have sought to delimit and define the essential features of *sean-nós*. All the while reflecting and reinforcing the judging decisions of the *Oireachtas*, scholars have focused on elements of pitch, timbre, dynamics, and language in attempts to justify the position of *sean-nós* as a truly authentic Irish high-art form. The two-traditions hypothesis is deeply implicated in these moves, as illustrated by a curious but recurring orientalizing strategy. Here, we will explore these issues and illustrate how the "festival culture" of traditional singing in Ireland is broadly constructed along the lines of the two-traditions hypothesis, with festivals predominantly specializing in one or the other language "tradition."

An tOireachtas

Singing competitions provide the most high-profile and popular outlets for those who sing in the Irish language. *An tOireachtas* offers a weekend of unaccompanied singing that is unrivaled for the intensity of the experience. For many the highlight of the singing year, this national competition has achieved the highest recognition of any among the singers themselves. No competition for singing in English has achieved anything like the same recognition. Like all competitions, the *Oireachtas* has often caused heated argument and bitter dispute over adjudications, which are often perceived to be idiosyncratic and biased. This would be an issue in any such competition in Ireland, whatever the language community, but the politics of *an tOireachtas* are made even more complex by the issue of *sean-nós*.

The establishment of the national *Oireachtas* festival in 1897, under the auspices of the Gaelic League, institutionalized the dominant lines of force that constituted the Irish cultural nationalist vision. Ó Súilleabháin (11–22) has documented that the stated aims of the festival were to develop literature in the Irish language and to promote other Irish-language cultural expressions. Gaelic singing, and what was considered a proper and national expression of it, was a symbolically central but highly contested domain at the early *Oireachtas* competitions. Many thought, for example, that harmonized versions of Gaelic songs for choral performance should be acceptable. Others, however, felt that this choral style was redolent of foreign influence and, moreover, that it was anathema to the Gaelic song tradition and should be completely disallowed. These people instead favored the unaccompanied, solo monophonic style used by country singers, holding it up as the pinnacle of aesthetic achievement among Irish-speaking people, to which all singers of songs in Irish should aspire (95–113). Thus the focus of debate over what was or was not considered "authentic" shifted to "the old Irish style" or, as expressed in Irish, "*sean-nós.*" Ó Súilleabháin records the gradual changeover from the term "old Irish style" used in English to the term "*sean-nós,*" as found in the directive issued for the 1911 *Oireachtas* competitions: *Ní éistfear ach le hamhránaíocht ar an sean-nós* (Only *sean-nós* singing will be listened to) (111). The phrasing of the term here, "*ar an sean-nós*" (on/in the old style) is adjectival. Increasingly, however, the label "*sean-nós*" achieved the status of a proper noun. What was included within the bounds of the term would remain pure, unadulterated, and implicitly, if not explicitly, not-English. This is in contrast to the entry requirements for the instrumental music competitions, which were open to all who could play. By 1924, the last *Oireachtas* before a fifteen-year hiatus, the term "*sean-nós*" was commonly used to delimit and partition elements of song considered more than ordinarily authentic. The term thus became a powerful, pivotal focus following the reestablishment of the *Oireachtas* festival in 1939, and although it is not without its critics (for example, Carson), "*sean-nós*" has remained the central label with which people refer to song and singing in the Irish language.

The renewed *Oireachtas* lent a new impetus to discourses of separation and bifurcation. Adjudication became increasingly meticulous, as the areas of uniqueness and distinction accorded to *sean-nós* singing style were refined. Attention focused on aspects of language, so that rhyme and prosody were maintained in accordance with older literary conventions and the melodic embellishments common to the style were analyzed and reified. A strict dichotomy between Gaelic and English languages was enforced in the *sean-nós* competitions, with entry being restricted to people from *Gaeltacht* or Irish-speaking regions. Furthermore, the Gaelic-speaking part of Connemara (the coastal south) and the Aran Islands began increasingly to provide the lion's share of the winners. As Shields notes, these styles were identified by adjudicators as more authentic because of the ornate melodic decoration favored by competitors from the region (124). This development was facilitated partly because of the prowess and talent of those competitors and partly because of the dominance of the myth-making discourses concerning the West in general and Connemara in particular. Adjudication had a tendency to become very severe. One example of the most salient moment of such impossible standards in the history of *Oireachtas* competitions is the 1967 prize-winner's competition, in which first prize was deliberately not awarded, ostensibly because the required standard had not been reached. Later, in the 1970s, Northern singers complained that their claims to being authentic traditional singers had been denounced publicly by adjudicators. This may be partly attributed to the perceived unacceptability of the Northern dialect and also to the comparative scarcity of embellishment found in Northern singing.

Some of the *Oireachtas* adjudicators have also written scholarly works on *sean-nós* style. This combination of adjudication and scholarship originated in the early Gaelic League days and continues today. In probably the best known of these works, Ó Canainn engages in a detailed musical analysis of *sean-nós* style. He discusses the various kinds of ornamentation used by singers, distinguishing between ornamentation and variation as stylistic devices and further categorizing various types such as melismatic and intervallic ornamentation and melismatic, intervallic, and rhythmic variation. Seán Ó Riada, discussed in more detail later, was a musician, composer, and academic for whom the *sean-nós* grand prix was renamed after his early and tragic death in 1971; he also contributed to this debate, and many of his insights profoundly influenced Ó Canainn. Detached formalist analysis became the hallmark of scholarship and adjudication, together further advancing the idea that *sean-nós* was an esoteric and rarified "high art" form. Its need of a corresponding "low" form (that is, English-language singing) as an antithetical reference point was crucial to the development of such discourse.

The Oriental Hypothesis

The two-traditions hypothesis is further reinforced in characterizations of *sean-nós* by the curious but recurring suggestion that the cultural forms of Irish music are not European in origin but are in fact more closely linked to the classical traditions of the Orient. Ó Riada, for example, argues that Irish music is not European in the least but is instead "closer to some [albeit unidentified] forms of Oriental music." He further claims that to understand Irish music, we must forget about European music: "Its standards are not Irish standards; its style is not Irish style; its forms are not Irish forms" (20). Similarly, in a brief survey of justifications for the possible "Asian origin of Irish music," Fanny Feehan argues on the basis of a rudimentary comparative musicology that Irish music, and the experience of Irish singers and musicians, is not European. Instead, she suggests "links between the music of North and South India, Persia, North Africa, Spain and Ireland" (335). "I have seen and heard enough," she writes, "to be convinced that there are links and even if some proof is lacking the suggestions remain tantalising" (ibid.).

If claims for the "oriental" origins of Irish music are to have any rhetorical weight, however, proving the links between "non-European" or "non-Western" musical forms and *sean-nós* is crucial. The Gaelic lineage of *sean-nós* is the sine qua non of this orientalizing assembly of associations. What is considered *sean-nós* is regularly characterized as the most authentic survival of the Irish musical tradition, "the key which opens every lock" (Ó Canainn 49) or even "the basis of all traditional Irish music" (Quinn 16). If there are cultural links anywhere, the argument goes, they would be found in *sean-nós*. This is clearly a concern in the work of Ó Riada:

In approaching our vocal music, that style of singing traditional songs which is called in Irish the "*sean-nós*"—the "old style"—it is best to listen as if we were listening to music for the first time, with a child's new mind; or to think of Indian music rather than European. (23)

Feehan writes of Moroccan singers,

It . . . has seemed to me for many years now, that the same combination of embroidery and ornamentation of the melody-line, in addition to the introspective attitude of the performer, might have been experienced in

Connemara, Ring, or in one of the now ruined cottages in the Comeragh Mountains or Nire Valley. (333)

The most extensive attempt to draw such links has been Bob Quinn's "Atlantean" thesis. In homage to Ó Riada's orientalist suggestions, Quinn uses the high-art form of *sean-nós* of the West Galway region as the starting point for an explanatory narrative of comparative inquiry that posits a shared maritime culture along the Atlantic coasts of Europe, if not also including the cultures of North Africa and the Mediterranean. These assertions strongly echo eighteenth- and nineteenth-century antiquarian arguments that advanced Ireland's claims to a great and ancient Gaelic civilization. Leersen draws particular attention to the Phoenician model championed by Charles Vallancey in the late eighteenth century:

The presupposition was that ancient Ireland had had a native tradition of high civility, which was now lost owing to the violent destruction and wholesale ruin that was brought upon the country in modern times. In the opposition between civility and barbarism, the Anglocentric view saw the Irish as savages and the English presence as a source of civility; the Phoenician hypothesis turned the tables, and predicated civility on the native Gaels while bracketing the English presence with the Viking spoliations, seeing them as violent disruptions. (74)

A similar logic of reversal and opposition arguably informs the orientalization of "Irish music" and, in particular, *sean-nós*. Though not obviously stated, there is a strong, implicit anti-English subtext to these arguments. Significantly, English-language song is always silently omitted from the general category of "Irish music" when orientalization is at stake. By a process of occlusion and exclusion, the two-traditions hypothesis is categorically asserted, the essential primacy of the Gaelic song tradition upheld. These representational strategies also undoubtedly spring from an underlying, implicit opposition between non-Western and Western societies (Carrier 5). *Sean-nós* is clearly identified as non-European and non-Western. Thus *sean-nós* can be recognized not merely as simple, European "folk song" but as a complex and ancient Gaelic art form of classical high civility, equal in status to the European art tradition but radically separate from it. English-language singing, in contrast, is represented as vulgar and European or, as an adjudicator once disparagingly remarked to an assembly of both Gaelic and Anglophone singers, "a very poor second to singing in Irish."[8]

Festivals

The dominance of "festival culture" in Irish singing circles often perpetuates the bifurcation and privilege of the two-traditions hypothesis. This shows that the hypothesis is not just a set of ideas in scholarly discourse but a set of ideas that has been partially enforced upon the everyday lives and practices of people who sing. Perhaps the first festivals of Irish music in the modern period were the Granard Balls of the 1780s sponsored by James Dungan, a wealthy Irish businessman who resided in Copenhagen. They prefigured the famed Belfast Harp Festival in 1792, at which the music was first written down. From then on, Irish music and song began to be defined as Gaelic. The competitors at the Belfast festival, for example, were forbidden from playing anything but Irish music, despite the fact that, as professional musicians, they played different kinds of music as their patrons demanded. This opposition was later enshrined in the *Oireachtas*, founded in 1897 and based on the Welsh *Eisteddfodau*, which had undergone considerable change from the 1860s on. Again, nostalgia for a once-glorious Gaelic ascendancy was evident in the title chosen, the word "*Oireachtas*" being a revitalization and recontextualization of the Gaelic term for a king's assembly. Many other lesser festivals were held at this time at different venues around the country and particularly around the Gaelic colleges that had been established for the purpose of second-language acquisition in Irish-speaking regions. These were often called "*feis*" (pl. *feiseanna*), another resurrected term meaning "a celebration." These new contexts became important venues for the performance of traditional verbal art, and people quickly grew accustomed to them. They became standard fixtures at local fairs of all kinds, which also might encompass many other kinds of events. The *Oireachtas* did not recognize Gaelic singing in English at its events since its brief was purely to promote Gaelic. Whatever stimulation existed for Gaelic singers then, there was little or nothing done for singing in English.

This position improved somewhat with the establishment of *Comhaltas Ceoltóirí Éireann* in 1951. This governmentally recognized and supported umbrella organization holds competitions, known as *Fleadhanna*, at all levels from county to provincial to national (*Fleadh Cheoil na hÉireann*) and international level. Under the auspices of this organization, English singing gained some ground. In fact, this is the most prestigious competitive venue for English-language traditional singing at present. There is also an

Irish-language competition, but although it is important, it has not ousted the supremacy of *An tOireachtas* as the major forum for Gaelic singing. Many other festivals throughout Ireland feature traditional song to some extent, with some gatherings being exclusively dedicated to song. Each of these festivals tends to be primarily associated with one of the polarities of the "two traditions." These include *Fleadh Amhrán agus Rince* (Festival of Song and Dance) held in Ballycastle, county Antrim, and organized by Comhaltas Ceoltóirí Éireann, which has competitive dancing competitions but only noncompetitive song; *Féile na Mí* (The Meath Festival), a prestigious Gaelic singing competition held in Rath Cairn, the small but vigorous Irish-speaking area of the county; *Féile Cois Cuain* (Festival by the Harbor), held in Louisburgh, county Mayo, every May; the Ennistymon Festival of Traditional Singing, county Clare, primarily an English-language gathering, although Gaelic- and English-language singing are promoted in a conscious effort at equality; and the Willie Clancy Summer School, which offers workshops on traditional song in both languages as part of a broader cultural scheme focusing particularly on music and dance. The "Willie Week," as it is popularly known, has spawned a number of imitators, such as the South Sligo Summer School and the Joe Mooney Summer School in Drumshanbo, county Leitrim. These two seem to concentrate on instrumental playing, and to judge from their programs, Irish-language singing seems to have been overlooked as part of the curriculum. We might also mention the International Ballad Seminar, organized by Jimmy McBride in Inishowen yearly, and *Sean-Nós Cois Life*, a festival that promotes Gaelic song through the organization of workshops and the presentation of awards to outstanding contributors to the Gaelic song tradition.

An increasingly popular and prestigious festival is *Éigse Dhiarmaid Uí Shúilleabháin* (The Diarmaid Ó Súilleabháin Gathering), held annually in early December since 1992 and named in commemoration of a noted Irish-language journalist and singer (1947–91), a member of a renowned singing family from Cúil Aodha in the West Cork *Gaeltacht* area of Múscraí, which also encompasses the village of Ballyvourney. Indeed, because of the renown its singers have achieved over the years, this region features prominently in our discussion later. The festival is run by Ó Súilleabháin's surviving brothers and sisters, all accomplished singers in their own right. This festival concentrates on singing, but it also includes much instrumental music and dancing and attracts many of the most prestigious traditional musicians.

When it is considered that this event is run in an Irish-speaking region and that the family who run it are one of the strongest bulwarks in the defense of Gaelic as a vernacular in the region, the welcome for English-language singing is remarkable. In 2000, Róisín White from county Down was a featured artist in a presentation of her recollections and singing life. In 2001, the featured singer was Brian Mullen, a broadcaster from Derry. Both of these singers are English speakers who have become fluent speakers of Irish to the extent that it constitutes a large part of their identity. They still, however, sing primarily in English and did so at their events at *Éigse Dhiarmaid Uí Shúilleabháin*. This integrated attitude to songs, singing, and language choice demonstrates a remarkable security and confidence regarding the value of English-language singing on the part of the organizers of *Éigse Dhiarmaid Uí Shúilleabháin* in that they are in no way threatened by English. This contrasts remarkably with the more official competitive events, where the competitors are separated by language and often also by gender, in a monologic compartmentalization. Many of the same people frequent both kinds of events and negotiate them differently as appropriate. It is clear, then, that while the two traditions can clearly be seen to operate in and through formally organized singing practices, people who sing are themselves often engaged in far more complex interactions than can be encompassed within the scope of the two-traditions hypothesis.

The Two-Traditions Hypothesis: Implications for Analysis

We have established that discourses and practices of song, singing, and singers in Ireland are often structured by the dominance and persistence of the two-traditions hypothesis. As we have seen, this process starts with an a priori assumption that there are entities that might be considered "song traditions." Such thinking leads, on the one hand, to the conceptual closure of a Gaelic song tradition as the paragon of authenticity and Irish identity and, on the other, to a barely developed conceptualization of an English song tradition that is defined within the binary opposition as the degenerate Other of the Gaelic tradition, if not omitted from analyses altogether. The "choice of languages" approach implied by the two-traditions hypothesis, however, provides an inadequate explanatory framework in the face of the complexity and multiplicity of singers' experiences. There is no either/or answer that can suffice where the experiences of singers are concerned. Our own experiences as singers and our ethnographic fieldwork clearly show that the situation is more complicated than that. In response to the two-traditions hypothesis, part of our task is to restore complexity to the explanatory analysis of song and singing in Ireland. By simplifying the interconnections at stake, attention is diverted from the politics of representation, away from issues of meaning and the socially situated dynamics of discourse and expectation. We seek to redirect attention to the need for particularism so that less simplistic, less generalized, less partial accounts of singers' experiences might come to light. More specifically, we suggest that the study of singers and singing in Ireland might be guided by the theoretical orientation of social interactionism.

Social Interactionism

Social interactionism has already been employed to great effect by Pickering and Green and other scholars in *Everyday Culture: Popular Song and the Vernacular Milieu,* a collection that focuses on what we might term "traditional" singers and singing in England. Identifying face-to-face interaction as a "genuine human universal," Pickering and Green propose that strategies informed by a centrality of social interaction militate against cultural abstraction and scholarly idealization, even if they cannot wholly prevent it. Pickering and Green do, however, also note that studies that focus on the local and the particular can slip into the murky waters of anecdotalism, sentimentalization, and even escapism. Particularist study must therefore be constantly reincorporated into a general theoretical framework (Pickering and Green 7).

It is, of course, important to clarify what is meant here by "social interaction." Erving Goffman's definition of social interaction, for example, is unusually narrow, understood as "that which uniquely transpires in social situations, that is, environments in which two or more individuals are physically in one another's response presence" (235). For Goffman, then, there are times when social interaction does not occur. Here, however, social interaction alludes broadly to the constant and dynamic environment of interrelationship that we experience in the course of our lives. In saying that social interaction is constant, our position is sympathetic with the approach of

Jonathan Turner, whose theoretical stance rests on the idea that social interaction is an "invariant property of the universe" (13). In saying that social interaction is dynamic, we can reiterate Becker's understanding that "the simplest notion of social interaction when applied to man is that of reciprocal influencing among persons or social forces" (657), Burns's statement that "individual acts and social pressures mutually modify each other" (13), and Turner's definition that "social interaction is the process whereby the overt movements, covert deliberations, and basic physiology of one individual influence those of another, and vice versa" (14).

Toward Particularity

This position allows us to draw on the field of social interactionism, or simply "interactionism," what Paul Rock refers to as "a deliberately unsystematic and often vague method of interpreting the ways in which people do things together" (843).[9] The unsystematic nature of the field leads to a proliferation of perspectives and the absence of a dominant orthodoxy (ibid.). J. R. Hall uses the phrase "the social interaction perspective" to refer to "the cluster of approaches that focus on meaning, action, symbols, and the interactive unfolding and historically contingent character of social life" (17). In this cluster, Hall includes interpretive sociology, symbolic interactionism, phenomenology, hermeneutics, and ethnomethodology.[10] Although interactionism is a field of diverse approaches, we might say that interactionists are united by an emphasis on the situational context of meaning, a focus on the ways "meanings emerge, are negotiated, stabilized and transformed" (Plummer ix). Burns summarizes the central principles of interactionist approaches as follows:

Firstly, humans respond to the environment on the basis of the meanings that elements of the environment have for them as individuals. Secondly, such meanings are a product of social interaction, and thirdly these . . . meanings are modified through individual interpretation within the ambit of this shared interaction. (12–13)

Social interactionism brings us face-to-face with the politics of representation. In the case of the two-traditions hypothesis, for example, it would require us to ask who is using this binary opposition of song traditions and why, how, and to what effect it is used. Rather than thinking of languages as hermetically sealed containers that enclose and embody radically distinct cultures, social interactionism allows us to confront the delicacies of language use in particular circumstances in particular company and to be aware of the importance of emergent meanings in singers' horizons of understanding and expectation. This theoretical orientation draws us away from the assumptions of the two-traditions hypothesis and brings us closer to the fluid boundaries and complexities of singing practices as people move in and out of a variety of contexts of social interaction.

Ethnographic Perspectives from Fieldwork

Up to this point, we have been trying to undo the entrenched and sclerotic two-traditions hypothesis by examining its component parts minutely. In this section, we will take a different approach to the problem and examine the lives of particular singers in order to see how their experience conforms or differs from such a rigid differentiation. In this examination, we briefly illuminate three singers' experiences in order to demonstrate how little a complete differentiation is applicable in any of the cases. First, we will explore the singing life and repertoire of Elizabeth (Bess) Cronin (1879–1954) from the Ballyvourney region. Second, we will look to the life and experience of Róisín White, from Attical in county Down in the North East of Ireland. Third, we will focus on the experience of Teresa McClafferty, a singer from Tory Island in the far North West of the country.

Elizabeth Cronin and the Mystery of the Glottal Stop

The Ballyvourney region has been known for many years as a stronghold of Irish-language traditions, of poets, and of excellent traditional singers in Gaelic and English. In fact, the song-makers of the region compose in both languages. Early in the twentieth century, it was jokingly referred to as the "capital" of the Irish-speaking regions because its inhabitants were such successful contestants at the early *Oireachtais*. Elizabeth Cronin numbered as one of the most renowned among them; in fact, she achieved iconic status regionally, nationally, and indeed internationally, partly because she was visited by many prominent song collectors, including Alan Lomax and Jean Ritchie. From our perspective, it is important to note that she was among the contestants at early *Feiseanna*, as Miss Bessie Herlihy, whose singing was admired for its "beauty" and "naive simplicity" (Ó Cróinín 22).

In fact, for this reason and because so many leading and influential characters in traditional music circles collected from her, she has achieved a reputation as a paragon of vocal style, her singing considered to be an excellent example of *sean-nós*.

In her grandson Dáibhí Ó Cróinín's collection of her songs, it becomes abundantly clear that Mrs. Cronin sang all kinds of songs in the same communal context. Her large repertoire of almost 200 songs included anonymous Gaelic love songs, formal laments and the occasional dirge, a milking song, the works of local poets in Irish and English, children's songs, macaronic songs (alternate verses in Gaelic and English), ballads (in English) of varying periods, and music hall songs: in other words, a representative selection of the whole range of musical items available to her. It would appear that her choices in song were directed aesthetically and that the idea that a song should be thought less of simply because it was in English and not in Gaelic was foreign to her. It would appear, indeed, that a greater concern to her was keeping the knowledge of late night singing activities from her immediate neighbors in order to avoid their severe disapproval (Ó Cróinín 16).

If Mrs. Cronin's singing is *sean-nós* when in Gaelic and if she sings her songs in English in a similar style, how can it be that one is completely different from and intrinsically superior to the other, simply because of the matter of the language? Yet such an opinion has been respectably advanced. With no apparent irony, in discussing *sean-nós*, Ó Canainn remarks that the glottal stop, a trope characteristic of the style, particularly in West Cork, is also found in the Anglo-Irish ballads of the region (73). The note of surprise in this observation is striking considering that, given the evidence we have discussed in relation to Mrs. Cronin's singing, the glottal stop would be much more noteworthy by its absence. Proponents of the two-traditions hypothesis then may blithely disregard the socially interactive context of an actual event in favor of detached and prescriptive analysis to perpetuate the validity of that hypothesis.

Róisín White

The dubiousness of this proposition is further highlighted by Róisín White's critique of its pejorative implications for her singing. A fluent Irish speaker, Róisín sings primarily in English but increasingly enjoys singing in Irish, too. A highly respected singer, she is welcomed wherever singers are gathered

together. As in the case of Elizabeth Cronin, we get some idea of the complexities and particularities of singers' experiences when we examine social
interaction. In an interview conducted in February 2001, Róisín's life experience as a singer of songs emerges and is foregrounded over any rhetorical
position of hypothetical linguistic separation. She was born and raised in
Attical, a small farming community in county Down, in English-speaking
Ireland, and her experiences as a singer encompass a vast range of social
registers: from singing in the family home while growing up to enjoying the
company of friends of many years' standing in her own home; from recording albums in the studio to leading song workshops in France; from teaching
songs in the classroom to helping organize singing festivals. She moves in
and out of English and Irish languages with a fluidity that often highlights
the inadequacies and even inappropriateness of simplistic linguistic categorization.

What we see very clearly in Róisín's testimony is the centrality of people
and the importance of personalities, friendships through music, and good
company in the way that Róisín thinks about songs and singing, language or
languages. She is unwilling to separate songs from people and does not make
a clear distinction between the Irish and English languages in her singing.
Her experiences highlight the inadequate and reductive oversimplicity of the
two-traditions hypothesis and the further inadequacy of the notion that, at
any given moment, the singing of songs with English- or Irish-language
lyrics might indicate a shifting between distinct music cultures.

Róisín's interview is living testimony to the centrality of songs and singing
in her life. She couldn't remember a time when she didn't sing. And though
not born into an Irish-speaking environment, her investment has led her to
become a secondary school teacher of that language. She also enjoys singing
and listening to songs in Irish. As she spoke, it became clear that she was perplexed about certain questions surrounding the languages for speech and
song in Ireland. She noted that people often make a big distinction between
unaccompanied traditional singing in the Irish language, which they label
sean-nós, and unaccompanied traditional singing in English, which they say
couldn't be *sean-nós* because of the language of its text. This didn't make any
sense to her. For one thing, she felt that it raised unaccompanied singing in
Irish to a higher position. "Now," she said, "what is the difference between,"
and she sang, "*Cois abhann ghleanna an Chéama*" [By the river in the glen of

Keim] and "I am a lonely exile"? These are the first lines of two songs associated with the West Cork region of Múscraí, in the surroundings of Ballyvourney, both of which she sang to the same melody and with similar pitch, intonation, and understated delivery, in a manner suitable for traditional singing. "What is the difference?" she asked. Again, she sang a line of a song in English and mirrored it with a line in Irish. "D'y'know?" she ventured, "I don't agree with raising one higher than the other."

Here, Róisín had sung snippets from two songs, both from the same region, using a similar metrical pattern for each as dictated by the melody. One, "Cath Chéim an Fhia" (The Battle of Keimaneigh) (Brennan 34–46), is an early-nineteenth-century song commemorating a fight between local vigilantes, or Whiteboys, and the State's Yeomen, which resulted in some deaths. It was composed by Máire Bhuí Ní Laoghaire, a poet of note, mother of one of the Whiteboys, and a strident opponent of the British. The other, "The Kilnamartra Exile," is an emigration song from a later period (around the 1920s) composed by John Brown from the same area, using the same tune, and employing a similar metrical pattern. It tells of an exile's travels across America in an unsuccessful attempt to make his fortune. Finally, his thoughts turn with regret to his home in West Cork, which he will never see again. When Róisín asks "What is the difference?" between the singing of the two songs, she clearly does not mean to collapse the obvious differences in text and history between the two. Rather, we can interpret her insistence that these songs are the same from the point of view of musical style.

By insisting that the musical style is the same in the performance of the two songs, Róisín means to draw attention to their equality as performed items in a particular repertoire. They are representations of different experiences of people in a particular region, both being authentic popular expressions of the history of that place. When performed in a communal context, as they frequently are, both reenact and reaffirm different aspects of the historical experience of and the relationship to place. This is done using more or less the same melody and vocal style, so that it may seem meaningless and arbitrary to privilege one above the other from the point of view of authenticity. Both, in fact, are equally relevant to the situatedness of a particular historically and physically located community and constitute a part of its active song repertoire, embodied in the memories and voices of its individual members. Such a phenomenon strongly suggests that, in present performance, one recalls and implies the other as items in a contemporary repertoire. From the perspective of a linear temporality that valorizes and reifies the past to the exclusion of the present, the Gaelic one is clearly older, more authentic, and thus more relevant than the other. It is precisely these differences that the two-traditions opposition invokes to privilege Gaelic songs. By calling attention to their musical commonalities, however, Róisín astutely foregrounds the notion that they are both coexistent contemporary works enacted in performance, sabotaging the power bind of linear temporality and presenting the possibility of viewing them as equally authentic. By emphasizing an undoubted performative contemporaneity in the present, she blurs and problematizes the boundary that would support a bifurcated view of two hermetically discrete traditions, with the Gaelic element hierarchically perched high above its English-language counterpart by virtue of age, language, and *sean-nós* singing style. In underscoring the musical and stylistic similarities of the two works, then, Róisín's critique of such an ideology is particularly fitting, since it clearly exposes an anomaly between rhetoric and actual practice.

Although not specifically relating it to her own difficulties with the anomalies of the two-traditions bifurcation, Róisín tells of an encounter at a small local music festival in Mayo where a particular song session was devoted to Gaelic songs only. She herself was a guest at the festival and felt obliged to appear and to perform at this session as part of her duties as an invited participant. She arrived when the session was in full swing. Present were some of the most prominent and respected singers of Gaelic songs. Róisín was accompanied by a friend who didn't know any songs in Irish. As Róisín tells it,

————was with me, and————doesn't sing in Irish at all, and we arrived on the Saturday afternoon and the singing session had been on from about three o'clock or something, and most of the singers were singing in Irish, and it was down as unaccompanied singing in Irish, it might even have been down as *sean-nós*, I'm not sure. Ah, there was Joe John, Josie wasn't there, but Treasa Ní Cheannabháin was there, and that boy Sweeney, and Mícheal Ó Seighin and . . . Ah there was a good crowd, and people who are fine singers, and I know their faces but I'm not sure of their names, and they're from Mayo, lovely singers, lovely natural singers. On the programme it probably said 'till five o'clock' or half five, and, sure, half five came, and six o'clock came, and the people were still singing. And then Treasa [MC and an accomplished singer in her own right] said, "It's near time to go to tea now, but there's a few more people have come in there," this is all in Irish, "There's a few more people have come in there, and I see Róisín White, and there's a girl with her, I'm not sure of her name, but they can't go unless them two women sing", so course it fell to my lot to sing and I sang [sings] *Ó tá iníon agam agus tá sí óg.* . . . And then it fell ———'s lot to sing and she says to me "I'm going to kill you, cause I have no effin songs in Irish!", and she said to Treasa, "Just leave me out, I have no songs in Irish." Treasa said, There's no difference, we're all the same here. Sing your pleasure!" And she didn't feel excluded, or she didn't feel that it was of lesser importance, and I thought that's the way it should be!

As Róisín reflected upon this incident, it was clear that she had no difficulty with the concept of a song session only for the singing of songs in Gaelic. Quite the contrary. Her difficulty with the two-traditions dichotomy is not concerned with the privileging of Gaelic song as such but rather with the inferior status unquestioningly accorded to English-language singing and singers because of it. The important point for Róisín was the generous and open way in which Treasa, the MC, had handled the situation—putting her friend at her ease, including her, and welcoming her participation in what could have been an alien environment. It was the reinforcement of such values that Róisín viewed as the important issue. The two-traditions separation was most definitely a factor in the initial tensions of the situation. Far more important, though, was the respect accorded to a fellow singer, the recognition that inclusive relationships between people in these contexts should take priority over the dominant discursive separations that weigh in on the side of exclusion in the cause of authenticity. Instead of strict divisions, we find here the flexible negotiation of uncertainty, appropriateness, and expectation.

Róisín is sensitive to and conscious of the challenges faced by the small community for whom the Irish language is an everyday mode of communication. She is part of a committee that annually organizes the Ennistymon Song Festival, devoted to unaccompanied traditional song in Irish and English. This committee itself has devoted a specific slot in the weekend timetable to encourage Gaelic singing so that its practitioners do not feel crowded out by their more numerous English-speaking counterparts. Consequently, it is clear that her difficulty with the two-traditions dichotomy is not concerned with the privileging of Gaelic song, which might be regarded as a kind of affirmative action, but rather with the inferior status unquestioningly accorded to English-language singing and singers because of it. Róisín's reasons for privileging Gaelic songs and singers are probably because of intrinsic merit, because there are fewer Gaelic singers, and because she enjoys the company and the singing of those who sing in Gaelic. None of these reasons automatically upholds the hierarchical superiority for Gaelic songs advocated by the two-traditions polarity. At the same time, however, these ideas clearly value Gaelic song and singers highly because of their continued unique enrichment of the overall linguistic and musical matrix of the island. Consequently, her argument for a realignment of the imbalance that effectively penalizes English-language singing and singers, rendering them second-class citizens in the singing world, is based on such democratic principles and seems to us a more ethically tenable position.

Teresa McClafferty

One further example from a different region in the "field" serves to underline strikingly the reasons for the acquisition of songs by particular singers. In an interview in 1997 regarding her experience of singing, Teresa McClafferty (born 1931), a Tory islander and a renowned singer, talked about the ways in which she acquired songs and proudly drew attention to the fact that she could pick up songs having heard them only once or twice. Tory, a small island off the northwest coast of Donegal in the Republic of Ireland, is noted for its maintenance of storytelling, singing, music, and dancing traditions and remains one of the most strongly Gaelic-dominant parts of Donegal. For this reason, English was very much a second language for Teresa in her teenage years: at one point during the interview, she stated that once she did not know the difference between "yes" and "no" in English. When she was a teenager, her exposure to English was confined to school lessons and to summer visits from relatives who lived in English-speaking East Donegal and across the North Channel in Scotland. In one story from this period of her life, she related the challenge she faced in acquiring a song from an English-speaking relative. This girl's name was Caitlín Kelly. Her mother was a native of Tory, but she herself had grown up in East Donegal, a part of the region known as *An Lagán* (the Lagan) to Irish speakers from Donegal and which is not to be confused with the Lagan River valley farther east. She was spending a holiday in Tory one summer, and in a particular house in the East End, called *teach Eddy* (Eddy's house), some singing had started. This is how Teresa told the story (to Lillis Ó Laoire):[11]

T: Caitlín Kelly was somewhat older than me, and
L: She was raised out in the Lagan.

T: She was raised out there, up in Ballindrait.

But her mother would come on holiday,

the same way as we do today,

and she would have the children with her according as they became older.

But this afternoon they came

and I used to be matey with her,

when she was at home,

the more that I had no English,

I was trying to be patching away.

But we were sitting back in the kitchen bed

and her aunt asked to sing a song.

She was a beautiful singer

and they say her father before her was also a

good singer,

as you might say.

But she sang this one *I left Ireland and mother*

because we were poor . . .

and I **took a fancy to the song**.[12]

I said to her, "Sing it for me again, for God's sake.

I have a great fancy for that song [*tá dúil iontach agam san amhrán sin*]."

And oh, I had to force her greatly, you know,

she wasn't pleased to sing it for me a second time.

But says I, "If you sing it again, Caitlín,"

says I, "I'll sing it after you."

"Well," says she,

"you won't be able to do that."

Because I had never heard it until then.

"Well," says I,

"sing it again," says I.

And she sang it again, and I sang it after her.

"Well," she says,

"that's the strangest thing I have ever seen done."

Well, the song that you have a fancy for [*a mbeidh dúil agat ann*] . . .

L: You'll pick it up.

T: You'll pick it up right away.

I had the air and the lot with me.

I had.

I never did that but that once.

But I had a fancy for the song [*bhí dúil agam san amhrán*]

and I was sort of understanding it . . .

Fig. 1. "There's a Dear Spot in Ireland" (sung by Teresa McClafferty; transcribed by Niall Keegan & Sandra Joyce, IWMC, University of Limerick)

Teresa's emphatic stress on her desire (*dúil* in Gaelic) for the song is clear from her narrative. The challenge of assimilating a song in the English language after two hearings is stressed, especially as it was the singer's second language.

The song Teresa assimilated after two consecutive hearings is itself of interest to a perspective regarding the interplay between Irish and English languages in singing. Its theme, that of emigration, is a standard one in traditional songs, particularly in the English language. Significantly, its air (see Fig. 1) cannot be regarded as acceptable in the canon of traditional song in Ireland; because of its tune, it does not *sound* "traditional" according to the usual norms of that canon. It is a relatively simple tune with which chordal harmonic accompaniment can easily be imagined. Although Teresa's performance of it uses free rhythm, the tune would fit easily into a strict or regular rhythmic tempo.

The song serves as an example that a living culture operates without regard to considerations of "artistic purity," or at least those of cultural nationalism, and that its carriers make distinct and assured choices about what it is that they like, as confirmed by the work of David Whisnant. If a particular artifact being transmitted from person to person is not "traditional" in the sense that it is a hoary survival from the ancient past, it will be assimilated if individuals remain interested in it. We conclude that this song originated in the United

States and that Teresa's "modern" tune became attached to it at some point during the chain of mainly oral transmission. Perhaps, indeed, the desire, the *dúil*, that inspired her feat of assimilation could be attributed directly to the fact that she found the tune novel and unusual. Like other songs in the repertoire, however, that were orally assimilated, the same process of acquisition applied. Clearly, the motivating factor was desire, *dúil*, and not the categorical bifurcating and isolating principles of cultural nationalism, which would, indeed, condemn such a choice as uninformed, at worst, on the grounds of extremely uncouth and unsuitable language and style. As one commentator, Donal O'Sullivan, put it, "It is surprising that people whose immediate forbears had enjoyed the riches of Gaelic poetry could stomach this type of verse" (7). It is quite clear from Teresa's narrative, however, that nothing remotely approaching nausea troubled her and that she embodied a varied spectrum of cultural forms without apparent tension or conflict.

Conclusion

As we have outlined, ideologies of folklore in Ireland are founded upon romantic theories that, recalling Herder, support a monolithic and essentialist idea that equates "language" and "nation." One song's journey into the Tory island song store gives a different picture of Irish-speaking Ireland to the traditional and discrete purity imagined in exoticizing and orientalizing discourses. It is not that we do not know that Irish speakers can read and write or speak the English language and choose to acquire elements of English culture; on the contrary, it is that for reasons linked to an entrenched two-traditions hypothesis, we choose to ignore such uncertain, uncomfortable truths when we imagine our disciplines and reify our traditions. Once and for all we must admit that, as James Clifford, quoting William Carlos Williams, says, the "pure products go crazy" (1)—if it was a case that they were ever otherwise.

We have tried to illuminate some of the assumptions that underpin attitudes to language and song in Ireland. Founded upon the romantic movement, a mythology has grown up around the Irish and the English languages that in some respects attempts to address the huge power differential between them. Somehow, it is felt that by raising Gaelic traditions above those of English, Irish speakers can devise an effective protecting strategy sufficient to counter the overwhelming strength of English. We have shown that this is not the case and that such assumptions are actually counterproductive to both languages and the interplay and social interaction between them. Such strategies give rise to suspicion and anomalous categories that, in privileging some and devaluing others, are damaging and limiting to all. We call for a realignment of these categories in a way that will still acknowledge the struggles of survival, maintenance, and development faced by local cultures in the face of the international culture industries. Such a realignment need not result in any practical losses. Indeed, putting all participants on a par, regardless of language choices, more surely empowers such necessary resistance to total assimilation.

Notes

1. The use of the phrase "two traditions" here very consciously echoes the "two-traditions" debate in Northern Ireland. The "two-traditions" hypothesis supposes that there are two traditions within Northern Irish politics, the pro-British community and the pro-Irish community, each with identifiable and unitary characteristics that remain authentic. Shirlow and McGovern have shown that this has been one of the central myths used in intergovernmental diagnoses of conflict in Northern Ireland. Yet it has also provided a central support for sectarian discord, deflecting attention away from issues of class and socioeconomics in favor of a binary ideological framework that keeps religion and history at the center of the conflicts.

2. The term used in the Irish language is "*Gaeilge.*" In English, the term "*Gaelic*" is rarely used within Ireland to refer to Irish, largely on account of the continued dominance of cultural nationalist associations. Furthermore, in a wider context, "*Gaelic*" more commonly refers in English to Scottish "*Gàidhlig*" (McCoy and Scott 1). However, we shall use the terms "Irish" and "Gaelic" interchangeably.

3. Literally, "old style" or "old way." A term commonly applied to unaccompanied, solo, monophonic singing found in Gaelic-speaking regions. See Ó Canainn and Vallely.

4. Shore and Wright observe:

> The task for an anthropology of the present . . . is to unsettle and dislodge the certainties and orthodoxies that govern the present. This is not simply a question of "exoticising the familiar." Rather, it involves detaching and repositioning oneself sufficiently far enough from the norms and categories of thought that give security and meaning to the moral universe of one's society in order to interrogate the supposed natural or axiomatic "order of things." (17).

5. As elaborated by Hutchinson, a distinction should be made between cultural nationalism and political nationalism. Cultural nationalists pursued the essentialism of cultural distinctiveness as a moral end in itself; for political nationalists, establishing cultural distinctiveness was often a means to the ends of secession and independent statehood.

6. As Carrier has noted of other such oppositions, this dichotomy springs from an underlying, implicit opposition between the non-Western and Western societies, and it is from this opposition that the two-traditions hypothesis receives much of its rhetorical force and intellectual appeal (5).

7. See note 3.

8. This remark was made by one of the adjudicators at *Cruinniú na mBád* (The Gathering of the Boats), a celebration of the Connemara sailing tradition held annually in Kinvara, county Galway. A traditional singing competition featuring music in Irish and English, *An tAmhrán Beo* (The Living Song) is a regular feature of the *Cruinniú na mBád* festival. Lillis Ó Laoire was a competitor in both categories of the event held in August 1990. The adjudicator who made the remark was Séamus Ó Dubhthaigh.

9. We use the terms "social interaction" and "social interactionism" here while also acknowledging that the more prevalent terms are "symbolic interaction" and "symbolic interactionism," retrospectively coined by Herbert Blumer in 1937 to refer to the research focus of sociologists and social psychologists working from the University of Chicago, in particular the work of George Herbert Mead, Charles Horton Cooley, W. I. Thomas, Robert E. Park, Florian Znaniecki, Robert Redfield, Louis Wirth, James Baldwin, and Blumer himself. "Symbolic interactionism" identifies symbols as the basis of social life. Individuals and society, it is proposed, develop in and through people's interaction, a process of reciprocal influencing mediated by symbols. This is illustrated in the essays in the Becker and McCall collection. By *symbol* is meant "a stimulus that has a learned meaning and value for people, and man's response to a symbol is in terms of its meaning and value rather than in terms of its physical stimulation of his sense organs" (Rose 5). Symbols, and the meanings and values to which they refer, are understood in symbolic interactionism to occur in associative clusters (10). Individuals develop a sense of themselves as they learn to use symbols and also as they learn to see themselves the way they believe others see them. Individuals in this way become objects to themselves and conscious of their condition of otherness. Although as Plummer reports, "symbolic interaction" and "symbolic interactionism" remain the more common terms, it has long been recognized that interactionist studies that actually focus on symbolic concerns are few and far between. The field, it could be argued, is misnamed. As Fred Davis, president of the Society for the Study of Symbolic Interaction, remarked in 1981, "What is noteworthy about (many good interactionist studies) is . . . the (at best) utter casualness or (at worst) complete neglect with which we attend to the actual symbolic materials by which the meaning generation process is carried forward" (qtd. in Plummer xiv). This neglect of symbol is largely due, Davis argues, to a dominant and influential structuralism in the rise of semiotics, an approach that is generally inconsistent with interactionist concerns for emergent, negotiated meaning. Symbolic interactionism, then, is here taken to be a subcategory of the broader field of social interactionism.

10. Denzin, for example, explicitly acknowledges a debt to this "cluster of approaches" in his development of what he terms "interpretive interactionism." From this perspective, Denzin explores the relationship between personal troubles and the public policies and institutions that have been created to address those problems, advocating that "the perspectives and experiences of those persons who are served by applied programs must be grasped, interpreted, and understood if solid, effective, applied programs are to be created" (12).

11. Interview in August 1997 with Teresa McClafferty, conducted by Lillis Ó Laoire in Irish as part of a research project into practices of transmission and performance of song in Tory. In translating the passage, I have given some of the key phrases in the original Irish in brackets after the translation. I append here the full text of the interview in Irish, for the benefit of those who read the language. I have broken the phrases in an attempt to give an approximation of the rhythms of Teresa's narrative:

> *T:* Bhí Caitlín Kelly, bhí sí rud inteacht níos sine ná mise agus . . .
> *L:* Tógadh amuigh ar an Lagán í.
> *T:* Tógadh amuigh thuas i mBallindrait.
>   But thiocfadh a máthair ar laethe saoire,

an dóigh chéanna a bhfuil muid ag goil go fóill,
agus bheadh na páistí léithe agus de réir mar bhí siad ag éirí mór.
But an tráthnóna seo tháinig siad
agus bheinn féin ag mateáil léithe nuair a bheadh sí sa bhaile,
the more nach raibh Béarla ar bith agam,
bhí mé ag iarraidh bheith ag paisteáil liom.
But bhí muid inár suí thiar sa leabaidh na cisteanadh agus d'iarr a haint uirthi
amhrán a cheol.
Bhí ceol galánta aici agus deir siad go raibh ceol
maith ag a hathair roimpi mar déarfá.
But cheol sí an ceann seo *I left Ireland and mother
because we were poor* . . . Agus chuir mé féin **dúil
insan amhrán**.
Dúirt mé léithe, "Ceol dom ar ais é'e gheall ar
Dhia.
Tá dúil iontach agam san amhrán sin."
Agus Ó bhí fórsáil iontach agam uirthi, you know,
cha raibh sí sásta a cheol athuair dom.
Ach deirimse, "Má cheolann tú ar ais é a Chaitlín," a deirimse,
"ceolfaidh mise do dhiaidh é."
"Bhail," a deir sí,
"cha bhíonn tú ábalta sin a dhéanamh."
Nó char chuala mise riamh é go dtí sin.
"Bhail," a deirimse,
"ceol ar ais é," a deirimse.
Agus cheol sí ar ais é agus cheol mise ina diaidh é.
"Bhail," a deir sí,
"sin," a deir sí,
"an rud is iontaí a chonaic mé déanta riamh."
Bhail an t-amhrán a mbeidh dúil agat ann . . .
L: Piocfaidh tú suas é.
T: Piocfaidh tú suas right away é. Bhí an guth is an
lot liom. Bhí. Cha dtear mé sin riamh ach an iarraidh
sin. But bhí dúil agam insan amhrán agus bhí mé
cineál a thuigbheáil . . .

12. Teresa placed great emphasis on these words. The bold type attempts to
represent this.

Works Cited

Becker, Howard S. "Social Interaction." *A Dictionary of the Social Sciences.* Ed. Julian Gould
    and William Kolb. London: Tavistock, 1964. 657–58.
Becker, Howard S., and Michal M. McCall, eds. *Symbolic Interaction and Cultural Studies.*
    Chicago: U of Chicago P, 1990.
Blumer, Herbert. *Symbolic Interactionism: Perspective and Method.* Englewood Cliffs,
    NJ: Prentice-Hall, 1969.
Brennan, Brian. *Máire Bhuí Ní Laoire: A Poet of her People.* Cork: Collins, 2000.
Burke, Kenneth. *A Grammar of Motives.* Berkeley: U of California P, 1969.
Burns, R. B. *The Self-Concept: In Theory, Measurement, Development and Behaviour.* London:
    Longman, 1979.

Byrne, Anne, Ricca Edmondson, and Kathleen Fahy. "Rural Tourism and Cultural Identity in the West of Ireland." *Tourism in Ireland: A Critical Analysis.* Ed. Barbara O'Connor and Michael Cronin. Cork: Cork UP, 1993. 233–57.

Carrier, James G., ed. *Occidentalism: Images of the West.* Oxford: Clarendon, 1995.

Carson, Ciarán. *Irish Traditional Music.* Belfast: Appletree, 1986.

Chakrabarty, Dipesh. "The Death of History? Historical Consciousness and the Culture of Late Capitalism." *Public Culture* 4.2 (1992): 47–66.

Chapman, Malcolm. *The Gaelic Vision in Scottish Culture.* London: Croom Helm, 1978.

Clifford, James. *The Predicament of Culture: Twentieth-century Ethnography, Literature, and Art.* Cambridge: Harvard UP, 1988.

Crowley, Ethel, and Jim MacLaughlin, eds. *Under the Belly of the Tiger: Class, Race, Identity and Culture in the Global Ireland.* Dublin: Irish Reporter, 1997.

Denzin, Norman, K. *Interpretive Interactionism.* Newbury Park: Sage, 1989.

Derrida, Jacques. *Of Grammatology.* Trans. Gayatri Chakravorty Spivak. Baltimore: Johns Hopkins UP, 1977.

Feehan, Fanny. "Suggested Links between Eastern and Celtic Music." *The Celtic Consciousness.* Ed. Robert O'Driscoll. New York: George Braziller, 1981. 333–39.

Gibbons, Luke. *Transformations in Irish Culture.* Cork: Cork UP, 1996.

Goffman, Erving. *The Goffman Reader.* Ed. Charles Lemert and Anne Branaman. Oxford: Blackwell, 1997.

Hall, J. R. "Social Interaction, Culture, and Historical Studies." *Symbolic Interaction and Cultural Studies.* Ed. Howard S. Becker and Michal M. McCall. Chicago: U of Chicago P, 1990. 16–45.

Hutchinson, John. *The Dynamics of Irish Cultural Nationalism: The Gaelic Revival and the Creation of the Irish Nation State.* London: Allen and Unwin, 1987.

Johnson, Nuala C. "Making Space: Gaeltacht Policy and the Politics of Identity." *In Search of Ireland: A Cultural Geography.* Ed. Brian Graham. London: Routledge, 1997. 174–91.

Leersen, Joep. *Remembrance and Imagination: Patterns in the Historical and Literary Representation of Ireland in the Nineteenth Century.* Cork: Cork UP in association with Field Day, 1996.

Mac Con Iomaire, Liam. "Sean-nós." *The Companion to Irish Traditional Music.* Ed. Fintan Vallely. Cork: Cork UP, 1999. 336–37.

MacDonagh, Oliver. *States of Mind: A Study of Anglo-Irish Conflict 1780–1980.* London: Allen and Unwin, 1983.

McCourt, Frank. *Angela's Ashes.* London: Flamingo, 1996.

McCoy, Gordon. "Rhetoric and Realpolitik: The Irish Language Movement and the British Government." *Culture and Policy in Northern Ireland: Anthropology in the Public Arena.* Ed. Hastings Donnan and Graham McFarlane. Belfast: Institute of Irish Studies, Queen's University Belfast, 1997. 117–38.

McCoy, Gordon, and Maolcholaim Scott, eds. *Aithne na nGael: Gaelic Identities.* Belfast: Institute of Irish Studies, Queen's University Belfast, 2000.

Nash, Catherine. " 'Embodying the Nation'—The West of Ireland Landscape and Irish Identity." *Tourism in Ireland: A Critical Analysis.* Ed. Barbara O'Connor and Michael Cronin. Cork: Cork UP, 1993. 86–112.

O'Boyle, Seán. *The Irish Song Tradition.* Dublin: Gilbert Dalton, 1976.

Ó Canainn, Tomás. *Traditional Music in Ireland.* London: Routledge, 1978.

Ó Cróinín, Dáibhí, ed. *The Songs of Elizabeth Cronin: Traditional Singer.* Dublin: Four Courts, 2000.

Ó Giolláin, Diarmuid. *Locating Irish Folklore: Tradition, Modernity, Identity.* Cork: Cork UP, 2000.

O'Leary, Philip. *The Prose Literature of the Gaelic Revival: Ideology and Innovation*. University Park: U of Pennsylvania P, 1994.

Ó Riada, Seán. *Our Musical Heritage*. Dublin: Fundúireacht an Riadaigh and Dolmen P, 1982.

O'Rourke, Brian. *Blas Meala: A Sip from the Honey Pot: Gaelic Folksongs with English Translations*. Dublin: Irish Academic, 1985.

Ó Súilleabháin, Donncha. *Scéal an Oireachtais* (The Story of *an tOireachtas*). Dublin: An Clóchomhar, 1984.

O'Sullivan, Donal. *Songs of the Irish: An Anthology of Irish Folk Music and Poetry with English Verse Translations*. Dublin: Mercier, 1981.

Ó Torna, Caitríona. "Constráid na Gaeltachta." *An Aimsir Óg* 2.1 (2000).

Ó Tuama, Seán, ed. *The Gaelic League Idea*. Cork: Mercier, 1972.

Pickering, Michael, and Tony Green, eds. *Everyday Culture: Popular Song and the Vernacular Milieu*. Milton Keynes: Open UP, 1987.

Plummer, Ken, ed. *Symbolic Interactionism*. Vol. 2. Aldershot: Edward Elgar, 1991.

Quinn, Bob. *Atlantean: Ireland's North African and Maritime Heritage*. New York: Quartet Books, 1986.

Rock, Paul. "Symbolic Interactionism." *The Social Science Encyclopedia*. Ed. Adam Kuper and Jessica Kuper. London: Routledge and Kegan Paul, 1985. 843–44.

Rose, Arnold M. "A Systematic Summary of Symbolic Interaction Theory." *Human Behavior and Social Processes*. Ed. Arnold M. Rose. London: Routledge and Kegan Paul, 1962. 3–19.

Said, Edward W. *Orientalism: Western Conceptions of the Orient*. London: Penguin, 1978.

Shields, Hugh. *Narrative Singing in Ireland: Lays, Ballads, Come-all-yes and Other Songs*. Dublin: Irish Academic, 1993.

Shirlow, Peter, and Mark McGovern, eds. *Who Are The People?: Unionism, Protestantism and Loyalism in Northern Ireland*. London: Pluto, 1997.

Shore, Cris, and Susan Wright, eds. *Anthropology of Policy: Critical Perspectives on Governance and Power*. London: Routledge, 1997.

Turner, Jonathan H. *A Theory of Social Interaction*. Stanford, CA: Stanford UP, 1988.

Vallely, Fintan, ed. *The Companion to Irish Traditional Music*. Cork: Cork UP, 1999.

Whisnant, David E. *All That Is Native and Fine: The Politics of Culture in an American Region*. Chapel Hill: U of North Carolina P, 1983.

Music

W

Language

CHOICE

in SONG and

Words:

Dialect

Performance

Part Three

"Trying to Break It Down"

MCs' Talk and Social Setting in Drum & Bass Performance

—Morgan Gerard and Jack Sidnell

Although music is increasingly available as an object of personal consumption as recordings circulated on disks and in electronic files, in one manifestation it is fundamentally social—embedded in public, socially organized events of performance. The situated activity of musical performance can be analyzed in terms of the social groupings that are organized within its course. In this essay, we argue that an anthropological account of drum & bass performance requires just such a situated analysis.[1] Thus, rather than treat social structures and categories (for example, race, social class, gender) as objective, external, and independent facts that constrain action, we ask about the organization of the activity itself and seek to reveal the categories implicated in its production. Our goal, then, is to explicate the methods that participants use in order to construct and understand the courses of action that are constitutive of the event in question: the performance of drum & bass music. Our argument is that such events involve an explicit rejection of received social categories based on ascribed criteria (that is, just those categories of race, social class, and gender that traditional accounts assume and employ in their analysis) and, simultaneously, a creative and methodic construction of alternative categories that are inherently tied to the situational particulars of the unfolding event.

In order to achieve our objectives, we undertake a detailed analysis of talk in three performances of drum & bass. Our investigation reveals that the MC draws upon a wide range of linguistic and performative resources that not only complement and enhance records played by a DJ; they also organize and maintain the audience's participation. Readers familiar with the music and performance conventions of drum & bass will immediately recognize the phenomena discussed in this essay. The analysis presented seeks to explicate these readily recognizable features of drum & bass performance through ethnographic description and, in so doing, explore one particular articulation of language and music.

The approach taken here is consistent with that developed by Christopher Small who, in *Musicking*, encourages theorists to engage with music in and as an event:

> a musical performance is a much richer and more complex affair than is allowed by those who concentrate their attention exclusively on the musical work and on its effect on an individual listener. If we widen the circle of our attention to take in the entire set of relationships that constitutes a performance, we shall see that music's primary meanings are not individual at all but social. Those social meanings are not to be hived off into something called a "sociology" of music that is separate from the meaning of the sounds but are fundamental to an understanding of the activity that is called music. (8)

Published works on drum & bass give scant attention to music as a performed activity embedded in complex and specific social contexts. Insider accounts, generally written by music journalists and fans, tend to construct a "historical" chronicle of drum & bass, its subgenres, and its personalities and thus give readers a sense of the subcultural scenario from which the music emerged in England (Collins; James; Reynolds) and Canada (Silcott; McCall). In the more limited scholarly writing on drum & bass, we find attempts to develop formal definitions of the drum & bass genre (Noys; Kronengold); concerns with blackness, authenticity, and the dialectic of urban/suburban identity (Noys; Thornton); and even one analysis of specific works as they relate to Kant's notion of the sublime (Chapman). Influenced by the Birmingham School of subcultural studies, scholars of drum & bass and other club and rave music tend to focus on "subjects" rather than on sites and on "articulations" rather than on activities. The result is that performances of music and dance—arguably the central concern and certainly the central activity of the participants—become exiled from any understanding of the music or the "subculture."

In fact, the only work we know of that addresses the connection between social meanings and performance interactions is Kai Fikentscher's study of underground dance music in New York City. Fikentscher centers his analysis on the dance floor, where social meanings are negotiated between people as they experience performers, music, dance, and each other. Acknowledging

Small's use of the term "musicking" to denote any form of participation in a musical event, Fikentscher suggests that mediated musical activity in dance clubs occurs through "collective performance" and an "interactive" relationship between DJs and dancers. His position is that "underground club dancing is characterized by collective performance on the floor as much as by the interaction of this performance with that of the DJ in the booth" (Fikentscher 58). While we would add that the collective performers on (and off) the dance floor are as interactive with each other as they are with the DJ, both conclusions follow from Small's understanding of what transpires in the event of music:

The act of musicking establishes in the place where it is happening a set of relationships, and it is in those relationships that the meaning of the act lies. They are to be found not only between those organized sounds which are conventionally thought of as being the stuff of musical meaning but also between the people who are taking part, in whatever capacity, in the performance; and they model, or stand as metaphor for, ideal relationships as the participants in the performance imagine them to be: relationships between person and person, between individual and society, between humanity and the natural world and even perhaps the supernatural world. (13)

In this respect, we find previous accounts of the MCs' interactional work largely inadequate. Simon Reynolds, for instance, observes that MCs utilize

an arsenal of non-verbal, incantatory techniques, bringing spoken language closer to the state of music: intonation, syncopation, alliteration, internal rhyme, slurring, rolling of r's, stuttering of consonants, twisting and stretching of vowels, comic accents, onomatopoeia. (232)

Whereas Reynolds talks of "free-associational delirium" (226), we show that these techniques are in fact constituent features of situated activities within which various social categories and claims to membership are embedded and through which MCs collaborate in intricate ways with both the audience and the DJ to build courses of action, organize the interactive context, and manage particular features of the local social setting (Schutz). In order to illustrate these activities, ethnographically specified examples are drawn from three performances that took place in Toronto, Canada. The first of these occurred at Industry Nightclub on 27 August 1999 and featured MC L Natural of Toronto and MC Fats and DJ Darren Jay, both from London, England; the second, at the Jet Nightclub on 31 July 1999, featured MC Fats, MC Fearless, and DJs the Usual Suspects, also from London; the third, at Turbo Niteclub on 26 May 2000, featured MC Ragga D alongside DJs D. Bridges and Maldini of Bad Company, again from London. (All of these performances are available on cassette tape; see Discography.)

Fikentscher examines relationships between DJs, dancers, and House music. A focus on drum & bass introduces a further complication due to the presence of language or talk within the course of the performance. In the context of contemporary club and rave music, drum & bass (or Jungle, as it is sometimes known) is distinguished from House by the fact that its performance includes a live vocalist, an MC. Drum & bass, in comparison with House music, can thus be characterized as talk-prominent: MCs are expected to interject sung, spoken, or rhymed vocals both to complement and enhance the predominantly instrumental music. Recognizing this difference, Noys draws a parallel between drum & bass MCs and rappers, referring to Jungle as a "Techno hip-hop" (321). Historical and ethnographic research, however, suggests a more important connection between drum & bass and reggae music. The majority of English and Toronto-based drum & bass MCs are of West Indian and, more specifically, Jamaican heritage, and this style of club and rave music is characterized by a significant degree of borrowing from the conventions of sound-system performances in Jamaican popular music. Either inspired by or getting their start chatting on British reggae sound systems as DJs, most of the veteran English performers then brought these experiences to drum & bass (and henceforth adopted the title "MC").[2] One such borrowing is a technique that figures prominently in drum & bass, known as the "rewind." As Simon Jones defines it, this consists of the "interruption and constant "cutting-back" of a popular record to its opening bars . . . to increase the sense of drama and anticipation amongst the audience," a practice that, along with "the DJ's exhortations and interjections . . . help[s] to socialize the dance event as a whole, by making it "live" and turning it into a creative performance" (30). This was the case in all of the Toronto performances we attended. For example, we observed MC L Natural, in the opening bars of a popular record, repeatedly call out, "Who wants it? Who needs it?" thus requesting a display of coparticipation from audience members and providing the DJ with an opportunity to spin back the record to its beginning. Such practices are crucially important to the organization of the performance as a whole as well as to the activities embedded therein.

Given that the MCs are often of West Indian descent, one might expect to find a significant number of Jamaican Creole (JC) (Patwa) linguistic features in drum & bass performances. Indeed, both James and Reynolds note that this was true of the live and pirate radio performances of the early 1990s that they studied. Our investigation, however, reveals relatively few distinctively Jamaican linguistic features (for discussion of JC, or Patwa, see Bailey; Cassidy and LePage; Cassidy). MC L Natural's performance included distinctive JC pronunciations (/ridim/ = "rhythm"), particular semantic nuances ("rough," "hard," "massive," "ride," "dance hall"), and morphosyntactic features characteristic of the dialect (/mi/ = "me" as first person singular subject pronoun, as in "Well now then massive, me say yes—time to ride!" and "Yes me comin' through"). While the number of such distinctive dialect features is relatively small, they have a disproportionate importance insofar as they are used in directives that call for responsive action from audience members. As such, an audience member's participation in the event often depends upon having some degree of competence in Patwa—those who cannot understand Patwa will not be able to participate with the rest of the audience in the actions that the MC is calling upon them to do. This said, our examination of three Toronto performances revealed relatively few distinctively Patwa formal linguistic features. As such, if language is understood solely as a formal system of phonological, morphological, and syntactic features, we will not be able to explain the "Jamaicaness" of the MC's talk and performance.

For this and other reasons, it would be a grave mistake to restrict one's conception of language to formal features of linguistic structure. Rather than taking language in structural terms as a symbolic system through which social action is represented, we focus here on talk as the primary mode of locally managed and situated human activity—sequentially organized and collaboratively built social action in and of itself. With regard to the specific case under examination, it seems clear that the Jamaican cultural tradition which MCs draw upon is not evidenced in the language they use so much as the way they use language to assemble, organize, and manage frameworks of participation in the situated activities that make up the performance as a whole. Drawing from the conventions of sound-system performances in Jamaica, drum & bass MCs, like their reggae DJ counterparts, "remain organically connected to the audience from whom they continually draw their inspiration and whose collective moods and concerns they seek to reflect" (Jones 29). We would modify this statement to include "direct" as well as "reflect," for in drum & bass, MCs and DJs direct the activity in overt ways. This kind of direction is predicated upon the coordination of the MC and the DJ (who are paired either regularly or periodically at live events), which in turn depends upon the MC's intimate knowledge of the music being played by the DJ, his recurrent monitoring of the progress and mixing of records on the turntables, and his recognition of the DJ's gestural or verbal indications of imminent musical changes.[3]

A starting point for the analysis of interaction in drum & bass performance is found in the concept of "call and response," which is frequently invoked to describe African and African diaspora musical forms (for example, Lomax; Chernoff). The patterns discussed under this rubric are clearly observable in drum & bass. Indeed, almost every MC has adopted a call-and-response chant; for instance, MC Ragga D (who performs with Bad Company) will say, "When I say "Bad" you say 'Company.'" Anticipating the audience's reply ("Company"), the DJ will cut out the volume of the record being played in order to fill the room with the audience's shouted response. Another frequently observed pattern draws upon Jamaican DJ Tappa Zukie's mid-1970s hit "O Lord" and requires the same joint participation of the DJ, MC, and audience. Generally used in the opening bars of popular tracks, the MC calls out, "People are you ready?" At the completion of the question the DJ cuts out the record in expectation of the audience's response: a combination of "Bo!" (to imitate a gunshot) and one hand raised in the air in the shape of a pistol.

Such coordinated social action requires the application of several different kinds of practical knowledge that are inadequately denoted by the term "call and response." In the first place, it is not clear what kind of an action a "call" is—there appears to be no clear analogue in ordinary conversation and, in fact, the actions subsumed under "call" appear to be more appropriately described by a range of glosses—"directive," "question," "request," and so on. The point here is that the action cannot be properly, once and for all, designated in advance of an examination of the particulars of the talk in question.

For this reason, we suggest that the phenomena designated by the phrase "call and response" is best analyzed in terms of what conversation analysts refer to as "adjacency pair organization" (Sacks, *Lectures*; Goodwin and Heritage). Conversation analysis shows us that one needs to look at the way the "call" (or first pair part) is treated by the coparticipants and, in particular, its recipients. The various examples discussed in this essay suggest that the call-and-response notion involves an essential and unwarranted abstraction from the contingent and reflexive processes of interpretation at work in interaction. Furthermore, as the "People are you ready?" example makes clear, the "call" does not in and of itself indicate what an appropriate response will be; rather, any given participant's production of a response draws on various forms of contextual and conventional knowledge. So, for example, the use of the hand raised in the shape of a pistol and the resounding "Bo!" is a Jamaican sound-system tradition and, in the context of drum & bass, points to experience with, or recognition of, a convention associated with membership in various identifiable social categories, as we will discuss later.

We now turn to the specific kinds of interactional work that an MC undertakes during the course of a performance. For the purposes of analysis, we have organized our discussion into a number of topical sections; having done so, however, we want to emphasize that the performance as a whole constitutes a perceivedly complete and sequentially organized course of action. That is, the various DJs, MCs, and audience participants at any given performance all collaborate to produce something that all parties can potentially recognize as a coherent, successful "night." We begin our analysis with a consideration of the MCs' use of person-referring forms before moving to consider the way in which descriptions of the social setting and the directives within which they are frequently embedded organize and make visible specific categorizations of the event's participants.

The MCs' Use of Pronouns and Other Person-Referring Forms

In the example that follows, MC L Natural, who had previously been emceeing for Toronto's DJ Sniper, is joined onstage by MC Fats. After DJ Darren Jay steps to the turntables, he waits for Sniper's record to play out completely and then proceeds to play his first record of the night, "Porno Style" by Danny Breaks and AK1200. This particular record belongs to a set-introduction piece; infamous for its highly sexualized moaning (from a pornographic movie), it works well as a first record because of the way in which its simple drum pattern repeats (in what is known as a "two-step" pattern in drum & bass) for approximately two minutes before the full accompaniment of more complex drums and the bass line come in. The following excerpt represents the talk that accompanied the first minutes of the record:

MC Fats:	**We**'re rolling on with the Darren Jay.
	The intro . . . ( ) Are **you** ready inside?[4]
MC L Natural:	Darren Jay, MC Fats, Natural.
	We come with a firing squad.
	We come with a firing squad.
	We come with a firing squad.
MC Fats:	Oh my God!
	The way the DJ shakes the sound.
	Whoa now.
	With an intro.
	With an intro.
MC L Natural:	All about that and **dem** no treat **dem** flow.
	Inside **you** ready, ready, ready, ready, ready, ready.
	Rough, rough, **they** comin' rough and steady.
	Anytime **you** ready, ready, ready.
	Darren Jay, Jay, Jay ( ) is ready.
	We're ready. Ready. Ready. Ready. What?!
MC Fats:	( ) to know that the way **we** step inside.
	I am **your** undercover bubbler ( )
	Here **we** go.

We have emphasized the pronouns here to draw attention to the way they are used to categorize the event's participants as primary addressed recipients (for example, "you"), nonrecipients (for example, "they"), and coauthors (for example, "we"). In most cases, the MC uses "you" to establish the audience as the recipient for the talk. Although this may seem self-evident, it is, of course, not the only option available. It would also be possible for the MC to construct the DJ or another MC onstage as a primary addressed recipient. This, however, happens only rarely. More often, the DJ and any other MCs are referred to, along with the MC (speaker), by the use of "we." In this way, MCs use pronouns to organize the individuals present into identifiable sets of participants who are differently positioned with regard to the ongoing activity implemented in the same talk. As such, and to foreshadow the discussion that follows, pronouns provide a rather neat illustration of the way in which language is a constituent feature of the settings it is used to describe

(Heritage). That is to say, "we come with a firing squad" is both *about* the setting insofar as it consists of a clearly self-directed description, and *of* the setting insofar as the "we" provides for the recognition of a particular dimension of that setting—for example, the framework of participation and the alignment of the participants vis-à-vis one another. While we cannot provide a full analysis of the various footings (Goffman; see also Goodwin & Goodwin) made visible through such pronominal usages, it is possible to see the way in which both MCs and DJs construct themselves as a group through their repeated and reciprocal uses of the first person plural pronoun "we." The ambiguity of "we" between inclusive and exclusive readings has often been noted (Sacks, *Lectures*), and here we find an instance of this: while it seems clear the "we" in "we come with a firing squad" refers to the MCs and the DJs (that is, the performers), the "we" in "We're rolling on with the Darren Jay" and in "Here we go" could potentially include members of the audience.

In several turns shown in the example, such as Fats's "Are you ready inside," the audience members are clearly categorized as primary addressed recipients for the talk. One may also note the way Fats establishes a more personalized and individualized dyad by his use of "I" and "your" in "I am your undercover bubbler." Finally, L Natural makes reference to a world outside the immediate framework of the activity through his use of "dem," in effect establishing the boundary of the event. These examples illustrate, then, the way in which the MCs are able to shape and manage the emergent participation framework as an ongoing accomplishment. Frameworks of participation are of basic importance insofar as they contribute to the self-explicating and accountable (observable, recognizable, reportable) character of the activity under way. That is to say, pronouns make an organization of participation visible. An understanding of the participation framework can then be used to draw further inferences about the character of the activity, its probable course, how one might be implicated in it, and so forth (for example, a request for coparticipation is more likely to be addressed to a "you" than to a "them"). Audience members, although they can to some extent either accept or not accept such proposals (for instance, by attending or not attending the talk), cannot actively shape the participation framework in the same way as the MC can. Clearly, then, the activities we discuss here have, as one of their consistent and pervasive features, a basic asymmetry between performers and audience. As will become clear in our discussion that follows, much of the MC's talk is directed to overcoming such asymmetry and creating an interactive context in which the setting's members actively coparticipate. However, the construction of such opportunities for audience coparticipation is at all times measured and managed by the MC.

Describing and Assembling Features of the Setting

During the course of the performance, the MC routinely uses language to describe features of the immediate social setting. Following Garfinkel and Sacks ("Sociological Description"), we treat such descriptions as complex forms of social action that cannot be properly understood if analyzed solely in terms of their relative "completeness" (Garfinkel and Sacks; Schegloff, "Description"). As Weber noted, no object or event can be described exhaustively. Rather, descriptions propose certain kinds of relevancies about the relation between an object or event described and the ongoing course of action within which the description is embedded. Speakers, then, do not passively "report" already obvious and observable features of the social setting. Instead, in the course of their practical engagement with each other, they actively investigate the social setting in which they find themselves and make proposals, in the form of descriptions, about which features are at the moment relevant to the ongoing course of action they are pursuing. Descriptions, then, are a public way of organizing social settings. In our observations of the three drum & bass events, we noted three forms of description: global/omnirelevant, spatial/temporal, and reflexive. We discuss each of these in turn.

In those examples we characterize as "global" or "omnirelevant," the MC describes features of the social setting in such a way as to highlight the absolute generality and "generalizability" of the referent. Such an orientation on the part of the MC is demonstrable insofar as co-occurring features of the talk make this clear. For example, L Natural repeatedly uses the framing device "It's all about" to convey such omnirelevance: "It's all about the way we play the sounds"; "It's all about the way you flex down the rhythm"; "It's all about the way we step inside your house." Such descriptions contrast with those that are quite clearly tied to some immediate, highly local, emergent feature of the interactive context. Note the way in which the third example combines the "omnirelevant" framing device—"It's all about"—with a spatial description, a matter to which we now turn.

MCs routinely describe the temporal and spatial parameters of the event. Particularly important in this respect is the MC's use of place-names. Consider the following sequence:

MC Fats: Representing drum & bass style
                 all the way from the UK.
                 The first part of the style . . .
MC L Natural: Yes, all the way
                 live and direct from the U.K.
                 London ( ) Y'all ready.

This example illustrates the way spatial descriptions provide for public displays of agreement. Note how MC L Natural orients to several features of MC Fats's description. In the first place, his turn-initial "yes" is properly placed to display his ongoing monitoring of Fats's talk. Furthermore, it explicitly indicates agreement with Fats's description. L Natural reinforces such agreement by displaying that it is founded upon an ongoing attention to and understanding of the turns to which it is directed. For instance, L Natural repeats certain elements ("all the way . . . from the UK") of the talk with which he is in agreement. In this way, MC L Natural is able to display, in no uncertain terms, his alignment toward Fats's talk.

Besides the opportunities they provide for the expression of agreement, spatial and temporal descriptions are important in a number of other respects. We note that spatial descriptions involving place-names are always phrased in such a way as to show the relevance of the spatial/location description to the immediate framework of the performance. Thus MCs appear never to say things such as "Hey! I'm from the UK" or "This is my hometown—Toronto!" Rather, place-names are embedded in turns of the following sort: "Live and direct from London," "All the way from the UK," "Toronto, you hear this sound." These turns share a clear orientation to the contingencies of the immediate local context of the performance. Place-names are often used to indicate one position in a movement that, in its totality, encompasses the current scene (for example, MC Ragga D describes himself and Bad Company as having "just come from Philly"). That is to say, the place-names point to an origin or endpoint for the performance. This is made explicit in the example "Live and direct from the U.K."

We dwell on the connection between place-names and the local framework of participation for two reasons. First, the theme of place is fundamental to what might loosely be understood as the politics of MC performances. Drum & bass MCs cite locations as if relaying messages between the centers of, to borrow Benedict Anderson's term, an "imagined community." For the British MC performing abroad, directing local audiences in the participation of the drum & bass event creates new employment markets and nurtures the development of new "scenes." While maintaining their position in an established, Anglo-centric hierarchy, MCs further a "political" agenda—one commonly invoked in interviews with British DJs and MCs—to take the music, its performance, and thus themselves to every corner of the globe. Through regular engagements in countries such as Canada, Brazil, and Japan (as well as nations throughout in Europe) and by the fact that it is their voice that conducts participation on dance floors, the MC might be understood as the primary mediator in the development of what Mark Slobin calls the "diasporic interculture." For Toronto MCs performing at home it is a case of, on the one hand, recognizing the guiding role played by their British counterparts and, on the other, engaging in a process of individuation by which they establish their own, local ranking in the hierarchy of drum & bass. Will Straw has argued that such polycentricity is a defining feature in the generation of scenes and communities in dance music. While his discussion of how social space and temporal processes shape the enculturation of new scenes and communities is relevant to the preceding discussion, it is not through media such as record labels, dance music magazines, and DJ play lists that dance music culture most successfully propagates itself but rather through the immediacy and experience of participating in live performance.

The second reason we emphasize the connection between the place-names and the local framework is because it highlights a persistent feature of the spatial descriptions we found in the MCs' performances—their orientation to the immediate social setting and emergent features of the activity. Such descriptions in fact constitute a major resource that the MC draws upon in managing both the framework of participation and the temporality of the unfolding event. For example, at the beginning of the performance, the MC was found to repeat the phrase "You ready?" in this way orienting to imminent yet "future" stages of the performance. Given that the MC is assumed to have access to privileged information about the scheduling of the event, "You ready?" is hearable as promissory of things to come.⁵ "You ready?" displaces the here-now of the interactive event by suggesting that it is preparatory to something that is about to happen. At a well-defined, indeed pivotal, point in the course of the performance, the MC dramatically shifts from "You ready?" to "Right here! Right now!" The temporality of the event is thus not an "external feature" of the performance but rather something that MCs manage and organize within the course of the activities in which they are engaged.

Temporal descriptions are a persistent and pervasive feature of the MC's talk; other examples that we found in the three performances referred to here, as well as in drum & bass performances generally, include phrases such as "Look out below, from head to toe, now we start the show" (MC Fats); "Time to break it down" (MC Fats); and "It's time to ride" (MC L Natural). In the following sections, we will argue that such a use of descriptions to manage and assemble features of the social setting is crucial to an understanding of the interactional work that constitutes an MC's performance. In particular, such spatial and temporal descriptions provide for the recognizability of the social setting as a temporally unfolding set of locations. These locations, which are emergent features of the interactive context, then become resources for building social categories in the talk of the MC.

A third type of description that we find throughout our transcripts of the performances might be characterized as self-directed or reflexive. For example, MC L Natural describes himself as "reaching out to the core" and "trying to break it down." Such descriptive statements offer characterizations of the interactional work in which the MC (along with the DJ) is currently engaged (see Garfinkel and Sacks on "glossing" and "formulating"); as such, they are a highly explicit way of managing and organizing the settings in which they are embedded in that they provide a characterization of the participation framework and the activity in progress. We found that such descriptions were routinely concerned with the quality of the relationship between performer and audience. Notice in this respect that MC L Natural's "reaching out to the core" offers a characterization of both the course of action under way (that is, reaching) and the audience (that is, as a heterogeneous population composed of recognizable subgroups, for example, the core versus the periphery).

Social Action in the MC's Talk: Directives and Questions

During his performance, MC Ragga D was heard to say to the audience, "Your request is our command." In citing this apparently simple cliché, the MC is in fact offering what we take to be a rather astute, reflexive description that points to a persistent point of trouble in the MC's performance as well as the steps routinely taken toward its solution. Note, then, that the phenomena we have discussed to this point are largely single turns abstracted in a number of ways from the actual interactive, sequentially organized contexts in which they were embedded. Of course, when MCs offer spatial descriptions that include place-names, these are often received with expressions of appreciation (for example, applause), and as such these descriptions provide opportunities for audience members to engage as active coparticipants. Public displays of appreciation positioned directly after the mention of a place-name are one way in which audience members can show that they are attending to the talk of the MC and that they are active participants in the ongoing, collaboratively built course of action. However, such shows of appreciation can do little more than this; they only demonstrate that the audience member has heard the name of a particular city. Such displays of appreciation do not presuppose the kind of detailed understanding that recipients develop in response to a turn-at-talk in ordinary conversation (Goodwin and Heritage; Goodwin and Goodwin).

Other displays, however, indicate that audience members do, in fact, have a detailed understanding of the unfolding character of the activity. We find in this respect that the participation framework that encompasses the MC, the DJ, and those audience members who occupy the space directly in front of the performers is highly structured. These front-members of the audience can be seen to participate in the proceedings in concert, both with each other and with the performers, and as such there must be some finely tuned mechanism by which this is accomplished.

In attempting to get at this issue, we would argue that directives are a critically important resource that MCs draw upon in an effort to build social action collaboratively with the audience and to organize the emergent features of the setting in ways that render them recognizable to others. Crucial to our understanding of directives is the recognition that they constitute first pair parts in adjacency pairs (Goodwin and Heritage). As such, we may appropriately speak of "directive-response sequences." We have already mentioned the importance of sequences in our earlier discussion of place-names and audience appreciation. There we suggested that the mention of place-names provided opportunities for audience members to express appreciation (and potentially to make claims about membership in social categories—such as "Torontonian"). Such sequences provide for the expression not only of appreciation but also, and simultaneously, of understanding. As noted, however, this can only be a claim to understanding. The specific content of the response/appreciation does not in such cases incorporate detailed information as to what the audience member is responding to or just what he or she appreciates. The expression of appreciation only indicates that the audience member is monitoring the talk of the MC and can interpret it sufficiently well so as to reveal particular contextual moments in which appreciation is appropriate or even expected (and if the expected appreciation is not forthcoming, its absence will be noticeable). Directive-response sequences go well beyond this and call for a more committed form of engagement from audience members as well as a more detailed monitoring and parsing of the MC's talk. For example, when the MC yells "Jump!" to properly respond to such a directive the audience member must not only project its possible completion, upon which response is due, but must also understand the specific content of the directive. The response to the directive—jumping—conveys the audience member's understanding of the MC's talk at each of these levels.

There are a number of other considerations that are relevant to the organization of action in these contexts. In the first place, not all audience members are expected to respond in this way to all directives. During the course of our ethnographic fieldwork, we noted that audience members routinely scanned their peers when directives were issued presumably to see whether and how others were responding to the directive. Collaborative social action is possible insofar as audience members are simultaneously able to monitor the behavior of others and respond to the directive themselves. When the MC says "jump," he is heard as calling for a rather specific kind of action, and it is certainly not the case that any form of jumping will count as an appropriate response (see Sidnell, "Ethnographic," for a consideration of what is involved here). Coparticipants, particularly those who occupy the space directly in front of the performers, monitor each other's behaviors and, we suspect, are capable of applying normative evaluations, judgments, and sanctions in response to behavior that is perceived as deviant or nonconforming. The application of normative conventions—both as resources for interpreting action, in effect rendering it recognizable, and as guidelines for how one should appropriately conduct oneself—can thus be seen as centrally implicated in the production of coordinated activities of this kind (Heritage).

In our ethnographic research and later examination of the transcripts, we found that directives were often quite specific in the types of social action they requested of the audience members. For example, at one point MC L Natural calls out, "Whistles, Lighters!" Such a directive indicates a set of resources that may appropriately be used in public displays of coparticipation (for example, blow your whistle, light your lighter). Moreover, when we consider such a turn as part of a directive-response sequence, we see that it provides a specific opportunity (a "next-position" or slot in a sequence) in which a display of coparticipation can be performed. Audience members who are able to use these resources (whistles, lighters) in the next position within the sequence show that they have both attended to and understood the MC's talk and are therefore actively engaged in the ongoing course of action being constructed.

Questions served similar functions in the MC's talk. Like directives, the occurrence of a question creates a conditionally relevant next position within which a recipient's talk or action is expected and noticeably absent if not forthcoming. MCs repeatedly provide opportunities for audience participation through the use of questions such as "Who is feeling this?" and "Toronto, you hear this sound?"

These various forms of talk may be combined to create important focal moments within the performance that are collaborative and dialogic. MCs were repeatedly found to combine directives with descriptions of the spatial setting; in so doing, they were managing the participation framework of the activity in quite specific ways. This is accomplished by creating a spatial grid described from the perspective of the MC. Thus, when MC L Natural says "let me hear the people on the left side," the appropriate audience members show their monitoring of this talk by responding on the beat at the completion of the request. MC L Natural then repeats the request, substituting right side, back, up front, and so on. Such devices make directives much more specific and effective insofar as they introduce principles for the production and recognition of heterogeneity within the audience. Requests that are more specific may also be more readily hearable by a recipient as being "for me." These opportunities for audience displays of coparticipation also clearly involve the collaborative work of the DJ. DJs and MCs construct opportunities for audience member displays by combining the specifically addressed questions or directives we have discussed with gaps in what is an otherwise constant stream of music. The MC and DJ accomplish this is in part through the use of requests that make specific reference to the soundtrack. Thus, for instance, it was observed that MC Ragga D called, "Who wants a rewind?" and MC L Natural asked, "Who wants it? Who needs it?" Following this, the DJ stopped the music, creating a silence within which the action of the audience's response was conditionally relevant.

Managing Membership and Social Categories

The issues we have discussed separately in terms of footings, descriptions, and directives are, in fact, all part of a single organization through which social categories and claims to membership within them are managed. This is the topic to which we now turn. We have already seen how, in their interactional work with the audience, MCs frequently make reference to categories that are tied to local and emergent features of the social setting—for example, the people on the left side, the people on the right side. Such categorizations are, in fact, symptomatic of a much broader phenomenon that involves the rejection of categories based on race, gender, and class in favor of those that are locally managed within the setting by the setting's members. We find this rejection made explicit in remarks by MC Fats ("Could a Black, Could a White, Indian, Chiny, inside tonight") and also by MC L Natural ("Whether White or Black, it don't mean jack!"). These rejected criteria are replaced by categories generated within the setting. As noted, these categories are inherently tied to the local particulars of the event and are often based on spatial principles of differentiation (those on the left side, right side, and so forth).

The explicit rejection of categories based on ascribed criteria (race, class, gender) is thus combined with the construction of alternatives in the MC's talk. For example, MC Ragga D consistently referred to the audience members occupying the space directly in front of the performers using a Patwa term that has played an important role in Jamaican pop music from ska onward: "rudeboy" (/ruudbwai/); that is, a person who is "forward, bold impertinent; wild, violent, reckless" (Cassidy and LePage 387). What is particularly interesting about the category is that, although clearly of Jamaican origin, it makes no reference to ethnicity or race. The MC was observed to use the category in a way consistent with its use in Jamaica and elsewhere— that is, a rudeboy is recognized on the basis of publicly observable behavior (and explicitly not ascribed characteristics). The MC consistently used "rudeboy" to refer to those people who were actively displaying coparticipation through energetic dancing, verbal and gestural signs of appreciation, and directed gaze. The occupation of a particular space within the setting (the "front") also appears to be particularly significant and, as such, there are important connections between the MC's use of spatial descriptions and his use of these membership categorizations such as "rudeboy." Illustratively, at one point MC Ragga D repeated the phrase "*dis-ya ruudbwai*" (these rudeboys here) several times, with the use of the deictic demonstrative "*dis*" (these) and locative "*ya*" (here) serving to highlight the extremely local, context-tied, context-informing character of the designation (Sidnell, "Deixis"). The evidence we have provided here thus strongly suggests that members of the category "rudeboy" are identifiable not on the basis of ascribed criteria such as race, class, and gender but on the basis of their publicly observable behavior within the immediately local and emergent context of the ongoing activity. This was made even more apparent by the fact that the MC would consistently call out not only to the "rudeboys" but also, and within the same unit of talk, to the "rudegirls."

In the late 1960s, Sacks (*Lectures*) noted that "hotrodder" was a category administered by the members of the group it designated; this category was set up in opposition to "adult-administered" categories such as "teenager" or "kids in cars." For the category "hotrodders," members decided on the characteristics of the category, and they policed and regulated its use. The use of "rudeboy" is similar in a number of respects. Membership in this category is not decided on the basis of ascribed, once-and-for-all characteristics but rather on the basis of publicly observable and locally managed behaviors. Furthermore, given that there is some sense in which the group's recognizability as "a group of people dancing together" is a collaborative accomplishment, it can be said that membership is actively managed by members (although clearly the MC has an important role to play in initially proposing *this* category for *this* recognizable group). Seeing a group of people moving about in the same general location as "dancing together" and thereby as constituting a locally managed "group" clearly involves a rather complex kind of investigation and analysis on the part of the observer.

Conclusion

The rejection of externally defined social categories and the adoption of alternatives appears to be in some sense built into the very architecture of the events we have examined. In examining drum & bass as an event rather than a subcultural product, we hope to supplement previous sociological investigations into how categories are organized with the course of situated activities. We have argued that various forms of descriptive practice, directives, and categorization techniques are combined in the talk of the drum & bass MC in such a way as to provide for the observable organization of the social setting. The analysis has attempted to work outward from the actions located in the talk of the MC to the larger social framework. Following Garfinkel, we have argued that particular actions and the social frameworks in which they are embedded stand, for the setting's members, in a mutually elaborative relationship. These findings may serve as a word of caution at a time when social scientists often assume that the self-same categories (for example, race, class, and gender) can be reasonably used to orient analysis of any and every social phenomenon. The analysis provided here argues against assuming the relevance of such categories in advance of a thoroughgoing examination of the data. Our method involves asking about what categories were relevant to the participants in some social activity and how the relevance of these categories informed the design and organization of that activity. The construction of alternatives is the product of methodic interactional work by the participants in the materials we examined here, and it is furthermore a testament to their creativity and optimism. Such materials require that social scientists stretch their sense of the possible and, in so doing, pay serious attention to the social actor's finely tuned and reflexive understanding of the social frameworks within which action is embedded. Above all, the foregoing analysis points to the potential dangers of imposing the analyst's concerns on the social situations being studied (Schegloff, "Whose

Text"). Whereas such acts of imposition run the risk of simply reinforcing the observers' preconceived sense of what is important, a responsiveness and attention to contexted action and practical reasoning potentially clears the path for new ways of understanding the social order. By focusing on the "complex spiral of relationships" that Small (48) finds between sound, participants, the performance space and the outside world as they are actively invoked by the MC during the course of performance, we mean to suggest that future studies of dance music such as drum & bass would be best served from the dance floor and not the armchair. If, as a number of authors (Straw; Langlois; Fikentscher; Thornton; Rietveld; Hutson) have suggested, these music and dance spaces can be likened to ritual events, we should approach them as such—not by severing enactment from text, as Bruce Kapferer has cautioned against, but by framing analysis in the immediate and locally organized contexts of performance.

Notes

Ordering of this essay's authors is strictly alphabetical.

1. "Drum & bass" refers to a distinct form of contemporary club and rave music and is chiefly characterized by the pairing of 160 beats per minute (bpm) breakbeats with 80 bpm bass lines (James x–xi; Noys; Collins). Whereas Techno and House music (two other popular rave forms) generally consist of instrumental DJ sets that may or may not incorporate tracks with brief vocal samples, drum & bass, as this essay will demonstrate, is talk-prominent, almost always featuring an MC.

2. Note that the terms have shifted somewhat: in the Jamaican context studied by Simon Jones, the MC is known as the DJ, and what we now call the DJ is called the "Selector."

3. We use the masculine pronoun here advisedly: all the MCs whose activity we observed were men.

4. Empty parentheses indicate that talk is audible but we were unable to transcribe it.

5. In this connection, see Meyer's discussion of how expectation structures emotion and meaning in music.

Works Cited

Anderson, Benedict. *Imagined Communities*. London: Verso, 1983.

Bailey, Beryl. *Jamaican Creole Syntax*. Cambridge: Cambridge UP, 1966.

Cassidy, Frederic G. *Jamaica Talk: Three Hundred Years of the English Language in Jamaica*. London: Macmillan, 1961.

Cassidy, Frederic G., and R. B. LePage. *Dictionary of Jamaican English*. Cambridge: Cambridge UP, 1980.

Chapman, Dale. "Hermeneutics of Suspicion: Paranoia and the Technological Sublime in Drum & Bass." International Association for the Study of Popular Music Conference (I.A.S.P.M.). Musical Intersections, Toronto, 2000.

Chernoff, John Miller. *African Rhythm and African Sensibility*. Chicago: U Chicago P, 1979.

Collins, Matthew. *Altered State: The Story of Ecstasy Culture and Acid House*. London: Serpent's Tail, 1997.

Fikentscher, Kai. "You Better Work! Music, Dance, and Marginality in Underground Dance Clubs of New York." Diss. Columbia U, 1996.

Garfinkel, Harold. *Studies in Ethnomethodology.* Englewood Cliffs, NJ: Prentice-Hall, 1967.

Garfinkel, Harold, and Harvey Sacks. "On Formal Structures of Practical Actions." *Theoretical Sociology: Perspectives and Developments*. Ed. John C. McKinney and Edward A. Tiryakian. New York: Appleton-Century-Crofts, 1970.

Goffman, Erving. *Forms of Talk*. Oxford: Blackwell, 1981.

Goodwin, Charles, and John Heritage. "Conversation Analysis." *Annual Review of Anthropology* 19 (1990): 283–307.

Goodwin, Charles, and Marjorie Goodwin. "Context, Activity, Participation." *The Contextualization of Language*. Ed. Peter Auer and Aldo Di Luzio. Amsterdam: John Benjamins, 1992. 77–99.

Heritage, John. "Ethnomethodology." *Social Theory Today*. Ed. Anthony Giddens and Jonathan H. Turner. Stanford, CA: Stanford UP, 1987.

Hutson, Scott R. "Technoshamanism: Spiritual Healing in the Rave Subculture." *Popular Music and Society* 23.3 (1999): 53–77.

James, Martin. *State of Bass: Jungle the Story So Far*. London: Boxtree, 1997.

Jones, Simon. *Black Culture, White Youth: The Reggae Tradition from JA to UK*. London: Macmillan Education, 1988.

Kapferer, Bruce. "Performance and the Structuring of Meaning and Experience." *The Anthropology of Experience*. Ed. Victor Turner and Edward Bruner. Chicago: U Illinois P, 1986.

Kronengold, Charles. "Form Making and Bass Bin Shaking: Sounds and Structures of Drum & Bass." Society for American Music—International Association for the Study of Popular Music Conference (S.A.M.–I.A.S.P.M.). Toronto: Musical Intersections, 2000.

Langlois, Tony. "Can You Feel It? DJs and House Music Culture in the UK." *Popular Music* 11.2 (1992): 229–38.

Lomax, Alan. *The Land Where the Blues Began*. New York: Pantheon Books. 1993.

McCall, Tara. *This Is Not a Rave*. Toronto: Insomniac, 2001.

Myer, Leonard. *Emotion and Meaning in Music*. Chicago: U Chicago P, 1956.

Noys, Benjamin. "Into the Jungle." *Popular Music* 14.2 (1995): 321–31.

Reynolds, Simon. *Energy Flash*. London: Picador, 1998.

Rietveld, Hillegonda C. *This Is Our House*. Aldershot: Ashgate, 1998.

Sacks, Harvey. "Hotrodders: A Revolutionary Category." *Everyday Language: Studies in Ethnomethodology*." George Psathas, Ed. New York: Irvington, 1997. 7–14.

——*Lectures on Conversation*. Cambridge, MA: Blackwell, 1995.

——"Sociological Description." *Berkeley Journal of Sociology* 8 (1963): 1–16.

Schegloff, Emanuel A. "Description in the Social Sciences I: Talk-in-Interaction." *IPrA Papers in Pragmatics* 2 (1998): 1–24.

——"Whose Text? Whose Context?" *Discourse and Society* 8.2 (1997): 165–88.

Schutz, Alfred. "Making Music Together: A Study in Social Relationship." *Collected Papers Vol. 2: Studies in Social Theory.* The Hague: Martinus Nijhoff, 1964. 159–78.

Sidnell, Jack. "Deixis." *Handbook of Pragmatics*. Ed. Jef Verschueren et al. Amsterdam: John Benjamins, 1998. 1–28.

——"An Ethnographic Consideration of Rule-Following." *Journal of the Royal Anthropological Institute*, forthcoming.

Silcott, Mireille. *Rave America*. Toronto: ECW, 1999.

Small, Christopher. *Musicking: The Meanings of Performing and Listening.* Hanover, NH: UP New England, 1998.

Straw, Will. "Systems of Articulation, Logics of Change: Communities and Scenes in Popular Music." *Cultural Studies* 5.3 (1991): 368–88.

Thornton, Sarah. *Club Cultures: Music, Media, and Subcultural Capital.* Hanover, NH: Wesleyan UP, 1996.

Weber, Max. *Max Weber on the Methodology of the Social Sciences.* Ed. and trans. Edward A. Shils and Henry A. Finch. Glencoe, IL: Free, 1949.

Discography

Turbo Mix Live Version 2: Bad Company. Audiocassette. Toronto, Canada. Tripledecks, 1999.

DJ Tappa Zukie. "Oh Lord." *From the Archives.* CD. RAS, U.S., 1996.

Darren Jay. *Renegades Sessions Volume 4.* 27 Aug. 1999. Audiocassette. Toronto, Canada. Tripledecks, 1999.

The Usual Suspects. *Deep in the Jungle, Lifeforce I.* 31 July 1999. Audiocassette. Tripledecks, Toronto, Canada. 1999.

Supplemental Discography: Representative Samples of the Drum & Bass Genre

Promised Land Vol.1. Various artists; mixed by LTJ Bukem feat. MC Conrad. Mutant Sound System, 1997.

Planet V. Various artists. V Recordings, 1999.

Fabio Presents Liquid Funk 2000. Various artists mixed by Fabio. Creative Source, 2000.

Points In Time Vol. 1–6. Various artists. Good Looking, 1999.

Funk the Millennium. Ganja Kru. True Playaz, 1999.

Genetically Unmodified. Various artists. Hard Leaders, 1999.

Armageddon. Various artists. Renegade Hardware, 1999.

Sound in Motion. Various artists. Ram Records, 1998.

Platinum Breaks. Various artists. Metalheadz, 2000.

Through The Eyes. Various artists. Full Cycle, 2000.

Singing Hawaiian and the Aesthetics of (In)Comprehensibility

—*C. K. Szego*

The last fifteen years has seen a variety of movements across the humanities and social sciences that critique the notion of cultural totality and attend to the active and variable interpretation of expressive forms within social groups. For those who study music in culture, the heterogeneities, discontinuities, and contradictions that these movements expose provide an increasingly compelling approach to the investigation of musical meaning. Indeed, ethnomusicology's alliance with anthropology almost half a century ago drew scholars toward theoretical paths that often led to similar, overdetermined outcomes, at least with regard to the meanings that human subjects invested in musical sounds. Whether the approach to music was guided by a search for sources of stability in society, for isomorphism between aesthetic and other domains of cultural life, or for key organizing symbols, the conclusions were virtually identical, that is, all fully socialized participants in a music culture got the same meanings "free" (Gee 12), leaving no one behind in the interpretive dust. Though some ethnomusicological accounts did register aesthetic difference, usually as a function of socioeconomic class or generation, only recently have scholars more fully acknowledged the ways that producers and consumers of music exercise their interpretive agency. Within the last decade, a number of ethnographic studies have demonstrated how meanings emerging from the apprehension of music are multiple and nonconsensual (for example, Meintjes), socially constituted yet individually variable and provisional (for example, Berger). Casting musicians and their audiences as enterprising meaning-makers does not, of course, portend the end of cultural systems; it simply recognizes that while apprehension may be guided or "used by" a shared set of aesthetic principles, so do interpretive agents "use" them.

Having turned this hermeneutic corner, we may be encouraged to explore specific problems or gaps in our knowledge of musical meaning-making. Little is known, for example, about how music means when it is received outside the culture of origin or, in autochthonous situations, what happens when consumers of music are so historically removed from their predecessors' expressive culture that they lack conventional, essential competences for interpreting it. One of these competences, considered foundational to the apprehension of most genres of vocal music, is language.

With important exceptions, ethnomusicological accounts of vocal musics have assumed the ability of their practitioners and receptors to engage texts semantically. That assumption has always been vulnerable, but especially so in an age when vocal music routinely crosses boundaries of linguistic proficiency; transnational music markets and culturally plural colonial and postcolonial societies make this a quotidian reality. In this essay, I examine some of the perceptual processes and "interpretive moves" (Feld) used by those who perform and apprehend music in an associated language, that is, a language tied to the identity of a social group but not necessarily spoken by its members (Eastman and Reese). Specifically, I look at how, in the early 1990s, a group of predominantly unilingual English-speaking Native Hawaiian high school students made meaning out of Hawaiian texts set to music. Fluent speakers of the Polynesian language naturally lamented students' inability to spontaneously retrieve the meanings of Hawaiian words they listened to or sang, claiming that the only source of affective response or signification left them lay in musical sound or in extramusical, contextual variables. While sound and social context were immeasurably important, students who were denied conventional access to texts due to lack of linguistic proficiency carved out their own text-centered interpretive pathways, creating what Harris M. Berger has called an "aesthetics of (in)comprehensibility" (pers. comm.).

This essay proceeds by outlining the historical forces that delivered the students I worked with (and Native Hawaiians generally) to the conditions of linguistic discontinuity they experienced. Then, following an orientation to Hawaiian-language genres and a description of students' pedagogical grounding in Hawaiian linguistic arts, I discuss the mechanics of students' meaning-making.

Kamehameha Schools and the History of Language Instruction

Ethnographic research upon which this essay is based was conducted at the Performing Arts Department in the Secondary Division of Kamehameha Schools, a private institution for students of Native Hawaiian ancestry located in Honolulu, Hawai'i.[1] Kamehameha, named for the dynasty that ruled the Hawaiian Islands from the late eighteenth to late nineteenth centuries, was (and is) funded by the estate of the last prominent member of that lineage, Bernice Pauahi Bishop (1831–1884). Mrs. Bishop, like many other members of Hawaiian royalty, was the product of a colonial American, Protestant education and willed the same to her benefactors. Thus in 1887 the Kamehameha School for Boys opened under the principalship of Rev. William B. Oleson, who drew most of his small, Protestant faculty from the United States.[2]

When King Kalākaua (r. 1874–1891) graced the school's opening with a speech in the students' native tongue, it was a gesture they could perhaps appreciate, for the project of linguistic colonization that would soon transform Hawaiian society was already well under way. Mrs. Bishop's request that Kamehameha's language of instruction be English was, in part, an acknowledgment of increasing Anglo-centrism; in fact, had she not provided such precise direction for her wards' schooling, English would very likely have been established as the medium of instruction (Kanahele), reflecting as it did broader educational trends in colonial Hawai'i. The linguistic ideology to which Rev. Oleson adhered, however, consigned Kamehameha students not only to unilingual English education but to unilingualism in every other sphere of their lives, thus prohibiting even casual discourse in Hawaiian.[3] Because indigenous music and dance were largely text-based, the path of language use and instruction set out for Kamehameha students had long-term implications for their aesthetic practice and meaning-making.

Systematic efforts to discourage Hawaiian speakers at Kamehameha Schools continued until the language fell into general disuse. By 1894, the year following American insurgents' deposition of the Hawaiian monarchy, enrollment in Hawaiian-language public schools had already dwindled to 2.8 percent of total enrollment (Reinecke), and instruction in Hawaiian ceased altogether soon after Hawai'i became a territory of the United States in

1898.[4] Lacking pedagogical support, no new generations of Hawaiian speakers emerged after the 1920s (Derek Bickerton, pers. comm.). Though the language was in an almost moribund state at Kamehameha and in Hawai'i generally, certain Hawaiian words continued to be used in daily English discourse but often with little regard for Hawaiian phonetics. Pronunciation and spellings, for example, consistently failed to recognize the '*okina* or glottal stop /'/ as a consonant, just as it had eluded early orthographers (Schütz).[5] Likewise, fidelity to vowel sounds, including vowel length, which is phonemic in Hawaiian, was disregarded;[6] even island names were misspelled and mispronounced, for example, Lanai [lənᾳi] for Lāna'i [lɑːnəʔi].[7]

Except for meager, ad hoc offerings in Hawaiian language at Kamehameha Schools during the 1920s and 1940s and again in the 1960s, Hawaiian was not officially spoken. Despite their role as stewards of Native Hawaiian education, senior Kamehameha administrators remained weakly committed to indigenous language study until the mid-1980s, when Hawaiian as a second language was fully established in the curriculum—a move spurred by the work of culture revivalists in the public sphere. The efforts of language activists, operating in the midst of a burgeoning movement to restore indigenous culture, were realized in Hawai'i's 1978 Constitutional Convention, which ratified Hawaiian as an official language of the state, and in a 1986 statute that legalized Hawaiian as a medium for teaching in public schools and made provision for private Hawaiian-language schools (State of Hawaii 110).[8] Following these advances, in the early 1990s Kamehameha began experimenting with Hawaiian immersion education at the primary levels. At the high school level, where the research for this essay was carried out, almost a quarter of the student population was enrolled in Hawaiian-language classes in the same period, though few had progressed beyond the elementary levels; students, and those who advised them, often thought it more advantageous to study languages with greater potential for commercial application, such as Japanese. Practically speaking, then, for the greater part of Kamehameha's history, Hawaiian language had life not in spoken discourse but in song.

From the late 1880s, daily exercises and chapel services made use of Hawaiian-language hymns, boarders sang grace in Hawaiian before meals, and during moments of leisure, students taught one another songs from their home islands. The most visible medium for Hawaiian language, however, was an extracurricular choral song competition initiated and organized by students in 1921. Favoring syncretic genres modeled after Western musics and continuing to exclude indigenous practices from its program of study, by the 1930s the school co-opted "Song Contest," as it came to be known, in an effort to "preserve . . . Hawaiian songs and add new songs to [students'] Hawaiian repertoire" (Brown 3). The event became a highly public, annual display of Hawaiian-language song that helped root the community's image of Kamehameha as "the singing school." Song Contest may have shouldered the burden of Kamehameha's self-appointed status as guardian and preserver of Hawaiian culture; however, as 1927 graduate Laura Smith recalled, "we sang the Hawaiian words . . . [but] we didn't even know what they meant, and that was a tragedy" (Smith 32). The great efflorescence of Hawaiian song at Kamehameha occurred only after students' native "voice"—that is, their ability to think and express themselves in Hawaiian—had atrophied.

Chanted *mele* (poetry), the foundational genre of indigenous expressive culture, and the *hula* choreography that accompanied it were only introduced to the high school's official "frontstage" performances (Goffman) during the emergent revival of Hawaiian culture in the mid-1960s.[9] The students I worked with, then, were "children of the Hawaiian Renaissance," born in the late 1970s to a sweeping cultural movement aimed at correcting over a century of American cultural domination. Students in the 1990s, therefore, had significant exposure to chanted *mele*, even if few were expert chanters themselves, and early-twentieth-century popular Hawaiian songs were still sung by the Concert Glee Club and by all 1,800 students at Song Contest—the televised, a cappella choral competition held each year among Kamehameha's high school classes.

Hawaiian Linguistic Arts and Their Pedagogy

Students' performance and apprehension of Hawaiian-language genres were deeply informed by an understanding of pre-European and nineteenth-century Hawaiian musical aesthetics, cultivated in required and elective courses. Each year, several classes in Hawaiian Culture were dedicated to the discussion of *mele* and its musical and kinaesthetic manifestations. Chant and Dance courses, on the other hand, were devoted to the subject entirely and partnered aesthetic theory with performance. *Hālau hula* (community-based *hula* schools), which enjoyed high rates of participation by young Kamehameha women, provided further exposure to a common body of ideas vis-à-vis Hawaiian linguistic arts.

At Kamehameha, students quickly learned that the poetic texts that gave rise to indigenous musical and kinaesthetic arts were prized for their linguistic sophistication. Both *mele oli* (chanted poetry) and *mele hula* (chanted poetry accompanied by dance) were driven by a text that was valued as much as, if not more than, the qualities of its intoned delivery (see Roberts 57; Wong 9). Chanted *mele* (and later sung *mele*, based on Euro-American musical models) served numerous purposes; they venerated gods and individuals of high rank, honored places, mapped genealogies, and even chronicled romantic intrigues. Rich in descriptive imagery and euphonious devices like linked assonance, *mele* used indirect, understated language and *kaona* (hidden meanings) to create polysemic texts by design.[10] Apprehending *mele*, students were told, was an exquisite exercise in the recovery of *kaona*, created primarily through metaphor but also through double entendre.[11] For example, *mele* made copious references to nature and to place-names, the latter serving as metaphorical reminders of people and events (Elbert). Reading metaphors, detecting and deciphering meanings that lay below the denotative surface of words, was oftentimes facilitated by dancers whose task it was to realize and interpret certain *mele* texts:

> Part of the interest in watching a *hula* was to discover how skillfully the choreographer had made the text visible in a culturally satisfying way, by enhancing or obscuring the meaning. In general, *hula* movements enhanced the *mele* and brought to the verbal form a more profound understanding through the addition of a visual dimension. (Kaeppler 13)

In Chant and Dance courses at Kamehameha, moving students to an understanding of the texts they were to dance followed a couple of trajectories. In one of the classes I observed, the instructor provided his students with the written Hawaiian text, and their first assignment was to create a literal translation using any resources that might be available to them, such as dictionaries or Hawaiian-speaking elders. Based on these initial efforts, they then pieced together a tentative translation in class, one that each individual would later submit in "nice, poetic language." Classroom translation was a negotiated process that explored polysemy created through allusion and metaphor. For example, analysis of the *mele* phrase *"Ku'u maha lehua"* (My grove of *lehua* trees) engendered many new understandings—that forests frequently referenced a lover; that while flowers were often feminized in contemporary Hawai'i, the *lehua* blossom was a symbol of masculinity in pre-European times; and that, depending on context, *lehua* could connote human or supernatural beings, for example, a mortal warrior or the goddess Laka. Relating this information to other, initially opaque chant phrases, the instructor concluded, "Now you know *lehua* must be special to Hawaiian people; it has so many *kaona*."

An alternative to collective translation was simply to provide students with texts and their English translations. Kamehameha's two Chant and Dance instructors were fluently bilingual and often supplied their own, but a common and favored source of translations generally was Nathaniel B. Emerson's 1906 publication, *Unwritten Literature of Hawaii*; even when they didn't borrow directly from Emerson, instructors drew on the syntactic constructions and vocabulary that marked his nineteenth-century style.

Students also learned of their ancestors' investment in an ontology that asserted the constitutive nature of language. Language was more than a countersign of thought or a representational system that reported on mental activity. By virtue of their inherent *mana* (spiritual power), words had a potency that could effect both positive and negative outcomes. For that reason, text was chosen judiciously, and specific words were declared *kapu* (prohibited) in certain contexts; any error in the recitation of text invited misfortune, even possible death (Wong 12). At this point in classroom narratives, instructors invariably quoted the Hawaiian proverb, *"I ka 'ōlelo nō ke ola; i ka 'ōlelo nō ka make"* (In the word is life; in the word is death).

One of the Chant and Dance instructors illustrated this belief in the latent energy of words by relaying the story of a Hawaiian college student who wrote a song for his sweetheart, likening her to a spirit. Within a few months of recording the song, its recipient died unexpectedly, drawing claims that the lyrics had literally brought about her transformation. The instructor also professed to having witnessed another person die as the same song was being sung. By sharing these examples, the instructor tendered the idea that it is "possible to cause someone to die by using the wrong word." Examples like these were imparted with a view to sensitizing students to a logocentric Hawaiian worldview and to impressing them with the importance of understanding the words they chanted and danced; the manner in which such examples were presented, however, was never doctrinaire. Information was typically couched in historical, personal, or deliberately ambiguous terms; thus students did not appear to be burdened by the possible consequences of breaking a word *kapu*. The instructor's caution—that "it's important to know our words and to know what power they have"—worked, nonetheless, to offset potentially casual attitudes toward *mele* and encourage greater accountability in class.

The vigor and particularity with which instructors approached the topic of *mele* was also an attempt to reset the inverted relationship between poetry and music/dance that was promulgated by the tourist industry. Putting text in its proper place was helped by glossing *mele* and its accompanying dance as storytelling—the latter a visual extension of the textual form. As one instructor explained to his students, "You really have to . . . internalize the words. Because *hula* is different from other dances . . . [like] the jerk, and the monkey, and the mashed potato. . . . [It] actually embodies a story."[12] The focus on storytelling was constantly reinforced. Prior to teaching a new dance, an instructor counseled his students to

watch how simple the motions are going to be. It's not anything that you're used to nowadays because many people don't understand the language and don't understand what's happening with a story. They need entertainment in the form of vigorous movements . . . because they don't understand the basic story.

Likewise, when dancers lost their concentration or when a particular attitude or feeling was lacking in their countenance and gesture, instructors would invariably ask, "What is the story you are trying to tell?" And, students were told, "in a culture that didn't have writing, the [*mele*] *oli* is the TV, the storybook."

No student could escape the message that textual understanding was essential to achieving competent, compelling performances of *mele oli, mele hula,* or *hula,* and classroom pedagogy privileged the semantic elements of *mele* by keeping the story trope in constant play. Instructors worked assiduously to inculcate students with the sense that traditional *mele* from the nineteenth and early twentieth centuries told stories and that *mele,* whether chanted or sung, were imbued with meanings deeper than could be indicated by any literal translation of words.

Hawaiian-Language Genres and Their Place at Kamehameha Schools

Understanding of *mele*, cultivated by instructors at Kamehameha and reinforced by students' *hālau* training, came to be applied with canonic force not only to chant but also to songs performed at Song Contest. Song Contest relied heavily, but not exclusively, on a genre known as *mele Hawai'i* (see Stillman, "Hula Hits"). The first acknowledged composers of *mele Hawai'i* were members of the *ali'i*, or chiefly class, who had been schooled by missionaries. Musically literate, they fused the subtleties of Hawaiian poetry with the music of Western common practice, creating hymnlike diatonic melodies set in verse-chorus form (Stillman, "Hawaiian Songbooks"). Indulging a late-nineteenth-century "Victorian romantic sensibility," *mele Hawai'i* tended to focus on themes of love (Stillman, "Beyond Bibliography," 480).

The earliest piece of published sheet music in Hawai'i, dating from 1867, is a song in this genre by future monarch Lydia Lili'uokalani (Lili'uokalani). By the 1920s, the *mele Hawai'i* repertoire had grown substantially, due in large measure to the prolific output of Charles E. King. Trained by Queen Lili'uokalani and his American teachers at the Kamehameha School for Boys, King's compositional oeuvre served as a common fund for succeeding generations of students and for a large network of school, workplace, and community-based glee clubs. An indicator of the popularity of the genre from the late nineteenth century to the late 1930s was its mass dissemination in printed, notated form; according to Stillman ("Beyond Bibliography" 481), *mele Hawai'i* "account for approximately 80 percent of the contents" of published Hawaiian songbooks.

Another popular song genre, *mele hula ku'i*, was performed infrequently at Kamehameha Schools but subject to choral arrangement when it was.[13] *Mele hula ku'i* joined (*ku'i*) old and new elements together. The texts embodied traditional Hawaiian poetics but were organized in strophic couplets and featured a common ending formula—*Ha'ina 'ia mai ana ka puana* (Tell the summary refrain) or some variant thereof—placed at the beginning of the last strophe.[14] Though clearly there were differences in poetic structure and content among Hawaiian-language genres of the nineteenth and early twentieth centuries, that is, chanted *mele* (*mele oli* and *mele hula*), *mele Hawai'i*,

and *mele hula ku'i*, it was their common storytelling and metaphorical properties that Kamehameha instructors chose to emphasize.

In addition to Song Contest, which called on every student's participation, a major vehicle for Hawaiian-language choral music at Kamehameha
Schools was the Concert Glee Club, whose repertoire also included Western
choral literature. Additionally, the hymns and doxology sung at biweekly
chapel services, as well as songs honoring Mrs. Bishop, all used Hawaiian
texts and were arranged for choral groups.

Choral musics at Kamehameha Schools conformed to a very simple classificatory system—those that employed Hawaiian language and those that
did not—a scheme that also delineated students' communicative ideals.
Both categories were founded on Western musical idioms, but many students still regarded Hawaiian choral music as "special" and distinguished it
from its Western counterpart, which they believed to be "much more for
entertainment than telling stories." Four Concert Glee Club women were
particularly cogitative and voluble on the perceived uniqueness of Hawaiian choral music and cited arrangers' use of musical iconicity that resonated
with their experience of living in Hawai'i and being Native Hawaiian. As
an example, the group offered Robert Cazimero's arrangement of "Rain
Tuahine O Mānoa" (Fig. 1), which uses repeated, descending broken chords
to represent the gently spraying mists of Mānoa Valley: "'Rain Tuahine'—
[the] ways it's presented, have certain parts to be things like the rain. . . . So
I think in a lot of ways Hawaiian choral music, it goes deeper in that it paints
the picture around you so you can understand it better."

Perhaps more than any other arranger, Randie Fong, head of Kamehameha's Performing Arts Department, consciously employed musical icons
and indices, especially those with historical valence. Though his were often
less transparent than the previous example, he took time with students to
elucidate music-text relationships. Of his 1992 Song Contest arrangement of
"Kaho'olawe" for the senior boys, Fong explained that

in the third verse of their song I was trying to capture . . . one of our [political] struggles
with [the island of] Kaho'olawe maybe fifteen years ago [which] took the life of George
Helm and Kimo Mitchell who were on surfboards. . . .[15] That moved me so . . . to the
point where I wanted that third verse to be almost like a memorial to them and [I]
played with modes a little bit—not too much; played with wind-like motion to capture
the elements and the second basses being surfers on the surfboard.[16]

Fig. 1. Descending Broken Chords, "Rain Tauhine O Mānoa," mm. 10–19 (Julia Walanika; arr. Robert Cazimero)

Students usually took these interpretations to heart, and the senior boys' Song Contest director frequently recalled Fong's musico-political exegesis to reinvigorate his group when singers became slack or unfocused.

Though this approach to text setting was not overly common, it remained salient in students' minds, causing one of them to comment that "the way the arrangements are made—it's like [they're] surrounded by . . . mystery and stuff." Student glosses on Hawaiian choral song also centered on its syncretic nature: "It is the connection between chant and [W]estern music"; "It has meaning—the message of the past in a modern way"; and "Culture culture. Very, very important. Interesting blend of two worlds." Clearly cognizant of the historical impact of Western music on Hawaiian expressive culture, still others viewed the genre as essentially Hawaiian in conceptualization or considered its most valued qualities to be Hawaiian: "The songs are nice, but done in the Western style of notation and structure. The value lies within the lyrics, and the rest of it isn't Hawaiian, if you think about it." Indeed, Hawaiian text was, to most students, the most significant marker of difference.

Making Meaning Out of Hawaiian-Language Texts

The question of how students made meaning out of Hawaiian-language texts was addressed, methodologically, in two primary ways. In 1992, five weeks following the seventieth annual Kamehameha Song Contest, I asked twenty-five students representing grades nine through twelve to write down as much of the Hawaiian text as they could remember of any one of the songs they had learned and performed for the event. They were encouraged to sing to themselves if that aided the process of recollection and were asked to provide a translation of as much of the text as they could. Then, whether or not they could complete the first two steps, they were asked to explain what they felt their chosen song was about and what kind of meaning it had for them; this they expressed in writing and/or in conversation with me.

In determining how students apprehended Hawaiian-language text as listeners, the goal was to obtain more phenomenologically nuanced descriptions. I was not as much interested in obtaining the stories students told to others as I was in the stories no one tells, in thoughts that are fleeting and fragmentary and often so mundane as to be unmemorable. To this end, Wineburg's research on historians' readings of historical texts, as well as Feld's exposition of "interpretive moves," which examines musical meaning-making in the stream of experience, provided some methodological cues. I asked students to listen to selections of Hawaiian-language music (chanted *mele*, *hula kuʻi* songs, and *mele Hawaiʻi*) and to monitor whatever came across the screen of their consciousness for those durations.[17] Listeners gave written or pictorial expression to the thoughts/emotions, images, and physical impulses they experienced moment by moment, and their responses became material for later discussion.[18]

In the recollection/translation exercise, six (24 percent) of the students were only able to recall portions of the Hawaiian text, usually the first verse or first couple of phrases, and were unable to provide any translation. Another eleven (44 percent) students were able to recall the text in its entirety but could provide no translation of the text, translate only the first line, or translate only isolated words. The remaining eight (32 percent) students could recall the entire text and translate all or significant portions of it. A total of seventeen (68 percent), therefore, had minimal or no recollected understanding of the words they had sung at Song Contest. Still, the overwhelming majority of students indicated a preference for Hawaiian choral music over comparable musical styles sung in English or other European languages; they did so, in part, because they possessed a variety of perceptual and cognitive schemes for generating meaning from Hawaiian-language song that were not predicated on an understanding of semantic content. Indeed, despite limited comprehension, Kamehameha students were drawn to language at other levels.

The following outlines singers/listeners' meaning-making processes from the "lowest" levels of auditory perception to "highest" levels of cognition (Tolbert). In addition to varying degrees of engagement with the denotative and connotative material of Hawaiian texts, singers/listeners were engaged in some fashion with the sonic properties of language and/or with language as sign.

Meaning Making I: Sonic Properties of Language

Pronunciation

Listening to and learning Hawaiian songs were processes that sensitized students to the sounds of Hawaiian, which, for the unilingual English speaker, invoked a novel phonemic system. Hawaiian uses a relatively small phonemic inventory with eighteen consonants and vowels in all: /p, k, ', h, l, m, n, w, a, e, i, o, u, ā, ē, ī, ō, ū/.[19] Allophonic variants of these phonemes require some adjustment for English-speaking singers of Hawaiian, especially /a/.[20] Newbrand (10) indicates that /a/ has two allophones, [ʌ] [a], and accordingly *A Handbook for Song Contest Student Directors* warns that when singing in Hawaiian, students should "be especially sensitive to the vowel 'a.' For example, the word 'lani' is so often sung with an 'a' that is too bright or spread. Think of an 'a' as being 'uh' as in 'Hawai'i' " (Noble 10).

Pronunciation was a matter of utmost concern, largely because students were judged heavily on that aspect of their performance during Song Contest. The emphasis on pronunciation had increased significantly over the years and especially since the Hawaiian Renaissance, to the extent that in 1992 two of the five judges devoted their attention to language exclusively. Their task was to evaluate diction ("pronunciation and enunciation of words in singing, as opposed to speaking"), interpretation ("poetic phrasing of text, conveyance of storyline"), and overall effect ("stage presence, posture, delivery, communication, feeling"). Excellence in language was also recognized by the ʻŌlelo Makuahine [Mother Tongue] Award, first bestowed in 1989.

In preparation for Song Contest, each class took direction on language matters from Hawaiian-speaking faculty, who supervised and occasionally led their rehearsals. Though the vast majority of rehearsal periods were spent learning and combining parts, time was taken to perfect articulation, with frequent reference to comments made by the previous year's language judges. Students learned, among other things, to produce a distinct glottal stop and to work through difficulties presented by the musical parsing of text. Singers, for example, were strongly inclined to geminate a word like *nani* (beautiful);[21] they would, in other words, anticipate the beginning of the second syllable at the end of the first syllable: na(n)-ni. The expectation, however, was to clearly separate the syllables, na-ni, a practice also consistent with the Western classical convention of singing on the vowel as long as possible.

Accurate pronunciation was inherently desirable and competitively astute, but it also demonstrated taking back the power of language that preceding generations of Native Hawaiian students were denied. In fact, even when singers were quick to demonstrate accurate pronunciation of a word, instructors continued to press the issue, as the following exchange illustrates:

Instructor: What island are you singing about?
Singers: Lānaʻi [correctly pronounced]
Instructor: Again?
Singers: Lānaʻi [correctly pronounced]
Instructor: Again?
Singers: Lānaʻi [correctly pronounced]
Instructor: What do you *not* want to say?
Singers: Lanai [lānai]
Instructor: What does *that* mean? Porch.[22]

This lighthearted but earnest interrogation set the tone for the first Song Contest meeting between an instructor and her high school charges. Her hypercorrection and reminder to students of the common mispronunciation of Lāna'i added a political subtext to the rehearsal dialogue, since mispronunciation and a lack of observance of orthographic conventions were most often attributed to Anglo-centric indifference (see Kamana).

Due to the emphasis on Hawaiian diction, it is in this domain of language that students felt most qualified and empowered to evaluate their own vocal performances and that of others. In fact, in the listening exercise, they frequently used their knowledge of Hawaiian articulatory phonetics to assess singers' and chanters' authenticity. The smooth, elided delivery of a Native Hawaiian singer like Gabby Pahinui, for example, was treated as testimony to the singer's comfort and familiarity with "real old Hawaiian language," evoking empathetic judgments. On the other hand, a *mele hula* performance that betrayed the chanter's American linguistic socialization inspired a torrent of pejorative descriptors. Though the chanter was, in fact, Native Hawaiian, his performance foregrounded a perceived ethical crisis—the appropriation and misuse of Hawaiian language and an indigenous expressive form by a *haole* (white/Euro-American)—provoking repudiation. Mere pronunciation of text, therefore, was the stuff of meaning-making, and for those who chose to use it as such, it was an indexical measure of authenticity and a singer/chanter's right to performance.

The Sounds of Sung Language

In addition to a small inventory of phonemes, Hawaiian also has a stock of only 162 possible syllables (Maddieson 22).[23] To create necessary distinctions in meaning, therefore, the language relies on flexible reduplicative and recombinative schemes. There is also an abundance of homonyms and near-homonyms (Elbert and Mahoe 10), and these features taken together create a strong sense of sonic homogeneity. According to Elbert and Mahoe, "In connected discourse . . . 60 percent of 3,347 successive sounds are vowels, 26.5 percent are *a* and *ā* and 42 percent are *a*, *i*, and *k*. Thus there is not only a small inventory but also a rather strong concentration in three of the eighteen possible sounds" (11). As students learn to sing or chant *mele* and as their auditory exposure to them increases, they become familiar with and accustomed to forming the distinct phonemic configurations afforded by the language, for example, syllable structure, developing mental representations of them. As a result, those who understand nothing or very little of what they are singing or listening to do not swim in a sea of infinite sonic variety but make ordered perceptions of the sounds they sing and hear. Hence, one response from the listening exercise indicated that the "sounds are familiar but [I] don't understand them—[I] hear them in other songs." Since the listener did not live in an environment where Hawaiian was spoken, song was one of the principal means for acquiring and exercising his perception of the language's phonological properties.[24]

Listeners also registered their lack of lexical and poetic understanding with assertions of feelingful engagement, for instance, "[I] don't understand [the words] but pleasing flow, rhyme and sound" and "[I] couldn't understand text, but felt it." I learned from talking with students that their valuation of the sonic properties of musically realized text was partly rooted in phonetics, partly in poetic sound design (hence, the reference to rhyme) and partly in vocal timbre, inspiring qualifiers like "flowing" and "sweet."[25] In addition to being a source of sonic appreciation, intoned Hawaiian poetry served as material for cognitive manipulation, as revealed by the listener who noted a pattern of keeping "the a(h) sound at [the] end of each line in my head" while attending to a *hula ku'i* song. Although the kind of self-awareness reflected in this statement was rather rare among listeners, my sense from speaking with other students is that Hawaiian language and language sounds in general could not only be monitored and used as objects of abstract poetic and phonosthetic pleasure but that they were resources for sonic play. Intentional cognitive achievements like sound retention were indications of productive, creative agency on the part of listeners.

For many of the instances that have just been cited, it is important to acknowledge that language was not apprehended or engaged independent of its musical context; in other words, the structural features of a song/chant such as rhythm and intonation formed a "matrix of intelligibility" (Lévi-Strauss xxiv) for language sounds. Listener references to the temporal and timbral characteristics of language sounds, such as flow and sweetness, actually point to gestalt experiences that fused language with musical sound. Sung utterances, then, can constitute meaningful sonic streams whether or not they achieve denotative resonance. An analogy might be made here to vocable texts used in Shoshone *Naraya* (Ghost Dance) songs, which Vander likens to abstract paintings: they are not intended to represent real objects but to create sensual patternings of color and shape (Vander 350). This is highly suggestive for a theory of musically grounded language reception where linguistic competence has not yet been developed. Unlike vocable texts, Hawaiian *mele* are semantically rich and are intended to evoke particular meanings and stimulate the imagination;[26] but regardless of the extent to which singers/listeners can grasp semantic intent, they can still hook into texts by discerning, savoring, and cognitively managing musico-linguistic acoustic qualities and patterns.

Vocal Timbre, Language, and Music

For members of the Concert Glee Club who performed a variety of musical styles in a variety of languages, there was a marked preference for singing Hawaiian-language material. There was, furthermore, a general predilection for singing in a language of origin; they were adamant, for example, about singing Italian songs in Italian and would scrutinize English translations given them for flaws in syntax, flow, and sentiment or mood evoked.

On one occasion, Concert Glee Club women rejected the English translation of a Finnish song that spoke of winter dreariness. Though in many ways the English text resembled Hawaiian poetry, with its copious references to nature and use of metaphor, it lacked the requisite sensibilities created by a union of phonetic sound and lyric sentiment. As one of the young women explained, "[We] would rather sing it in Finnish simply because it doesn't make sense [in English]; it loses effect totally. It's so remorse[ful]." Not only did the English translation not live up to the students' most cherished romantic sentiments, but they preferred to sing in the original language because "Finnish sounds so much more sweeter to say." It was better, they thought, to sound "sweet" and compromise comprehension than it was to be understood and experience a disappointing affect. This approach to text is indicative of an acute perceptivity to the sounds of language embedded in a musical matrix.

Many took great pleasure in the sounds of sung Hawaiian and believed that their performances of Hawaiian choral music were audibly distinct in terms of timbral quality. One student described the particular acoustic attributes of Kamehameha's choral groups, using a mainland university choir visiting the Kamehameha campus as her point of reference:

I talked to students that came from the university. They said they listened to the way we sing and there's this roundness, this darkness, this golden sound to it, the way we sing and blend in *a cappella* compared to when they sing. . . . After hearing Western literature being sung by maybe a college [choir] and listening to Hawaiian music being sung by Concert Glee, there's a slight difference in it and to me the sound sounds romantic . . . 'cause it's focused, it's the same notes as the Western but the interpretation just comes out so different—the tone, the quality is just so different.

These observations have been shared by some very knowledgeable choral conductors, and though she did not make a direct connection between Hawaiian language and timbral quality, it seems an obvious choice.[27]

My own impression, and that of conductor Howard Swan (Dale Noble, pers. comm.), is that the Concert Glee Club's choral tone changed with the repertoire they performed; singing the music of Bach or Mozart in, say, German or Latin produced an edgier, more incisive sound. There are several potential explanations, but implicated here is Robert Cogan's work on vocal timbre and his notion of "sonic morphologies" (Cogan 17)—formal units of musical analysis created at the intersection of music and language. Just as linguists were slow to recognize suprasegmental features such as stress, accent, and intonation, so have Western music theorists only recently begun to examine timbre as a parameter equal in importance to harmony, melody, rhythm, and formal organization. Cogan's approach, based on rudimentary musical and phonetic acoustics, recognizes the codependence of language and musical sound in vocal composition, that is, that in pitched vocalization, the human voice generates complex tones: singers create and sustain pitches on vowels principally, and each intoned vowel has a characteristic spectral profile consisting of a fundamental frequency (or tone) and a number of overtones. Within this acoustic structure there are regions of intense resonance known as formants that correspond to each vowel;[28] it is the listener's perception of the intensity and position/distribution of formants that corresponds to his or her experience of vocal timbre.[29] Thus "words, especially their vowels, *orchestrate* the music, giving each melodic note (the notated fundamental pitch) a specific array of resonating spectral elements (vowel formants)" (27). In this way, detailed descriptions of a linguistically based style or composition can be obtained from an analysis of acoustic spectra.

Since spectral data were not collected, this discussion is necessarily speculative and limited to generating hypotheses. I am suggesting that if one were to create a spectral flow chart of a piece of Hawaiian-language choral song, that the sonic fabric would as a whole look significantly different from that of an English-language choral song in the same style. Sung Hawaiian would be distinguished not only by (1) its compact phonemic inventory and by (2) the allophonic realization of each phoneme (for example, [a] and [ʌ] for /a/) but by (3) the arrangement of successive phonemes into larger units, dictated by the phonotactic rules of the language (for example, no consonant clusters like /pl/), (4) by the relative frequency of usage of each phoneme (for example, the high proportion of /a/, /i/, and /k/), and (5) by the proportion of each phoneme's soundedness in a musical context (for example, the fact that vowels can be sustained but stops cannot).[30] These elements, combined with elements of arrangement (for example, vocal range and register, texture) and vocal production (for example, laryngeal position), would contribute to the particular sonic character of Hawaiian choral music as sung by Kamehameha students. Although accounting for an acoustic stimulus is not the same as accounting for its perception, applying Cogan's analytical procedures to Hawaiian choral song may still shed considerable light on a largely ignored dimension of musical apprehension and text-based meaning-making—vocal timbre—a dimension that may become even more salient in circumstances where linguistic competence is negligible.

Meaning Making II: Semantic Properties of Language

Semantic Anchoring
In addition to being absorbed by the sonic properties of sung language, Kamehameha students attempted to make sense out of Hawaiian language at a semantic level. Those who had acquired sufficient skill to make immediate sense out of Hawaiian song lyrics, or a significant portion of them, often took great pride and pleasure in doing so: "I love to listen to the text of a song (and define it if possible)," wrote one male student. But regardless of their ability or proclivity for doing so, students' perceptual and cognitive apparatus was primed for extracting semantic meaning. Most students recognized and understood certain words in any song text, such as general nouns (for example, *pua* [flower], *makani* [wind], *manu* [bird]), adjectives (for example, *nani* [beautiful], *kilakila* [majestic]), verbs (for example, *ho'oipo* [to make love, court]), definite particles (for example, *ke/ka* [the]), and directional particles (for example, *mai* [come, come here]). They were

also familiar with many of the place-names that proliferate in *mele* generally (for example, Haleakalā), as well as the formulaic song ending, *Haʻina ʻia mai ana ka puana*, used in *hula kuʻi* songs. These words and phrases functioned as semantic anchors in their musico-linguistic field of apprehension. As students listened to Hawaiian-language songs and even as they performed them, they tracked lyrics for recognizable sounds and injected semantic content where there was an appropriate match. In this way, they fashioned a rather selective, if sparse, text of their own. Supporting the idea of tracking is one listener's response to the chanted *mele*, "Aia Lā ʻO Pele I Hawaiʻi," acknowledging that there were "Hawaiian words with 'Pele' in there somewhere."[31]

Because of many homonyms and near-homonyms in the language and the difficulty students had in discerning the initial position glottal stop (for example, *ʻo*) and in distinguishing between short and long vowels (for example, *o* and *ō*), especially in musical settings, meaning substitution occurred often. Take, for instance, one student's perceptual untying of the word *ʻōpua* (billowing clouds) into the more familiar lexical items, *o* (of) and *pua* (flower), potentially giving rise to the image of a flower or any of its connotative referents, such as "sweetheart," where billowing clouds were denoted.

Musical structure, that is, the relative pitch, stress, and duration of syllables, often guided the perceptual parsing of texts. An example from the song "Nani Koʻolau" demonstrates this aptly.

Original text:
I laila kāua i walea ai (It is there that you and I were acquainted)

Students' parsed texts, guided by musical structure:
A. *ila ila ka ua iwa lei a i*
B. *Ila Ila ka ua I ua leahi*

Fig. 2. "Nani Koʻolau," mm. 17–18 (Traditional; arr. Robert Cazimero)

In both cases (A and B), the singers did not recognize the diphthong /ai/ in *laila* because musical structure separated the vowels. That, combined with the rhythmic stresses of the arrangement, makes the singers' orthographic representations quite understandable, given their lack of facility with the language. Perception of the word *lei* (garland of flowers) in the first case can be accounted for by considering the familiarity of the word, its frequency in Hawaiian song texts, the similarity between /e/ (in *walea̱*) and the diphthong /ei/,[32] and the possible elision of the /a/ sounds in *walea̱ a̱i*, facilitated by pitch repetition. Although the respondent did not translate her words, by inference her use of the word *lei* also constitutes an example of semantic anchoring, as does the second case: "Leahi" [Lē'ahi] is familiar to most island residents as the Hawaiian name for Diamond Head.[33] Clearly, the written text, from which all student singers began the process of learning these songs and to which they referred until it was time to sing from memory, did not guarantee perceptions that were consistent with it, nor did it guarantee assignations of meaning that were congruent with the denotative or connotative range of particular words.

Building Narratives: "Interpretive Moves"

Though listeners unfamiliar with a song or chant often had little to ground their understanding of the Hawaiian lyrics they apprehended, most singers had a general sense of the meaning of the Hawaiian texts they sang. In some cases a single verse or line of text presented an image that became the sole focus of students' interpretation, especially when that image was singled out for discussion by one of their instructors or leaders and was particularly provocative or moving. For example, "Nani Ko'olau" is a song about two lovers who play rapturously among the waterfalls in O'ahu's Ko'olau mountain range. One of the singers recalled the way in which she came to understand the sexual connotations of the text:

The reason why I remember that [is] because when we sang it we had no energy at first, and then when we found out the meaning, you know our leader was telling us, "you know what this *means*?" You know there was a climax point and everything, and we thought "oh my gosh!" It was kind of shocking and kind of funny. He made it kind of funny so that we'd get more energy in it and that's the part that he kind of emphasized on because it made us laugh.

Not only was the director's portrayal of text humorous, but certain words were particularly memorable and easy to translate. Verses one, three, and four of this *hula ku'i* song ended with the phrase "*Me ka wai o ka 'ūlala 'e hō*" (In the water that makes us silly). The second verse, furthermore, contains the phrase couplet "*A hiki kāua i Nu'uanu / A inu i ka wai Silosila*" (We arrived at Nu'uanu / And drank the water of Silosila). Here, students were told, the word "*Silosila*" is ambiguous: it could refer to a specific pool of water where the lovers met or, in a song thick with allusions to intimacy, Silosila may have been used to disguise the name of one of the individuals, a common poetic strategy. Furthermore, the second half of the word, "sila," was understood to be a Hawaiianization of the English word "silly," echoing the theme of the refrain. Thus "*sila*" was foregrounded in singers' consciousness because of the playful mood it helped portray, its likeness to a familiar English word, and the distinctive use of the /s/ in a phonemic environment that usually did not use sibilants.

The "dignified risqué" tone of the song, as one instructor characterized it, appealed to the young singers, who often personalized its meaning. One young man wrote that "I like it, [it] makes me think about loving someone in a nice romantic way," and another disclosed that "it made me feel warm inside and feel like I was on top at Koolau [*sic*] watching the 2 lovers and kind of actually feeling what they felt when they were up there." In a reminiscence of Song Contest, a young woman described the shifting foci of her attention: hovering on the horizon of her consciousness as she followed the song director were mental images of the Ko'olau mountains because, as she explained, "I lived in Kāne'ohe and I love the mountains. And since it does talk about the Ko'olau mountains . . . just the name reminds me of it . . . hearing it or saying it reminds me of it."

Students' ability to develop meaning from text, then, is not predicated entirely on their linguistic competence. Even those students who could not comprehend most of the words they sang or could not recall any of the text were engaged in some kind of interpretive move, based sometimes on the general mood or message of the text in combination with musical features. The song "Ua Nani Kaua'i" (Kaua'i Is Beautiful), where the title alone is all that one student understood, evoked childhood memories of driving through the island with a family member and of the island's lush greenery. Another student who knew only that the song "Kamalani O Keaukaha" was "about the love of two people and how the love of them [was] perpetuated" thought fondly of her parents and "how their love brought them together." Highly personal, internal narratives of this kind were not contained in the lyrics, but neither were they contrary to traditional modes of interpretation.

As one might expect, however, the students who could provide full or partial translations were also able to provide the richest descriptions of the text/story. One senior male wrote of the song "Kaho'olawe,"

> I have a lot of love for this song. It is a very famous song, made famous by the Makaha Sons's [*sic*] version. Their version is very fast and forceful. The island of Kaho'olawe is sort of representative of the Hawaiian struggle to maintain and care for their lands. This song is strong and it conjures images of George Helm and Kimo Mitchell who were sort of martyrs to their cause of the Hawaiian people today. This song puts pride and strength into Hawaiians all over Hawai'i *nei* and is something that all Hawaiians can grasp and hold close to the heart. When the boy[s] in this class sang this song we all held hands. I feel this represented the strong feelings we had and the unity we felt.

The narrative energy of Randie Fong's metaphoric interpretation is felt in this student's description of the song. The student's experience of "communitas" (Turner), which he presumed to share with his classmates, is linked not only to the song and the historical passions it evokes but to the Hawaiian social ideals of *lokahi* (unity) and *'ohana* (family) that were constantly voiced by rehearsal directors in an effort to move singers to greater levels of cooperative effort. Voice and word choice also distinguish this from previous student narratives; use of the third person plural pronoun ("we") and the broad claim the singer makes for the feelings of "all Hawaiians" locate it in contemporary Hawaiian political discourse. Narratives like this were not uncommon, and while many were inspired by an arranger's or Hawaiian speaker's textual exegesis, they were often of the singer's own making.

Sound Symbolism

Few of the students who participated in the text recollection exercise and with whom I spoke were sufficiently competent in Hawaiian language to appreciate sound symbolism, that is, "the direct linkage between [the] sound [of a word] and [its] meaning" (Hinton, Nichols, and Ohala 1).[34] In fact, only one student, the senior male quoted earlier, who was studying Advanced Hawaiian, mentioned that he apprehended texts in this way. For instance, the sounds of both *anuanu* and *koʻekoʻe* (or alternately, *toʻetoʻe*) suggested their meaning—coldness—to him, heightening his engagement with song lyrics. While sound symbolism was a resource available only to students with a strong command of Hawaiian language, narrative construction was a part of most, though certainly not all, students' interpretive palettes.

Meaning Making III: Sign Properties of Language

The vestiges of a vital oral tradition are contained in the assertion that Hawaiian *mele* and thus the Hawaiian choral song repertoire that Kamehameha sustained tell stories. The extent to which student singers engaged the "stories" suggested by the lyrics or imagined their own varied considerably. Nonetheless, the musico-linguistic principle of telling a story through song (or chant) was a cornerstone of their aesthetic and communicative ideals. To recall, it helped distinguish Hawaiian choral music from its Western counterparts. And though singers/listeners may have been limited in their ability to attend to a song's intimate and finely wrought descriptions of person, place, or sentiment, they delighted and took pride in the very idea of telling a story to an audience. Unable to contain her enthusiasm, one young woman explained that singing "makes me feel like I am totally Hawaiian and relaying messages." The indexical act of poetic communication, an act that self-consciously linked her to her ancestral heritage, is what mattered most to her and to many others.

Indeed, singing "traditional words" was perceived as being continuous with the practice of chanted *mele* and other genres of oral performance:

in the Hawaiian culture [much] is passed on through songs and things. . . . That's the history right there. It's all in the song, everything is. . . . So be it choral music or whatever way it's [set musically]—that has meaning all of its own, that's the foundation, the way it's presented . . . through song.

By virtue of its connection to pre-European expressive practice, Hawaiian song was an exalted medium; additionally, sung *mele* were valuable because they often recorded images of premodern Hawaiian life, inscribing history in collective memory. Thus as singers, some Kamehameha students also saw themselves as select keepers of the past.

For members of the Concert Glee Club, a group that performed for a wide variety of audiences, understanding of the text by an audience of knowledgeable Hawaiian speakers was gratifying but rare and certainly not essential. What Kamehameha administrators had developed in forums like Concert Glee Club recitals and Song Contest were contexts for Hawaiian-language display in which audiences recognized associated language as a symbolic expression of social identity (Eastman and Stein 189). Song Contest was a secular ritual event that, in its rhetorical setup and material enactment, framed the primary activity within it, that is, singing *mele*, as "traditional," as Hawaiian, and as distinctively Kamehamehan. In this way, upper-level Kamehameha administrators of the early 1990s could use Song Contest to polish their public image by showing their support for the Native Hawaiian identity project. Students, on the other hand, had no choice but to participate in Song Contest and had little control over the ways in which they did participate. Still, the rhetorical power of the event incorporated most students, heightening awareness of their minority status as Native Hawaiians and the symbolic significance of singing in their associated language.

For the group of four Concert Glee Club women referred to earlier, a lack of textual understanding was actually thought to enhance the listening experience, especially when the audience was composed of nonisland residents: "People, when they hear us sing Hawaiian, then they really get into it 'cause they never heard anything like that before. So they enjoy it more, yeah? 'Cause they don't know what it means." Even with more familiar audiences, singing in a semicomprehensible language was believed to imbue their performances with a mystique that resonated with what they identified as the "mysterious" quality of their songs, that is, the *kaona* (veiled messages or layers of meaning) that they knew existed in many lyrics but could not detect on their own, as well as the musical icons and indices employed in some of the arrangements they sang. In a sense, the mystique and the audience's lack of comprehension made it more possible for students to imagine themselves as oral historians/storytellers and to realize any tendency they may have had toward "self-exoticization" (Hosokawa 509); any such inclination seems to have grown out of students' relationship to ancestral Hawaiians, whom they often spoke about as distant-but-related Others driven by an intense aesthetic sensibility. The hyperconsciousness of statements that connected self with song (for example, "It makes me feel like I'm totally Hawaiian and relaying messages") betrayed the gap between students' pragmatic appraisals of their own linguistic abilities and the public projections of identity that singing Hawaiian provided them.

There were individuals, of course, who failed to engage and/or denied engaging the musico-linguistic and sociomusical processes that have been described in this section because of their lack of interest in the style of music and/or singing generally. They usually attributed any investment in or attachment to a song to a different set of social variables, as, for example, the young man who remarked simply that "this song makes me feel happy because we won [Song Contest with it] even though I didn't even sing much of it." For the most part, however, it was students' pedagogically nurtured valuation of Hawaiian poetics and oral transmission that led to their self-ascription as storytellers, a status linked to their prototypical definitions of Hawaiianness. One can only presume that their ability to create stories internally, that is, to comprehend some element of the messages they sang or to construct personal narratives, enriched their claims to this status.

An Aesthetic of (In)Comprehensibility

Further scrutinizing the relationship between language, music, and meaning, the data suggest that students' preoccupations with Hawaiian language have consequences for listening not only to Hawaiian-language but to English-language musics as well. This was made apparent during the listening exercise and in students' responses to a performance by the visiting mainland choir. In both instances, students apprehended English-language pieces that made extended use of vocables. The former was a lyric song arrangement that substituted two verses of text with the vocable "do" /du/, and the latter was a collage of invented vocables and recognizable but syntactically fragmented words intended to evince the sound-images of an industrial cityscape. Uncomfortable with the nonlexical items in both instances and the nonlinear, nonnarrative qualities of the live performance, many students simply dismissed them as "silly" or "dumb." I initially had some difficulty reconciling students' predominantly negative response to vocables in English-language vocal music, on the one hand, with their veneration of Hawaiian language, which many barely understood, on the other. It appears that in addition to the rather considerable symbolic significance that indigenous language holds,

Kamehameha students engaged Hawaiian music texts with an assumption of their underlying semanticity. They presumed that Hawaiian words had assigned meanings even if they were unaware of them and that the Hawaiian musico-linguistic system could not be equivocated in this regard. Semanticity was necessary and privileged for its potential to convey stories, which students considered the paradigmatic function of Hawaiian-language musics. The corollary is that language that failed to meet the criterion of semanticity was inauthentic, and music lacking the legitimacy of "real" language was diminished in value. English-language vocables, to which no specific meanings are assigned, compromised young Native Hawaiians' conviction in the function of language, especially when these vocables dominated text.

The indigenous principle of *mana* contained in the Hawaiian proverb—"In the word is life; in the word is death"—is implicated here. Students heard and quoted the proverb often; for them it was hooked, both pedagogically and in principle, to a related tenet of Hawaiian expressive culture, that is, that music and dance are language-driven. Students learned and absorbed the principles of word *mana* and logogenesis, but these principles did not accommodate their lack of Hawaiian linguistic competence or a language they did understand—English—whose speakers generally invested so little autonomous power in the word. Left to their own interpretive devices, most students seem to have cognitively blended traditional principles with their experience as English speakers to fashion a more workable aesthetic, which might be stated as follows: musical text ought to have semantic integrity and tell stories; text divorced from this fundamentally social purpose renders vocal music inauthentic or less valuable. This reconstituted principle maintains the conceptual centrality of language but removes the absolutist, life-and-death punch, making it applicable to a broader range of musics and interpretive scenarios. In terms of interpretive weightings, this aesthetic downplays the inherent, supernaturally derived power of intoned language, which students regarded with both fascination and ambivalence, and shifts emphasis to the denotative and symbolic cogency of language, that is, the ability to relay information or "messages" even when they are beyond full comprehension, to record history, and to represent Hawaiianness.

The extent to which students considered language comprehension desirable varied as a function of their Hawaiian-language proficiency; advanced Hawaiian speakers, few that they were, were uncompromising in their insistence on semantic awareness. For most others, like the four Concert Glee Club women, comprehension was an ideal that was difficult to satisfy and therefore not regarded as an absolute requisite for their own or their audience's pleasure. However, while they did not deem understanding of a musical text to be necessary, they insisted on understanding in principle and in terms familiar to them. Thus they were amenable to singing in Finnish because they were confident that the words had semantic properties and could convey a story, if not to them, then to someone else.

Summary

Methodical suppression of spoken Hawaiian in the first three and a half decades of Kamehameha Schools' history was only seriously redressed in the last two decades of the twentieth century. The swell of student interest in Hawaiian-language study in the early 1990s, however, held no immediate promise of widespread fluency, and the vitality of Hawaiian language at Kamehameha Schools was, even then, still principally limited to songs performed and apprehended by a group of largely unilingual English speakers. Linguistic asymmetry was problematic for a vocal tradition that was text driven and that focused aesthetic appreciation on poetic intricacy and subtlety. This study of Kamehameha student singers and listeners suggests, however, that their encounters with Hawaiian texts engendered multiple levels of meaning-making. Generally speaking, the lower-level perceptual processes that students performed were accompanied by more general and holistic cognitive understandings of the meanings of a song.

At the semantic level, even a limited amount of vocabulary seems to have generated enough material for meaning-making so that texts did not remain impermeable to their perceivers, though understanding was hardly guaranteed and misunderstanding was entirely possible. It would, furthermore, be unwise to confuse lack of vocabulary with a lack of general comprehension, though the conflation may often be apt. Receptors of musical text approach semantic meaning in many ways—from broad, generalized types of interpretation to those that treat text as a collection of words.

In terms of the recollection and listening exercises in which students participated, singers had a broader repertoire of interpretive strategies than did listeners. Singers could rely on isolated words or single lines or verses learned from translations as well as instructors' textual glosses to focus their semantic interpretation and construct internal narratives. Student singers could also apprehend *kaona*—though their apprehension of it was studied—while listeners, who also lacked the spontaneous interpretive sophistication of their ancestors, were not privy to it at all (see Roberts 57–58). For those very few who possessed a high level of linguistic competence, sound symbolism was another potential interpretive resource.

Perceptual and cognitive processes that exploited the sonic qualities of sung language were evident in both singers and listeners. Their interpretive achievements, however, ranged widely. They tracked texts for familiar sounds, (re)arranged them into lexical units, and decoded them to create a kind of patchwork semantics. Building on their attention to euphony and the temporal flow of sung language, students also demonstrated the potential for manipulating phonemes in auditory imagination, in one instance producing a virtual polytextual sound piece. I have also hypothesized that vocal timbres resulting from a union of musical and linguistic sound created sonic morphologies that were at work in student understandings of their choral sound, that is, its perceived "darkness." While exploiting Hawaiian language for its sonic properties was part of the pleasure to be derived from text, it was by itself not instrumentally sufficient: students needed to know that below their acoustic surface, sounds were not semantically empty but were capable of fulfilling their designative purpose.

Little trace of an indigenous philosophy of language that invested metaphysical power in the sounded word and that anticipated the potential effects of mispronunciation was evident. Given also the privileged position of semantics in Hawaiian ethnoaesthetics, the emphasis on pronunciation by both singers and listeners might be interpreted as a superficial approach to textual engagement. But by turning auditory percepts into concepts and then treating them as signs, student singers and listeners were engaged in "several interacting levels of meaning formation" (Tolbert 8). As correct pronunciation indirectly honored the pre-European disposition toward words as potent generative and degenerative forces (a principle most students respected but were not overly concerned with), it decried a century of language oppression, mispronunciation, and disparagement.

If, on the one hand, students exercised their interpretive independence by overlooking the *mana* principle—which had been gently but painstakingly nurtured in the classroom—they surrendered to the narrative principle entirely, even imagining themselves as Hawaiian storytellers. Working at the level of sign, singing Hawaiian *mele* was emblematic of being Hawaiian, because an essentialized trait of "being Hawaiian" for many students was to tell stories that remembered loved ones and honored gods, nature, and the high-born. While singing *mele Hawai'i* directly indexed indigenous expressive genres and the poetic values students had been taught to value, their lack of linguistic competence introduced several degrees of remove from pre-European and nineteenth-century indigenous practice, transforming the singing of Hawaiian into a sign of "possibility and imagination" (Turino 245). Song Contest, the traditionalizing ritual that showcased student singing, then became directly implicated in the political discourse on identity that had been generated by the Hawaiian Renaissance. Like other contexts for language display, Song Contest was a site where Native Hawaiian youth could imagine themselves to be like their ancestors, thus publicly insinuating "who [they] would like to be in the world" (Eastman and Stein 187).

Young Native Hawaiians singing and listening to music in their associated language demonstrate how text performed and apprehended outside the domain of language fluency can yield to sonic, semantic, and symbolic interpretation. That their experiences were not devoid of meaning is a conclusion that neither forgives Hawai'i's history of linguistic colonization nor sanctions its present and continuing forms.

Conclusions

Performing in and apprehending an associated language is distinct from other musico-linguistic practices where text is completely or semicomprehensible, and yet this study suggests how meaning might be drawn from a paucity of semantic material or none at all. As examples, text is often made intentionally incomprehensible through garbling (Kaeppler 152) or some other means of distortion in order to hide information or protect the uninitiated. Alternatively, text becomes indecipherable when words/language are so archaic they no longer have a place in collective or individual memory, or, having been borrowed from another culture, they were never understood or quickly forgotten (Kuschel 53). Sometimes song vocabulary and syntax are recognized as belonging to another, for example, supernatural, realm and are thus thought to be beyond human cognizance (Powers). And of course, some texts elude certain conventions of understanding because they have no semantic referent; nonlexical syllables or vocables serve as the most commonly cited examples of this phenomenon (see Bagemihl; Campbell and Collinson; Frisbie; Yung). Applications of this study expand further still with the recognition that apprehending an associated language shares many resemblances with the cultural boundary-crossing that is currently being played out in postcolonial cultural revivals, in world music programs, and in potentially every sweep of the radio dial that invites music to float into the soundscape culturally unanchored.

One of the most vivid examples of cultural boundary-crossing is contained in Hosokawa's study of musical transnationalism in Japan. His elegant analysis of the Japanese salsa band Orquesta de la Luz speaks to the complexity of Japan's history of appropriating foreign musics and simulating them by means of *kata* learning. *Kata* refers to both a didactic mode (based on strict imitation) and an aesthetic approach that privileges surface effects, attention to detail, formal patterning, and process. Hosokawa is highly successful in recuperating the meanings of Japanese salsa through the voices of band members, music critics, and analysis of song texts. Moreover, his data suggest the profitability of examining the perceptual and cognitive processes that its consumers invoke as they engage the genre. In light of the Hawaiian case study, we might ask how Japanese audiences apprehend Spanish lyrics, which they "seldom understand," and confect meanings from them. Do unintelligible words simply serve as signs of foreignness? If *kata* encourages absolute fidelity to foreign acoustic models in terms of sonic production, how does it affect listeners' experiences? Does it enable phonosthetic pleasure to be derived from the text by channeling perception to the acoustic surface of words? Do members of Japan's salsa scene consult liner notes or Web sites for translations, in search of interpretive direction, and if they do, how do they use that information? And do aficionados' understandings of Latino/a aesthetics merge unproblematically with a Japanese aesthetic approach, or must they be reconciled? If we are to take anything from the Hawaiian example, it is that situations of cross-cultural musico-linguistic apprehension can force a selection on the part of the apprehender. Kamehameha students cobbled together an aesthetic from their experience as English speakers and their knowledge of Hawaiian ethnopoetics, an aesthetic, moreover, that served them in a variety of musico-linguistic scenarios.

Addressing the issue of cross-cultural musico-linguistic apprehension more generally, anthropologist Ulf Hannerz asks, "Could there be affinities which allow us, for example, to appreciate what Nigerians or Indonesians do as they sing or dance, even as what they say when they speak sounds to us as only gibberish?" (22).[35] Since the early 1980s, ethnomusicologists have typically shied away from this kind of question, and from the matter of intercultural reception in general, for fear, perhaps, of sounding a universalist theme. But by speaking of affinities, Hannerz is not alluding to some deep structural connection between people of different cultures; recommending another approach, he goes on to suggest that "perhaps we have to draw different boundaries of intelligibility for each symbolic mode" (ibid.). While we need to be cautious toward any sharp differentiation between speech and song that might be implied by these collective statements, the Hawaiian case study suggests that if our approach to the reception of musically realized texts is confined to the denotative, representational properties of language, then the perceptual achievements and significations of those who apprehend associated language in song, as well as those who apprehend any sung language beyond their ken, will remain lost to us.[36] Hannerz's speculations are generally congruent with Native Hawaiian students' musical perceptions, which revealed that they experienced musically realized text as a gestalt, that when language was fused with musical sound, the interpretive possibilities expanded.

This essay began with some observations on current theoretical trends in the humanities and social sciences and on ethnomusicology's relationship to anthropology. Another legacy of that partnership is the ethnographic method and the overarching objective that guides it, namely, to understand and communicate human subjects' practices in a way that accurately reflects their perspectives, their meanings. In contemporary scholarship, that objective is usually sought with the knowledge that while we can stretch our capacity to understand and perceive things as our consultants do, our ability to share in their experience will be limited in some fashion (Geertz)—by their incomplete renderings and translations of experience, by our inability to move past deeply rooted conceptual schemes, and so on. Where our shared experience stops, however, experience itself does not. There is always something else, and that something else—those interpretations of and responses to other people's musical practices—will be filtered through a set of cultural and personal presuppositions. Likewise, when our consultants cross boundaries of cultural competence, we can expect that their apprehensions and understandings will be shaped by their own centricities. Rather than dismiss or invalidate these apprehensions and understandings as "distortive of original meanings," as ethnomusicologists have been wont to do, scholarship might more fruitfully be applied to investigating how "affect and meaning [are] created anew in the specific social and historical circumstances of each instance of music's creation and use" (Shepherd 4).

Without abandoning the central notion of shared, socially grounded experience and signification, humanists and social scientists have already started to think beyond the essentialized and stable meanings that have, historically, carried so much authority in their disciplines. Situations of cross-cultural production and reception provide particularly fertile ground for examining the dynamics of musico-linguistic interpretation and for revealing the dialectics of structure and agency in the meaning-making enterprise.

Notes

1. Native Hawaiians are descendants of the aboriginal people inhabiting the Hawaiian islands prior to the arrival of Europeans in 1778; the majority of Native Hawaiians today are of mixed ancestry, for example, Hawaiian Chinese. Because students at Kamehameha Schools typically referred to their ethnicity and culture as "Hawaiian" rather than "Native Hawaiian," that is the expression used throughout most of this essay.

2. Land rich but cash poor, the estate could not fulfill the Hawaiian benefactress's desire to establish a parallel institution for girls; the founding of the Kamehameha School for Girls in 1894, therefore, was a gift of her American-born husband, Charles Reed Bishop. Today, the Kamehameha Schools are administered as one unit and remain the sole beneficiary of the Bishop Estate.

3. Sunday services at Kaumakapili Church were the only sanctioned opportunities for spoken Hawaiian, and even then students were more likely to be receptors rather than speakers.

4. Instruction in Hawaiian came to a legal halt with the revision of Hawaiian statutes in 1896 (see Territory of Hawaii 156), and by 1902 there were no Hawaiian schools left (Reinecke 72).

5. Customary notation for the glottal stop is /ʔ/; however, following Schütz, I use the same symbol used in contemporary Hawaiian orthography, /'/.

6. A phoneme, placed between slashes (see above), is an abstract representation of a class of sounds recognized by native speakers as making meaningful distinctions in their language. In Hawaiian, vowel length is phonemic; it creates semantic contrast. For example, *aka* means "shadow," and *akā* means "but."

7. Another arena for linguistic misuse, seldom acknowledged in language debates, was American popular song. One of the most important media for mainland Americans' exposure to Hawaiian language in the early twentieth century was song, and one of the earliest forums for Hawaiian-language singers on the American mainland was the 1915

Panama-Pacific Exposition in San Francisco. Capitalizing on performers' successes there, Tin Pan Alley began turning out music that mimicked Hawaiian song (see Tatar). Having perceived some of the distinctive features of Hawaiian, such as the small phonemic inventory and reduplication of syllables, Tin Pan Alley lyricists created nonsense texts that parodied the language, for example, "Yacka Hula Hicky Dula" and "Oh How She Could Yacki Hacki Wicki Wacki Woo."

8. With the guarantee of legal protection, the next step was to establish schools for exclusive instruction in Hawaiian. The first Pūnana Leo (literally "language nests")—private Hawaiian-language immersion preschools—had already opened in 1984, and in 1987 a state-sponsored Hawaiian-language immersion program began in six selected public elementary schools (Dunford; Schütz). In February 1992, the state's Board of Education approved a policy that would allow public school students beyond the fifth grade to receive almost total Hawaiian immersion education (Infante).

9. See note 14.

10. Linked assonance is a specific type of echoism that "consists in beginning a new line with a word or words sounding the same or very like the last words of the preceding line or some words in it which are of outstanding importance" (Roberts 66). Elbert (127) provides the following example:

> *Ke kua 'ia maila i ke kai ka hala o Puna / E hala'o' a ana mehe kanaka lā*
> [Chopped to bits by the sea are the hala trees / Standing up like human beings]

11. According to Zaneta Ho'oūlu Cambra (pers. comm.), alternate meanings could also be suggested by articulatory shifts of stress in the delivery of *mele*.

12. "Story" has become a culturally loaded word in local parlance (Eastman). As a spoken form, storytelling was a popular pastime within the family and has continued to exist in more or less elaborated forms in certain Hawaiian subpopulations, within particular families, and among children (see Watson-Gegeo and Boggs). Storytelling shares some features with and is subsumed by another narrative category, "talk-story," a discursive form that flourishes in Hawai'i in which an interlocutor engages another in extended conversation through verbal play, teasing, and storytelling. A local expression, talk-story—or talking story—involves reminiscence and even gossip (Boggs) to create "a rambling personal experience narrative mixed with folk materials" (Watson 154). The expression signals the salience of story-ing in contemporary Hawai'i as well as the flexibility of its conceptualization.

13. There are several potential explanations for the infrequent performance of *mele hula ku'i*. One is that *hula*, which accompanied the genre, was not allowed at Kamehameha until the 1940s, and then only in sitting position. In 1965, the ban on standing *hula* was overturned, but musical practices were by then well entrenched.

14. Each verse had two phrases of equal musical and poetic length, performed to the same music in duple meter. Melodies consisted of pitches from the Western diatonic scale, arranged to imply tonic-dominant relationships (Stillman, "The *Hula Ku'i*," 69, 90), and an instrumental "vamp" or interlude was inserted between strophes.

15. The U.S. Navy leased Kaho'olawe for target practice in 1940, and after the attack on Pearl Harbor the American government assumed complete authority over the island under martial law. Gradually, the natural environment was devastated. In 1976, concerned Hawaiians began protesting bomb testing on Kaho'olawe, and in 1977, Walter Ritte and Richard Sawyer, two members of the group Protect Kaho'olawe 'Ohana (PKO), successfully occupied the island. Not realizing that Ritte and Sawyer had returned from the island, fellow PKO members George Helm and Kimo Mitchell attempted to reach them by surfboard and perished in the attempt.

16. Fong's explanation, provided in an interview with me (Fong), was the same given to students.

17. The listening exercise involved seventy-six students and was completely open-ended (students were not directed to listen for anything at all). Though students listened to many different types of music, this essay deals only with student responses that are relevant to their apprehension of Hawaiian text.

18. In both exercises, I worked with groups of four to five students at a time. This provided an opportunity immediately following the reflective tasks to talk individually with them or to engage in small group discussions when students felt so inclined.

19. "In the Ni'ihau dialect, and in the speech of some of the older generation, /k/ has both [k] and [t] allophones" (Newbrand 6). Hence, the song title "Rain Tuahine O Mānoa."

20. An allophone is an acoustic manifestation of a phoneme and is placed within square brackets, for example, [*a*].

21. "Gemination" refers to the doubling of a consonant or vowel.

22. The Hawaiian word meaning "porch" is "lānai."

23. By way of contrast, Yoruba has 582, Cantonese has 3,456, and Vietnamese has 14,430 possible syllables (Maddieson 22).

24. Gaining familiarity with the phonological properties of Hawaiian was not simply a function of learning songs at school. Students were avid consumers of contemporary Hawaiian music, much of which also uses Hawaiian language.

25. Rhyme is actually rare in traditional Hawaiian *mele*, but did occur in the song the student is referring to. Timbre refers to the color or quality of a sound, often described in sensory terms, for example, bright, fuzzy, warm.

26. Chanted *mele* can use vocables, for example, '*ea lā*, but they generally play a secondary role to denotative language.

27. For example, Erkki Pohjola, founder and conductor of Finland's Tapiola Choir, has had two opportunities to hear the Concert Glee Club live and noted its distinctly "warm" sound (pers. comm.). Anthony Barresi, choral music education specialist at the University of Wisconsin–Madison, is another who has commented on the group's "rich" timbre (pers. comm.).

28. To explain in more detail, most pitched instrumental and vocal sound consists of several tones heard simultaneously. This complex tone consists of a fundamental frequency, the lowest and loudest of the tones and hence the most audible, and a number of overtones at frequencies higher than the fundamental but usually not individually discernable by listeners. Nonetheless, it is the relative loudness or intensity of these overtones and the way they are distributed within the acoustic spectrum that contributes to the listener's experience of timbre.

In vocal terms, Potter explains that

> as an instrument, the voice consists of three elements: a power supply (the lungs), and oscillator (the cords, or vocal folds as they are sometimes called) and a resonator (the vocal tract, consisting of the mouth and throat cavities). The airstream from the lungs passes through the folds, which vibrate, producing the raw material for speaking or singing. This raw sound is a complex one consisting of a fundamental frequency determined by the cordal vibration, and a large number of overtones or partials. As in any acoustic space there is a frequency at which the tract itself resonates. There are, in fact, four or five such resonances, known as formants, which have their own vibrating frequency (which, of course, changes with the shape of the tract). The closer the [overtones] correspond to this frequency, the louder will be the resulting sound leaving the lips. This relationship also determines the colour of vowels, a hugely complex process of continually shifting frequencies involving also the lips, jaw and tongue. (52–53)

29. In the case of choral music, there is less research and therefore more speculation about the specific factors that contribute to the perception of timbre. Sundberg supposes that the

distribution of formant frequencies among individual choir members contributes to choral timbre (145).

30. All languages have constraints on the ways that phonemes are distributed, and phonotactics refers to the linear sequences of sounds that are allowed in a given language.

31. Pele is the name of the goddess associated with Hawaiian volcanoes. As a supernatural being, she figures prominently in many Native Hawaiians' belief systems; as a figure of folkloric importance, she is familiar to most state residents, regardless of ethnicity.

32. This still seems possible even though the second element of the Hawaiian diphthong "has more vowel quality than the off-glide in an English diphthong" (Pukui and Elbert xvii).

33. Diamond Head is the volcanic crater adjacent to the Waikīkī district in Honolulu. Its distinct profile has made it a popular image for photographic and other forms of visual representation, especially in tourist literature.

34. Sound symbolism in English can be illustrated with the word "tap." It begins and ends with the stops /t/ and /p/ respectively, which are both short, abrupt sounds, and are used in this instance to denote a short, abrupt sound or action. Of the many types, this is an example of imitative sound symbolism (see Hinton, Nichols, and Ohala).

35. Part of this passage is also quoted in Hosokawa.

36. Hannerz's generalization should not be taken as universalism, recognizing, as ethnomusicologists have, that speech and song share many parameters and that in culture-specific instances there is sometimes little distinction between the two categories (where they apply) or even between broader classificatory rubrics like music and language (see, for example, Bagemihl).

Works Cited

Bagemihl, Bruce. "The Morphology and Phonology of Katajjait (Inuit Throat Games)." *Canadian Journal of Linguistics/Revue canadienne de linguistique* 33.1 (1988): 1–58.

Berger, Harris M. *Metal, Rock and Jazz: Perception and the Phenomenology of Musical Experience.* Hanover, NH: Wesleyan UP, 1999.

Boggs, Stephen T. *Speaking, Relating, and Learning: A Study of Hawaiian Children at Home and at School.* Assisted by Karen Watson-Gegeo and Georgia McMillen. Norwood, NJ: Ablex, 1985.

Brown, Laura E. "Choral Music in the Kamehameha School for Girls. Outline Presented at Faculty Meeting, April 11, 1935." Ms. Kamehameha Schools Bishop Estate Archives.

Campbell, J. L., and Francis Collinson. "The Meaningless Refrain Syllables and their Significance." *Hebridean Folksongs.* Vol. 1. Oxford: Clarendon P, 1969. 227–37.

Cogan, Robert. *New Images of Musical Sound.* Cambridge: Harvard UP, 1984.

Dunford, Bruce. "Language and Heritage." *Executive Educator* 13.12 (1991): 38–39.

Eastman, Carol M. "'Culture-Loaded' Vocabulary and Language Resurrection." *Current Anthropology* 20.2 (1979): 401–02.

Eastman, Carol, and Thomas Reese. "Associated Language: How Language and Ethnic Identity Are Related." *General Linguistics* 21.2 (1981): 109–16.

Eastman, Carol M., and Roberta F. Stein. "Language Display: Authenticating Claims to Social Identity." *Journal of Multilingual and Multicultural Development* 14.3 (1993): 187–202.

Elbert, Samuel H. "Connotative Values of Hawaiian Place Names." *Directions in Pacific Traditional Literature Essays in Honor of Katharine Luomala.* Ed. Adrienne Kaeppler and H. Arlo Nimmo. Honolulu: Bishop Museum P, 1976. 117–33.

Elbert, Samuel H., and Noelani Mahoe. *Nā Mele O Hawai'i Nei: 101 Hawaiian Songs.* Honolulu: U of Hawaii P, 1970.

Feld, Steven. "Communication, Music, and Speech about Music." *Yearbook for Traditional Music* 16 (1984): 1–18.

Fong, Randie K. Personal interview. Honolulu. 15 Feb. 1992.

Frisbie, Charlotte J. "Vocables in Navajo Ceremonial Music." *Ethnomusicology* 24.3 (1980): 347–92.

Gee, James P. *The Social Mind: Language, Ideology, and Social Practice.* New York: Bergin and Garvey, 1992.

Geertz, Clifford. " 'From the Native's Point of View': On the Nature of Anthropological Understanding." *Local Knowledge: Further Essays in Interpretive Anthropology.* New York: Basic, 1983. 55–69.

Goffman, Erving. *The Presentation of Self in Everyday Life.* Woodstock, NY: Overlook P, 1973.

Hannerz, Ulf. *Transnational Connections: Culture, People, Places.* London/New York: Routledge, 1996.

Hinton, Leanne, Johanna Nichols, and John Ohala. "Introduction: Sound-symbolic Processes." *Sound Symbolism.* Cambridge: Cambridge UP, 1994. 1–14.

Hosokawa, Shuhei. " 'Salsa No Tiene Frontera': Orquesta de la Luz and the Globalization of Popular Music." *Cultural Studies* 13.3 (1999): 509–34.

Infante, Esme M. "Hawaiian Language Study OK'd for All Through the 12th Grade." *Honolulu Advertiser* 7 Feb. 1992.

Kaeppler, Adrienne L. *Hula Pahu: Hawaiian Drum Dances.* Honolulu: Bishop Museum P, 1992.

Kamana [Kamanā], Kauanoe. "Language Languish; Time to Inject New Respect for Hawaiian." *Honolulu Star-Bulletin* 17 Feb. 1987.

Kanahele, George S. *Pauahi: The Kamehameha Legacy.* Honolulu: Kamehameha Schools P, 1986.

Kuschel, Rolf. "Games on a Polynesian Outlier Island: A Case Study of the Implications of Cultural Change." *Journal of the Polynesian Society* 84.1 (1975): 25–66.

Lévi-Strauss, Claude. "Preface." *Six Lectures on Sound and Meaning.* Roman Jakobson. J. Mepham, tr. Cambridge: MIT P, 1978. xi–xxxvi.

Lili'uokalani. Dorothy K. Gillett, text and notation; Barbara B. Smith, ed. *The Queen's Songbook: Her Majesty Queen Lili'uokalani.* Honolulu: Hui Hānai, 1999.

Maddieson, Ian. *Patterns of Sounds.* Cambridge: Cambridge UP, 1984.

Meintjes, Louise. "Paul Simon's Graceland, South Africa, and the Mediation of Musical Meaning." *Ethnomusicology* 34.1 (1990): 37–73.

Newbrand, Helene Luise. "A Phonemic Analysis of Hawaiian." M.A. thesis. U of Hawaii, 1951.

Noble, Dale. *A Handbook for Song Contest Student Directors.* Honolulu: Kamehameha Schools, 1990.

Potter, John. *Vocal Authority: Singing Style and Ideology.* Cambridge: Cambridge UP, 1998.

Powers, William K. *Sacred Language: The Nature of Supernatural Discourse in Lakota.* Norman: U of Oklahoma P, 1986.

Pukui, Mary Kawena, and Samuel H. Elbert. *Hawaiian Dictionary: Hawaiian-English, English-Hawaiian.* Rev. and enl. ed. Honolulu: U of Hawaii P, 1986.

Reinecke, John. *Language and Dialect in Hawaii: A Sociolinguistic History to 1935.* Ed. Stanley M. Tsuzaki. Honolulu: U of Hawaii P, 1969.

Roberts, Helen H. *Ancient Hawaiian Music.* 1926. Gloucester, MA: Peter Smith, 1977.

Schütz, Albert J. *The Voices of Eden: A History of Hawaiian Language Studies.* Honolulu: U of Hawai'i P, 1994.

Shepherd, John. "Cross-Cultural Musical Reception: A Theoretical Perspective." Society for Ethnomusicology annual meeting, Chicago. 12 October 1991.

Smith, Laura. Interview with Mandy Bowers. Honolulu. 15 July 1991. Kamehameha Schools, Hawaiian Collection.

State of Hawaii. *Hawaii Revised Statutes: Comprising the Statutes of the State of Hawaii, Consolidated, Revised and Annotated.* Supplement, Vol. 5. [Honolulu]: n.p., 1985. Replacement, 1991.

Stillman, Amy K. "Beyond Bibliography: Interpreting Hawaiian-Language Protestant Hymn Imprints." *Ethnomusicology* 40.3 (1996): 469–88.

———. "Hula Hits, Local Music and Local Charts: Some Dynamics of Popular Hawaiian Music." *Sound Alliances: Indigenous Peoples, Cultural Politics and Popular Music in the Pacific.* Ed. Philip Hayward. London: Cassell, 1996. 89–103.

———. "The *Hula Ku'i*: A Tradition in Hawaiian Music and Dance." M.A. thesis, U of Hawaii, 1982.

———. "Published Hawaiian Songbooks." *MLA Notes* 44 (1987): 221–39.

Sundberg, Johan. *The Science of the Singing Voice.* De Kalb: Northern Illinois UP, 1987.

Tatar, Elizabeth. *Strains of Change: The Impact of Tourism on Hawaiian Music.* Honolulu: Bishop Museum P, 1987.

Territory of Hawaii. *Revised Laws of Hawaii; Comprising the Statutes of the Territory, Consolidated, Revised and Annotated.* Honolulu: Hawaiian Gazette, 1905.

Tolbert, Elizabeth. "Theories of Meaning and Music Cognition: An Ethnomusicological Approach." *World of Music* 34.3 (1992): 7–21.

Turino, Thomas A. "Signs of Imagination, Identity and Experience: A Peircian Semiotic Theory for Music." *Ethnomusicology* 43.2 (1999): 221–55.

Turner, Victor. *The Ritual Process.* Chicago: Aldine, 1969.

Vander, Judith. *Shoshone Ghost Dance Religion: Poetry Songs and Great Basin Context.* Urbana: U of Illinois P, 1997.

Watson, Karen Ann. "Transferable Communicative Routines: Strategies and Group Identity in Two Speech Events." *Language in Society* 4.1 (1975): 53–72.

Watson-Gegeo, Karen Ann, and Stephen T. Boggs. "From Verbal Play to Talk Story: The Role of Routines in Speech Events among Hawaiian Children." *Child Discourse.* Ed. Susan Erwin-Tripp and Claudia Mitchell-Kernan. New York: Academic P, 1977. 67–90.

Wineburg, Samuel S. "On the Reading of Historical Texts: Notes on the Breach Between School and Academy." *American Educational Research Journal* 28.3 (1991): 495–519.

Wong, Kaupena. "Ancient Hawaiian Music." *The Kamehameha Schools 75th Anniversary Lectures.* Honolulu: Kamehameha Schools P, 1965. 9–15.

Yung, Bell. "Padding Syllables." *Cantonese Opera: Performance as Creative Process.* Cambridge: Cambridge UP, 1989. 92–105.

"*Chanter en Yaourt*"

Pop Music and Language Choice in France

—Cece Cutler

Quite by chance, a musician friend of mine was asked to write some English lyrics for a French pop-rock group called Montecarl. He explained to me that there were already vocal tracks on the demo but that they were just *yaourt*, or "yogurt," and did not really mean anything. In France, *chanter en yaourt* refers to singing that imitates English and is often glossed as *le faux anglais*, or "fake English." In its most general sense, *chanter en yaourt* involves the use of an assortment of real and nonsense English words and sounds sung in phonologically and prosodically convincing approximations of English. French pop singers use *yaourt* as a tool for writing songs in English: first, they compose a song, record the basic drum and guitar tracks, and then put *yaourt* lyrics on top to get a sense of how the song would sound if it were sung in English. Then they write English lyrics (or have them written by a native speaker) that fit the melodic, harmonic, and rhythmic structure of the song.[1] These final lyrics may even mimic the phrasing and the sounds of the original *yaourt* lyrics in some ways. Although *yaourt* lyrics may at times sound quite a bit like English, vocalists insist they are not actually singing in English. *Yaourt* in this context should thus be seen as a kind of verbal and musical art form that requires an ear finely attuned to aspects of English structure and English usage in popular music. Every French child studies English for at least six years in school, but it is not uncommon for young people in France to have rather limited verbal fluency. *Yaourt* is thus a natural method for pop singers to overcome their limited English verbal skills while satisfying the market demands to write songs in English.

Montecarl, the group whose music this essay investigates, is made up of four male musicians in their midtwenties who play music that can fairly be described as pop-rock with a "retro" 1960s edge. Montecarl's music is described by the French music press as "uncomplicated," "close to the spirit of the

1960s," with "wild guitars" and "tortured vocals embellished with vibrato" ("Bienvenue sur le site internet de Montecarl"). Their tight, driving pop rhythms and catchy melodies are reminiscent of French pop groups like Télélphone and Jacques Dutronc as well as classic 1960s British rock groups like the Who and the Kinks. Montecarl toured mainly in France and some in England between 1996 and their breakup in early 2000. The lead singer in the band, according to several of his English-speaking friends, has limited verbal skills in English, although his oral comprehension is quite good. Montecarl record and perform songs in English as well as in French. The unreleased demo used for this analysis consists of six tracks totaling 24:53 minutes. Four of the six songs are sung in *yaourt*, one is in French, and one is a mixture French and *yaourt*.

This essay will present an analysis of the linguistic strategies artists employ when singing in *yaourt*. On close inspection, *yaourt* lyrics demonstrate patterns that reveal a fair degree of linguistic competence. Transcribed excerpts of the lyrics will be analyzed with respect to phonetics, phonology, morphosyntax, prosody, and lexis. A modified phonetic transcription of the *yaourt* lyrics will show how various formal features are employed to create the semblance of English. The non-French sounds that appear most frequently in the lyrics can give us a better idea of which prosodic and phonological elements of English are most salient for nonnative speakers, particularly for French speakers. The sounds these speakers associate with English can be examined as indexical elements that, in effect, connote or embody some essential (or even essentialized?) notion of what it means to sound like one is speaking English. This essay will also explore the aesthetics of singing in a language one does not fully command and the role of English as a lingua franca in the international pop music market. The phenomenon of pop artists employing an accent other than their own is quite widespread; however, the phenomenon of imitating a language one does not speak very well has not been looked at in depth.

English in World Pop Music

Recent work in a fast-growing interdisciplinary field called English as an International Language (EIL) has highlighted the rapid expansion of English across the globe (Kachru). The prestige attached to English around the world and its role as an international language make it a natural choice for many pop music artists in non-English speaking countries. Many European pop musicians since the 1960s have written or at least recorded songs in English in hopes of reaching a broader market (for example, Swedish groups like Abba and the Cardigans, the Icelandic artist Björk, and others).[2] In many cases, there is enormous pressure from record label companies for groups to sing in English so that their music can be distributed globally. But in France, where the French language is aggressively protected by the Academie Française and where since 1996 it has been mandated that 40 percent of the music on the radio be in French (Ludden), it may come as a surprise that many artists with primarily French-speaking audiences still opt to sing in English. One notable deviation from this trend has been the enormous success of French rap sung in French. France has witnessed the proliferation of local rap groups such as MC Solaar, F.F.F., and Crew Assassin, particularly among the disenfranchised North African and sub-Saharan African youth living on the outskirts of Paris. Although English expressions like "get down" and "dealer" do show up in French rap, most artists rap entirely in French.[3] The borrowing of American English rap jargon by French rappers is, however, a separate topic from the imitation of English we find in *yaourt*.

Linguistic Analysis

The following sections examine some of the *yaourt* lyrics in terms of phonetics, phonology, morpho-syntax, prosody, and lexis. To make the text accessible to an interdisciplinary audience, I have transcribed the lyrics using a modified English orthography that approximates the actual pronunciation on the tape. The reader, however, should refer to the full transcription using symbols from the International Phonetic Alphabet (IPA) in Appendix A for a more accurate representation.[4] One verse plus the chorus from Tracks 1 and 6 have been transcribed using the modified English orthography. It cannot be emphasized enough how subjective the following transcription is. I tried as much as possible to use English words when they were quite unambiguous, but where a word's status was questionable, I avoided giving it an English spelling so as to leave its interpretation as open as possible. When the songs were played for others, these listeners heard different English words than I did, and unanimous decisions about a word's status were rare. These two songs and respective verses were chosen because the vocal tracks were the most audible and because they were also sung entirely in *yaourt*.

Track 1, Verse 1 (3:53)
1 tahm is sweet
2 an' a low ah
3 weev you sumah babe
4 ahm only ada go
5 ahm much in lucky
6 nobody's low
7 ahm now chi wone

Chorus
8 ahm trynu be mah ideal lucky
9 widah sumfin'
10 why not to jay
11 ah wou
12 in lucky new change of mind
13 ahma be mah luck yo
14 justa one naht
15 luvah baby
16 check it oh sumfing whadevah lucky
17 what is a lowkey
18 ahm facin'

Track 6, Verse 2 (3:27)
1 ah feel the ((burn is?)) en wayteen
2 ya try out an' honey en mah thing
3 you come mah lil' honley anothah
4 but it sumfin' (( )) if ya look even 'igher
5 trah to you gotta look even 'igher
6 you duh gotta wah look even 'igher
7 ahm justa baby the somethin' deniah
8 ahm justa no paying attention deniah

Chorus
9 ah wannu lockin everyday
10 ahm justa thinkin' of a ((bla?)) blue
11 ah wanna turn it up an' ye'siday
12 ah trahda live / leave an' nothin' bothah you
13 ah cry to live / leave an' nothin' pay

Phonetics/Phonology

The phonetics and phonology of a language involve the inventory of sounds in that language and how these sounds are put together in speech. The consonant sounds found in English but not in French include "th" as in "this" and "thing," the American "r," which differs in terms of manner and place of articulation from the French uvular "r," the "ch" sound in "church," the "j" sound in "jog," and the "h" sound in "happy." Although French has a wider range of vowels than English (including nasalized vowels and front rounded vowels), it lacks the vowel sound represented by the IPA symbol /ɪ/ as in the English word "bit." Likewise, it lacks the sound /æ/ as in "hat" and /ʊ/ as in "book," as well as diphthongs (or double vowels) like /ay/ in "bike," /aw/ in "house," and /oy/ in "boy." In terms of phonetics, the lead vocalist demonstrates a command of most of the basic vowel sounds of English, including /æ/ as in Track 1, line 2 (an' a); /ʊ/ in Track 1, line 11 (wou(ld)); and the diphthongs /ay/ and /aw/ in Track 6, line 12, and in Track 1, line 7. The vocalist also controls the English affricates "ch" and "j" (see Track 1, lines 12 and 14) and even the /d/ sound in the American pronunciation of the word "whatever" (see Track 1, line 16).[5]

The "r" sound and its patterning in the lyrics require some explanation. The French "r" is called a uvular fricative and is transcribed /ʁ/ in the IPA system. It differs from the English or American "r" with respect to place and manner of articulation (that is, where and how the tongue is placed with respect to the roof of the mouth and how the air passes through the oral/nasal tract). The English "r" is formed by bunching up or curling back the tongue slightly in the prepalatal part of the mouth, whereas the French "r" is formed by constricting the back of the tongue near the uvula. The vocalist avoids words that start with "r" in his singing—ostensibly the most difficult phonological environment for a French speaker to pronounce the American "r." There are some syllables that start off with a consonant plus "r," and in these instances the vocalist produces quite a close approximation of the English variant. There are no words that end in "r" in the lyrics. This may be due to the fact that vocalist is following the typical British pattern of "r-lessness"—the omission of "r" when it follows a vowel as in "far" (for example, fah).

One of the most notable features evident here is the vocalist's tendency to produce monophthongs in words like "I" and "my" so they sound more like "ah" and "mah." Although this may be partially influenced by French, which has no such diphthongs, it is also a typical feature of English in the American South and is a widespread feature in the music of pop groups that do not necessarily have any geographical connection or cultural affinity to that part of the United States.[6]

Also of interest are the examples in the lyrics of the sort of phonological reduction typical of the rapid speech of native English speakers. The singer employs "-ing dropping" in gerunds and other -ing words like "facin'" and "somethin'" in Track 1, lines 9 and 18. In Track 1, line 2, "an' a" sounds like a reduction of "and a," and "trynu" in line 8 sounds like a reduction of "trying to." In Track 6, lines 9 and 11, "ah wannu" appears to be a reduction of "I want to," and "ah trahda" in lines 12 and 13 may likewise be a reduction of "I try to." Finally, the first word in line 13 of Track 1, "ahma," is possibly an extreme reduction of "I'm going to." The singer has either acquired a fair degree of knowledge about the assimilation and reduction rules of English speech or has simply picked up these forms as units from other English pop lyrics. The "d" sound, however, may well represent the acquisition of the so-called flapping rule, since it appears in all the places we would expect it, even across word boundaries.[7]

Although the singer's pronunciation of "th" in Track 6, lines 7, 10, and 12, seems quite good, there is some phonological interference from French in his pronunciation of the "th" sound in words like "something," "through," and "with." Since French does not have this sound, speakers often approximate one of the nearest sounds in terms of manner and place of articulation. This results in pronunciations like "sumfing" for "something" in Track 1, line 16, and "weev" for "with" in Track 1, line 3. In Track 6, his pronunciation of the vowel in "look" and "looking" reflects standard pronunciation in lines 5 and 6, but he employs a more centralized vowel in line 4 (sounding more like "lucking"). There is a third variant in Track 6, line 9, which sounds like "lockin." As was the case with sounds like "th," the vowel in the word "look" does not exist in French, and the singer's pronunciation reflects an attempt to get the sound right. With some vowels, there is potential semantic confusion (see Track 6, line 12, "leave"). French lacks the short English vowel /ɪ/, and there is a tendency for French speakers to substitute the sound "ee" in a word like "live" so that it becomes homophonous with "leave." It is not clear that the singer was trying to produce one or any of either of these words in the song, but if that had been his intention, the meaning would be ambiguous.

The kinds of syllables we see in the *yaourt* lyrics are also noteworthy. There is a preference among many world languages (including French) for open syllables, that is, syllables ending in vowels rather than consonants (McCarthy and Prince). Many such languages, however, do allow some kinds of consonants at the end of a syllable, namely nasal consonants like "m" and "n." An analysis of the *yaourt* lyrics shows a full 75 percent of the syllables end in vowels compared with 17 percent that end in nasal consonants and just 8 percent that end in other consonant sounds (fricatives, stops, and liquids).[8] These figures reflect French syllable structure constraints (phonotactics) more closely than English, which does permit most consonants and even allows multiple consonants at the ends of syllables.

Furthermore, there are virtually no consonant clusters in the lyrics. A consonant cluster is defined as two or more consonants within the same syllable. Bearing in mind that orthography does not always reflect pronunciation, French does not allow clusters at the end of syllables, although word initial clusters are acceptable (for example, _station_, _tromper_). Where two consonants do appear side-by-side in the *yaourt* lyrics, they form the coda and onset of adjacent syllables within a word. (The coda is the final segment or segments of a syllable, for example, the "t" in "ha_t_" or the "st" in "pa_st_"; the onset is the first consonant or set of consonants in a syllable, for example, "r" in "_r_ack" or "tr" in "_tr_ack"). The word "just," which contains the consonant cluster "st" in the coda, is resyllabified via the addition of an "epenthetic" vowel at the end of the word. This breaks up the cluster so that it conforms better to French phonotactic constraints (see Track 1, line 14, "justa one naht," and Track 6, lines 7, 8, and 10). The word "just" in English consists of only one syllable, but adding a vowel on the end breaks up the final consonant cluster so that the "s" becomes the coda of the first syllable and the "t" becomes the onset of the second syllable (for example, just → jus.ta). These examples show that the vocalist has a good grasp of English sounds and phonological processes, but in terms of syllable structure, his *yaourt* conforms more to French phonotactic constraints than those of English.

Morpho-syntax

Morphology refers to the suffixes and prefixes (referred to generically as affixes) appended to nouns and verbs, and syntax refers to the structure of sentences. A morpho-syntactic analysis of *yaourt* is hampered by the questionable lexical status of many of the words, so it is important to emphasize that the following remarks are based on one interpretation of the possible referents these words have in English. Derivational affixes include prefixes and suffixes like un- in "<u>un</u>steady" and -able as in "know<u>able</u>." Inflectional affixes in English indicate past tense, -ed as in "walk<u>ed</u>," third person -s as in "He goe<u>s</u>," and progressive -ing as in "I am walk<u>ing</u>." There are a few examples of inflection in the lyrics: Track 1, lines 4, 5, 8, and 13, appear to contain first person inflected forms of "to be" (I'm). There are a couple of possible examples of progressive verbs—Track 6, lines 1 ("wayteen" or "waiting"?) and 10 ("thinkin"). French has inflectional morphology to indicate plurality, person, number, and tense, so inflection is not a foreign concept. However, many French speakers run into trouble with English plural marking since they do not actually pronounce plural -s in words like *chiens* "dogs" and therefore have a tendency to omit it when speaking English. French indicates possession by way of the preposition *de* as in *C'est le chien de mon frere.* (lit. It's the dog of my brother), whereas English uses the inflectional possessive -s ("It's my brother's dog.") The singer seems to have correctly employed the English possessive -s in Track 1, line 6 ("nobody's"), although this could alternatively be an example of third person verbal -s in its contracted form.

When *yaourt* words closely resemble English, the natural tendency is to try to identify the larger phrase to which they belong. Many such putative phrases seem to be fragments as in Track 1, line 14, "justa one night"(?), and Track 6, line 12, "I try to live/leave"(?). As minimal units, these phrases are grammatically correct, but they lack the requisite specifiers and/or complements to form complete sentences. For example, "change of mind"(?) in Track 1, line 12, would normally require a preceding subject and verb (for example, "<u>I had</u> a change of mind."). Line 3 appears to be a prepositional phrase beginning with "with" ("weev you sumah babe") but lacking a preceding verb phrase. (In English, prepositional phrases are generally preceded by verb phrases or noun phrases in complete sentences.) The singer appears to be inserting the preposition "to" in front of progressive verbs as in "you gotta looking"(?) in Track 6, line 5, and "I wannu lockin' everyday" in Track 6, line 9. This may be an overgeneralization of the use of infinitival "to" due to the influence of French which would use infinitival verbs in equivalent sentences (for example, *Je veux regarder* [I want to look]).

Similar syntactic confusion occurs in wh- phrases (sentences that begin with words like "why," "who," "where," and "when"). In Track 1, line 10 starts with "why" followed by "not to" ("why not to jay"). Here, the singer seems to have placed the preposition "to" after the negator—a pattern that is not grammatical in English regardless of the kind of word that follows it. In fact, this sentence more clearly follows the pattern we would find in colloquial French wh- phrases, such as we see in example 1 where the wh- word is followed by a negator and then an infinitival verb.

1. *Pourquoi pas faire ça?*
"Why not (to) do this?"

There is some quite predictable confusion with quantifiers in the lyrics. The singer has employed "much" rather than "very" to qualify the adjective "lucky" in Track 1, line 5, "ahm much in lucky." He may have heard expressions like "in love," or "in luck" and sentences like "I'm much obliged" and overgeneralized to form the sentence "I'm much in lucky." In French, the quantifier *trés* would be used in all of these contexts, as we see in example 2.

2. *Je suis trés amoureuse.*
"I am very (much) in love."

Despite some minor confusion regarding prepositions, these limited examples suggest that the singer has a basic grasp of how to form noun phrases, verb phrases, and prepositional phrases in English. He also seems to have a basic understanding of English word order, although it must be noted that the patterns in French with respect to phrase structure and sentence structure do not differ significantly from English.

Prosody

Prosody in linguistics refers to the study of intonation, tone, and stress in language. Stress is relevant to this discussion in that English and French differ in how stress is assigned. In English, stress may fall on the first or second syllable in bisyllabic words. In words of three syllables or more, stress usually falls on the penultimate syllable. Stress placement in English may also change the part of speech of a word (for example, ábstract *noun* versus abstráct *adj.*). In sum, stress in English varies quite a bit and may not always be predictable, but it rarely falls on the final syllable of a word. In contrast, stress in French almost always falls on the last syllable in a word, although in rapid speech it may fall on the final syllable of a group of words (Vaissirèae). Stress in music, however, is dictated in many ways by the phrasing and rhythm of the song in interaction with the prosody of the language of the lyrics. It is therefore quite difficult to separate the prosody of the language from that of the song. One observation can be made in this regard: the vocalist tends to place the stress on the penultimate syllable in two- and three-syllable words and rarely on the last syllable. He may not have a firm grasp of English stress rules, but he seems to have realized the pattern is different from French and that part of creating a realistic semblance of English involves making sure that stress does not fall on the final syllable as it does in French.

Lexis

What is most revealing in a lexical analysis of the lyrics is the repetition of certain monosyllabic and bisyllabic nouns, like "time," "babe," "love," "lover," and "night." These nouns come from a stock of words commonly found in pop lyrics. Research into code switching, otherwise known as the mixing of two languages (for example, Spanglish, Chinglish, or Franglais) shows that the most commonly switched items tend to be nouns (Poplack). This pattern seems to hold for *yaourt*, although there is about an equal number of verbs, half of which are gerunds. These verbs are also quite common and represent the kinds of verbs second-language learners typically learn first. The suffix -ing in gerunds may well have special salience for nonnative speakers since it is such a frequently occurring feature of English. There are very few function words (such as "it," "to," and "a"), but there are many examples of first person singular pronouns (seven examples in Track 1 and eight in Track 6) followed closely by second person singular pronouns (one example in Track 1 and five in Track 6). This, too, is predictable given the often personal nature of songwriting and the frequency with which pronouns occur in everyday speech.

A breakdown of the putative lexical items in Tracks 1 and 6 and their grammatical categories is shown in Table 1.

Words that fall into nonlexical categories are more rare and include quantifiers such as *one* in Track 1, line 14, and conjunctions (or apparent ones) like "oh" or "or" in line 16.

As was the case for the morpho-syntactic analysis, the uncertain status of lexical items makes certain kinds of linguistic interpretation questionable. The

	TRACK 1	TRACK 6
Nouns	time, babe, nobody's, idol, something, change, mind, night, lover, baby, luck	thing, something, baby
Adjectives	sweet, lucky	——
Verbs	is, trying, am, facing, wou? or would	feel, waiting, come, looking, try, got, look, thinking, try, pay
Pronouns	ah (I) (line 4), mah (my) (lines 8, 13)	ah (I) (lines 1, 7, 8, 11–13), mah (my) (line 2) you (lines 2, 3, 6, 9, 12)
Prepositions	with, in, of	to, of
Wh- words	what, whatever, why	——
Adverbs	——	——

Table 1. Lexical Categories of Plausible English Words in the Lyrics

	TRACK 1	TRACK 6
Determiners	——	duh (the) (lines 1, 6)
Degree words, qualifiers, quantifiers	much (line 5) just (line 14) one (line 14)	——
Auxiliaries	be (lines 8, 13)	——
Conjunctions	an' (and) (line 2) oh (or) (line 16)	but (line 4)

Table 2. Nonlexical Categories of Plausible English Words in the Lyrics

frequency with which nouns and verbs occur is predictable in terms of cognitive salience. When challenged to come up with words of another language, most people will respond with nouns and verbs rather than auxiliaries, prepositions, and the like. Furthermore, nouns like "baby" and verbs like "love" occur so frequently in English pop music that it is quite natural that they would turn up in the spontaneous attempts to reproduce English that we see in *yaourt*.

Discussion

Linguistically, we can say that the singer in Montecarl has quite a good grasp of the sounds of English. He has identified certain vowels and consonants that do not exist in French and used them repeatedly throughout the two songs. The same can be said of his frequent use of progressive verbs (gerunds). In essence, these linguistic elements ("ch," /ay/, /aw/, the suffix -ing, and so forth) appear to have a high degree of salience for the vocalist, indeed perhaps for French speakers in general. As such, these elements function as metonyms for the entire language, and their frequent repetition constitutes a convincing representation of English. Certain phonological and prosodic features in the *yaourt* lyrics suggest that the singer may have a better understanding of certain aspects of English than his verbal ability implies. The degree of phonological assimilation he employs in strings of words suggests he has at least some grasp of how sounds and syllables are elided in rapid speech as well as an awareness that English stress patterns are different from those of French. He also has a basic grasp of English phrase structure and word order rules. But in terms of syllable structure, the phonotactic constraints of French are winning out over English (that is, the syllables in the lyrics conform to the shape of syllables in French more than English).

There are many pop and rock musicians around the world who sing in English rather than, or in addition to, their native tongue. Contemporary Spanish pop groups like Sexy Sadie, Dover, and Amphetamine Discharge sing virtually all their songs in English even though most of their fans are Spanish speaking. Pop artists employing an accent other than their own is equally if not more common. Peter Trudgill documents British pop singers (for example, the Beatles, the Rolling Stones) using American (and African American) accents during the 1960s and 1970s. In subsequent decades, white singers in mixed British pop groups like Madness, the Specials, and UB40 employed Jamaican Creole accents and expressions in their songs. Most recently, white rappers in the U.S. such as the Beastie Boys, Eminem, and Vanilla Ice have appropriated African American English accents and expressions from hip hop culture.

Although American (especially African American) speech features have been the target of much linguistic appropriation or imitation by pop musicians outside the United States, sometimes the trend is reversed and other groups (including the British) become the target. American rock groups like Guided by Voices and Green Day appropriate stereotypically British pronunciations in their music. Green Day, in particular, adopt Estuary English features in their revisitations of British punk rock vocal styles (for example, the glottalization of word medial and final stops and postvocalic r-lessness) (see Wells). These appropriations, although rather liminal and incomplete, seem to represent the ardent desire on behalf of these musicians to identify themselves with certain British musical traditions. It may be that a full affectation of a British accent would come too close to an overt claim of identity (that is, British) and ultimately alienate listeners, whereas the partial adoption of selected linguistic features is a more subtle and acceptable way of referencing one's musical roots. Other groups like the American band the Upper Crust employ British accents satirically in songs like "Friend of a Friend of the Working Class." In other cases, vocalists tone down or eliminate linguistic features that link them to a particular musical or cultural tradition. Trudgill notes that from 1963 to 1969, the Beatles subsequently distanced themselves from American pronunciations, switching from the American /æ/ in words like *can't* and *half* to the British /aː/ as part of a shift from rock and roll to more contemplative works.

Linguistic appropriation, regardless of directionality, can be viewed as an attempt by individuals to align themselves symbolically with the speakers they imitate and thereby participate in the prestige these groups enjoy in the larger community or within a subculture (Bell). In this line of analysis, white American hip hop artists like Eminem who rap in African American English are claiming a kind of African American identity through language—an identity that is enormously prestigious within the hip hop community.

The *yaourt* phenomenon is a bit more complex, although it bears some similarities to the cases just mentioned. Affective feelings toward the English language, Britain, or the United States will inevitably vary from person to person, but it can be fairly stated that the French do not have a comfortable relationship with the English language or British and American culture. Far from a general expression of desire for things British or American, groups like Montecarl selectively align themselves with a particular genre of English rock—1960s and 1970s rock groups like the Who, the Kinks, and the Buzzcocks. By singing in English, Montecarl are claiming to be a part of that tradition rather than attempting to claim a British identity. The presence of

American speech features in the *yaourt* lyrics may be because such features also tend to occur in British pop music from the 1960s and 1970s—precisely the genre after which Montecarl style themselves. Another explanation could be based on the work of Allan Bell, who argues that the farther away one is linguistically from the target language, the vaguer one is, and can afford to be, about the linguistic target. The imperfect execution of the linguistic target, "rather than being lamentable, may be a highly successful strategy" that is "sufficient to evoke the model for the home audience" (Bell 194).

For many pop bands, the choice to sing in English (or *yaourt*) is also mediated in some sense by the international prestige of English. Within the subculture of Anglophile pop, English plays the role of the "official language," and those who want to be taken seriously must pay tribute to its status through musical and linguistic reference. This is not to deny the role of institutional power and capital in shaping language ideologies: language varieties clearly derive part of their value from large-scale sociohistorical processes (Rampton 311), and English undeniably benefits from the global scale of American economic and political clout. The reasons why bands like Montecarl choose to sing songs in English may be more complex than this brief account permits. The hope of tapping into English-speaking markets certainly plays a role, but Montecarl has its biggest fan base in France. Are there other reasons why the band would choose English?

There is a commonly held language ideology among many European pop and rock musicians that it is "easier" to write lyrics in English, and several nonnative speaking musicians have told me they think rock music simply "sounds better" in English. This preference may stem from the long tradition of English-language pop and rock music that serves as a point of reference for generations of non-English-speaking musicians and fans. Songwriters can draw from a huge inventory of English words and expressions that, according to them, "sound more authentic" than the equivalent expressions in their native languages. A musician from the New York rock band Nada Surf recounted to me the mixed reception the group received after performing one of their songs in French while on tour in Normandy. Another friend of mine from Spain said that Sting was nearly booed off the stage during a concert Madrid in 1999 when he sang a song in Spanish. I know of no studies that demonstrate whether certain languages lend themselves better to certain musical genres. It may be that such claims are partially or wholly based on social rather than linguistic or musical factors (that is, local or subcultural language ideologies). Since Montecarl broke up, the singer went on to put out a CD in English and continues to perform and record the majority of his music in English. From my brief discussions with him prior to the release of the band's last album, he repeated the view that the songs sound better sto him in English. Although it is clear that this opinion is at least in part derived from language ideologies surrounding English, the fact of structural differences in English and French phrasing should not be ignored. The band members' musical influences—1960s British pop—and their adulatory mimicry of this genre may also play a role in their choice of English. It may be necessary to sing in English in order to achieve the retro sound and rhythm as closely as they do, particularly when we consider the differences between English and French stress patterns.

Affective and psychological explanations for the linguistic appropriation of another group's way of speaking can be found in the work of Ben Rampton and of Bell. Rampton terms the appropriation of another group's language or dialect as "crossing" and analyzes it as part of a growing tendency for individuals to construct their identities from the wide array of commodified cultural elements surrounding them. Accordingly, "crossing" constitutes a kind of ethnolinguistic border transgression and reflects the desire to inhabit an alternative identity. A related concept is Bell's "outgroup referee design," a model characterized by speakers "[laying] claim to a speech and identity which are not their own but which hold prestige for them on some dimension" (188). Referees are third persons not physically present at an interaction but possessing such salience for a speaker that they influence speech even in their absence (186). In this model, speakers "diverge from the speech of their [own] ingroup—and thus in some sense from their own 'natural' speech—towards an outgroup with whom they wish to identify" (188). For many non-English-speaking pop singers, the referees and the linguistic target are, in the broadest sense, British or American pop singers, but they may not be able to distinguish the two varieties in a systematic way. Montecarl adopt several phonological patterns that are characteristic of American English rather that British English (for example, a "d" sound in "whatever" or the pronunciation of "I" as "ah"), but it is unlikely that they are aware these are features of American English.

Common to all referee design is the absence of direct feedback—something that has crucial consequences for a speaker's performance. "The speaker has no access to the outgroup, and therefore lacks adequate models of outgroup speech" (Bell 190). The singer in Montecarl does not generally have much access to English in his everyday life, resulting in a notable lack of fluency. According to Bell, "when the outgroup and its dialect are distant, attempted shift is partial and imperfect. It focuses on a few salient features in which the referee's dialect differs from the speaker's" (190). Bell goes on to say that "the aim of referee design is for your speech to put the audience in mind of a particular reference group. A few token shifts should successfully convince the immediate audience" (ibid.). As the analysis has shown, the singer in Montecarl adopts particular features of American English and uses them to index the speech of British pop artists. Montecarl's nominal use of English sounds suffices to alert non-English-speaking audience members to the fact that they are referencing English speakers but fails to match (quantitatively) the use of such features in the speech of the target group.

Along these lines, we can think of the *yaourt* phenomenon in terms of how it represents some kind of essentialized re-presentation of English. Among other writers, Keith Walters has suggested that second-language learners are most aware of features that differ most from their own variety.[9] The *yaourt* lyrics on the demo contain multiple examples of English sounds like /æ/, and "-ing," suggesting that these sounds are perhaps more salient on some level (and therefore representative of English) since they do not exist in French. In his attempts to re-create English, the vocalist in Montecarl uses these English sounds repeatedly in both tracks. Such highly recognizable sounds and words become indexical of English itself and, in some ways, its speakers. This process resembles what Rampton calls "pejorative secondary foreigner talk." This mock register displays a similar kind of indexicalization whereby particular features of pronunciation, words, and expressions that have come to represent an ethnic out-group are exaggerated or overused for dramatic or humorous effect (Hill). Another parallel can be found in the orthographic debates in Haiti surrounding the letter "k." Schieffelin and Doucet report that some Haitian-language planners regarded "k" as too "Anglo-Saxon" (read: American imperialist) and rejected its inclusion into the Haitian *kreyol* alphabet. These examples suggest that foreign words, but also sounds and even symbols, can have aesthetic meaning for people—meaning that is culturally specific and linked to the unique historical and cultural relationship individuals have to a foreign language and its speakers.

Conclusion

The *yaourt* phenomenon exists in many other non-English-speaking parts of the world (for example, *huachi huachi* in Spain). Additional studies of other "pseudo" forms of English in pop music and in other musical or verbal genres would certainly reveal interesting interactions between the singer's first language and English. Examining which linguistic features are most salient, and thereby in some ways indexical of English, for speakers of other languages as well as their subjective attitudes toward these features would allow for important cross-linguistic and cross-cultural comparisons.

Acknowledgments

I would like to thank Harris M. Berger for helpful comments and suggestions. I would also like to give my thanks to Daniel Lorca, Matthew Caws, and Ira Elliott for editing suggestions pertaining to pop music and, most of all, to the French band Montecarl, for allowing me to analyze their most recent demo.

Notes

1. Fino Oyonarte, who plays in the Spanish rock group Los Enemigos, reported the widespread use of similar practices in Spain where the "fake" English used in song writing is called "*huachi huachi*" or "*huachinglis*" (pers. comm.).

2. There are and always have been healthy local markets in Europe for pop music performed in local languages and dialects. Herbert Grönemeyer, Einstürzende Neubauten, and Nena are a few German groups that come to mind. In Spain, local bands like Los Enemigos, who only sing in Castilian, regularly tour Spain and have a respectable national following. In France, Serge Gainsbourg, Téléphone, and Johnny Halliday had unprecedented success singing in French. See also Chamberlain on pop music singers who sing in French being regarded as "poets" in France.

3. Expressions like "get down," "underground," "wack," "*kique ta merde*" (calqued on "kick that shit"), "hardcore," "*le dealer*," and "*le ridime*" appear in the lyrics of a group called Crew Assassin and can be viewed at http://www.anthologeek.net/%7Eassassin/textes_set.htm. Calvet posits that the forms of many of these English loan words will eventually be "frenchified" as their meanings evolve from technical to more general usage. According to a 1998 report filed by Jennifer Ludden for National Public Radio, France is the world's second largest market for rap music, and the recording industry has relied on American producers like Charles Alexander to re-create the musical sound that is identified with rap. In French, word stress always falls on the last syllable, and intonation contours across sentences do not necessary fall toward the end as they do in English. As a result, there is a tendency for syllables to "bleed" over the main rhythmic peaks in a measure. Alexander

tries to get French rappers to make their lyrics conform to English prosody to create a more "authentic" American sound (Ludden).

4. The IPA is superior to any conventional or nonconventional spelling system for linguistic analysis because it provides a neutral and consistent way to represent all possible sounds in any language. An IPA transcription can also reveal some of the phonological processes at work in the speech of someone whose native language is not English but French. There are several problems involved in trying to represent pronunciation without the IPA. For example, nonconventional orthographies often carry unintended sociocultural connotations. But the main problem here is that it is not always clear whether the singer in Montecarl is using an actual English word, so using English spelling—even in a modified form—effectively assigns to it a semantic and grammatical role that may not be justified. The tendency to insert word boundaries and to parse these units as English words is difficult to avoid, but an IPA transcription still allows greater room for analysis and interpretation than standard orthography would permit.

5. This "d" sound in words like "butter" and "whatever" is a distinctively American phonological pattern. This "d" sound (called the "flap") appears when written "t" occurs between two vowels and where primary stress falls on the preceding syllable. Most British English speakers would pronounce the "t" in this position.

6. Monophthongization involves the reduction of a diphthong or double vowel to a single vowel. This is commonly found in the American South where the pronoun "I" (/ay/ of Standard American English) loses its second element and becomes /a:/ (sounding a bit like ahh).

7. See note 5.

8. Open syllables are syllables that end in vowels rather than consonants. Examples are "ma" and "bee," which both end in vowels. Closed syllables are found in words like "cat" and "asp." Nasal consonants are /n/, /m/, and the -ng sound in "sing." Stops include the sounds /p/, /t/, /k/, /b/, /d/, and /g/ in English. Fricatives are sounds like /s/, /z/, /f/, /v/, and the "th" sound. Liquids are sounds like /l/ and /r/.

9. Walters describes whites who called into a talk show to complain about the African American pronunciation of "ask" as /æks/. He writes that the whites selected this one feature, raised it to the level of stereotype, and attributed the low status of African Americans to their use of it.

Appendix

The conventions used in the IPA transcriptions are as follows:
[ ]   IPA phonetic transcription
(( ))   speech inaudible
ká   an accent over the syllable indicates stress.

Track 1, Verse 1 (3:53)
19 [tá::m izwí::t]
20 [ænə lóʔa::]
21 [wiv yu sʌmə béy::b]
22 [áim ónli ʔaedə gó::]
23 [a:m mʌtʃin lʌki::]
24 [nobádiz ló:d]
25 [áim náw tʃíwó:n]

Chorus

26 [áim trá:nu bí mái á:díl lʌ́ki::]
27 [widə sʌ́mfɛn]
28 [way nátu dze:]
29 [áy wÚ]
30 [in lʌ́ki nu: tʃénʒ əv máy::nd]
31 [áimə bí má: lʌ́kjó]
32 [dʒʌ́stə wʌ́n ná:t]
33 lʌ́və bé:bí]
34 [tʃékɪt o sʌ́mfɪŋ wʌ́dévʌ́ lʌ́:ki::]
35 [wʌ́dɪzə lʌ́wki::]
36 [á:m féisen]

Track 6, Verse 2 (3:27)

14 [á: fil ðə ((___ ən)) weɪdin]
15 [jə drái awdɛn hʌ́ni ɛ́n má: θm̩]
16 [ju kʌ́m ma: lɪl hʌ́nli ənʌ́ðə]
17 [bʌ́d ɪ sʌ́mfɪn (( ))də lʌ́kɪŋ ənáiə]
18 [tráy tú yú gádə lʊ́kiŋ ənáiə]
19 [ju də gádewə lʊ́kiŋ ənáiə]
20 [a:m dʒʌ́stə béibi ðə sʌ́mθɪn dənáiə]
21 [a:m dʒʌ́stə nópeŋətɛ́nʃən dənáiə]

Chorus

22 [a:wánu lókín ɛ́vridé]
23 [a:m dʒʌ́stə θɪŋkən ʌ́və ((blæka blú))]
24 [a:wánə tánɪdʌ́pɛn jésədé]
25 [a:tráydə liv ən nʌ́θɪn báðə jú]
26 [a:tráydə liv ən nʌ́θɪn pé]

Works Cited

Bell, Allan. "Language Style as Audience Design." *Language in Society* 13 (1984): 145–204.

"Bienvenue sur le site internet de Montecarl." 3 August 2000.

Calvet, Louis Jean. "Les Mots du Rap et de la Techno." *Français dans le Monde* 289 (May-June 1997): 24–25.

Chamberlain, Alan L. "Modern French Music and Language Teaching." *Journal of the Australian Federation of Modern Language Teachers' Associations* 10 (1974): 15–18.

Hill, Jane H. "Is It Really 'No Problemo'? Junk Spanish and Anglo Racism." First Annual Symposium About Language and Society. U of Texas, Austin. 10–12 April 1993.

Kachru, Braj B. "Introduction: The Other Side of English and the 1990s." Ed. Braj B. Kachru. *The Other Tongue: English Across Cultures.* Chicago: U of Illinois P, 1992. 1–19.

Ludden, Jennifer. "French Rap." *Morning Edition.* National Public Radio. 23 Sept. 1998.

McCarthy, John, and Alan S. Prince. "Prosodic Morphology I: Constraint Interaction and Satisfaction." Unpublished manuscript, 1993.

Poplack, Shana. "Sometimes I'll Start a Sentence in Spanish Y TERMINO EN ESPAÑOL: Toward a Typology of Code-Switching." *Linguistics* 18.7/8 (1980): 581–618.

Rampton, Ben. *Crossing: Language and Ethnicity among Adolescents.* New York: Longman, 1995.

Schieffelin, B., and R. Doucet. "The 'Real' Haitian Creole: Ideology, Metalinguistics, and Orthographic Choice." *American Ethnologist* 21 (1994): 175–202.

Trudgill, Peter. "Acts of Conflicting Identity: The Sociolinguistics of British Pop-Song Pronunciation." Ed. Nikolas Coupland et al. *Sociolinguistics: A Reader*. New York: St. Martin's, 1997. 251–65.

Vaissière, J. "Rhythm, Accentuation, and Final Lengthening in French." *Music, Language, Speech, and Brain*. Ed. J. Sundberg et al. Stockholm: Wenner-Gren, 1992. 108–20.

Walters, Keith. "Black English, White Speakers, and Language Ideology." Fourth Annual Symposium about Language and Society. U of Texas, Austin. 12–14 April 1996.

Wells, John. "Estuary English." http://www.phon.ucl.ac.uk/home/estuary/home.htm. 24 June 2000.

Contributors

Harris M. Berger is an associate professor of music in the Department of Performance Studies at Texas A&M University. He is the author of *Metal, Rock, and Jazz: Perception and the Phenomenology of Musical Experience* (Wesleyan University Press / University Press of New England, 1999) and the founder and chair of the Popular Music Section of the Society for Ethnomusicology. His articles have appeared in the journals *Ethnomusicology*, *Popular Music*, the *Journal of American Folklore*, and the *Journal of Folklore Research*.

Michael Thomas Carroll is professor of English at New Mexico Highlands University. He is the author of *Popular Modernity in America: Experience, Technology, Mythohistory* (2000) and co-editor, with Eddie Tafoya, of *Phenomenological Approaches to Popular Culture* (2000). His work has been published in *Literature/Film Quarterly* and *Studies in Popular Culture*.

María Elena Cepeda is a doctoral candidate in the Department of Romance Languages and Literatures at the University of Michigan, Ann Arbor. Her research to date focuses primarily on U.S. Latina/o popular music, language politics, and literature. She has published pieces in *Revista Canadiense*, *Popular Music and Society*, *Discourse*, and *Latino Studies* (forthcoming), among other publications, and served as editorial assistant for *Musical Migrations: Transnationalism and Cultural Hybridity in Latin/o America* (Cándida F. Jáquez and Frances R. Aparicio, editors). Cepeda is currently completing a dissertation on Colombian popular music and Miami's transnational Colombian community.

Cece Cutler received her Ph.D. in linguistics from New York University in 2002. Her research focuses on the relationship between language and identity and more specifically on the language practices of white teenagers who affiliate with hip-hop.

John Fenn is a Ph.D. candidate in folklore and ethnomusicology at Indiana University, Bloomington. His dissertation (in process) investigates performance and social practice of rap and ragga musics in Malawi. He is active in the Applied Ethnomusicology section of the Society for Ethnomusicology and will guest edit a volume of *Folklore Forum* (Spring 2003) exploring the past, present, and future of ethnomusicology in the public realm.

Morgan Gerard is a former graduate student in social anthropology at the University of Toronto. His doctoral dissertation investigates ritualization in rave and club performances.

Paul D. Greene is an assistant professor at Pennsylvania State University, specializing in musical cultures of India and the Himalayas. His research engages popular and traditional musics, Buddhist musics, and sound technologies in world musical cultures. He is editor of several book volumes and journal issues in ethnomusicology, and has authored over twenty articles in *Ethnomusicology, Popular Music, The World of Music, Asian Music*, and elsewhere.

David Henderson is a visiting assistant professor of music at Saint Lawrence University in Canton, New York. His work, based in the Kathmandu Valley of Nepal, has appeared in the journals *Ethnomusicology* and *Asian Music*, and he is co-editor, with Ron Emoff, of *Mementos, Artifacts, and Hallucinations from the Ethnographer's Tent* (Routledge, 2002).

Dave Laing is a writer, editor, and lecturer based in London. His other works include *The Sound of Our Time* (1969), *One Chord Wonders: Power and Meaning in Punk Rock* (1985) and, with Phil Hardy, *The Da Capo Companion to 20th Century Popular Music* (1995). He is an editor of the *Continuum Encyclopedia of Popular Music of the World* whose first volumes were published in 2003.

Edward Larkey is an associate professor of German in the Department of Modern Languages and Linguistics at the University of Maryland, Baltimore County. He has published articles on the intersection of the global and local popular music of German-speaking countries, particularly on issues of cultural industries, identity constructions, and discourse and genre boundaries in German popular music.

Anthony McCann received a Ph.D. in ethnomusicology from the University of Limerick, Ireland, for a study of the dynamics of intellectual property practices as enclosure. He has held positions as a Fulbright Scholar and Postdoctoral Research Fellow at the Smithsonian Center for Folklife and Cultural Heritage. Other awards have included a Government of Ireland Scholarship and the Charles Seeger Prize.

Tony Mitchell is a senior lecturer in writing and cultural studies at the University of Technology, Sydney. He is the author of *Dario Fo: People's Court Jester* (Methuen, 1999) and *Popular Music and Local Identity: Rock, Pop, and Rap in Europe and Oceania* (University of Leicester Press, 1996), as well as numerous articles. From 1997 to 1999, he was chairperson of IASPM (the International Association for the Study of Popular Music). He is also editor of *Global Noise: Rap and Hip-hop outside the USA* (Wesleyan University Press, 2001).

Lillis Ó Laoire lectures in Irish language and literature at the University of Limerick, Ireland. His research interests include performance studies, ethnographic ethics, nationalism, and Gaelic song studies. He directs Ionad na nAmhrán (The Song Centre), an archive and performance project at the Irish World Music Centre, University of Limerick.

Alex Perullo is a Ph.D. candidate in ethnomusicology and African studies at Indiana University. He is currently completing his dissertation on the postsocialist popular music scene in Dar es Salaam, Tanzania.

Jack Sidnell is an assistant professor of anthropology at the University of Toronto. His research focuses on the empirical study of talk-in-interaction. He has conducted ethnographic research in Toronto, Guyana, and, most recently, St. Vincent, West Indies.

Maria Paula Survilla is an assistant professor of music at Wartburg College in Waverly, Iowa. Her research includes the interplay between popular (rock) genres and traditional music in post-soviet Belarus. Her book, *Of Mermaids and Rock Singers: Placing the Self and Defining the Nation Through Belarusan Contemporary Music* was published by Routledge in 2002.

C. K. Szego is an assistant professor in the School of Music and Department of Folklore at Memorial University of Newfoundland. She is co-editor of *Musics of the World's Cultures: A Source Book for Music Educators* (1997).

Sue Tuohy is an assistant professor at Indiana University where she teaches courses on ethnomusicology, ethnographic theory and method, and East Asian musics and cultures. She has conducted field research in the People's Republic of China, particularly on folksongs and festivals in Northwest China and on Chinese cultural studies scholarship. She is completing a book on the making of music and meaning in contemporary China. She has published articles on topics such as music and nationalism, early Chinese film music, and the social life of genre.

Jeremy Wallach recently received his doctorate from the Department of Anthropology at the University of Pennsylvania. His dissertation is an ethnographic study of youth, popular music, and social change in contemporary Indonesia.